Motivational Factors in the Etiology of Drug Abuse

Volume 50 of
the Nebraska Symposium
on Motivation

University of Nebraska Press
Lincoln and London

Volume 50 of the Nebraska Symposium on Motivation

Motivational Factors in the Etiology of Drug Abuse

Richard A. Dienstbier — *Series Editor*

Rick A. Bevins and Michael T. Bardo — *Editors*

Presenters

George F. Koob — *The Scripps Research Institute*

Harriet de Wit — *The University of Chicago*

R. D. Spealman — *New England Primate Research Center, Harvard Medical School*

Jaak Panksepp — *Bowling Green State University*

Michael T. Bardo — *University of Kentucky*

Roy A. Wise — *National Institute on Drug Abuse, NIH*

Jane Stewart — *Concordia University, Montreal, Quebec, Canada*

M. Vogel-Sprott — *University of Waterloo*

Motivational Factors in the Etiology of Drug Abuse is Volume 50 in the series
CURRENT THEORY AND RESEARCH
IN MOTIVATION

Manufactured in the United States of America
International Standard Book Number
0-8032-1340-9 (Clothbound)

∞

Preface

The volume editors for this 50th edition of the Nebraska Symposium are Rick A. Bevins and Michael T. Bardo. Rick is an Associate Professor of Psychology at the University of Nebraska. However, for the first time the volume includes an editor from outside the University of Nebraska system. Mike is a Professor of Psychology at the University of Kentucky. Rick and Mike coordinated the symposium that led to this volume with enthusiasm and dedication, and they worked with the Symposium Advisory Committee in developing plans for celebrating this half-century of our Symposium. Coordinating the volume means that Rick and Mike did most of the "heavy lifting," from planning the volume, to selecting and inviting the contributors, and to coordinating all aspects of the editing. My thanks to them and the contributors for the very timely production of their chapters.

As with Symposium sessions of the last several years, to allow other scholars to travel to the Symposium as participants, we invited posters relevant to the main theme of addiction. This poster session included 35 submissions from researchers in places such as Boston University, UNC–Chapel Hill, Denison University, University of Giessen, University of South Dakota, and University of Minnesota. Since this is a tradition we will continue, we urge you, our readers, to consider such poster submissions when you receive future Symposium announcements.

This Symposium series is supported largely by funds donated in the memory of Professor Harry K. Wolfe to the University of Nebraska Foundation by the late Professor Cora L. Friedline. This Symposium volume, like those of the recent past, is dedicated to the memory of Professor Wolfe, who brought psychology to the University of Nebraska. After studying with Professor Wilhelm Wundt, Professor Wolfe returned to this, his native state, to establish the first undergraduate laboratory of psychology in the nation. As a student at Nebraska, Professor Friedline studied psychology under Professor Wolfe.

We are grateful to the late Professor Friedline for this bequest, and to the University of Nebraska Foundation for continued financial support for the series. For this 50th anniversary year, and for subsequent years, the amount of funding granted by the Foundation has been increased. We are particularly grateful to Senior Vice Chancellor for Academic Affairs Richard Edwards for assistance in securing that increase.

It is time to give a special thanks to Claudia Price-Decker, who regularly helps with the coordination of the sessions themselves, overseeing the many details that must be considered for the Symposium to run smoothly. Claudia is great, she is appreciated, and we have come to take smooth running for granted. Others who help and deserve thanks include Becki Barnes, who has been helping for years, and Joy Menke who has joined this effort more recently.

Richard A. Dienstbier
Series Editor

Contents

Introduction: Motivation, Drug Abuse, and 50 Years of Theoretical and Empirical Inquiry

Rick A. Bevins
University of Nebraska–Lincoln

Michael T. Bardo
University of Kentucky

In reviewing the 25-year history of the Nebraska Symposium on Motivation, Benjamin and Jones (1979) noted that the Symposium was "the longest-lived topical series in American psychology, with a national and international reputation" (p. ix). On March 28 and 29 of 2002, with a packed auditorium on the campus of the University of Nebraska–Lincoln, this record was doubled in life. As the reader will quickly see from the list of contributors, the reputation of the Symposium was also maintained on its 50th Anniversary. Before continuing, we would like to reiterate the thanks in the Preface for all those who supported the Symposium with their hard work, thoughtful effort, and generous support. We are also grateful to the selection committee for choosing our proposal for the 50th Nebraska Symposium on Motivation. We believe it is fitting that drug abuse be the topic for this Symposium. Drug abuse and its associated personal and fiscal costs reflect the largest health problem in the United States (Robert Wood Johnson Foundation, 2001). Psychology, as a broad integrated field of inquiry, has much to contribute to understanding and solving this serious problem. The contents of this volume clearly support this claim.

The contributors in the early volumes of the Symposium tended to be from disparate areas, but they had an empirical and theoretical focus that informed the field of psychology about motivation and its affiliated constructs (e.g., arousal, drive, etc.). Gerald McClearn, in Volume 16, was the first contributor to have a significant portion of a chapter devoted to discussing drug-abuse-related research. However, the data were presented in the spirit of understanding motivational processes rather than drug abuse. In the words of McClearn (1968):

> It should be emphasized that mouse alcohol preference is not regarded as a simple analog of human alcoholism, although it is reasonable to expect that studies on the inheritance of alcohol preference in mice, and on the genetics of differential behavioral response to alcohol, will contribute to the pool of basic knowledge that will ultimately result in better understanding of human alcoholism. For present purposes, however, I should like to emphasize the motivational aspects of the research. From the point of view of motivational dynamics, the systems influencing ingestion of any substance are relevant, and the fact that the ingested substance is alcohol is incidental. (p. 61)

In the 1970s the Symposium became focused such that the contributors in a given year tended to have an aligned theme to their research programs (cf. Benjamin & Jones, 1979). For example, in 2000 the Symposium addressed the importance and role of evolutionary psychology to understanding psychological phenomena (Leger, Kamil, & French, 2001). As reflected in the title "Alcohol and Addictive Behavior," the 34th Nebraska Symposium on Motivation was the first to focus its attention on drug abuse, especially alcoholism. In the closing paragraph of the Introduction of that volume, Clay Rivers (1987), the organizer and editor for that year, revealed that his main "hope" of the Symposium and the volume was to "help narrow the gap between what we know and what we do when working with addictive behavior in general and alcoholics in particular" (p. xx). We hope this volume will contribute further to this crucial step in the prevention of drug addiction.

When we decided that the title of the present volume would be "Motivational Factors in the Etiology of Drug Abuse," it was no accident that we placed "motivational" as the first word. Such placement served to remind us of an important yet often ignored issue in the drug abuse field. That is, we need to more explicitly explore the meaning of the current motivational-like constructs that are so widely used in the drug abuse literature (e.g., cravings, seeking, incentive, urges, etc.), but which often remain undefined. Indeed, we did an Internet Medline search from 1998–2002 that cross-listed the word "motivation" with each of the following drugs: alcohol, amphetamine, cocaine, nicotine, and heroin. This simple search resulted in 729 hits. The contributors to the present volume are helping to provide us with the direction needed to grapple with the elusive constructs and theories related to the motivational aspects of drug taking.

For readers familiar with the history of psychology, it will be recognized that this task is not easy. After reading this volume, we encourage folks to read some of the past volumes your library likely has on its shelf. They are a treasure trove of critical thinking on the issue. The following are quotes reflecting some of the different approaches past contributors have taken to treating motivation—some embrace, some reject, and others find a middle ground.

Judson S. Brown (1953)

It is perhaps safe to assert that in every serious attempt to account for the behavior of living organisms, the concept of motivation, in one guise or another, has played a major explanatory role. But it is not safe to assert that students of behavior have reached appreciable agreement as to how drives can be most meaningfully defined, what mechanisms are involved in each case, how many drives there are, or precisely how drives function as behavior determinants. (p. 1)

Robert C. Bolles (1958)

Five years ago J. S. Brown cautioned against confusing acquired drives with acquired response tendencies (9). He had particular reference to a social drive, the "drive for money," which he argued in only a descriptive label for money-getting responses. Perhaps we should extend Brown's argument to the "primary" drives, and guard against confusing *any* drive with response tendencies. Thus, the "hunger drive" may be only a descriptive label for food-getting responses. Perhaps the drive concept has no more usefulness than to provide a basis for describing different kinds of behavior. (p. 24)

T. C. Schneirla (1959)

Motivation, broadly considered, concerns the causation and impulsion of behavior. The question here is what impels the approach and withdrawal reactions of very different animals from protozoans to man and how each level develops its characteristic pattern. Have these levels anything in common, or does each have a basis very different from the others? (p. 1)

David Birch (1961)

In common with quite a number of my predecessors in these symposia I will take advantage of this opportunity to make some comments of a general, systematic nature revealing my view on motivation as a theoretical construct. I suspect that the term is, in fact, not a very useful one technically, though probably quite important in communication that is nontechnical or relatively so. (p. 179)

W. Edgar Vinacke (1962)

Littman (1958), in one of these symposia, presented a brilliant review of the multiplicity of motivational concepts. He suggested that "motivation" is a very general term to cover any and all sorts of psychological "actives." I agree very strongly with this point of view, but I disagree with what he seems to conclude: namely, that psychologists might just as well abandon the study of motivation, as such, and concentrate on the properties of behavior without worrying whether or not such properties are motivational. Perhaps he merely means to suggest that there are no simple or unitary motivational phenomena. I agree. But I would object to the possible imputation that these are purely illusory variables. Instead, I shall insist that "motivation" does really refer to definable classes of influence upon performance, and that it is an essential responsibility of psychology to identify and measure them. But we must face squarely the complexity that may result. (pp. 2–3)

Howard H. Kendler (1965)

I must confess that my initial aspiration to present the psychology of motivation as a nice, neat, orderly array of facts and principles was not fully realized. I would like to believe that the fault was not entirely my own but was due in part to the refractory quality of motivation. It is apparent to me that the topic of motivation is more confusing, more disorderly, more vexing than are the fields of sensation, learning, and perception. Why do we psychologists have so much difficulty with the problems of motivation? Why does motivation represent a backward area of psychology? What can be done? (p. 2)

C. R. Gallistel (1975)

Processes that potentiate and inhibit the lower-level mechanisms of sensorimotor coordination in order to ensure an overall coherence and direction to behavior are what I refer to as motivational processes. The existence of such processes, regardless of what one chooses to call them, seems beyond dispute. (p. 189)

Timothy B. Baker, Elsimae Morse, & Jack E. Sherman (1987)

We would like to revive interest in urges because we believe their analysis will foster a clearer understanding of motivational processes important in addiction. We view urges as affects that, like other affects, have prototypic phenomenological, behavioral, and physiological correlates . . . We believe the motivational significance of urges is clear; they occupy the position relative to approach behavior that fear occupies with respect to avoidance. (pp. 257–258)

Douglas Derryberry & Don M. Tucker (1991)

Complex as well as elementary motives must be implemented by neural mechanisms, yet it has been difficult to relate such mechanisms to the psychological processes of human motivation. The difficulty in the past has been a lack of knowledge about the workings of the brain. In recent years there have been important advances in the neurosciences, but this knowledge is typically to specific neural mechanisms, rather than general brain function, and it is held by researchers who are seldom conversant with psychological theory. (p. 289)

It is a good thing that controversy is one of the fuels of science. Although we have a long way to go, our field has made amazing progress in the 50 years of this Symposium. We hope that the present volume contributes to this progress—perhaps by evoking further conversation and controversy about motivational processes involved in drug abuse. With that conversation, new hypotheses will undoubtedly emerge and individuals will pursue them empirically. It is through this process that our science will help solve the major health problems of this century. In this pursuit, however, we must remember that few of us, if anyone, can predict from where and in what system the next critical insight will emerge (Dethier, 1966; Laidler, 1998).

References

Baker, T. B., Morse, E., & Sherman, J. E. (1987). The motivation to use drugs: A psychobiological analysis of urges. In P. C. Rivers (Ed.), *Alcohol and addictive behavior. Nebraska symposium on motivation, 1986* (pp. 257–323). Lincoln: University of Nebraska Press.

Benjamin, L. T., Jr., & Jones, M. R. (1979). From motivational theory to social cognitive development: Twenty-five years of the Nebraska Symposium. In R. A. Dienstbier (Ed.), *Nebraska symposium on motivation, 1978* (pp. ix–xix). Lincoln: University of Nebraska Press.

Birch, D. (1961). A motivational interpretation of extinction. In M. R. Jones (Ed.), *Nebraska symposium on motivation, 1961* (pp. 179–197). Lincoln: University of Nebraska Press.

Bolles, R. C. (1958). The usefulness of the drive concept. In M. R. Jones (Ed.), *Nebraska symposium on motivation, 1958* (pp. 1–33). Lincoln: University of Nebraska Press.

Brown, J. S. (1953). Problems presented by the concept of acquired drives. In M. R. Jones (Ed.), *Current theory and research in motivation: A symposium* (pp. 1–21). Lincoln: University of Nebraska Press.

Derryberry, D., & Tucker, D. M. (1991). The adaptive base of neural hierarchy: Elementary motivational controls on network function. In R. A. Dienstbier (Ed.), *Perspectives on motivation. Nebraska symposium on motivation, 1990* (pp. 287–342). Lincoln: University of Nebraska Press.

Dethier, V. G. (1966). Insects and the concept of motivation. In D. Levine (Ed.), *Nebraska symposium on motivation, 1966* (pp. 105–136). Lincoln: University of Nebraska Press.

Gallistel, C. R. (1975). Motivation as a central organizing process: The psychophysical approach to functional and neurophysiological analysis. In J. K. Cole, & T. B. Sonderegger (Eds.), *Nebraska symposium on motivation, 1974* (pp. 183–250). Lincoln: University of Nebraska Press.

Kendler, H. H. (1965). Motivation and behavior. In D. Levine (Ed.), *Nebraska symposium on motivation, 1965* (pp. 1–23). Lincoln: University of Nebraska Press.

Laidler, K. J. (1998). *To light such a candle: Chapters in the history of science and technology.* Oxford: Oxford University Press.

Leger, D. W., Kamil, A. C., & French, J. A. (2001). Introduction: Fear and loathing of evolutionary psychology in the social sciences. In J. A. French, A. C. Kamil, & D. W. Leger (Eds.), *Evolutionary psychology and motivation. Nebraska symposium on motivation, 2001* (pp. ix–xxiii). Lincoln: University of Nebraska Press.

Littman, R. A. (1958). Motives, history and causes. In M. R. Jones (Ed.), *Nebraska symposium on motivation, 1958* (pp. 114–168). Lincoln: University of Nebraska Press.
McClearn, G. E. (1968). Genetics and motivation of the mouse. In W. J. Arnold (Ed.), *Nebraska symposium on motivation, 1968* (pp. 47–83). Lincoln: University of Nebraska Press.
Rivers, P. C. (1987). Introduction. In P. C. Rivers (Ed.), *Alcohol and addictive behavior. Nebraska symposium on motivation, 1986* (pp. ix–xx). Lincoln: University of Nebraska Press.
Robert Wood Johnson Foundation (2001). *Substance abuse: The nation's number one health problem.* Princeton NJ: RWJF.
Schneirla, T. C. (1959). An evolutionary and developmental theory of biphasic processes underlying approach and withdrawal. In M. R. Jones (Ed.), *Nebraska symposium on motivation, 1959* (pp. 1–42). Lincoln: University of Nebraska Press.
Vinacke, W. E. (1962). Motivation as a complex problem. In M. R. Jones (Ed.), *Nebraska symposium on motivation, 1962* (pp. 1–46). Lincoln: University of Nebraska Press.

Allostatic View of Motivation: Implications for Psychopathology

George F. Koob
The Scripps Research Institute

Motivation as a concept has many definitions. Donald Hebb (1949) argued that motivation is "stimulation that arouses activity of a particular kind" (p. 172), and C. P. Richter (1927) argued that "spontaneous activity arises from certain underlying physiological origins," and such "internal" drives are reflected in the amount of general activity (p. 307). Dalbir Bindra (1976) defined motivational function as a "rough label for the relatively persisting states that make an animal initiate and maintain actions leading to particular outcomes or goals" (p. 363), and a more behavioristic view is that incentive motivation is "given the properties of energizing behavior (along with other motivational factors) and of being proportional to the amount and quality of the reinforcer" (Bartoshuk, 1979, p. 695).

All of these definitions point to certain common characteristics of our concept of motivation. It is a state that varies with arousal and guides behavior in relationship to changes in the environment. The environment can be external (incentives) or internal (central motive states or drives), and such motivation or motivational states are not constant and vary over time. The concept of motivation was linked inextricably with hedonic, affective, or emotional states in the context

This is publication number 15049-NP from The Scripps Research Institute. The author would like to thank Mike Arends for his assistance with manuscript preparation.

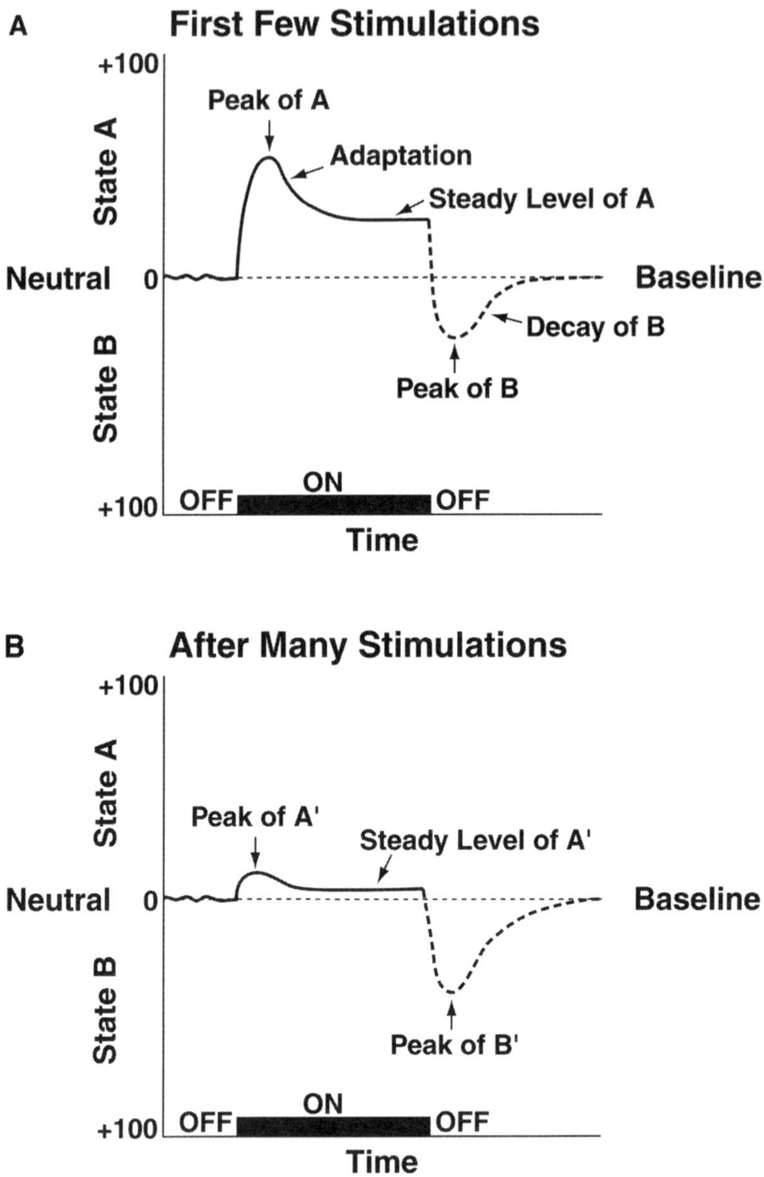

Figure 1. (A) The standard pattern of affective dynamics produced by a relatively novel unconditioned stimulus. (B) The standard pattern of affective dynamics produced by a familiar, frequently repeated unconditioned stimulus. (From Solomon, 1980. Copyright © 1980 by the American Psychological Association. Reprinted with permission.)

of temporal dynamics by Solomon's opponent-process theory of motivation. Solomon and Corbit (1974) postulated that hedonic, affective, or emotional states, once initiated, are automatically modulated by the central nervous system with mechanisms that reduce the intensity of hedonic feelings. Termed the "opponent-process" theory of motivation, Solomon argued that there is affective or hedonic habituation (or tolerance) and affective or hedonic withdrawal (abstinence). He defined two processes: the *a-process* and the *b-process.* The *a-process* could consist of either positive or negative hedonic responses. It occurs shortly after presentation of a stimulus, correlates closely with the stimulus intensity, quality, and duration of the reinforcer, and shows tolerance. In contrast, the *b-process* appears after the *a-process* has terminated and is sluggish in onset, slow to build up to an asymptote, slow to decay, and gets larger with repeated exposure. Thus, the affective dynamics of opponent-process theory generate new motives and new opportunities for reinforcing and energizing behavior (Solomon, 1980; Figure 1).

From a neurobehavioral perspective it was hypothesized that in brain motivational systems the initial acute effect of an emotional stimulus or a drug is opposed or counteracted by homeostatic changes in brain systems. Certain systems in the brain were hypothesized to suppress or reduce all departures from hedonic neutrality (Solomon & Corbit, 1974). This affect control system was conceptualized as a single negative feedback, or opponent, loop that opposes the stimulus-aroused affective state (Solomon & Corbit, 1974; Siegel, 1975; Poulos & Cappell, 1991). In this opponent-process theory, tolerance and dependence are inextricably linked (Solomon & Corbit, 1974), and affective states—pleasant or aversive—were hypothesized to be automatically opposed by centrally mediated mechanisms that reduce the intensity of these affective states. In the context of drug dependence, Solomon argued that the first few self-administrations of an opiate drug produce a pattern of motivational changes similar to that observed in Figure 1A. The onset of the drug effect produces euphoria that is the *a-process,* and this is followed by a decline in intensity. Then, after the drug wears off, the *b-process* state emerges as an aversive craving state (Figure 2).

More recently, opponent-process theory has been expanded into the domains of the neurocircuitry and neurobiology of drug addiction from a physiological perspective. An allostatic model of the brain

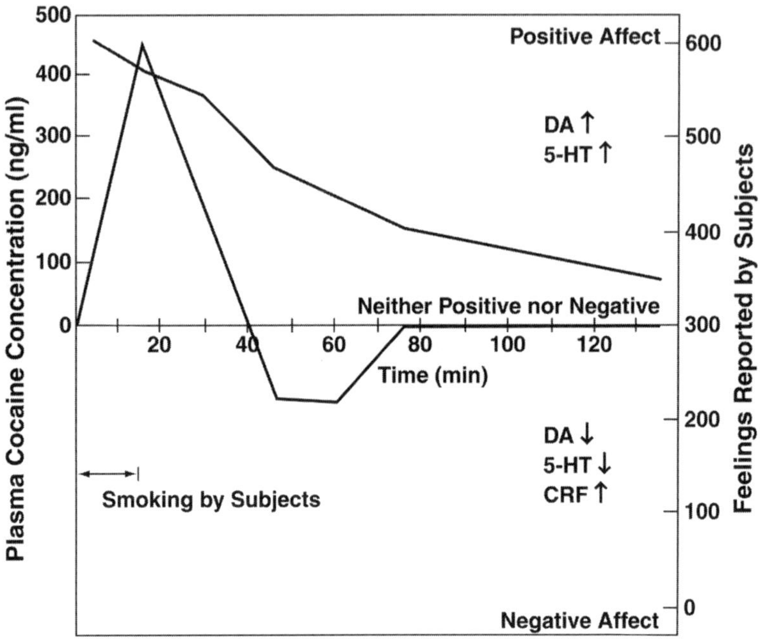

Figure 2. Demonstration of the opponent-process theory *b-process* state emerging as an aversive craving state. Dysphoric feelings followed the initial euphoria in experimental subjects who smoked cocaine paste, even though the concentration of cocaine in the plasma of the blood remained relatively high. The dysphoria is characterized by anxiety, depression, fatigue, and a desire for more cocaine. The peak feelings for the subjects were probably reached shortly before the peak plasma concentration, but the first psychological measurements were made later than the plasma assay. Hence, the temporal sequence of the peaks shown cannot be regarded as definitive. (Adapted from Van Dyke & Byck, 1982. Copyright © 1982 by Scientific American, Inc. All rights reserved. Printed with permission.)

motivational systems has been proposed to explain the persistent changes in motivation that are associated with vulnerability to relapse in addiction, and this model may generalize to other psychopathology associated with dysregulated motivational systems. In this framework, addiction is conceptualized as a cycle of spiraling dysregulation of brain reward systems that progressively increases resulting in the compulsive use of drugs. Counteradaptive processes such as opponent-process that are part of the normal homeostatic limitation of reward function fail to return within the normal homeostatic range and are hypothesized to form an allostatic state. This

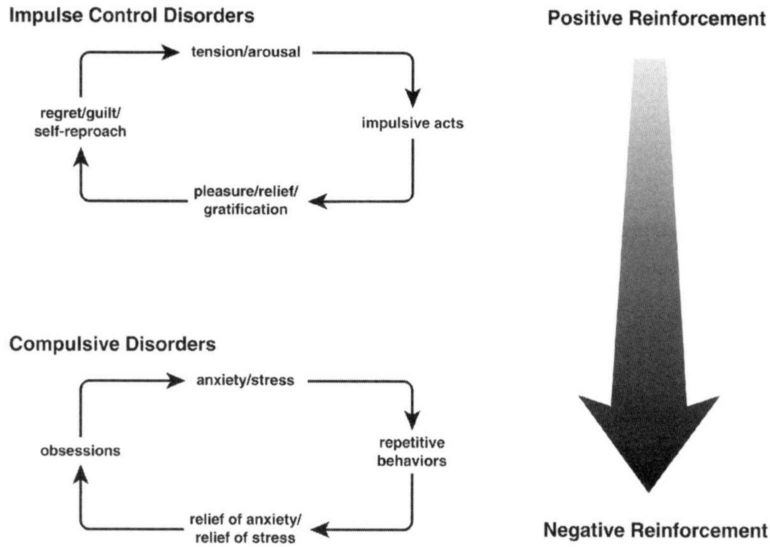

Figure 3. Diagram showing stages of impulse control disorder and compulsive disorder cycles related to the sources of reinforcement. In impulse control disorders an increasing tension and arousal occurs before the impulsive act, with pleasure, gratification or relief during the act. Following the act there may or may not be regret or guilt. In compulsive disorders, there are recurrent and persistent thoughts (obsessions) that cause marked anxiety and stress followed by repetitive behaviors (compulsions) that are aimed at preventing or reducing distress (American Psychiatric Association, 1994). Positive reinforcement (pleasure/gratification) is more closely associated with impulse control disorders. Negative reinforcement (relief of anxiety or relief of stress) is more closely associated with compulsive disorders.

allostatic state is further hypothesized to be reflected in a chronic deviation of reward set point that is fueled not only by dysregulation of reward circuits per se but by recruitment of brain and hormonal stress responses.

Drug addiction has been conceptualized as a chronic relapsing disorder characterized by compulsive drug-taking behavior with impairment in social and occupational functioning. From a psychiatric perspective, drug addiction has aspects of both impulse control disorders and compulsive disorders (Figure 3). Impulse control disorders are characterized by an increasing sense of tension or arousal before committing an impulsive act; pleasure, gratification, or relief at the time of committing the act; and following the act there may or may not be regret, self-reproach, or guilt (American Psychiatric

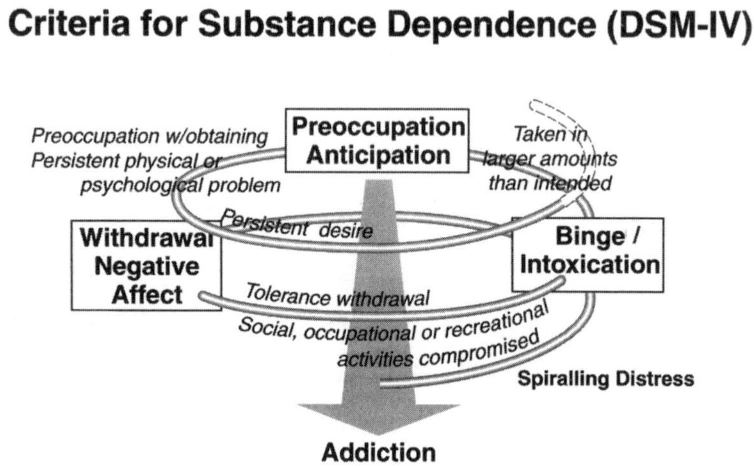

Figure 4. Diagram describing the spiraling distress-addiction cycle from a psychiatric perspective, including the three major components of the addiction cycle (preoccupation/anticipation, binge/intoxication, and withdrawal/negative affect) with the different criteria for substance dependence from the *Diagnostic and Statistical Manual of Mental Disorders* incorporated. (From Koob & Le Moal, 1997. Copyright © 1997 by the American Association of the Advancement of Science. Reprinted with permission.)

Association, 1994). In contrast, compulsive disorders are characterized by anxiety and stress before committing a compulsive repetitive behavior, and relief from the stress by performing the compulsive behavior. As an individual moves from an impulsive disorder to a compulsive disorder there is a shift from positive reinforcement driving the motivated behavior to negative reinforcement driving the motivated behavior. Drug addiction has been conceptualized as a disorder that progresses from impulsivity to compulsivity in a collapsed cycle of addiction comprised of three stages: preoccupation/anticipation, binge/intoxication, and withdrawal/negative affect (Figure 4). Different theoretical perspectives ranging from experimental psychology, social psychology, and neurobiology can be superimposed on these three stages that are conceptualized as feeding into each other, becoming more intense, and ultimately leading to the pathological state known as addiction (Koob & Le Moal, 1997).

Cocaine is a powerfully reinforcing psychostimulant with high addiction potential and provides a model with which to bridge the domains of motivation and psychopathology. Cocaine increases the availability of monoamines at the synaptic level in the brain, and much is known about the neuropharmacological basis of its acute reinforcing effects. Early work suggested a primary role for the mesolimbic dopamine system that projects to the basal forebrain (Koob, 1992). More recent evidence suggests that both dopaminergic and serotonergic terminals within a basal forebrain macrostructure termed the extended amygdala (central nucleus of the amygdala, bed nucleus of the stria terminalis, and a transition area in the region of the shell of the nucleus accumbens) have a particularly important role in the acute rewarding effects of cocaine (Koob, Sanna, & Bloom, 1998). Significant evidence also exists to show that these systems can be dysregulated by prolonged self-administration of cocaine yielding an opponent-process-like change in the neurochemistry of the extended amygdala. Continuous self-administration of cocaine for 12 hours produces decreases in extracellular levels of dopamine and serotonin in the nucleus accumbens as measured by *in vivo* microdialysis (Figure 5). However, there are even more dramatic increases in extracellular levels of the brain stress neurotransmitter corticotropin-releasing factor (CRF) in the central nucleus of the amygdala during acute withdrawal (Figure 6). Both of these changes could be hypothesized to contribute to the brain neurochemical representation of the "opponent loop" conceptualized by Solomon (1980).

However, drug addiction, and cocaine addiction in particular, is considered a chronic relapsing disorder where subjects episodically administer the drug and become abstinent. What is unknown is what neurochemical/neurocircuitry changes occur that provide the motivational basis for vulnerability after the acute withdrawal during periods of abstinence and how such changes lead to escalation in drug intake over time. Animal models of escalation of drug intake have been established using prolonged access to drugs that are beginning to provide some insights into the neurobiological changes that may lead to vulnerability to escalation in drug intake and relapse.

Historically in animal models of cocaine self-administration the focus was restricted to stable behavior from day to day in order to reliably interpret within-subject designs aimed at exploring the pharmacological and neuropharmacological basis for the acute reinforcing effects of cocaine. Typically, rats allowed access to fewer than 3 hours of cocaine per day, after acquisition of self-administration, establish highly stable levels of intake and patterns of responding

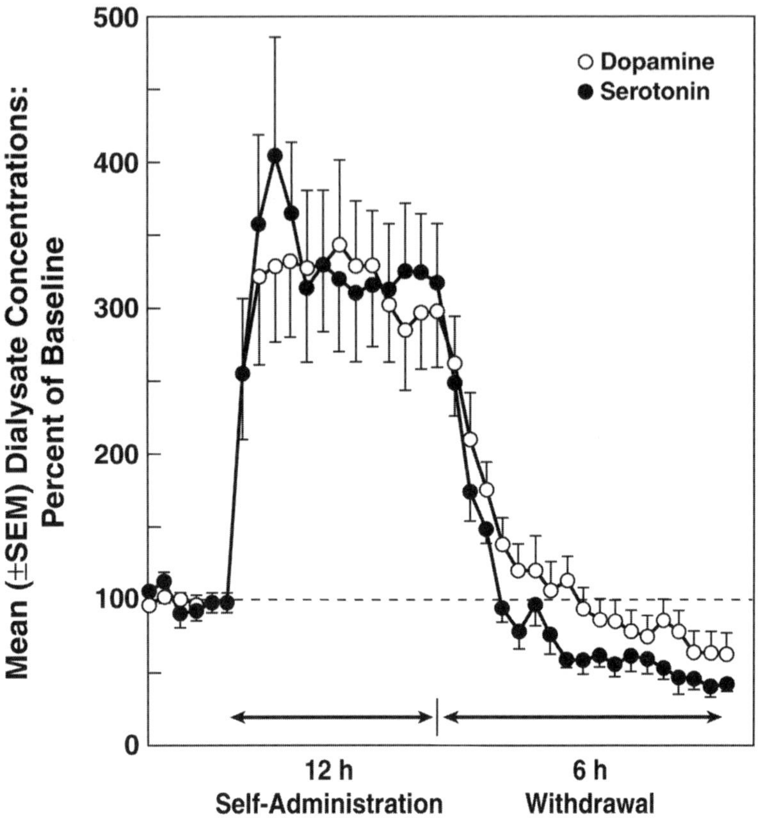

Figure 5. The profile of dialysate serotonin and dopamine concentrations and a corresponding representative reinforcer delivery record during a 12-hour extended-access cocaine self-administration session. The mean (± SEM) presession baseline dialysate concentrations of serotonin and dopamine were 0.98 ± 0.1 nM and 5.3 ± 0.5 nM, respectively (*n* = 7). (Adapted from Parsons et al., 1995. Printed with permission.)

between daily sessions. To explore the possibility that differential access to intravenous cocaine self-administration in rats may produce different patterns of drug intake, rats were allowed access to intravenous self-administration of cocaine for 1 hour and 6 hours per day. With 1-hour access (short access) to cocaine per session via intravenous self-administration, drug intake remained low and stable, not changing from day to day as observed previously. In contrast, with 6-hour access (long access) to cocaine drug intake gradually escalated over days (Ahmed & Koob, 1998; Figure 7). In the escalation group,

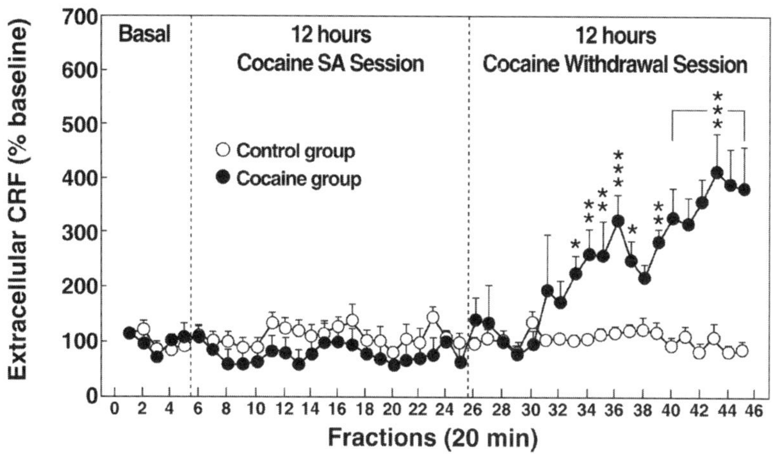

Figure 6. Mean (± SEM) dialysate CRF concentrations collected from the central nucleus of the amygdala of rats during baseline, a 12-hour cocaine self-administration session, and a subsequent 12-hour withdrawal period (Cocaine Group, $n = 5$). CRF levels in animals with the same history of cocaine self-administration training and drug exposure, but not given access to cocaine on the test day, are shown for comparison (Control Group, $n = 6$). The data are expressed as percentages of basal CRF concentrations. Dialysates were collected over 2-hour periods alternating with 1-hour nonsampling periods. During cocaine self-administration, dialysate CRF concentrations in the cocaine group were decreased by about 25% relative to control animals. In contrast, termination of access to cocaine resulted in a significant increase in CRF efflux, which began approximately 5 hours postcocaine and reached about 400% of presession baseline levels at the end of the withdrawal session. * $p < 0.05$; ** $p < 0.01$; *** $p < 0.001$; Simple Effects after overall mixed factorial ANOVA. (Adapted from Richter & Weiss, 1999. Copyright © 1999 by Wiley-Liss, Inc. Printed by permission of Wiley-Liss, Inc., a subsidiary of J. Wiley and Sons, Inc.)

there was an increased early intake as well as sustained intake over the session and an upward shift in the dose-effect function suggesting an increase in hedonic set point. When animals were allowed different doses of cocaine during self-administration the long access animals titrated cocaine effects as well as the short access rats, but the long access rats consistently self-administered almost twice as much cocaine at any dose tested, further suggesting an upward shift in the set point for cocaine reward in the escalated animals (Ahmed & Koob, 1998).

According to the hedonic allostasis hypothesis described above, tolerance to drug hedonic effects and increased motivation for these effects are inextricably linked to the same chronic perturbation in

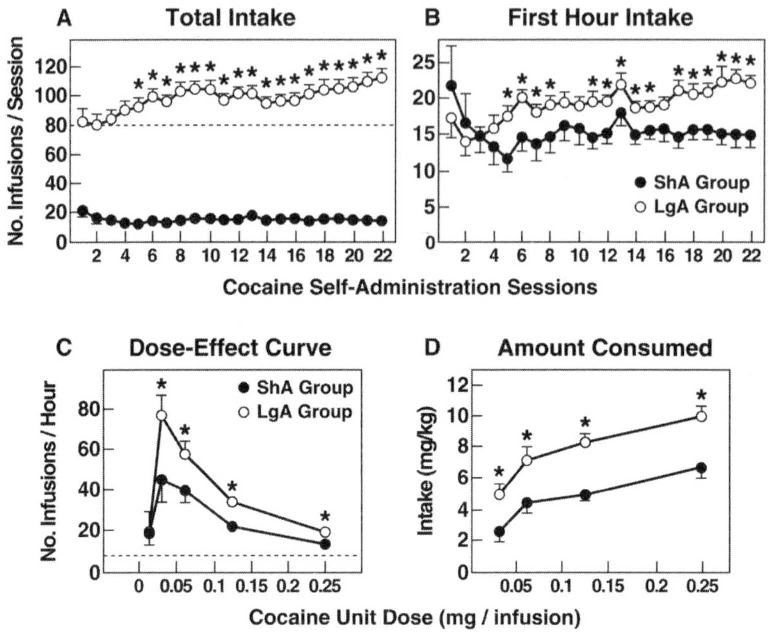

Figure 7. Effect of drug availability on cocaine intake (mean ± SEM). (A) In long access (LgA) rats ($n = 12$) but not in short access (ShA) rats ($n = 12$), mean total cocaine intake started to increase significantly from session 5 ($p < 0.05$; sessions 5 to 22 compared to session 1) and continued to increase thereafter ($p < 0.05$; session 5 compared to sessions 8–10, 12, 13, 17–22). (B) During the first hour, LgA rats self-administered more infusions than ShA rats during sessions 5–8, 11, 12, 14, 15, and 17–22 ($p < 0.05$). (C) Mean infusions (± SEM) per cocaine dose tested. LgA rats took significantly more infusions than ShA rats at doses of 31.25, 62.5, 125, and 250 μg/infusion ($p < 0.05$). * $p < 0.05$ (Student's *t* test after appropriate one-way and two-way analysis of variance). (From Ahmed & Koob, 1998. Copyright © 1998 by the American Association for the Advancement of Science. Reprinted with permission.)

brain reward homeostasis (or allostasis). To directly test this hypothesis, two groups of rats were differentially exposed to cocaine self-administration as described above (i.e., 1-hour short access and 6-hour long access groups). The animals first were prepared with bipolar electrodes in either the right or left posterior lateral hypothalamus. One week postsurgery they were trained to respond for electrical brain stimulation. Intracranial self-stimulation (ICSS) thresholds measured in μA were assessed according to a modified discrete-trial current-threshold procedure (Markou & Koob, 1993). During the *screening phase,* the 22 rats tested for self-administration were allowed to self-administer cocaine during only 1 hour on a fixed-ratio 1 schedule after which two balanced groups with the same weight, cocaine intake and ICSS reward thresholds were formed. During the *escalation phase,* one group had access to cocaine self-administration for only 1 hour per day (short access or ShA rats) and the other group for 6 hours per day (long access or LgA rats). The remaining eight rats were exposed to the same experimental manipulations as the other rats, except that they were not exposed to cocaine. ICSS reward thresholds were measured in all rats two times a day, 3 hours and 17–22 hours after each daily self-administration session (ShA and LgA rats) or the control procedure (drug-naive rats). Each ICSS session lasted about 30 minutes.

Elevation in baseline ICSS thresholds temporally preceded and was highly correlated with escalation in cocaine intake (Ahmed, Kenny, Koob, & Markou, 2002). Further observation revealed that postsession elevations in ICSS reward thresholds failed to return to baseline levels before the onset of each subsequent self-administration session, thereby deviating more and more from control levels. The progressive elevation in reward thresholds was associated with a dramatic escalation in cocaine consumption in LgA rats as previously observed. Within 12 days, the first-hour cocaine intake in LgA rats rose to a level almost two times greater than that observed in ShA rats. Total intake in LgA rats also increased almost continually over the same period of time from 75.5 (± 13.9) to 125 (± 4.3) cocaine injections. The gradual elevation in ICSS reward thresholds associated with drug intake escalation did not result from a general inability to respond, as demonstrated by the lack of differences between groups in response latencies for ICSS (Ahmed et al., 2002). Finally, the rate of elevation in reward thresholds measured 1 hour before the daily access to cocaine (i.e., slope of elevation) was highly correlated ($r = 0.78$, $p < 0.01$) with the intensity of escalation in total cocaine intake. Finally, after escalation had occurred, an acute cocaine challenge failed to facilitate brain reward responsiveness to the same degree as before. These results show that the elevation in brain reward thresholds following prolonged access to cocaine failed to return to baseline levels between repeated, prolonged exposure to cocaine self-administration (i.e., residual hysteresis), thus creating a greater and greater elevation in baseline ICSS thresholds. These data provide compelling evidence for brain reward dysfunction in escalated cocaine self-administration and strong support for the hedonic allostasis model of drug addiction.

Similar changes in self-administration of heroin and alcohol have been observed in animals with more prolonged access (Ahmed, Walker, & Koob, 2000) or a history of dependence (Roberts, Heyser, Cole, Griffin, & Koob, 2000). Ethanol-dependent rats will self-administer significantly more ethanol during acute withdrawal than rats in a nondependent state. In these studies, Wistar rats are trained using a sweet solution fadeout procedure to self-administer ethanol in a two-lever operant situation where one lever delivers 0.1 ml of 10% ethanol and the other lever delivers 0.1 ml of water. Nondependent animals typically self-administer doses of ethanol sufficient to produce blood ethanol levels averaging 25–30 mg% at the end of a 30-minute session, but rats made dependent on ethanol self-administer almost twice as much ethanol. With unlimited access to ethanol during a full 12 hours of withdrawal, animals will maintain blood ethanol levels above 100 mg% (Roberts, Cole, & Koob, 1996). When animals were subjected to repeated withdrawals and ethanol intake was charted over repeated abstinence, operant responding was enhanced by 30–100% for up to four–eight weeks postwithdrawal. These results suggest an allostatic-like increase in ethanol self-administration in animals with a history of dependence on ethanol that is not observed in animals maintained on limited access of 30 minutes per day.

Neuropharmacological studies have shown that enhanced ethanol self-administration during acute withdrawal and protracted abstinence can be dose-dependently reduced by intracerebroventricular pretreatment with a γ-aminobutyric acid (GABA) agonist (Roberts et al., 1996) and a competitive CRF antagonist (Valdez et al., 2002). Identical doses and administration of these neuropharmacological agents to nondependent rats has no effect on self-administration of ethanol. These results suggest, during the development of dependence, not only a change in function of neurotransmitters associated with the acute reinforcing effects of ethanol (GABA) but also recruitment of a key element of the brain stress systems (CRF).

Acute withdrawal from drugs of abuse produces opponent-process-like changes in reward neurotransmitters in specific elements of reward circuitry associated with the extended amygdala as well as recruitment of brain stress systems that motivationally oppose the hedonic effects of drugs of abuse. Such changes in these brain systems associated with the development of motivational aspects of withdrawal are hypothesized to be a major source of potential allostatic changes that drive and maintain addiction. In this context, *allostasis* is defined as the process of achieving stability through change; *allostatic state* is a state of chronic deviation of the regulatory system from its normal (homeostatic) operating level; and *allostatic load* is the cost to the brain and body of the deviation, accumulating over time, and reflecting in many cases pathological states and accumulation of damage. More specifically, allostasis from the drug addiction perspective is the process of maintaining apparent reward function stability by changes in reward and stress system neurocircuitry. Decreases in the function of dopamine, serotonin, and opioid peptides are hypothesized to contribute to a shift in reward set point as well as recruitment of brain stress systems such as CRF (Figure 8). All of these changes are hypothesized to be focused on a dysregulation of function within the neurocircuitry of the basal forebrain macrostructure of the extended amygdala.

The present formulation is an extension of Solomon's opponent-process to an allostatic framework with a hypothesized neurobiologic mechanism (Figure 8). The initial experience of a drug with no prior drug history shows a positive hedonic response *(a-process)* and a negative hedonic response *(b-process)*, each represented respectively by increased and decreased functional activity of reward transmitters. The *b-process* is hypothesized to involve modest recruitment of brain stress neurotransmitter function. However, insufficient time between re-administering the drug to retain the *a-process* and limit the *b-process* leads to a transition to an allostatic reward state as has been observed in escalation of cocaine intake and ethanol intake in animal models. Under conditions of an allostatic reward state the *b-process* never returns to the original homeostatic level before drug taking begins again, thus creating a greater and greater allostatic state in the brain reward systems, and by extrapolation a transition to addiction. The counteradaptive opponent-process does not balance the activational process *(a-process)* but in fact shows a residual hysteresis. The results with cocaine escalation and brain reward thresholds provide empirical evidence for this hypothesis. This residual hysteresis can be hypothesized to involve not only decreases in reward neurotransmission such as dopamine, GABA and opioid peptides, but also recruitment of brain stress systems such as corticotropin-releasing fac-

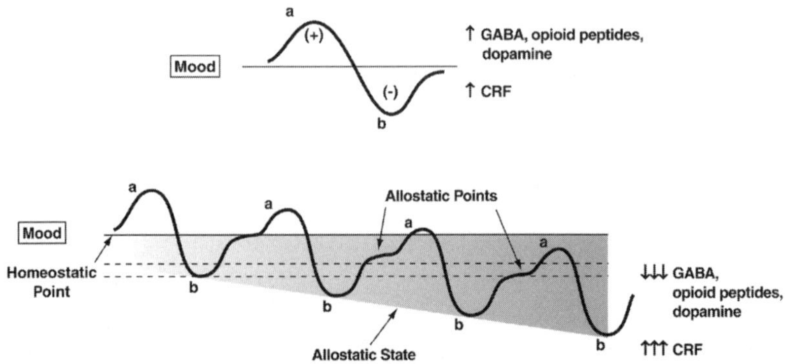

Figure 8. Diagram illustrating an extension of Solomon and Corbit's (1974) opponent-process model of motivation to outline the conceptual framework of the allostatic hypothesis. Both panels represent the affective response to the presentation of a drug. (Top) This diagram represents the initial experience of a drug with no prior drug history. The *a-process* represents a positive hedonic or positive mood state, and the *b-process* represents the negative hedonic or negative mood state. The affective stimulus (state) has been argued to be a sum of both an *a-process* and a *b-process.* An individual who experiences a positive hedonic mood state from a drug of abuse with sufficient time between re-administering the drug is hypothesized to retain the *a-process.* In other words, an appropriate counteradaptive opponent-process *(b-process)* that balances the activational process *(a-process)* does not lead to an allostatic state. (Bottom) The changes in the affective stimulus (state) in an individual with repeated frequent drug use that may represent a transition to an allostatic state in the brain reward systems and, by extrapolation, a transition to addiction. Note that the apparent *b-process* never returns to the original homeostatic level before drug taking is reinitiated, thus creating a greater and greater allostatic state in the brain reward system. In other words, the counteradaptive opponent-process *(b-process)* does not balance the activational process *(a-process)* but in fact shows a residual hysteresis. While these changes are exaggerated and condensed over time in the present conceptualization, the hypothesis here is that even during postdetoxification, a period of "protracted abstinence," the reward system is still bearing allostatic changes. In the nondependent state, reward experiences are normal, and the brain stress systems are not greatly engaged. During the transition to the state known as addiction, the brain reward system is in a major underactivated state while the brain stress system is highly activated. Small arrows refer to increased or decreased functional activity of the neurotransmitters. DA, dopamine; CRF, corticotropin-releasing factor; GABA, γ-aminobutyric acid. The following definitions apply: *allostasis,* the process of achieving stability through change; *allostatic state,* a state of chronic deviation of the regulatory system from its normal (homeostatic) operating level; *allostatic load,* the cost to the brain and body of the deviation, accumulating over time, and reflecting in many cases pathological states and accumulation of damage. (Modified from Koob & Le Moal, 2001. Copyright © 2001 by American College of Neuropsychopharmacology. Printed with permission.)

tor (Figure 8). Finally, these neurochemical/neurocircuitry changes observed during acute withdrawal may persist in some form even during postdetoxification defining a state termed "protracted abstinence."

An allostatic view of motivation provides an interesting framework for the development of psychopathology in a variety of domains. Allostasis originally was formulated as a hypothesis to explain the physiological basis for changes in patterns of human morbidity and mortality associated with modern life (Sterling & Eyer, 1988). High blood pressure and other pathology was linked to social disruption by a brain-body interaction. Using the arousal/stress continuum as their physiological framework, Sterling and Eyer argued that homeostasis was not adequate to explain such brain-body interactions, and the concept of allostasis has several unique characteristics that lends itself to more explanatory power. These characteristics include a continuous reevaluation of the organism's need and continuous readjustments to new set points, depending on demand. Allostasis can anticipate altered need and the system can make adjustments in advance. Allostatic systems also were hypothesized to use past experience to anticipate demand (Sterling & Eyer, 1988).

Extended to the domains of stress and the hypothalamic pituitary axis by McEwen (1998; 2000) and anxiety disorders and central CRF by Schulkin, McEwen, and Gold (1994) the concept of allostatic load was introduced, which is the price the body pays to adapt to adverse psychosocial or physical situations (McEwen, 2000). Allostatic load represents either external demands, such as too much stress, or internal demands, such as inefficient operation of the stress hormone response system. Similar connections have been made between allostatic changes in brain stress systems and posttraumatic stress disorder and anxiety disorders (Lindy & Wilson, 2001; Schulkin et al., 1994). A positive feedback interaction between glucocorticoids and CRF in the extended amygdala was hypothesized by Schulkin and colleagues (1994) as a substrate for specific symptoms of depressed patients such as expectation of adversity or negative outcomes. They argued that the loss of predictability and loss of perceived control leads to perpetual anticipation, is mediated by CRF in the amygdala, is modulated by glucocorticoids, and as such represents a neurobiological basis for the allostatic load and pathological arousal associated with melancholic depression. This early extension of the concept of allostasis clearly anticipated some of the observations associated with reward deficits in animal models of drug dependence.

Others similarly have argued that since depression is an established outcome of stress (and indeed, an ongoing depressive episode itself can constitute a chronic stress) that depression also fits an allostatic model (Carroll, 2002). The neuroendocrinology of human depression closely resembles that of chronic stress in the laboratory, including increased hypothalamic pituitary axis activity, reduced glucocorticoid feedback, and dysregulated diurnal rhythms or cortisol (Checkley, 1996). Reflecting back to the concept of allostatic load, there is a strong relationship between the number of depressive symptoms exhibited by subjects, and premature mortality and depression are associated with many cardiovascular risk factors (Carroll, 2002). In addition, one can reasonably see how both developmental and genetic domains can modify allostatic load that may determine vulnerability to pathology (McEwen, 2000). The challenge for future research will be to explore how the neurochemical/neurocircuitry changes associated with drug addiction, including the dysregulation of brain stress systems, extend to other mood disorders and motivational disorders that fall in the impulsive/compulsive disorder domain.

References

Ahmed, S. H., & Koob, G. F. (1998). Transition from moderate to excessive drug intake: Change in hedonic set point. *Science, 282,* 298–300.

Ahmed, S. H., Kenny, P. J., Koob, G. F., & Markou, A. (2002). Neurobiological evidence for hedonic allostasis associated with escalating cocaine use. *Nature Neuroscience, 5,* 625–626.

Ahmed, S. H., Walker, J. R., & Koob, G. F. (2000). Persistent increase in the motivation to take heroin in rats with a history of drug escalation. *Neuropsychopharmacology, 22,* 413–421.

American Psychiatric Association (1994). *Diagnostic and statistical manual of mental disorders* (4th ed.). Washington DC: American Psychiatric Association.

Bartoshuk, A. K. (1971). Motivation. In J. W. Kling, & L. A. Rigs, (Eds.), *Woodworth and Schlosberg's experimental psychology* (3rd ed.). New York: Holt, Rinehart and Winston.

Bindra, D. (1976). *A theory of intelligent behavior.* York: Wiley.

Carroll, B. J. (2002). Ageing, stress and the brain. In D. J. Chadwick, & J. A. Goode (Eds.), *Novartis foundation symposium: Vol. 242. Endocrine facets of ageing* (pp. 26–45). New York: Wiley.

Checkley, S. (1996). The neuroendocrinology of depression and chronic stress. *British Medical Bulletin, 52,* 597–617.

Hebb, D. O. (1949). *Organization of behavior: A neuropsychological theory.* New York: Wiley.

Koob, G. F. (1992). Drugs of abuse: Anatomy, pharmacology and function of reward pathways. *Trends in Pharmacological Sciences, 13,* 177–184.

Koob, G. F., & Le Moal, M. (1997). Drug abuse: Hedonic homeostatic dysregulation. *Science, 278,* 52–58.

Koob, G. F., Sanna, P. P., & Bloom, F. E. (1998). Neuroscience of addiction. *Neuron, 21,* 467–476.

Lindy, J. D., & Wilson, J. P. (2001). An allostatic approach to the psychodynamic understanding of PTSD. In J. P. Wilson, M. J. Friedman, & J. D. Lindy (Eds.), *Treating psychological trauma and PTSD* (pp. 125–138). New York: Guilford Press.

Markou, A., & Koob, G. F. (1993). Intracranial self-stimulation thresholds as a measure of reward. In A. Sahgal (Ed.), *Behavioural neuroscience: A practical approach: Vol. 2* (pp. 93–115). New York: Oxford University Press.

McEwen, B. S. (1998). Protective and damaging effects of stress mediators. *New England Journal of Medicine, 338,* 171–179.

McEwen, B. S. (2000). Allostasis and allostatic load: Implications for neuropsychopharmacology. *Neuropsychopharmacology, 22,* 108–124.

Parsons, L. H., Koob, G. F., & Weiss, F. (1995). Serotonin dysfunction in the nucleus accumbens of rats during withdrawal after unlimited access to intravenous cocaine. *Journal of Pharmacology and Experimental Therapeutics, 274,* 1182–1191.

Poulos, C. X., & Cappell, H. (1991). Homeostatic theory of drug tolerance: A general model of physiological adaptation. *Psychological Review, 98,* 390–408.

Richter, C. P. (1927). Animal behavior and internal drives. *Quarterly Review of Biology, 2,* 307–343.

Richter, R. M., & Weiss, F. (1999). In vivo CRF release in rat amygdala is increased during cocaine withdrawal in self-administering rats. *Synapse, 32,* 254–261

Roberts, A. J., Cole, M., & Koob, G. F. (1996). Intra-amygdala muscimol decreases operant ethanol self-administration in dependent rats. *Alcoholism: Clinical and Experimental Research, 20,* 1289–1298.

Roberts, A. J., Heyser, C. J., Cole, M., Griffin, P., & Koob, G. F. (2000). Excessive ethanol drinking following a history of dependence: Animal model of allostasis. *Neuropsychopharmacology, 22,* 581–594.

Schulkin, J., Gold, P. W., & McEwen, B. S. (1998). Induction of corticotropin-releasing hormone gene expression by glucocorticoids: Implication for understanding the states of fear and anxiety and allostatic load. *Psychoneuroendocrinology, 23,* 219–243.

Schulkin, J., McEwen, B. S., & Gold, P. W. (1994). Allostasis, amygdala, and anticipatory angst. *Neuroscience and Biobehavioral Reviews, 18,* 385–396.

Siegel, S. (1975). Evidence from rats that morphine tolerance is a learned response. *Journal of Comparative and Physiological Psychology, 89,* 489–506.

Solomon, R. L., & Corbit, J. D. (1974). An opponent-process theory of motivation: 1. Temporal dynamics of affect. *Psychological Review, 81,* 119–145.

Solomon, R. L. (1980). The opponent process theory of acquired motivation. *American Psychologist, 35,* 691–712.

Sterling, P., & Eyer, J. (1988). Allostasis: A new paradigm to explain arousal pathology. In S. Fisher, & J. Reason (Eds.), *Handbook of life stress, cognition and health* (pp. 629–647). New York: Wiley.

Valdez, G. R., Roberts, A. J., Chan, K., Davis, H., Brennan, M., Zorrilla, E. P., et al. (2002). Increased ethanol self-administration and anxiety-like behavior during acute withdrawal and protracted abstinence: Regulation by corticotropin-releasing factor. *Alcoholism: Clinical and Experimental Research, 26,* 1494–1501.

Van Dyke, C., & Byck, R. (1982). Cocaine. *Scientific American, 246,* 128–141.

Dual Determinants of Drug Use in Humans: Reward and Impulsivity

Harriet de Wit and
Jerry B. Richards
The University of Chicago

Drug use results from a convergence of many factors, including biological, pharmacological, psychological, and cultural influences. The focus of most research in the area of substance abuse has been on the factors that motivate or facilitate drug use, especially those relating to the rewarding properties of drugs. However, equally important in the etiology of problematic drug use in humans are the factors that *deter* individuals from using drugs. Failure of the processes that normally regulate behavior plays a key role in the development and maintenance of maladaptive drug use in humans. Although many studies have demonstrated the involvement of both reward and impulsivity processes in the etiology of drug abuse, the two processes have most often been studied in separate contexts, by different investigators, using different research techniques. In this chapter, we will discuss the respective contributions of the two general categories of factors, those that facilitate, and those that limit drug use. We will review how these factors each independently contribute to drug use during three stages in the natural history of drug abuse: initial exper-

Present address for Jerry B. Richards: State University of New York at Buffalo

This article was supported by DA09133 and DA02812

imentation with drugs, progression to repeated or excessive use, and during abstinence.

Positive, rewarding effects of drugs refer broadly to factors that promote the use of the drugs, including reinforcing effects of drugs in animals, as well as the euphoric effects in humans. Reward related influences on drug seeking include, for example, individual differences in sensitivity to reward in general (i.e., including nondrug rewards), the degree of reward or euphoria derived from a drug, the strength of responses to drug related stimuli (including desire or craving for the drug), and the strength of positive drug memories. Individual differences in the strength of these positive motivational factors affect susceptibility to drug seeking. The underlying neurobiology of drug related reward processes have been studied extensively, and it is generally believed that they involve activation of the mesolimbic dopamine system (Wise & Bozarth, 1987; Wise, 1996).

Impulsivity, broadly defined, refers to factors that regulate the performance of inappropriate or maladaptive behaviors. These factors are involved in the control of the normal tendency to repeat experiences that are rewarding. In humans, drug use is often inappropriate or has negative consequences, requiring the individual to actively refrain from using drugs in many situations. The failure to control unwanted behaviors or the failure of inhibitory processes, referred to here as "impulsive" behavior, increase the likelihood of using drugs. The term "impulsivity" has been used to refer to personality constructs, as well as to specific behavioral measures, both in the natural setting and in specific tests in the laboratory. As a personality construct, impulsivity has been conceptualized and measured in many different ways (Barratt & Patton, 1983; Eysenck, 1993; Tellegen 1982; Zuckerman, 1994). As a pattern of observable behavior in the natural setting, it has been measured using checklists and surveys by parents, teachers, and other observers (e.g., Achenbach & Edelbrock, 1979; Kendall & Wilcox, 1979). In the laboratory, impulsivity has been operationally defined and measured with tasks measuring specific constructs such as insensitivity to delayed or probabilistic consequences, insensitivity to negative consequences, inability to wait, or inability to withhold a prepotent response (Logan & Cowan, 1984; Rachlin & Green, 1972). It has been difficult to reconcile these various indices of impulsivity, and it is unlikely that these behaviors reflect a single underlying process (Milich & Kramer, 1984). Nevertheless, grouped together they provide a heuristic model for characterizing a dimension of behavioral dysregulation. A key challenge to researchers will be to identify and separate the behavioral and neurobiological processes underlying the expressions of impulsive behavior.

The combined factors of positive reward seeking and impulsivity influence behavior at all stages of human drug use. Both reward reactivity and behavioral restraint play a role in the initiation of drug use. Their influence continues and evolves after the first use of a drug and through the stages of continued use. Even during abstinence, after regular use has stopped, reward and impulsivity can each increase the likelihood of relapse, through separate mechanisms. In this chapter, we will discuss how the reward and impulsivity processes can function alone and together to influence the tendency to use drugs during each of these three stages of use: initiation, maintenance, and relapse.

Initiation of Use

The earliest stage of drug use, that of initially experimenting with drugs, is likely to be influenced by positive, reward seeking tendencies in the individual, as well as by a relative insensitivity to adverse or delayed consequences and poor behavioral inhibition. Both of these factors (reward and impulsivity) appear, in various forms, in the extensive literature on the personality and behavioral risk factors and the developmental trajectories that lead to drug use (e.g., Anthony & Petronis, 1995; Cherpitel, 1999; Dawes et al, 2000; Kandel, Yamaguch, & Chen, 1992). Studies linking risk factors to drug use have utilized primarily personality measures, behavioral checklists, or psychiatric symptoms and diagnoses to predict drug use. Although some studies depend on retrospective reports of early personality styles predating drug use, there are also a number of strong, prospective, longitudinal studies linking personality types to drug use (Gotham, Sher, & Wood, 1997). In addition, a few studies have used animal models to support the idea that certain behavioral tendencies predict a likelihood to take drugs (Poulos, Lê, & Parker, 1995).

REWARD PROCESSES IN INITIATION

At least two recent major theories of personality have postulated that individuals high on the trait of extraversion are particularly sensitive to reward, and that this reward sensitivity may be related to dopamine function. These theories propose that extraverted individuals are more likely to use drugs because they are more sensitive to reward in general (Cloninger, 1987; Depue & Collins, 1999). For example, Depue and Collins describe extraversion as behavioral activation, arousal, sociability, positive emotions, and "positive incentive motivation." They propose that individual differences in extraversion are related to variations in function of dopamine projections originating in the ventral tegmental area, which they argue is directly involved in the intensity of incentive motivation. Depue, Luciana, Arbisi, Collins, and Leon (1994) provided empirical support for the link between extraversion and dopamine activity by showing that individuals who score high on the personality measure of extraversion exhibit more pronounced endocrine (prolactin) and behavioral (eye blink) responses to a dopamine receptor agonist, bromocriptine. They link the trait to individual differences in the rewarding effects of drugs as follows: "Because degree of state dopamine activity affects the salience of incentive stimuli, the subjective emotional and motivational experiences that are naturally elicited by incentive stimuli and are part of extraversion—elation/euphoria, desire, incentive motivation, sense of potency or self-efficacy—will also be more enhanced [by drugs] in individuals high on this trait" (Depue & Collins, 1999, p. 511).

Survey studies support the association between reward sensitivity and initiation of drug use. Extraversion has been linked to drinking episodes in a longitudinal study of students who were followed for three years after college (Gotham et al., 1997). Using the NEO Five Factor Inventory to measure extraversion, these authors found a significant positive correlation between extraversion and frequent intoxication during the three years of the study. Another influential biobehavioral theory of personality by Cloninger (1987) links "reward dependence" and "novelty seeking" to noradrenergic and dopaminergic function, and links these to genetically based individual differences in susceptibility to alcoholism. Support for this model was obtained from an empirical study (Cloninger, Sigvardsson, & Bohman, 1988) in which personality data from 431 11-year-old Swedish children were used to predict their alcohol abuse or alcoholism at age 27. High novelty seeking, together with low scores on harm avoidance, another personality dimension, were highly predictive of alcohol abuse. To the extent that novelty seeking is related to reward sensitivity, these findings suggest an association between reward function and drug use. However, the concept of novelty seeking, like the concept of sensation seeking, may reflect a combination of sensitivity to reward *and* insensitivity to negative outcomes. Moreover, other investigators (e.g., Sher, Bartholow, & Wood, 2000) have suggested that the association between extraversion and drug use is indirect, occurring only because extraverts are more likely to be exposed to drugs because of their tendency to socialize. These observations suggest that impulsivity may play a role in the increased tendency for drug use in high novelty and sensation seeking individuals. Nevertheless, there is some support for the idea that individuals who are more sensitive to reward, a tendency associated with the trait of extraversion, are more likely to experiment with drugs.

The association between reward sensitivity and susceptibility to drug use has also derived support from models of drug use in laboratory animals (Bardo, Donohew, & Harrington, 1996; Piazza, Deminiere, Le Moal, & Simon, 1989). Exploratory activity in a novel environment can be interpreted as sensitivity to the rewarding effects of novel stimuli. Based on this interpretation, Piazza and coworkers found that rats that exhibited the most exploratory behavior in a novel environment also most readily acquired a response to obtain injections of a self-administered stimulant drug. Over the last 13 years this finding has been extended to other drugs, other species, and other drug reward paradigms (e.g., Klebaur & Bardo, 1999). In their review of the evidence for a relation between novelty seeking and drug use, Bardo et al. argue that exposure to novelty, like drugs of abuse, activates the mesolimbic dopamine system. Further, they suggest that individual differences in the dopamine system may account for individual differences in both novelty seeking and drug use. They review evidence that both genetic and environmental factors, such as rearing experiences and environmental enrichment, can account for individual differences in both novelty seeking and susceptibility to use drugs.

IMPULSIVITY IN INITIATION

The susceptibility to initiate use and to experiment with drugs has also been linked to various forms of impulsivity. Individuals high on personality measures of impulsivity begin to smoke and use alcohol at an earlier age (McGue, Iacono, Legrand, Malone, & Elkins, 2001; White, Pandina, & Chen, 2002). Psychiatric patients with impulsive symptoms such as failure to plan ahead and insensitivity to punishment (e.g., those with Antisocial Personality Disorder, American Psychiatric Association [APA], 1994) have a high risk for developing drug or alcohol abuse (Hesselbrock, Meyer, & Keener, 1985; Regier et al., 1990; Sher & Trull, 1994). Individuals with impulsive aggression, including impulsive violent offenders, impulsive arsonists, and individuals with intermittent explosive disorder also have higher rates of substance abuse than the general population (Brady, Myrick, & McElroy, 1998). In a cross-sectional study of risk factors for alcoholism, Sher (1991) found that antisocial, aggressive, and impulsive traits were characteristic both of individuals who were at risk for later developing alcohol problems themselves, and also of offspring of alcoholic subjects. More recently, in a prospective study of personality and substance abuse, Sher, Bartholow, and Wood (2000) found that traits related to disinhibition and undercontrol most consistently predicted substance abuse, both prospectively and cross-sectionally. Disinhibition and undercontrol were more potent predictors than negative emotionality, extraversion, neuroticism, or psychoticism.

Developmentally there is also a strong association between childhood diagnoses of Oppositional Defiant Disorder, Conduct Disorder, and Attention Deficit Disorder and early drug use (APA, 1994; Dawes et al., 2000; Disney, Elkins, McGue, & Iacono, 1999; Sullivan & Rudnik-Levin, 2001). These diagnoses are characterized by behavioral undercontrol and disinhibitory psychopathology, and boys with these diagnoses are more likely to use drugs and develop problems with substance abuse than control children (Tarter et al., 1999). These children may be more at risk for using drugs because they are impaired in their ability to suppress behaviors with adverse consequences. Dawes et al. concluded that behavioral "dysregulation" is the core disorder of early onset substance use problems. They define dysregulation as "a deficiency in the degree to which an individual can modulate his or her reactivity to environmental challenges," and they link this dysregulation to deficits in prefrontal cortical function. In a study investigating predictors of the first drink in a study of early adolescents, McGue et al. (2001) found that measures of behavioral disinhibition, including oppositionality, hyperactivity/impulsivity, and inattentiveness at age 11, predicted drinking onset by age 14. They concluded that individuals who have their first drink relatively early manifest higher rates of disinhibitory behavior and psychopathology *even before they first try alcohol.* They suggest that this vulnerability to disinhibitory behavior may also predict subsequent alcoholism.

The range of definitions and measures of "impulsivity" across studies makes it difficult to identify the exact deficit(s) that make some individuals more vulnerable to experimenting with drugs. A further difficulty with the personality approaches to impulsivity reviewed above is that they do not provide agreed-upon operational definitions of the concept that can be used in laboratory settings to study the ability of behavioral or physiological manipulations. In this chapter, we discuss laboratory procedures that are based on validated, operational measures of impulsive behavior. Use of these procedures will help to identify specific behavioral and neural processes that constitute subtypes of the larger class of impulsive behaviors. At least two subtypes of impulsivity have been characterized. One form of impulsivity that may predict drug use is a relative insensitivity to delayed consequences. Insensitivity to delayed consequences, or preference for immediate rewards, is a widely used definition of impulsivity that has been validated in a variety of contexts (Logue, 1988; Rachlin & Green, 1972; Figure 1). By this definition, impulsive individuals exhibit stronger preferences for immediate rewards (e.g., taking a drug) over more delayed rewards (e.g., succeeding in work or school), even though the delayed rewards are larger. Figure 1 shows how the value of rewards are "discounted" as a function of the delay to their delivery, and how more impulsive individuals discount delayed rewards more steeply. Similarly, when they are choosing between an immediate positive outcome (e.g., a drug) and the possibility of a delayed negative consequences (e.g., punishment), they will be relatively less sensitive to the possibility of punishment. Individuals who are more impulsive by this definition will be more likely to experiment with illicit drugs. A second form of impulsivity, which is also pertinent to drug abuse, is a deficit in behavioral inhibition, or in the ability to inhibit prepotent behaviors (Logan & Cowan, 1984). By this definition, impulsive children may use drugs because they are unable to inhibit strongly prepotent behaviors (e.g., the inclination to use drugs in response to peer pressure). Both of these subtypes of impulsivity, delay discounting and behavioral inhibition, have face validity and empirical support. However, few studies have examined the correspondence between the two to determine whether hey co-occur in the same individuals. Interestingly, Sonuga-Barke (2002) recently examined performance on both of these measures of impulsivity, sensitivity to delay, and behavioral inhibition in children with ADHD. The researchers found that ADHD children in general were impaired on both tasks, but that the two measures were not correlated. Instead, there appeared to be two subpopulations of ADHD patients, one that exhibited sensitivity to delay and the other that had poor inhibitory control. It would be very interesting to determine prospectively whether either of these impairments predicted initiation of drug use.

There is also some evidence that impulsive behavior is predictive of likelihood of drug self-administration in laboratory animals. Poulos et al. (1995) assessed impulsivity in rats using a delay of reward procedure, in which the animals chose between immediate, smaller rewards and larger, delayed rewards. Impulsivity in this task is defined as preference for immediate rewards. Then the animals were given the opportunity to self-administer alcohol. Animals that performed most impulsively on the delay of reward task also consumed the most alcohol in the self-administration test. The authors speculated that this relationship between impulsivity and alcohol consumption is mediated by common serotonergic pathways. The relationship between impulsivity and drug preference, as well as the involvement of serotonin in impulsive behavior, were partially supported by findings by Brunner and Hen (1997) in a study with 5-HT1B receptor knockout mice. The knockout mice exhibited more impulsive aggression (although they did not perform more impulsively on a delay discounting task), and also acquired cocaine self-administration more rapidly and consumed more alcohol than wild-type control mice. Although these results are intriguing and consistent with human data, it is not intuitively clear why impulsivity in animals should be predictive of alcohol use. Humans must limit or control their drug use because it is inappropriate to use drugs in many situations. In contrast, in animal models of drug use there are no obvious constraints on their drug consumption, and therefore it is not clear how impulsivity, as defined by delay of reward or impulsive aggression, should be related to consumption of the drug.

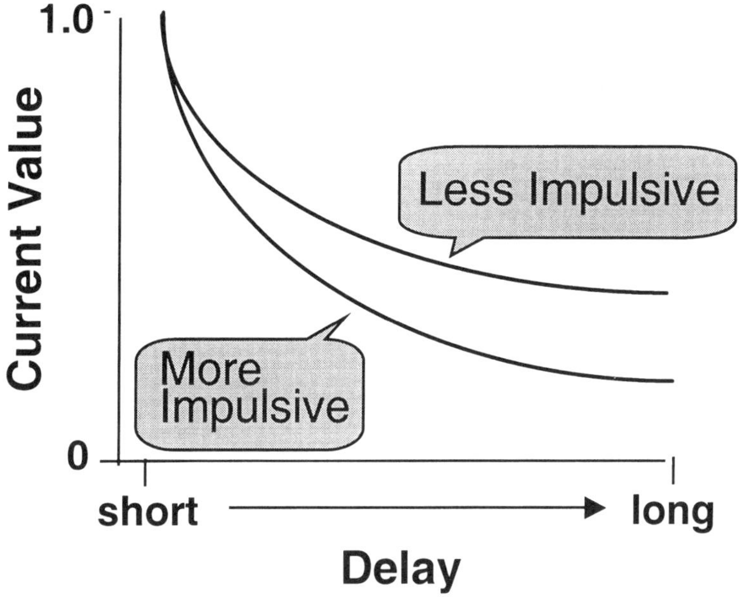

Figure 1. Hypothetical delay discounting curves illustrating more and less impulsive behavior. Plotted points are indifference points at which the delayed and immediate amounts are judged to be of equal value.

Maintenance of Use

Once an individual experiences the effects of a drug at least once, the direct effects of the drug, and the memories and conditioned responses relating to this experience, come to influence future drug-seeking behavior. Thus, variations in any of these elements of the rewarding effects of drugs will influence future drug-seeking behavior. In addition, variations in the ability to resist the temptation to repeat the drug use will also affect drug seeking. There is substantial interindividual variability in whether individuals continue to use drugs, after their first use. Although most people at some time in their lives try drugs, even drugs that are known to be highly abused, only a small number go on to use drugs regularly or excessively. For example, although 79% of adults report having used an illicit drug at some time in their lives by age 40, only 11% report using in the previous 30 days, and it can be assumed that many of these are not daily users and do not use drugs at problematic levels (National Institute of Drug Abuse [NIDA], 2000). Thus, only a small proportion of the people who try drugs progress to regular daily use of drugs. The variation among individuals in the maintenance and progression of drug use is likely to be determined by many factors. We propose that the combined influence of the rewarding effects of the drugs and variations in the ability to refrain from using a rewarding substance are major determinants of continuation of drug use.

The influence of reward and impulsivity in the susceptibility to use drugs may also change over the course of repeated or chronic use of drugs, and thereby affect the progression from use to abuse. Jentsch and Taylor (1999) suggest that chronic use of drugs may increase the rewarding effects of drugs and cause impairments in inhibition. They note that the rewarding, or positive motivational, effects of drugs may increase with repeated drug use, in accordance with the theory of incentive sensitization proposed by Robinson and Berridge (1993). At the same time, they argue, chronic use of drugs may impair the individual's ability to refrain from drug use by damaging brain areas involved in inhibitory control, especially frontal cortical areas. The combined influence of increased rewarding effects and decreased ability to refrain from drug use after chronic drug exposure may contribute to the uniquely compulsive nature of drug-seeking behavior in addicted individuals.

REWARD PROCESSES IN MAINTENANCE

Most drugs of abuse directly or indirectly activate the neural systems that mediate reward in the brain. In particular, studies with laboratory animals indicate that drugs activate the mesolimbic dopamine system, which is thought to mediate the rewarding effects of other reinforcing stimuli including food and water (Phillips & Fibiger, 1990; White, 1996; Wise, 1996). Imaging studies with humans provide further evidence that highly rewarding drugs, such as cocaine, activate the mesolimbic dopamine system at the same time that they produce the subjective experience of euphoria (Brieter, Rosen, & Ann, 1999). Experimental interventions (e.g., lesions, receptor antagonists, selectively bred animals) that decrease dopamine function typically decrease the rewarding effects of drugs, and interventions that enhance dopamine function increase rewards (Koob, 1992).

In humans, drug reward is generally associated with the subjective experience of pleasure, or "euphoria," which can be measured with standardized self-report questionnaires (de Wit & Griffiths, 1991; Fischman & Foltin, 1991). It is apparent from controlled studies with humans that individuals differ in degree of euphoria they experience from drugs, and that these individual differences are related to variations in drug-seeking behavior. We have conducted a series of double blind, placebo-controlled studies of drug preference in healthy volunteers to examine the relation between the quality or magnitude of subjective effects and the reinforcing effects of drugs. We found that subjects who reported the greatest euphorigenic effects from drugs (including alcohol, diazepam, and *d*-amphetamine) were also most likely to choose to consume these drugs over a placebo, in a choice test (de Wit, Uhlenhuth, & Johanson, 1986; de Wit, Uhlenhuth, Pierri, & Johanson, 1987; de Wit, Pierri, & Johanson, 1989). Contextual factors that dampen the subjective effects of drugs also decrease drug consumption (Doty & de Wit, 1996), and in at least one study (Enggasser & de Wit, 2001), a dopamine receptor antagonist that dampened the euphoric effects of alcohol also reduced consumption of alcohol. These findings with humans support the idea that there is a direct link between the positive, mood-enhancing effects of drugs and repeated drug use.

The processes of positive motivation, or reward, that facilitate drug use include conditioned motivational effects, such as Pavlovian conditioned incentive effects and conditioned reinforcement. After an organism has experienced the direct rewarding or reinforcing effects of a drug, environmental stimuli associated with this experience acquire positive motivational properties through classical and operant conditioning processes (Stewart, de Wit, & Eikelboom, 1984). These conditioned responses, together with processes related to memory and retrieval (Berke & Hyman, 2000), play a key role in the maintenance of drug use and influence the return to drug use after varying periods of abstinence (see next section). Many studies using laboratory animals have demonstrated the powerful control of conditioned stimuli in drug-seeking behavior (Caggiula et al., 2001; O'Brien, Childress, Ehrman, & Robbins, 1998; Robinson & Berridge, 1993). Factors that affect these conditioned responses, including individual variability in conditioning or memory, can influence the likelihood of cue-induced drug seeking. For example, Kambouropoulos and Staiger (2001) recently reported that individual differences in sensitivity to reward, as measured by responsiveness to a monetary incentive, was positively related to reactivity to alcohol-related cues in social drinkers. Thus, both unconditioned and conditioned rewarding effects of drugs exert a powerful influence over the maintenance of drug-seeking behavior.

IMPULSIVITY IN MAINTENANCE

In the absence of any countervailing influence, an organism that experiences pleasurable effects from a drug or any other positive stimulus is likely to try to repeat the experience. Almost by definition, a response that leads to a positive outcome (without concomitant negative consequences) will subsequently increase in frequency. In most animal models of drug use (self-administration), rats or monkeys have the opportunity to take drugs that are rewarding, without any observable negative consequences. In humans, however, drug use usually has some adverse consequences in addition to its positive consequences, and therefore drug use involves some conflict, and abstaining from drugs requires some inhibition or restraint. Adverse consequences, including social, legal, or medical problems such as violating cultural norms, breaking laws, or risking physical harm to self or others, normally limit an individual's tendency to use drugs. Impulsivity, including factors that decrease sensitivity to delayed negative consequences or factors that impair the ability to inhibit behavior, increase the likelihood of drug use, independently of the rewarding effects of the drug.

In drug-experienced individuals, impulsivity can increase the likelihood of using a drug both before the drug has been ingested on a particular occasion, as well as after the drug is taken. First, before a drug is ingested, drug-related conditioned stimuli (i.e., stimuli that have been associated with the drug in the past) and discriminative stimuli (i.e., stimuli that have signaled the availability of the drug) increase the likelihood, or motivation, to seek and use drugs. Individuals who are dispositionally more impulsive are less able to resist the impulse to take drugs induced by these stimuli, even though use is maladaptive (i.e., has adverse consequences). Thus, impulsive individuals are more likely to use alcohol in the face of known adverse consequences such as disapproval by authorities, punishment, and unpleasant physical symptoms of excessive consumption (Barnes, Welte, Hoffman, & Dintcheff, 1999; Cherpitel, 1999; Fergusson, Lynskey, & Horwood, 1995; Kilbey, Downey, & Breslau, 1998; McGue et al., 2001; Nagoshi, Wilson, & Rodriguez, 1991; Petry & Casarella, 1999). In addition, there may be alterations in state that affect impulsive decision making. For example, before the drug is ingested on a particular occasion, acute environmental events that induce stress may increase impulsive decision making (Gray, 1999; Tice, Bratslavsky, & Baumeister, 2001), thereby momentarily increasing preference for immediate rewards (e.g., getting the drug effect) over delayed reward (e.g., benefiting from abstinence). Thus, various factors may increase the likelihood of taking a drug on a particular occasion, independently of how rewarding the drug is. Second, after the drug has been ingested, the pharmacological effects of the drug may further increase the likelihood that the individual will extend the bout of drug use, by impairing the influence of both immediate and delayed consequences on behavior. For example, an individual may consume a drink with the intention of limiting herself to a single dose, with plans to engage in other, more productive activities after the drink. However, after consuming the alcohol, the pharmacological effects of the drug may modify the decision-making process, so that now more immediate rewards (e.g., consuming another drink) take precedence over the previously planned delayed rewards of productive work. Thus, the drug itself may increase impulsive behavior, thereby increasing the likelihood of further drug use. These examples illustrate that an individual's ability to withhold inappropriate responses and to make choices based on the value of delayed rewards plays an important role in whether they use drugs, independently of the rewarding effects of the drug.

To investigate the direct effects of drugs on measures of impulsivity, our laboratory has conducted a series of studies using parallel procedures in both humans and rats, to characterize the effects of drugs on impulsivity. The studies utilize two operationally defined measures of impulsivity, delay discounting and the Stop Task, a measure of behavioral inhibition. The delay-discounting task assesses a form of cognitive impulsivity, characterized by a preference for more immediate or certain rewards, relative to delayed or uncertain rewards (Logue, 1988; Rachlin & Green, 1972). Impulsive individuals, such as gamblers, impulsive psychiatric patients, and substance

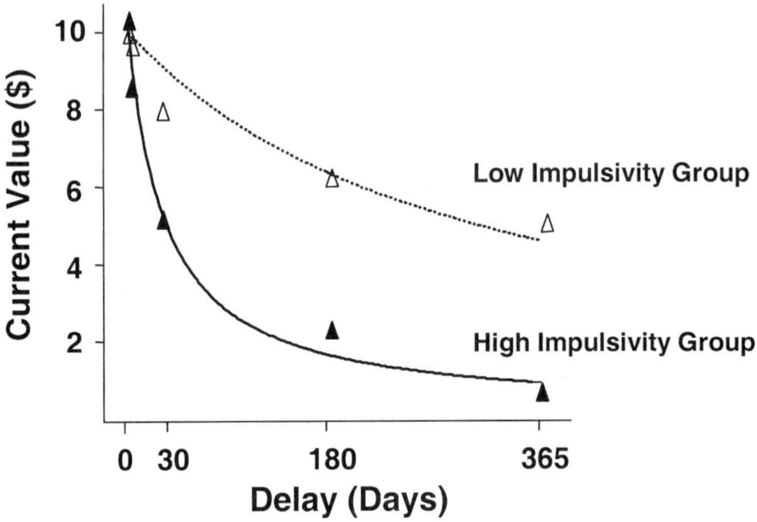

Figure 2. Delay discounting curves for high ($N = 12$) and low ($N = 12$) impulsive psychiatric patients, showing that the high impulsive group discounted more, especially at longer delays. Points show indifference points, lines show that the curves are well described with a hyperbolic function.

abusers, consistently prefer more immediate rewards in these tasks (Crean, de Wit, & Richards, 2000; Petry, 2000a, 2000b; Figure 2). For example, Figure 2 shows the discounting curves for psychiatric outpatients who either did, or did not, exhibit impulsive symptoms as part of their clinical profile. Small but significant correlations have been found between delay discounting and personality measures of discounting (Mitchell, 1999; Richards, Zhang, Mitchell, & de Wit, 1999). The Stop Task, in contrast, assesses the ability to inhibit a prepotent response (Logan & Cowan, 1984; Figure 3). Figure 3 shows schematically the sequence of events for a "go" trial and for a "stop" trial, and how the stop reaction time is calculated. This task measures the speed at which subjects are able to inhibit a response (Stop Reaction Time), relative to the speed with which they perform the response (Go Reaction Time). Children with ADHD, who are known to be highly impulsive, are impaired on the Stop Reaction Times, and methylphenidate, which reduces the symptoms of ADHD, also reverses this deficit. In young adults, Stop Reaction Time was also positively correlated with a personality measure of impulsivity (Lo-

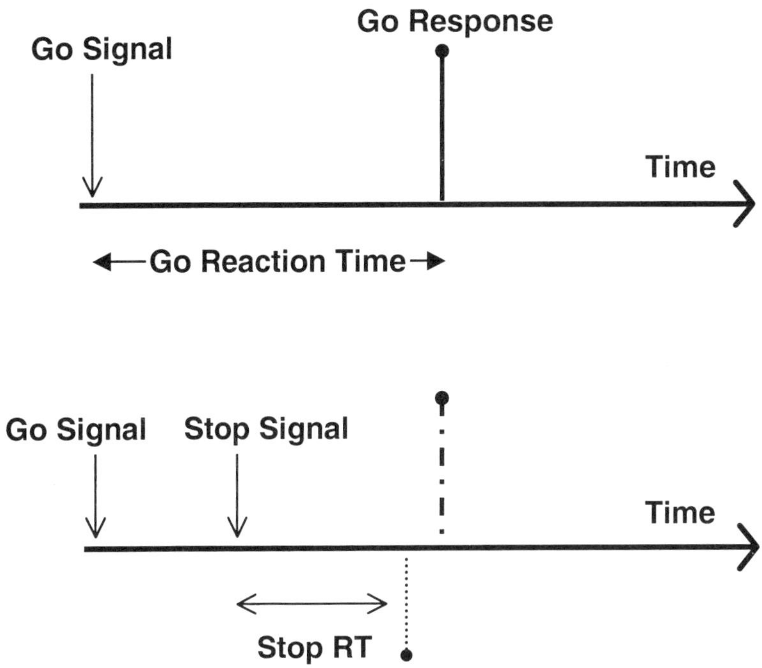

Figure 3. Schematic of Stop Task protocol. Top panel shows a Go trial, on which Go Reaction Time is determined. Bottom panel shows sequence of events for a Stop trial, on which the subject successfully inhibited the response. The inferred Stop RT response and 50% inhibition are estimated by varying the interval from Go to Stop Signal across trials.

gan, Schachar, & Tannock, 1997), although the correlation was small. These two tasks appear to measure different types of impulsivity, but both may be involved in inappropriate drug use. As was described previously, these two laboratory measures of impulsivity appear to identify distinct subsets of children with ADHD (Sonuga-Barke, 2002). We have assessed performance on these tasks after acute administration of drugs and after neurochemical manipulations on impulsive behavior. We have conducted studies in parallel, using similar procedures and drug manipulations in rats and in healthy human volunteers. The procedures and the results of our studies are described in the following sections.

Delay Discounting. Delay discounting provides a measure of how much the value of reward decreases (i.e., is discounted) as a function of the delay to receiving the reward. We use a computerized adjusting amount procedure to measure discounting of delayed reinforcers. In the studies with rats, the reinforcers are varying amounts of water, delayed by 0 to 16 seconds. In the parallel procedure with humans, the reinforcers are varying amounts of money, delayed by 0 to 360 days. The subjects choose between a smaller reinforcer amount available immediately and a larger amount available after a delay, in a series of adjusting trials. The choices, or trials, are presented according to an adjusting amount procedure (Richards et al., 1997; Richards, Zhang, Mitchell, & de Wit, 1999), in which the magnitude of the immediate reinforcer is adjusted across successive trials while the delayed option remains constant. The magnitude of the immediate reinforcer is varied systematically until an immediate value is reached at which the subject chooses the delayed and immediate options about 50% of the time. This is referred to as the "indifference point." Indifference points are determined for several different delays, which can then be plotted and discount functions derived through curve-fitting analysis. The curves that result from the devaluation of reward value by delay are well described by the hyperbolic function of Mazur (1987) $V = A/(1 + kD)$, where V is value, A is the amount of the delayed reward, D is the delay to reward, and k is a free parameter. Larger values of k indicate more rapid devaluation of reinforcer value by delay and greater impulsivity. Despite markedly different parameters in the rat and human studies, in terms of reinforcer type, magnitude, delay, and immediacy of consumption, the discount functions obtained in the two species are remarkably similar (Figure 4). Figure 4 shows that in both species the value of a delayed reinforcer decreases as the delay becomes longer, and how the resulting "discount function" is well described by the hyperbolic function. The results are stable within individuals in test-retest, and the discount functions vary both across individuals and after pharmacological interventions.

Several studies have shown that individuals with a history of drug use or abuse perform more impulsively (i.e., discount more steeply) on delay discounting tasks. For example, heroin addicts discount more than nondrug-using control subjects (Kirby, Petry, & Bickel, 1999; Madden, Petry, Badger, & Bickel 1999), problem drinkers discount more than lighter alcohol drinkers (Vuchinich & Simpson, 1998), cigarette smokers discount more than nonsmokers (Mitchell,

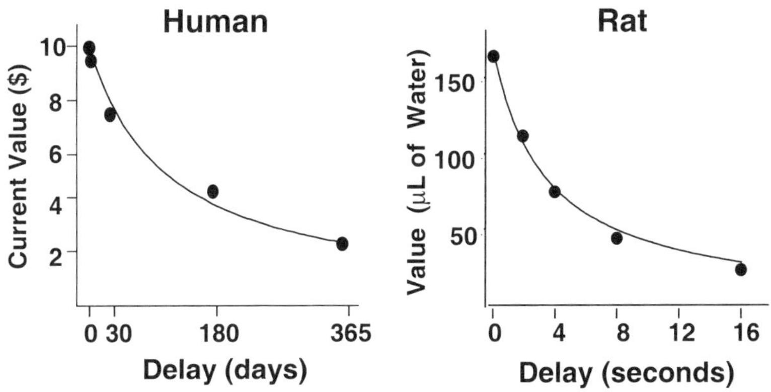

Figure 4. Delay discounting curves obtained from parallel adjusting amount procedures in humans and rats. In humans, the reinforcers are monetary values (0–$10) and in rats the reinforcers are small quantities of water (0–200 microliters). Hyperbolic curves fit the indifference points in both species.

1999), and current cigarette smokers discount more than exsmokers (Bickel, Odum, & Madden, 1999). These findings confirm clinical impressions that drug users are more impulsive than nondrug users, and they are also consistent with studies comparing drug users and nonusers on personality measures of impulsivity (e.g., Petry, 2001). However, these comparisons across populations are correlational and do not reveal whether the group differences resulted from the drug use (and its attendant lifestyles) or whether the differences predated, and perhaps contributed to, the drug use. This relationship will have to be examined in a longitudinal, prospective study in which the behavioral measure of delay discounting is used as a predictor of future drug use.

In humans, we have studied the effects of acute administration of several drugs on delay discounting, to investigate the direct effects of these drugs on impulsive behavior in healthy young adults. We have conducted double-blind, placebo-controlled studies to examine the effects of single doses of ethanol (0.5 or 0.8 g/kg; N = 24, for each dose; Richards, Zhang, Mitchell, & de Wit, 1999), oral delta^9-tetrahydrocannabinol (THC; 7.5 and 15 mg; N = 36; McDonald et al., 2003), oral *d*-amphetamine (10 and 20 mg; N = 36; de Wit, Enggasser, & Richards, 2002), and tryptophan depletion (N = 25; Crean, Richards, & de Wit, 2002). Tryptophan depletion is a dietary interven-

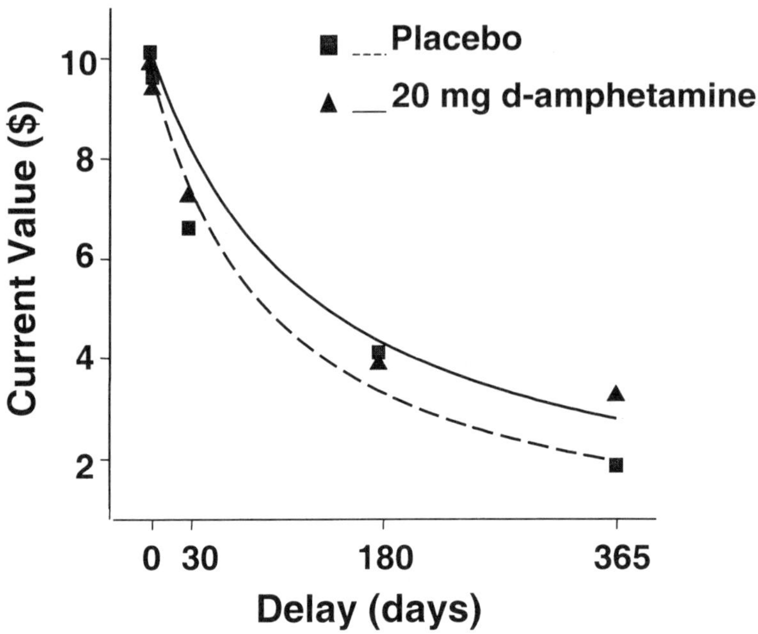

Figure 5. Effects of an acute oral dose of *d*-amphetamine (20 mg) or placebo on delay discounting in 36 healthy volunteers. *D*-amphetamine decreased delay discounting, that is, it decreased impulsive behavior.

tion that acutely decreases brain levels of serotonin. It was tested because low serotonin levels have been associated with impulsivity in humans and other primates (Higley, Suomi, & Linnoila, 1996; Linnoila, Virkkunen, & Scheinin, 1983; Virkkunen, Nuttila, Goodwin, & Linnoila, 1987). Ethanol, THC and *d*-amphetamine were tested because these drugs are abused, and may have adverse behavioral effects corresponding to decreases in the value of delayed, compared to immediate, rewards. Of these four interventions, the only one that altered delay discounting in healthy human volunteers was *d*-amphetamine, which *decreased* delay discounting, that is, it decreased impulsive behavior (Figure 5). Figure 5 shows that subjects valued delayed rewards slightly more after administration of amphetamine. The lack of effect with ethanol was unexpected, in view of suggestions that alcohol increases impulsive behavior (alcohol "myopia," Steele & Josephs, 1990; MacDonald, Zanna, & Fong, 1995), and the

Table 1. *Summary of Drugs Tested with Delay Discounting in Rats and Humans Using the Delay Discounting Procedure*

	Rat	Human
d-amphetamine (acute)	↓	↓
Methamphetamine (acute)	↓	
Methamphetamine (chronic)	↑	
D2 antagonist	↑	
5-HT lesion	n.e.	
DA lesion (NAC)	↑	

Note: ↓ = decrease in impulsivity
↑ = increase in impulsivity
n.e. = no effect

lack of effect with tryptophan depletion did not correspond with evidence that low serotonin is associated with impulsivity. The absence of effects with these manipulations may have been due to insensitivity of the procedure, the true (lack of) effects of these treatments, or the resistance to change of the subjects' behavior. It was interesting that *d*-amphetamine decreased impulsive behavior in these healthy subjects. First, this indicates that the procedure is at least sensitive to certain acute manipulations. Second, it is interesting because the direction of the effect is consistent with clinical findings that stimulant drugs decrease impulsive behavior in children with ADHD (Schachar, Tannock, & Logan, 1993), and also with delay discounting studies using stimulant drugs and dopamine antagonists in rats (see following discussion). It should be noted that the participants in these acute studies were highly functioning young adults, recruited mainly from a university community. It remains to be determined whether acute administration of these drugs would alter delay discounting in individuals who may be at higher risk, especially those who are high on the trait of impulsivity.

In rats, we (Richards, Sabol, & de Wit, 1999a; Wade, de Wit, & Richards, 2000) have used a similar, adjusting amount procedure to study the effects of drugs on delay discounting (Table 1). As in the studies with humans, acute doses of *d*-amphetamine and methamphetamine decreased delay discounting. In contrast, treatments that decreased dopamine function, including D2 receptor antagonists flupenthixol and raclopride (although not the D1 antagonist SCH 23390) and lesions of the nucleus accumbens, increased delay discounting, that is, made the animals more impulsive (Cardinal, Pennicott, Sugathapala, Robbins, & Everett, 2001; Wade et al., 2000). Notably, lesions that depleted serotonin in the forebrain by more than 90% had no effect on delay discounting, suggesting that this form of impulsive behavior is mediated more by dopamine than serotonin. It was also found that rats treated chronically with a high dose of methamphetamine became *more* impulsive, suggesting that the tendency to behave impulsively may increase after repeated exposure to stimulant drugs. Thus there are consistencies between the findings with rats and humans that suggest the delay discounting procedures, despite their many differences, are mediated by the same underlying processes. This homology increases our confidence in the animal models and in our ability to study the neurobiological processes mediating human impulsive behavior using the animal model.

Stop Task (Logan et al., 1997). The Stop Task is designed to assess the subject's ability to inhibit a prepotent response. In the human studies, subjects are instructed to respond as quickly as possible when a specific letter (Go signal) is presented on a computer screen, and to inhibit (Stop) their responses when a tone is presented very soon after the Go signal. In the rat studies, animals are trained to perform one response when one stimulus (Go signal) is presented, but to perform a different response when another stimulus (Stop signal) is presented. In both procedures, the Stop signal is presented on random trials and at different delays following the Go signal. The delays to the Stop signal are varied systematically according to the subject's performance: the delay to the Stop signal is adjusted until the subject inhibits (Stops) the Go responses on approximately 50% of trials. After the Stop signal delay has been adjusted to this 50% criterion, the time required for the subject to stop the Go response (Stop reaction time; Stop RT) can be inferred. The Stop RT is calculated by subtracting the final mean delay at which the Stop signal is presented from the mean Go RT. This is the primary dependent measure of the task. The Go reaction time (Go RT), or latency to respond to the Go signal, is a measure of simple reaction time and a secondary dependent measure that can be used to control for nonspecific changes in reaction times. Both Go RTs and Stop RTs are measured in milliseconds.

We have used this procedure with healthy human volunteers, using placebo-controlled procedures, to test the direct effects of ethanol (0.4 and 0.8 g/kg; de Wit, Crean, & Richards, 2000; Figure 6), THC (7.5

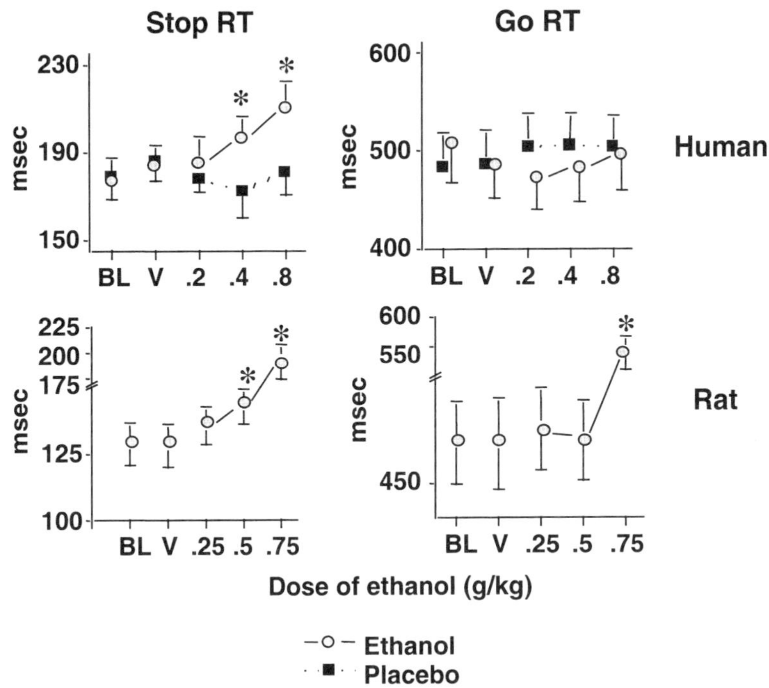

Figure 6. Effects of ethanol on the Stop Task in humans (top panels; N = 24) and rats (bottom panels; N = 12). In the human study, alcohol was administered in a single session in cumulating doses (0.2, 0.4, 0.8 g/kg; circular symbols), and placebo beverages were administered on another session (square symbols). In the rat study, each dose of ethanol was tested on a separate session. BL refers to baseline, V refers to vehicle. In both species, ethanol increased Stop RT at a dose that did not affect Go RT, indicating a specific impairment of inhibition. These figures are based on images previously published (de Wit et al., 2000; Feola et al., 2000).

and 15 mg; McDonald, Schleifer, Richards, & de Wit, 2003; Figure 7), *d*-amphetamine (10 and 20 mg; de Wit et al., 2000; Figure 8) and tryptophan depletion in males with or without a family history of alcoholism (N = 25; Crean, Richards, & de Wit, 2002). Figures 6 and 7 show that both ethanol and THC increased Stop RTs at doses that did not affect Go RT, indicating that they specifically increased the ability to inhibit responding. In contrast, Figure 8 shows that *d*-amphetamine *decreased* Stop RT (i.e., *decreased* impulsivity), consistent with its effects on the delay discounting procedure and consistent with its effects on the Stop Task in rats (see following discussion). Tryptophan deple-

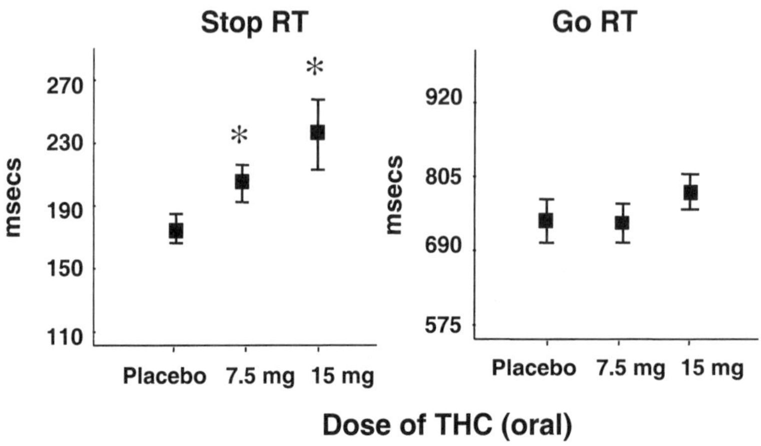

Figure 7. Effects of delta[9]-tetrahydrocannabinol (THC; 7.5 and 15 mg) on Stop and Go Reaction Times in healthy volunteers ($N = 36$). Both doses of THC increased Stop RT without affecting Go RT, indicating a specific impairment in inhibition.

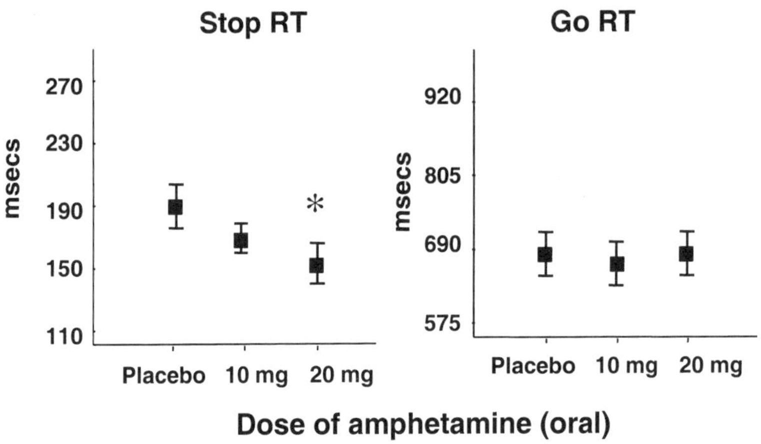

Figure 8. Effects of *d*-amphetamine (10 and 20 mg) on Stop and Go Reaction Times in healthy volunteers ($N = 36$). The higher dose of *d*-amphetamine decreased Stop RT without affecting Go RT, indicating a specific improvement in inhibition.

tion, a procedure that decreases brain levels of serotonin, increased Stop RT in subjects with a family history of alcoholism, compared to the subjects with no alcoholic relatives. Serotonin has been linked to risk for alcoholism and impulsive aggression (Linnoila, DeJong, &

Table 2. *Summary of Drugs Tested with the Stop Task in Rats and Humans*

	Rat	Human
d-amphetamine (acute)	↓	↓
Alcohol	↑	↑
THC		↑
5-HT lesion or depletion	↑	↑
DA lesion (NAC)	↑	

Note: Decrease in Stop RT = decrease in impulsivity
↑ = increase in impulsivity
↓ = decrease in impulsivity

Virkkunen, 1989). Finally, in the first study to compare drug-using populations on Stop Task performance, Fillmore, Rush, and Hays (2002) recently reported that cocaine users exhibit longer Stop RTs than control subjects on the Stop Task. Together, these results show that acute or chronic ingestion of drugs may impair the ability to inhibit responses. This impairment may affect not only performance on activities that require rapid response control, but also impair the ability to inhibit goal-directed behaviors in general.

We have also used the Stop Task procedure with rats to test the effects of drugs and treatments targeting specific neurotransmitter systems (Table 2). In concordance with the findings in humans, *d*-amphetamine (0.75 mg/kg) decreased Stop RT, whereas alcohol (doses 500 mg/kg) increased Stop RT, without affecting Go RT (Feola, Richards, & de Wit, 2000). Lesioning the serotonin system using 5, 7 DHT, resulted in impairments in Stop RTs without affecting Go RT (Richards, Kline, Miller, Crean, & de Wit, 2002).

Taken together, these findings indicate that both delay discounting and the Stop Task provide valid indices of impulsive behavior in both rats and humans, and that these two tasks measure separate behavioral and neural processes. This is an important finding, because it provides the groundwork for further research into the neurobiology of different types of impulsivity, the genetics of impulsivity, and the effects of drugs or other manipulations (e.g., stress) on impulsive behavior.

Relapse

One of the most puzzling and persistent issues in substance abuse research is why former drug users, who have successfully achieved abstinence often for extended periods of time, relapse at such an extraordinarily high rate. It is estimated that up to 80% of drug users who achieve initial abstinence (i.e., beyond the duration of acute withdrawal symptoms) return to using drugs, usually at their prequit rates (Hunt, Barnett, & Branch, 1971). A reward-related process that is believed to play an important role in relapse is that of conditioned responses to environmental cues previously paired with the drug. These cues elicit druglike responses, including the induction of craving for the drug (Stewart et al., 1984). An impulsivity-related process that can lead to a restoration of drug use is impaired behavioral inhibition. Abstinence from drug use may require an active inhibitory process of suppressing a prepotent drug-seeking response. Events that impair the individual's ability to maintain active response suppression will lead to a reinstatement of the response. Thus, both reward-related and impulsivity-related events may lead to restoration of drug use, even after extended periods of abstinence. These are described in more detail in the following sections.

REWARD PROCESSES IN RELAPSE

Among the factors that are known to precipitate relapse in human drug users are positive affective states (Shiffman, 1982; Shiffman, Paty, Gyns, Kassel, & Hickcox, 1996), ingestion of drugs that produce feelings of well being, and exposure to stimuli associated with rewarding drugs (de Wit, 1996). In an early study examining antecedents of relapse in 183 abstinent smokers who called a relapse counseling hotline, Shiffman (1982) reported that about one-third of relapse crises were associated with positive affective states. In a later study, Shiffman et al. (1996) studied the events that immediately preceded instances of relapse in smokers, using real-life monitoring of feelings and activities. They found that positive affective states such as "good mood" and "relaxing" accounted for 24–33% of the relapse episodes. To our knowledge, no laboratory-based studies have examined the effect of acute (nonpharmacological) induction of positive affect on relapse or craving for drugs in abstinent (ex)users. However, several studies have examined the effects of positive affective states induced by drugs, on craving for drugs or consumption of drugs (de

Wit, 1996). Single, experimenter-delivered doses of drugs of abuse, administered at a time when the subject is not currently using the drug, readily increase both subjective ratings of craving for the drug, and the tendency to self-administer the drug. For example, administration of cocaine to abstinent cocaine users increased ratings of craving and wanting more cocaine (Haney, Ward, Foltin, & Fischman, 2001; Jaffe, Cascella, Kumor, & Sherer, 1989). Small doses of alcohol administered to either alcoholics or social drinkers increase both ratings of wanting more alcohol and amount of alcohol consumed (Chutuape, Mitchell, & de Wit, 1994; Hodgson, Rankin, & Stockwell, 1979). One study (Chornock, Stitzer, Gross, & Leischow, 1992) examined the effects of smoking a single cigarette after four days of abstinence, and found that smoking a single cigarette increased the likelihood of returning to regular smoking over the subsequent 24-hour period. These naturalistic and laboratory-based studies indicate that drug-induced or naturally occurring positive mood states have the potential to reinstate drug-seeking behavior after a period of abstinence.

Administration of small doses of a formerly self-administered (rewarding) drug also reliably reinstates responding in rats, in an animal model of relapse (de Wit & Stewart, 1981; Gerber & Stretch, 1975; Shaham, Erb, & Stewart, 2000; Stewart et al., 1984). In these studies, rats are first trained to self-administer a drug, and then they undergo a period of extinction during which responses are no longer reinforced. Stimuli and events that reinstate responding after extinction are thought to model events that precipitate relapse in human drug users. In this model, experimenter-delivered injections of cocaine or heroin reinstate responding in rats that were previously trained to self-administer these drugs. A large number of studies have been conducted to investigate the neurochemical substrates and brain circuits involved in drug-induced reinstatement (Comer & Carroll, 1996; Lê, Quan, Juzystch, Fletcher, Joharchi, & Shaham, 1998; Lê, Poulos, Harding, Watchus, Juzytsch, & Shaham, 1999; Self, Barnhart, Lehman, & Nestler, 1996; Self & Nestler, 1998). Based on their own research and a review of the literature, Shaham et al. (2000) concluded that drug-induced reinstatement is mediated primarily by dopaminergic and, to a lesser extent opioid, mechanisms.

IMPULSIVITY IN RELAPSE

Given the powerful motivational influence of the rewarding effects of drugs and drug-related stimuli, abstaining from drugs after an extended period of drug use requires an active and sustained process of response suppression. Consequently, any events or states that interfere with this suppression increase the likelihood of relapse. Even after an individual has stopped using drugs, well-learned responses, strong positive memories of the drugs, contextual cues, and associations related to the drugs continue to promote drug-seeking behavior. In human drug users who are attempting to abstain from use these proactive influences must be countered by a battery of skills and strategies to suppress the urge to use drugs, including distraction, thought-stopping, relaxation, long-term planning, and cue extinction procedures. Most of these strategies require effort and concentration, and therefore it is not surprising that events or states that interfere with the individual's ability to inhibit responses also increase the likelihood of relapse.

Stress and negative affect states are also, like positive mood states, common antecedents to relapse in human drug users. Stress and negative mood states are likely to precipitate relapse by interfering with the ability to inhibit responses. In a real-time analysis of smoking relapse episodes, based on a smoking cessation hotline, Shiffman (1982) found that about one third of abstinent smokers reported that negative affect (anger, anxiety, and depression) elicited a strong urge to relapse. In a more recent study (Shiffman et al., 1996), it was found that "bad mood" and stress preceded 32–46% of relapse episodes. The idea that stress and negative mood states increase relapse is by impairing decision-making capacity derives some support from economic decision-making studies, which show that stress and negative affect increase impulsive (short-term) decision making (Gray, 1999; Leith & Baumeister, 1996; Tice et al., 2001).

Shaham et al. (2000) have shown that stress also reliably reinstates drug-reinforced responding in rats. Stressors such as foot-shock or cues previously associated with foot-shock, food deprivation, restraint, fox odor, or administration of a stress hormone reinstate responding that was previously reinforced by injections of cocaine or heroin. Further, these investigators have investigated the neural circuits that mediate stress-induced reinstatement, and they

Table 3. *Summary of Studies Showing That Reinstatement by Heroin Priming Injections Involve Different Processes from Reinstatement by Stress*

Treatment	Heroin prime	Stress
Naltrexone	↓	n.e.
D1 antagonist	↓	n.e.
D2 antagonist	↓	n.e.
CRF antagonist	n.e.	↓
Alpha2 agonist	n.e.	↓

Source: Shaham et al. (2000)
Note: ↓ = dampening of response
n.e. = no effect

have demonstrated that the mechanisms that mediate drug-induced reinstatement are separate from the mechanisms that mediate stress-induced reinstatement (Table 3). Unlike drug-induced reinstatement, stress-induced reinstatement appears to depend on the integrity of hypothalamic-pituitary and adrenergic systems. In particular, adrenolectomy or administration of corticotropin releasing factor antagonists and alpha2 adrenergic agonists attenuate stress-induced reinstatement, but have no effect on drug-induced reinstatement. In contrast, the treatments (described previously) that attenuate drug-induced reinstatement have no effect on stress-induced reinstatement. This apparent dissociation between reward-related and stress-related reinstatement provides further evidence for the existence of separate facilitative (reward and impulsivity) factors in the control of relapse and the return to drug-seeking behavior.

General Discussion

The evidence outlined here makes a case for independent processes of reward and impulsivity, both of which affect the likelihood of drug use. However, these two processes may interact or be linked by common behavioral or neural processes. For example, reward-sensitivity and impulsivity have been tied to the same underlying process in certain theories of personality. Early versions of Eysenck's personality theory classified impulsivity as a subcategory under the definition of extraversion (Eysenck & Eysenck, 1975). Other researchers (e.g., Cloninger, 1987) have linked reward sensitivity and novelty seeking to impulsivity. By this reasoning, the trait of sensation seeking or novelty seeking may result from either a susceptibility to rewards or from an insensitivity to negative outcomes. It is difficult to evaluate these conceptual schemes in the absence of clear operational definitions of the underlying factors, and controlled empirical research.

It is also possible that sensitivity to reward and impulsivity are separate processes, but that they tend to co-occur in certain individuals. There is empirical evidence that both sensation seeking and impulsivity are high in substance abusing populations. In one study, Conrod, Peterson, and Pihl (1997) examined relationships between personality and both self-reported and laboratory measures of alcohol consumption, in individuals with or without family histories of alcoholism. They found that disinhibition, as measured by personality questionnaires, and sensitivity to reinforcement strongly and independently predicted alcohol consumption both outside and in the laboratory, and that both of these influences were stronger in individuals genetically at risk for alcoholism. Sensitivity to alcohol reinforcement was related to quantity of alcohol consumed and frequency of excessive consumption, whereas disinhibition was related to self-reported negative consequences with alcohol. In another study, Conrod, Peterson, and Pihl (2001) studied personality risk factors in 293 substance-abusing women, and found that both sensation seeking and impulsivity were associated with higher rates of alcohol dependence. In another study, Dervaux et al. (2001) examined impulsivity (using the Barratt Impulsivity Scale; Barratt & Patton, 1983), sensation seeking (using the Sensation-Seeking Scale; Zuckerman, 1984) and anhedonia (using the Chapman Physical Anhedonia Scale) as risk factors for substance abuse in schizophrenic patients. They found that drug use was related to impulsivity and sensation seeking but not to anhedonia.

The co-incidence of high reward reactivity and high impulsivity among drug users could indicate that the two processes are related, or it could indicate that substance use results from both of these factors. From simple observation of behavior it is difficult to determine whether a particular (maladaptive) behavior occurs because its reward value is greater, or because the inhibitory processes are weaker. Only careful empirical research in well-controlled laboratory studies will allow these issues to be resolved. Precise and standardized operational definitions are needed to characterize different forms of impulsive behavior, in humans and in laboratory animals. Studies investigating the neurochemistry and neural circuits underlying these different forms of impulsive behavior will further delineate the processes that control impulsivity.

Another question that arises from this review is whether impulsivity can best be characterized as a trait that is stable over time or a state that is transient and sensitive to environmental influences. Traditionally, the trait of impulsivity has been measured using personality questionnaires. In contrast, behavioral measures of impulsivity used in the laboratory are commonly used to measure states that may be transient. For, example, as reviewed previously, we have found that alcohol decreases behavioral inhibition as measured by the Stop Task. It is not clear that acute alcohol consumption would lead to a similar change on a self-report personality measure of impulsivity. It is also not clear whether the two types of measures are related. Efforts to correlate trait (personality) measures of impulsivity with operationally defined behavioral indices have met with only limited success (Milich & Kramer, 1984; Richards, Zhang, Mitchell, & de Wit, 1999). This may be in part because personality approaches attempt to characterize impulsivity as a single trait, whereas behavioral studies described in this paper strongly suggest that there are separate forms of impulsive behavior (e.g., related to inhibitory control or evaluation of consequences). To our knowledge, these subtypes of impulsivity have not been defined or studied in personality formulations of impulsivity. In sum, the discipline would benefit from research attempting to harmonize these two traditionally separate approaches, each of which are bedded in rich theoretical and empirical foundations.

References

Achenbach, T., & Edelbrock, C. (1979). The child behavior profile: II: Boys aged 12–16 and girls aged 6–11 and 12–16. *Journal of Consulting and Clinical Psychology, 47,* 223–233.

American Psychiatric Association. (1994). *Diagnostic and statistical manual of mental disorders* (4th ed.). Washington DC: American Psychiatric Association.

Anthony, J. C., & Petronis, K. R. (1995). Early-onset drug use and risk of later drug problems. *Drug and Alcohol Dependence, 40,* 9–15.

Bardo, M. T., Donohew, R. L., & Harrington, N. G. (1996). Psychobiology of novelty seeking and drug seeking behavior. *Behavioural Brain Research, 77,* 23–43.

Barnes G. M., Welte J. W., Hoffman J. H., Dintcheff, B. A. (1999). Gambling and alcohol use among youth: Influences of demographic, socialization, and individual factors. *Addictive Behaviors, 24*(6), 749–767.

Barratt, E. S., & Patton, J. H. (1983). Impulsivity: Cognitive, behavioral, and psychophysiological correlates. In M. Zuckerman (Ed.), *Biological bases of sensation seeking, impulsivity, and anxiety* (pp. 77–116). Hillsdale NJ: Erlbaum.

Berke, J. D., & Hyman, S. E. (2000). Addiction, dopamine, and the molecular mechanisms of memory. *Neuron, 25*(3), 515–532.

Bickel, W. K., Odum, A. L., and Madden, G .J. (1999). Impulsivity and cigarette smoking: Delay discounting in current, never, and ex-smokers. *Psychopharmacology, 146*, 447–454.

Brady, K. T., Myrick, H., & McElroy, S. (1998). The relationship between substance use disorders, impulse control disorders, and pathological aggression. *American Journal on Addictions, 7*(3), 221–230.

Breiter, H. C., Rosen, B. R., & Ann, N. Y. (1999). Functional magnetic resonance imaging of brain reward circuitry in the human. *Annals of the New York Academy of Sciences, 877*, 523–47.

Brunner, D., & Hen, R. (1997). Insights in to the neurobiology of impulsive behavior from serotonin receptor knockout mice. *Annals of the New York Academy of Sciences, 836*, 81–105.

Caggiula, A. R., Donny, E. C., White, A. R., Chaudhri, N., Booth, S., Gharib, M. A., et al. (2001). Cue dependency of nicotine self-administration and smoking. *Pharmacology Biochemistry and Behavior, 70*(4), 515–530.

Cardinal, R. N., Pennicott, D. R., Sugathapala C. L., Robbins T. W., & Everett, B. J. (2001). Impulsive choice induced in rats by lesions of the nucleus accumbens core. *Science, 292*, 2499–2501.

Cherpitel, C. J. (1999). Substance use, injury, and risk-taking dispositions in the general population. *Alcoholism: Clinical and Experimental Research, 23*(1), 121–126.

Chornock, W. M., Stitzer, M. L., Gross, J., & Leischow, S. (1992). Experimental model of smoking re-exposure: Effects on relapse. *Psychopharmocology (Berlin), 108*(4), 495–500.

Chutuape, M. A. D., Mitchell, S. H., & de Wit, H. (1994). Ethanol preloads increase ethanol preference on a concurrent random-ratio schedule in social drinkers. *Experimental and Clinical Psychopharmacology, 2*, 310–318.

Cloninger, C. (1987). Neurogenetic adaptive mechanisms in alcoholism. *Science, 236*, 410–416.

Cloninger, C., Sigvardsson, S., & Bohman, M. (1988). Childhood personality predicts alcohol use in young adults. *Alcoholism, 12*, 494–505.

Comer, S. D., & Carroll, M. E. (1996). Oral caffeine pretreatment produced modest increases in smoked cocaine self-administered in rhesus monkeys. *Psychopharmacology (Berlin), 126*(4), 281–285.

Conrod, P. J., Peterson, J. B., & Pihl, R. O. (1997). Disinhibited personality and sensitivity to alcohol reinforcement: independent correlates of drink-

ing behavior in sons of alcoholics. *Alcoholism: Clinical and Experimental Research, 21,* 1320–1332.
Conrod, P. J., Peterson, J. B., & Pihl, R. O. (2001). Reliability and validity of alcohol-induced heart rate increase as a measure of sensitivity to the stimulant properties of alcohol. *Psychopharmacology (Berlin), 157*(1), 20–30.
Crean, J., de Wit, H., & Richards, J. B. (2000). Reward discounting as a measure of impulsive behavior in a psychiatric outpatient population. *Experimental and Clinical Psychopharmacology, 8*(2), 155–162.
Crean, J., Richards, J. B., & de Wit, H. (2002). Impulsive behavior in men with and without a family history of alcoholism: Effects of tryptophan depletion. *Behavioural Brain Research, 136*(2), 349–357.
Dawes, M. A., Antelman, S. M., Vanyukov, M. M., Giancola, P., Tarter, R. E., Susman, E. J., et al. (2000). Developmental sources of variation in liability to adolescent substance use disorders. *Drug and Alcohol Dependence, 61,* 3–14.
Depue, R. A., & Collins, P. F. (1999). Neurobiology of the structure of personality: Dopamine, facilitation of incentive motivation, and extraversion. *Behavioral and Brain Sciences, 22,* 491–569.
Depue, R. A., Luciana, M., Arbisi, P., Collins, P., & Leon, A. (1994). Dopamine and the structure of personality: Relation of agonist-induced dopamine to positive emotionality. *Journal of Personality and Social Psychology, 67*(3), 485–498.
Dervaux, A., Baylé, F. J., Laqueille, X., Bourdel, M. C., Le Borgne, M. H., Olié, J. P., & Krebs, M. O. (2001). Is substance abuse in schizophrenia related to impulsivity, sensation seeking, or anhedonia? *American Journal of Psychiatry, 158,* 492–494.
de Wit, H. (1996). Priming effects with drugs and other reinforcers. *Experimental and Clinical Psychopharmacology, 4,* 5–10.
de Wit, H., Crean, J., & Richards, J. (2000). Effects of *d*-amphetamine and ethanol on a measure of behavioral inhibition in humans. *Behavioral Neuroscience, 114,* 830–837.
de Wit, H., Enggasser, J. L., & Richards, J. B. (2002). Acute administration of *d*-amphetamine decreases impulsivity in healthy volunteers. *Neuropsychopharmacology, 27,* 813–825.
de Wit, H., & Griffiths, R. R. (1991). Methods of accessing the abuse liability of sedatives in humans. *Drug and Alcohol Dependence, 28,* 83–111.
de Wit, H., Pierri, J., & Johanson, C. E. (1989). Assessing individual differences in ethanol preference using a cumulative dosing procedure. *Psychopharmacology, 98,* 113–119.
de Wit, H., & J. Stewart. (1981). Reinstatement of cocaine-reinforced responding in the rat. *Psychopharmacology, 75,* 134–143.
de Wit, H., Uhlenhuth, E. H., & Johanson, C.E. (1986). Individual differences in the behavioral and subjective effects of amphetamine and diazepam. *Drug and Alcohol Dependence, 16,* 341–360.

de Wit, H., Uhlenhuth, E. H., Pierri, J., & Johanson, C. E. (1987). Individual differences in behavioral and subjective responses to alcohol. *Alcoholism: Clinical and Experimental Research, 11,* 52–59.

Disney, E. R., Elkins, I. J., McGue, M., & Iacono, W. G. (1999). Effects of ADHD, conduct disorder, and gender on substance use and abuse in adolescence. *American Journal of Psychiatry, 156,* 1515–1521.

Doty, P., & de Wit, H. (1996). Effects of naltrexone on subjective responses to ethanol in social drinkers. In L. S. Harris (Ed.), *Problems of drug dependence, 1995* (p. 328). NIDA *Research Monograph Series, 162.*

Enggasser, J., & de Wit, H. (2001). Haloperidol reduces the stimulant and reinforcing effects of ethanol in humans. *Alcoholism: Clinical and Experimental Research, 25,* 1448–1456.

Eysenck, H. J. (1993). The nature of impulsivity. In W. G. McCown, J. L. Johnson, & M. B. Sure (Eds.), *The impulsive client: Theory, research, and treatment.* Washington DC: American Psychological Association.

Eysenck, H. J. & Eysenck, S. B. G. (1975). *Manual of the Eysenck personality questionnaire.* London: Hodder & Stoughton.

Feola, T. W., Richards, J. B., & de Wit, H. (2000). Effects of *d*-amphetamine and ethanol on a measure of behavioral inhibition in rats. *Behavioral Neuroscience, 114,* 838–848.

Fergusson, D. M., Lynskey, M. T., & Horwood, L. J. (1995). The role of peer affiliations, social, family, and individual factors in continuities in cigarette smoking between childhood and adolescence. *Addiction, 90,* 647–659.

Fillmore, M. T., Rush, C. R., & Hays, L. (2002). Acute effects of oral cocaine on inhibitory control of behavior in humans. *Drug and Alcohol Dependence, 67*(2), 157–167.

Fischman, M. A., & Foltin, R. W. (1991). Utility of subjective effects measurements in assessing abuse liability of drugs in humans. *British Journal of Addiction, 86,* 1563–1570.

Gerber, G. J., & Stretch, R. (1975). Drug-induced reinstatement of extinguished self-administration behavior in monkeys. *Pharmacology Biochemistry and Behavior, 3*(6), 1055–1061.

Gotham, H. J., Sher, K. J., & Wood, P. K. (1997). Predicting stability and change in frequency of intoxication from the college years to beyond: Individual-difference and role transition variables. *Journal of Abnormal Psychology, 106*(4), 619–629.

Gray, J. R. (1999). A bias toward short-term thinking in threat-related negative emotional states. *Personality and Social Psychology Bulletin, 25,* 65–75.

Haney, M., Ward, A. S., Foltin, R. W., & Fischman, M. W. (2001). Effects of ecopipam, a selective dopamine D1 antagonist, on smoked cocaine self-administration by humans. *Psychopharmacology (Berlin), 155*(4), 330–337.

Hesselbrock, M., Meyer, R. E., & Keener, J. J. (1985). Psychopathology in hospitalized alcoholics. *Archives of General Psychiatry, 42,* 1050–1055.

Higley J. D., Suomi S. J., and Linnoila, M. (1996). A nonhuman primate model of type II alcoholism? Part 2. Diminished social competence and excessive aggression correlates with low cerebrospinal fluid 5-hydroxyindoleacetic acid concentrations. *Alcoholism: Clinical and Experimental Research, 30,* 643–650.

Hodgson, R., Rankin, H., & Stockwell, T. (1979). Alcohol dependence and the priming effect. *Behavior Research and Therapy, 17,* 379–387.

Hunt, W. A., Barnett, L. W., & Branch, L. G. (1971). Relapse rates in addiction programs. *Journal of Clinical Psychology, 27,* 355

Jaffe, J. H., Cascella, N. G., Kumor, K. M., & Sherer, M. A. (1989). Cocaine-induced cocaine craving. *Psychopharmacology (Berlin), 97*(1), 59–64.

Jentsch, J. D., & Taylor, J. R. (1999). Impulsivity resulting from frontostriatal dysfunction in drug abuse: Implications for the control of behavior by reward-related stimuli. *Psychopharmacology (Berlin), 146*(4), 373–390.

Kambouropoulos, N., & Staiger, P. K. (2001). The influence of sensitivity to reward on reactivity to alcohol-related cues. *Addiction, 96*(8), 1175–1185.

Kandel, D. B., Yamaguch, K., & Chen, K. (1992). Stages of progression in drug involvement from adolescence to adulthood: Further evidence for the gateway theory. *Journal of Studies on Alcohol, 53,* 447–457.

Kendall, P. C., & Wilcox, L. E. (1979). Self-control in children: Development of a rating scale. *Journal of Consulting and Clinical Psychology, 48*(1), 80–91.

Kilbey, M. M., Downey, K., & Breslau, N. (1998). Predicting the emergence and persistence of alcohol dependence in young adults: The role of expectance and other risk factors. *Experimental and Clinical Psychopharmacology, 6*(2), 149–156.

Kirby, K. N., Petry, N. M., & Bickel, W. K. (1999). Heroin addicts discount delayed rewards at higher rates than non-drug using controls. *Journal of Experimental Psychology: General, 128,* 78–87.

Klebaur, J. E., & Bardo, M. T. (1999). Individual differences in novelty seeking on the playground maze predict amphetamine conditioned place preference. *Pharmacology Biochemistry and Behavior, 63*(1), 131–136.

Koob, G. F. (1992). Drugs of abuse: Anatomy, pharmacology and function of reward pathways. *Trends in Pharmacological Sciences, 13,* 177–184.

Lê, A. D., Quan B., Juzystch W., Fletcher P. J., Joharchi, N., & Shaham, Y. (1998). Reinstatement of alcohol-seeking by priming injections of alcohol and exposure to stress in rats. *Psychopharmacology, 135,* 169–174.

Lê, A. D., Poulos C. X., Harding, S., Watchus, W., Juzytsch, W. & Shaham, Y. (1999). Effects of naltrexone and fluoxetine on alcohol self-administration and reinstatement of alcohol seeking induced by priming injections of alcohol and exposure to stress in rats. *Neuropsychopharmacology, 21,* 435–444.

Leith, K. P., & Baumeister, R. F. (1996). Why do bad moods increase self-defeating behavior? Emotion, risk-taking, and self-regulation. *Journal of Personality and Social Psychology, 71*(6), 1250–1267.

Linnoila, M., Virkkunen, M., & Scheinin, M. (1983). Low cerebrospinal fluid 5-hydroxyindoleacetic acid concentrations differentiates impulsive from non-impulsive violent offenders. *Life Sciences, 33,* 2609–2614.

Linnoila, M., DeJong, J., & Virkkunen, M. (1989). Family history of alcoholism in violent offenders and impulsive fire setters. *Archives of General Psychiatry, 46,* 613–616.

Logan, G. D., & Cowan, W. B. (1984). On the ability to inhibit thought and action: A theory of an act of control. *Psychological Review, 91,* 296–327.

Logan, G. D., Schachar, R. J. & Tannock, R. (1997). Impulsivity and inhibitory control. *Psychological Science, 8,* 60–64.

Logue, A. W. (1988). Research on self-control: An integrated framework. *Behavioral and Brain Sciences, 11,* 665–709.

MacDonald T. K., Zanna, M. P., & Fong, G. T. (1995). Decision making in altered states: Effects of alcohol on attitudes toward drinking and driving. *Journal of Personality and Social Psychology, 68*(6), 973–985.

Madden, G. J., Petry, N. M., Badger, G. J. & Bickel, W. K. (1997) Impulsive and self control choices in opioid dependent patients and non-drug-using control participants: Drug and monetary rewards. *Experimental and Clinical Psychopharmacology, 5,* 256–262.

Mazur, J. E. (1987). An adjusting procedure for studying delayed reinforcement. In M. L. Commons, J. E. Mazur, J. A. Nevin, & H. Rachlin (Eds.), *Quantitative analysis of behavior: The effects of delay and of intervening events on reinforcement value:* Vol. 5 (pp. 55–73). Hillsdale NJ: Erlbaum.

McDonald, J., Schleifer, L., Richards, J. B., & de Wit, H. (2003). Effects of delta^9-tetrahydrocannabinol on behavioral measures of impulsivity in humans. *Neuropsychopharmacology, 28,* 1356–1365.

McGue, M., Iacono, W. G., Legrand, L. N., Malone, S., & Elkins, I. (2001). Origins and consequences of age at first drink. I. Associations with substance-use disorders, disinhibitory behavior and psychopathology, and P3 amplitude. *Alcoholism: Clinical and Experimental Research, 25*(8), 1156–1165.

Milich, R., & Kramer, J. (1984). Reflections on impulsivity: An empirical investigation of impulsivity as a construct. *Advances in Learning and Behavioral Disabilities, 3,* 57–94.

Mitchell, S. H. (1999). Measures of impulsivity in cigarette smokers and non-smokers. *Psychopharmacology (Berlin), 146*(4), 455–464.

Nagoshi, C. T., Wilson, J. R., & Rodriguez, L. A. (1991). Impulsivity, sensation seeking, and behavioral and emotional responses to alcohol. *Alcoholism: Clinical and Experimental Research, 15,* 661–667.

National Institute of Drug Abuse. (2000). National survey results on drug use from monitoring the future study, 2000. U.S. Department of Health and Human Services, NIH, Bethesda MD.

O'Brien, C. P., Childress, A. R., Ehrman, R., & Robbins, S. J. (1998). Conditioning factors in drug abuse: Can they explain compulsion? *Journal of Psychopharmacology, 12*(1), 15–22.

Paty, J. A., Perz, W. G., Gnys, M., Kassel, J. D., & Hickcox, M. (1997). A day at a time: Predicting smoking lapse from daily urge. *Journal of Abnormal Psychology, 106*(1), 104–116.

Petry, N. M. (2000a.). Psychiatric symptoms in problem gambling and nonproblem gambling substance abusers. *American Journal on Addictions, 9,* 163–171.

Petry, N. M. (2000b.). Gambling problems in substance abusers are associated with increased sexual risk behaviors. *Addiction, 95,* 1089–1100.

Petry, N. M. (2001). Reliability of drug users' self-reported HIV risk behaviors using a brief, 11-item scale. *Substance Use and Misuse, 36*(12), 1731–1747.

Petry, N. M., & Casarella, T. (1999). Excessive discounting of delayed rewards in substance abusers with gambling problems. *Drug and Alcohol Dependence, 56,* 25–32.

Phillips, A. G., & Fibiger, H. C. (1990). Role of reward and enhancement of conditioned reward in persistence of responding for cocaine. *Behavioural Pharmacology, 1,* 269–282.

Piazza P. V., Deminiere, J. M., Le Moal, M., & Simon, H. (1989). Factors that predict individual vulnerability to amphetamine self-administration. *Science, 245,* 1511–1513.

Poulos, C. X., Lê, A. D., & Parker, J. L. (1995). Impulsivity predicts individual susceptibility to high levels of alcohol self-administration. *Behavioral Pharmacology, 6,* 1–5.

Rachlin, H., & Green, L. (1972). Commitment, choice, and self-control. *Journal of the Experimental Analysis of Behavior, 17,* 15–22.

Regier, D. A., Farmer, M., Rae, D., Locke, B., Keith, S., Judd, L., et al. (1990). Co-morbidity of mental disorders with alcohol and other drug abuse. *Journal of the American Medical Association* (JAMA), *264,* 2511–2518.

Richards, J. B., Chock, M. A., Carlson, B., de Wit, H., & Seiden, L. S. (1997). Comparison of two models of impulsive behavior: Effects of amphetamine and haloperidol. *Society for Neuroscience Abstracts, 23*(2), 2406.

Richards, J. B., Kline, T., Miller, D. B., Crean, J. P., & de Wit, H. (in press). Reduction of brain serotonin impairs response inhibition in rats. *Behavioural Brain Research.*

Richards, J. B., Mitchell, S. H., de Wit, H., & Seiden, L. S. (1997). Determination of discount functions in rats with an adjusting amount procedure. *Journal of the Experimental Analysis of Behavior, 67,* 353–366.

Richards, J. B., Sabol, K. E., & de Wit, H. (1999). Effects of methamphetamine on a model of impulsive behavior in rats. *Psychopharmacology, 146,* 432–439.

Richards, J. B., Zhang, L., Mitchell, S. H., & de Wit, H. (1999) Delay or probability discounting in a model of impulsive behavior: Effect of alcohol. *Journal of the Experimental Analysis of Behavior, 71*(2), 121–143.

Robinson, T. E., & Berridge, K. C. (1993). The neural basis of drug craving: An incentive-sensitization theory of addiction. *Brain Research Reviews, 18,* 247–291.

Schachar, R. S., Tannock, R., & Logan, G. (1993) Inhibitory control, impulsiveness, and attention deficit hyperactivity disorder. *Clinical Psychology Review, 13,* 721–739.

Self, D. W., Barnhart, W. J., Lehman, D. A., & Nestler, E. J. (1996). Opposite modulation of cocaine-seeking behavior by D1- and D2-like dopamine receptor agonists. *Science, 271*(5, 255), 1586–1589.

Self, D. W., & Nestler, E. J. (1998). Relapse to drug seeking: Neural and molecular mechanisms. *Drug and Alcohol Dependence, 51*, 49–60.

Shaham, Y., Erb, S., & Stewart, J. (2000). Stress-induced relapse to heroin and cocaine seeking in rate: A review. *Brain Research Reviews, 33*, 13–33.

Sher, K. J. (1991). *Children of alcoholics: A critical appraisal of theory and research.* Chicago: University of Chicago Press.

Sher, K. J., Bartholow, B. D., & Wood, M. D., (2000). Personality and substance use disorders: A prospective study. *Journal of Consulting and Clinical Psychology, 68*(5), 818–829.

Sher, K. J., & Trull, T. J. (1994). Personality and disinhibitory psychopathology: Alcoholism and antisocial personality disorder. *Journal of Abnormal Psychology, 103*, 92–102.

Shiffman, S., (1982). Relapse following smoking cessation: A situational analysis. *Journal of Consulting and Clinical Psychology, 50*(1), 71–86.

Shiffman, S., & Balabanis, M. (1996) Do drinking and smoking go together? *Alcohol Health and Research World, 20*, 107–110.

Shiffman, S., Paty, J. A., Gnys, M., Kassel, J. A., & Hickcox, M. (1996). First lapses to smoking: Within-subject analysis of real-time reports. *Journal of Consulting and Clinical Psychology, 64*(2), 366–379.

Sonuga-Barke, E. J. S. (2002). Psychological heterogeneity in AD/HD—a dual pathway model of behavior and cognition. *Behavioural Brain Research, 130*, 29–36.

Steele, C. M., & Josephs, R. A. (1990). Alcohol myopia: Its prized and dangerous effects. *American Psychologist, 45*, 921–933.

Stewart, J., de Wit, H., & Eikelboom, R. (1984). The role of unconditioned and conditioned drug effects in the self-administration of opiates and stimulants. *Psychological Review, 91*, 251–268.

Sullivan, M. A., & Rudnik-Levin, F. (2001). Attention deficit/hyperactivity disorder and substance abuse. Diagnostic and therapeutic considerations. *Annals of the New York Academy of Sciences, 931*, 251–270.

Tarter, R. E., Vanyukov, M. M., Giancola, P., Dawes, M. A., Blackson, T., Mezzich, A. C., et al. (1999). Etiology of early age onset substance use disorder: A maturational perspective. *Development and Psychopathology, 11*, 657–683.

Tellegen, A. (1982). *Multidimensional personality questionnaire manual.* Minneapolis: University of Minnesota Press.

Tice, D. M., Bratslavsky, E., & Baumeister, R. F. (2001). Emotional distress regularion takes precedence over impulse control: If you feel bad, do it! *Journal of Personality and Social Psychology, 80*, 53–67.

Virkkunen, M., Nuttila, A., Goodwin, F. K., & Linnoila, M. (1987). Cerebrospinal fluid monoamine metabolite levels in male arsonists. *Archives of General Psychiatry, 44*(3), 241–247.

Vuchinich, R. E., & Simpson, C. A. (1998). Hyperbolic temporal discounting in social drinkers and problem drinkers. *Experimental and Clinical Psychopharmacology, 6,* 292–305.

Wade, T. R., de Wit, H., & Richards, J. B. (2000). Effects of dopaminergic drugs on delayed reward as a measure of impulsive behavior in rats. *Psychopharmacology, 150,* 90–101.

White, H. R., Pandina, R. J., & Chen, P. (2002). Developmental trajectories of cigarette use from early adolescence into young adulthood. *Drug and Alcohol Dependence, 65,* 167–178.

White, N. (1996). Addictive drugs as reinforcers: Multiple partial actions on memory systems. *Addiction, 91*(7), 921–949.

Wise, R. A. (1996). Neurobiology of addiction. *Current Opinion in Neurobiology, 6,* 243–251.

Wise, R. A., & Bozarth M. A. (1987). A psychomotor stimulant theory of addiction. *Psychological Bulletin, 94,* 369–492.

Zuckerman, M. (1984) Sensation seeking: A comparative approach to a human trait. *Behavioral and Brain Sciences, 7,* 413–471.

Zuckerman, M. (1994). *Behavioral expressions and biosocial bases of sensation seeking.* New York: Cambridge University Press.

Triggers of Relapse: Nonhuman Primate Models of Reinstated Cocaine Seeking

R. D. Spealman, B. Lee, S. Tiefenbacher, D. M. Platt, J. K. Rowlett, and T. V. Khroyan

New England Primate Research Center, Harvard Medical School

Drug addiction is a chronic disorder characterized by recurring episodes of persistent drug use, abstinence, and relapse (Jaffe, 1990; Leshner, 1997; Simpson, Joe, Fletcher, Hubbard, & Anglin, 1999). Increased appreciation of the cyclic nature of addiction has led to the emergence of relapse prevention as a major clinical target for the long-term management of compulsive drug use (Dackis & O'Brien, 2001; DeJong, 1994). Considered from this perspective, identification

Animals used in the authors' studies were maintained in accordance with the guidelines of the Committee on Animals of the Harvard Medical School and the "Guide for Care and Use of Laboratory Animals" of the National Research Council (1996). Research protocols were approved by the Harvard Medical School Institutional Animal Care and Use Committee.

This work was supported by grants from the National Institute on Drug Abuse (DA 00499, DA 11054, and DA 11928) and the National Center for Research Resources (RR 00168). We thank D. Reed and M. Duggan for assistance in preparing the manuscript.

Present address for T. V. Khroyan: Center for Health Sciences, SRI International, Menlo Park CA 94025.

of pharmacological and environmental factors that trigger relapse, and of neurobiological mechanisms that underlie this process, is of crucial importance for the development of effective treatment strategies.

Growing evidence implicates acute drug reexposure (drug priming), environmental stimuli associated with drug use (drug cues), and stress as powerful motivational triggers of relapse in people (Jaffe, Cascella, Kumor, & Sherer, 1989; O'Brien, Childress, Ehrman, & Robbins, 1998; Rohsenow, Niaura, Childress, Abrams, & Monti , 1990–1991; Sinha, 2001), as well as reinstatement of previously extinguished drug seeking in animals (See, 2002; Shaham, Erb, & Stewart, 2000; Shalev, Grimm, & Shaham, 2002; Spealman, Barrett-Larimore, Rowlett, Platt, & Khroyan, 1999). A comprehensive analysis of these triggers in animal models is likely to provide a better understanding of the relapse process in people and to improve treatment interventions. This review will focus on recent advances in our understanding of relapse triggers and underlying mechanisms in nonhuman primate models of reinstated cocaine-seeking behavior. Our emphasis will be on integration of research in monkeys with the rapidly growing literature on rodent models, as well as human studies of relapse and craving. The latter areas have been the focus of several recent reviews (e.g., See, 2002; Shaham et al., 2000; Shalev et al., 2002, rodent models; Dackis & O'Brien, 2001; Kreek & Koob, 1998; Sinha, 2001, human studies).

Environmental and Pharmacological Triggers of Relapse

COCAINE CUES

Abstinent cocaine abusers frequently report symptoms of craving, arousal, and negative affect in response to environmental stimuli (e.g., drug-related paraphernalia and locations) previously associated with active drug use (Childress, McLellan, Ehrman, & O'Brien, 1988; Foltin & Haney, 2000; O'Brien, Childress, McLellan, & Ehrman, 1992). Although a causal relationship between craving and relapse has not been established, conditioned drug cues clearly can increase the self-reported desire to seek out and take drugs (Carter & Tiffany, 1999; Childress, Hole, Ehrman, Robbins, McLellan, & O'Brien, 1993; Foltin & Haney, 2000).

Because of the recognized importance of drug cues in promoting compulsive drug use by people, a growing number of researchers have begun to investigate the role of drug-associated stimuli as triggers of reinstated drug seeking in laboratory animals. In one of the earliest studies of this type, Davis and Smith (1976) trained rats to self-administer morphine under conditions in which an auditory stimulus was paired with each drug injection. Drug self-administration was then extinguished by substituting vehicle for drug and omitting the drug-paired stimulus. During subsequent test sessions, in which only vehicle was available for self-administration, reintroduction of the stimulus temporarily restored drug seeking to levels approaching those maintained by active drug self-administration. Other studies have extended these findings by showing that visual and auditory stimuli previously associated with cocaine self-administration can induce a temporary reinstatement of extinguished drug seeking in rodents (See, 2002; Shalev et al., 2002) and nonhuman primates (Bradberry, Barrett-Larimore, Jatlow, & Rubino, 2000; Spealman et al., 1999).

In our studies, for example, squirrel monkeys were trained to self-administer cocaine under a second-order schedule of reinforcement (cf. Goldberg, Kelleher, & Morse, 1975) in which operant responding (pressing a lever) was maintained jointly by injections of cocaine and a visual stimulus that was paired with cocaine injections. After high rates of responding were maintained for several months under these conditions, drug seeking was extinguished by substituting vehicle for cocaine and omitting the cocaine-paired stimulus. Reintroduction of the stimulus during subsequent test sessions produced a significant increase in response rate despite the fact that cocaine was not available for self-administration (Figure 1). In the majority of cases, cue-induced reinstatement of drug seeking was modest compared to the more pronounced effects of cocaine priming (see next section); however, large individual differences were observed among subjects, with some monkeys showing pronounced increases in drug seeking and others exhibiting little or no change (Figure 1, bottom panels). These individual differences mirror clinical reports of individual variations in the impact of drug cues on craving and relapse among human cocaine abusers (Childress, Mozley, McElgin, Fitzgerald, Reivich, & O'Brien, 1999; Foltin & Haney, 2000; Robbins, Ehrman, Childress, & O'Brien, 1997). Also in keeping with

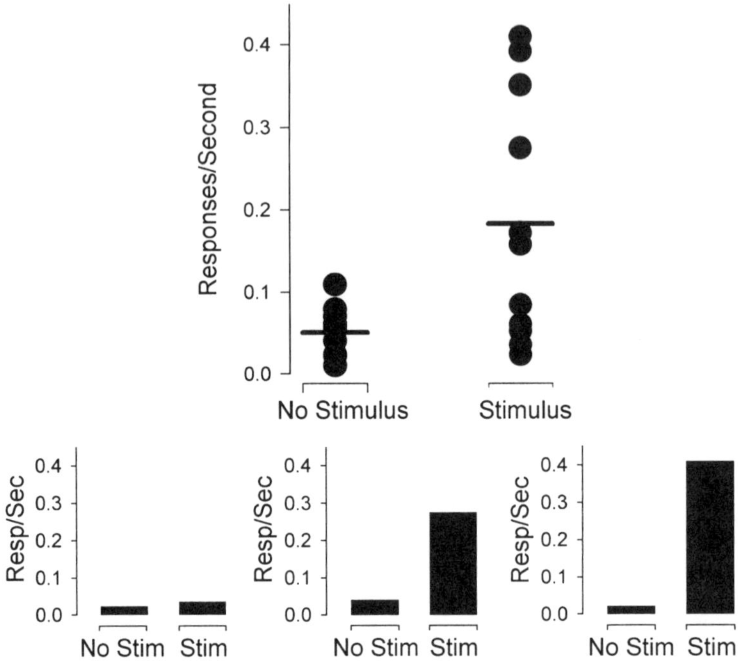

Figure 1. Reinstatement of drug seeking by presentations of a cocaine-paired stimulus contingent on lever pressing in monkeys with histories of i.v. cocaine self-administration. Top panel: Individual response rates (points) and means (horizontal lines) in the presence vs. absence of stimulus presentations ($p < 0.01$, paired t test, $N = 11$). Bottom panels: effects in representative subjects illustrating individual differences.

clinical observations, the impact of the cocaine-paired stimulus in our studies, as well as studies in rats (e.g., Grimm, Hope, Wise, & Shaham, 2001; Meil & See, 1996), persisted over weeks-to-months of drug abstinence, suggesting that vulnerability to cue-induced relapse extends beyond the initial stages of detoxification and withdrawal (cf. Gawin & Kleber, 1986).

COCAINE PRIMING

Acute exposure to cocaine (priming) has been found to induce craving in human cocaine abusers (Jaffe et al., 1989; Preston, Sullivan, Strain, & Bigelow, 1992), as well as robust reinstatement of cocaine seeking in rodents (Self & Nestler, 1998; Shalev et al., 2002) and non-human primates (Khroyan, Barrett-Larimore, Rowlett, & Spealman, 2000; Spealman et al., 1999). In studies from our laboratory, for example, monkeys were given extended histories (> 6 months) of i.v. cocaine self-administration under the second-order schedule described previously before moving to a protracted extinction phase, which was interrupted only by periodic tests to determine the effects of cocaine priming. Under these conditions, priming with cocaine induced pronounced reinstatement of cocaine-seeking behavior following extinction periods of up to 30 days (Spealman et al., 1999). Although the degree of reinstatement sometimes declined over the course of this period, the overall effect of cocaine priming was remarkably enduring given that there were no intervening opportunities to self-administer cocaine.

Additional studies showed that although cocaine priming induced appreciable reinstatement of drug seeking even in the absence of the cocaine-paired stimulus, a greater effect typically was seen when the stimulus was restored in conjunction with cocaine priming (Figure 2). Under the latter condition, priming-induced drug seeking was dose-dependent and, at maximally effective doses, engendered response rates as high as those maintained by active cocaine self-administration (Khroyan et al., 2000; Spealman et al., 1999). The robust reinstatement of drug seeking induced by priming combined with restoration of the cocaine-paired stimulus suggests a potentially important interaction between environmental and pharmacological triggers of relapse, possibly reflecting conditions analogous to those encountered by addicts in real-world situations.

STRESS

Stress and associated negative mood states have been repeatedly implicated as risk factors in drug addiction and relapse (Kreek & Koob, 1998; Sinha, 2001). Although clinical observations suggest that exposure to stress can induce drug craving and relapse in human drug abusers, the mechanisms by which stress triggers renewed drug seeking remain largely unknown (Sinha, 2001; Sinha, Catapano, & O'Malley, 1999; Sinha, Fuse, Aubin, & O'Malley, 2000). In an effort to better understand the biological basis of stress-induced relapse, recent studies have investigated the effects of stressful interventions

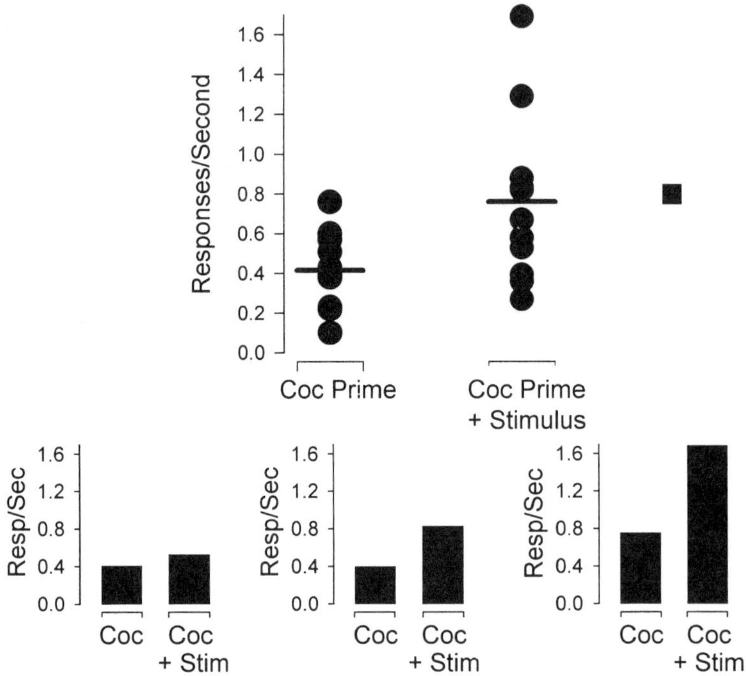

Figure 2. Enhancement of cocaine priming by response-contingent presentations of a cocaine-paired stimulus in monkeys with histories of i.v. cocaine self-administration. Top panel: Individual response rates (points) and means (horizontal lines) induced by cocaine (0.1–0.3 mg/kg, depending on subject) in the presence vs. absence of stimulus presentations ($p < 0.01$, paired t test, $N = 12$). Bottom panels: effects in representative subjects illustrating individual differences.

using animal models similar to those developed to investigate drug priming and cue-induced reinstatement of drug seeking. The majority of these studies have employed inescapable foot-shock to induce a presumably stresslike state in rats. With suitable parameter values (e.g., 10–30 minute periods of brief, intermittent shock in the test environment), this type of stress induces reliable reinstatement of drug seeking, sometimes to levels exceeding those induced by cocaine priming (Ahmed & Koob, 1997; Erb, Shaham, & Stewart, 1996; Mantsch & Goeders, 1999a; Sutton, Karanian, & Self, 2000).

The effects of foot-shock appear to be at least partially selective for drug-seeking behavior because shock typically does not induce significant reinstatement of operant behavior previously maintained by conventional reinforcers such as food or sucrose (Ahmed & Koob, 1997; Buczek, Lê, Wang, Stewart, & Shaham, 1999; Lê, Quan, Juzystch, Fletcher, Joharchi, & Shaham, 1998; Mantsch & Goeders, 1999a). The factors underlying the more dramatic effects of shock on reinstatement of drug-seeking as compared to food-seeking behavior are not known, but conceivably could reflect neuroadaptations resulting from chronic drug self-administration that increase vulnerability to stress-induced relapse (cf. Shaham et al., 2000). The ability of foot-shock to reinstate drug seeking also appears to depend on the environmental context in which shock is delivered. Although exposure to shock in an environment previously associated with drug self-administration engenders high levels of drug-seeking behavior, the same shock delivered in an unfamiliar environment has little or no effect on subsequent drug seeking in the test situation (Shalev, Highfield, Yap, & Shaham, 2000). While the generality of this apparent context dependency needs to be explored more fully, the results imply a potential interaction between stress and environmental drug cues that may elevate the risk of relapse.

The experimental utility of the rodent foot-shock model notwithstanding, electric shock is a unique physical stimulus that is not likely to impact relapse in human drug abusers. Several laboratories are attempting to develop models of stress that do not rely solely on electric shock and, thus, may be more analogous to the types of stress experienced by people. Although preliminary studies using various models of social stress in rodents and nonhuman primates have been explored, few definitive results have emerged. Initial experiments in our laboratory, for example, indicate that social confrontations with conspecifics or human intruders do not induce consistent reinstatement of cocaine seeking in squirrel monkeys (unpublished observations) despite the fact that these types of confrontations induce characteristic behavioral and physiological signs of stress in this species (Coe, Franklin, Smith, & Levine, 1982; Newman & Farley, 1995; Weerts & Miczek, 1996). Exposure to the scent of a predator (fox urine), presumably an ethologically relevant stressor for rodents, also fails to reinstate cocaine seeking in preliminary studies with rats (Shaham et al., 2000), and stress as a result of food deprivation has mixed effects in these models (Carroll, 1985; Shalev et al., 2000).

Neurobiological Basis of Relapse

DRUG PRIMING

Cocaine is a relatively nonselective monoamine transport inhibitor, but converging lines of evidence suggest that mesocorticolimbic dopaminergic (DA) mechanisms play an especially important role in cocaine's abuse-related effects, including its ability to trigger relapse (Self & Nestler, 1998; Shalev et al., 2002; Spealman et al., 1999). In addition to cocaine, for example, drugs that share cocaine's inhibitory effects on DA uptake, such as GBR12909, as well as drugs that directly stimulate D_2-like DA receptors, such as quinpirole and propylnorapomorphine (NPA), mimic the priming effects of cocaine in monkeys (Figure 3; Khroyan et al., 2000; Platt, Rowlett, & Spealman, 2001) and rodents (De Vries, Schoffelmeer, Binnekade, Vanderschuren, 1999; de Wit & Stewart, 1981; Self, Barnhart, Lehman, & Nestler, 1996; Wise, Murray, & Bozarth, 1990). Conversely, D_2-like receptor antagonists, including eticlopride, nemonapride and raclopride, block cocaine-induced reinstatement of drug seeking in monkeys (Khroyan et al., 2000) and/or rats (Weissenborn, Deroche, Koob, & Weiss, 1996). These findings are complemented by further observations that a cAMP-dependent protein kinase inhibitor administered directly into the nucleus accumbens induces reinstatement of cocaine-seeking behavior, presumably by mimicking the intracellular consequences of D_2-like receptor stimulation (Self, Genova, Hope, Barnhart, Spencer, & Nestler, 1998). In contrast to D_2-like receptor full agonists, however, low-efficacy (i.e., partial) agonists such as terguride and SDZ 208–911 block, rather than reinstate, cocaine-seeking behavior in monkeys, suggesting that high intrinsic activity may be required to reproduce cocaine's priming effect (Khroyan et al., 2000).

The D_2-like family of receptors is comprised of three primary receptor subtypes (D_2, D_3, and D_4; Sokoloff & Schwartz, 1995). Indirect evidence suggests that the D_2 receptor subtype may play an especially prominent role in the relapse-inducing effects of cocaine. In contrast to other D_2-like receptor agonists, the preferential D_3 receptor agonists PD 128,907 and 7-OH-DPAT do not consistently reinstate cocaine-seeking behavior in monkeys, nor do they alter drug seeking induced by cocaine priming (Khroyan et al., 2000; Spealman et al., 2000). Moreover, preferential D_3 receptor antagonists, including

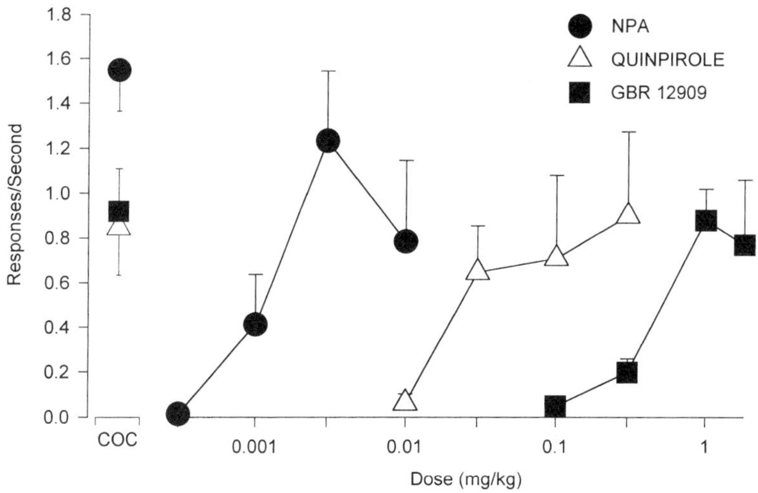

Figure 3. Dose-dependent reinstatement of drug seeking by priming with the DA uptake inhibitor GBR12909 and the D_2-like receptor agonists quinpirole and NPA in monkeys with histories of i.v. cocaine self-administration. Points above COC show priming with a maximally effective dose of cocaine. Data are means (± *SEM*, *N* = 3–5). Adapted from Khroyan et al. (2000) and Platt et al. (2001).

the highly selective antagonist AVE 5997, neither block nor mimic the priming effects of cocaine (Khroyan et al., 2000; Spealman et al., 2002). Although less is known about the role of the D_4 receptor subtype in cocaine's priming effects, high affinity at this receptor does not appear to be necessary for antagonists to block cocaine-induced reinstatement of drug seeking (Khroyan et al., 2000; Spealman et al., 2002).

The D_1-like receptor family (comprised of the D_1 and D_5 receptor subtypes) also plays an important role in the relapse-inducing effects of cocaine, but understanding its contribution has been unexpectedly challenging. In this regard, numerous studies have shown that D_1-like receptor agonists such as SKF 81297 and SKF 82958 partially mimic the discriminative stimulus effects of cocaine (Spealman, Bergman, Madras, & Melia, 1991; Witkin, Nichols, Terry, & Katz, 1991) and have reinforcing effects in animals with histories of i.v. cocaine self-administration (Grech, Spealman & Bergman, 1996; Self & Stein, 1992; Weed & Woolverton, 1995). Surprisingly, however, these drugs show little or no tendency to mimic the priming effects of

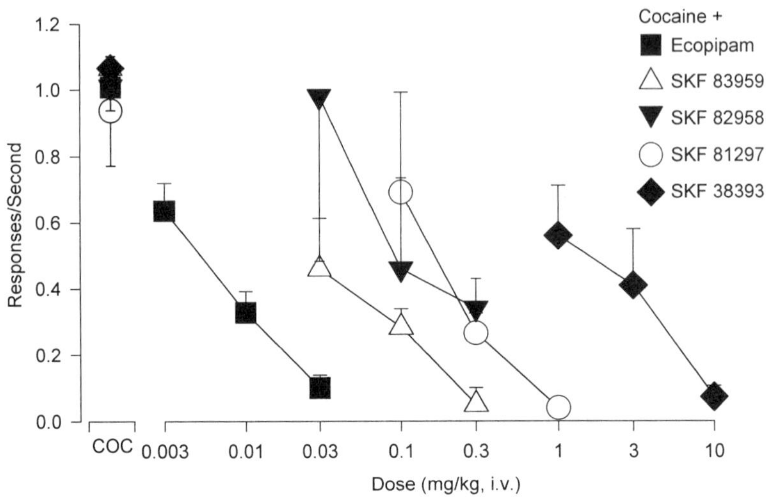

Figure 4. Dose-dependent inhibition of cocaine priming by D_1-like receptor agonists and antagonists in monkeys with histories of i.v. cocaine self-administration. Points above COC show priming with cocaine alone. Data are means (± *SEM*, *N* = 3–5). Adapted from Khroyan et al. (2000, 2003).

cocaine and instead inhibit cocaine-induced reinstatement of drug seeking in both monkeys (Figure 4; Khroyan et al., 2000) and rats (De Vries et al., 1999; Self et al., 1996). These findings suggest that stimulation of D_1-like receptors plays mainly an inhibitory role with respect to reinstatement of cocaine-seeking behavior. Complicating this interpretation, however, is the additional observation that D_1-like receptor antagonists such as ecopipam (SCH 39166) and SCH 23390 also inhibit cocaine's priming effects in monkeys (Figure 4; Khroyan et al., 2000; Khroyan, Platt, Rowlett, & Spealman, 2003) and rats (Norman, Norman, Hall, & Tsibulsky, 1999; Weissenborn et al., 1996). Despite the similar effects of D_1-like receptor agonists and antagonists when tested individually, the two types of drugs partially counteracted each other's effects when administered together (Khroyan et al., 2001), suggesting that D_1-like receptor agonists and antagonists inhibit cocaine-induced reinstatement of drug seeking via common receptor substrates, but through opposing pharmacological actions.

Recent evidence suggests that, in addition to DA, other monoaminergic mechanisms may play important modulatory roles in cocaine's ability to reinstate drug-seeking behavior. Noradrenergic (NE)

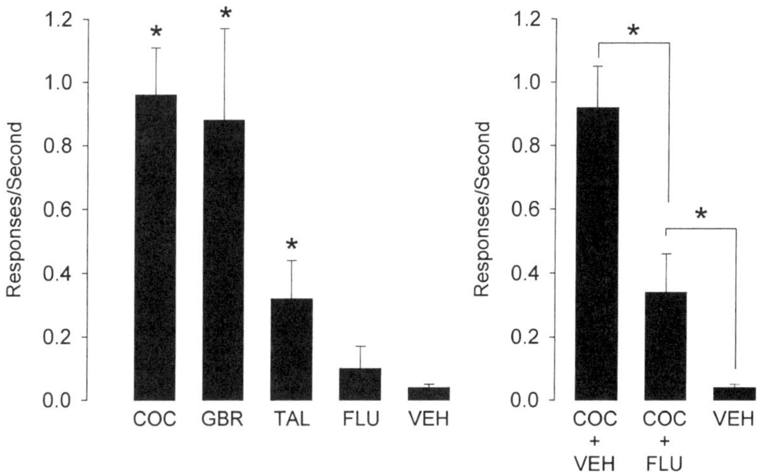

Figure 5. Effects of selective DA, NE, and 5-HT uptake inhibitors on reinstatement of drug seeking in monkeys with histories of i.v. cocaine self-administration. Left panel: priming with maximally effective doses of cocaine (COC; 1.0 mg/kg), GBR12909 (GBR; 1.8 mg/kg), talsupram (TAL; 5.6 mg/kg), and fluoxetine (FLU; 5.6 mg/kg). Right panel: priming with 1.0 mg/kg cocaine + vehicle or 5.6 mg/kg fluoxetine. Data are means (± SEM, $N = 4$). Asterisks show significant differences from vehicle or cocaine + vehicle ($p < 0.05$, Dunnett's test). Adapted from Platt et al. (2001).

projections from the locus coeruleus and the lateral tegmental nuclei and serotonergic (5-HT) projections from the dorsal raphe nucleus have been implicated in the regulation of mesocorticolimbic DA activity (Kelland, Freeman, & Chiodo, 1990; Marien, Lategan, & Colpaert, 1994), and pharmacological modulation of NE and 5-HT transmission can correspondingly influence many of the behavioral effects of cocaine related to its abuse (Spealman, 1993, 1995; Tessel, 1990; Walsh & Cunningham, 1997). The same may be true for cocaine-induced reinstatement of drug seeking. Along these lines, selective NE uptake inhibitors such as talsupram and nisoxetine partially reinstate cocaine-seeking behavior in squirrel monkeys, whereas selective 5-HT uptake inhibitors such as fluoxetine attenuate cocaine-induced reinstatement of drug seeking (Figure 5; Platt et al., 2001). Consistent with the latter finding, depletion of brain 5-HT with the selective neurotoxin 5,7-dihydroxytryptamine has been reported to enhance cocaine-induced reinstatement of drug seeking in rats (Tran-Nguyen, Bellew, Grote, & Neisewander, 2001).

Glutamate activity in the nucleus accumbens also has been linked to the abuse-related effects of cocaine in animals, particularly cocaine's ability to induce neuroadaptations associated with behavioral sensitization (Kalivas, Pierce, Cornish, & Sorg, 1998; Pierce, Bell, Duffy, & Kalivas, 1996; Wolf, 1998). Similarly, recent studies have revealed a possible role for glutamate neurotransmission in cocaine-induced reinstatement of drug seeking (Cornish, Duffy, & Kalivas, 1999; Cornish & Kalivas, 2000; De Vries et al., 1999; Park et al., 2002). Stimulation of AMPA/kainate receptors by administration of AMPA directly into the nucleus accumbens, for example, induced selective reinstatement of cocaine-seeking behavior in rats and, conversely, microinjection of the AMPA/kainate receptor antagonist CNQX into this brain region attenuated cocaine-induced reinstatement of responding (Cornish et al., 1999; Cornish & Kalivas, 2000; Park et al., 2002). In contrast, intra-accumbens or systemic injections of NMDA receptor antagonists, such as AP-5 or dizocilpine, failed to block cocaine-induced reinstatement of drug seeking and instead mimicked the priming effects of cocaine under some conditions (De Vries et al., 1999; Park et al., 2002). Although a definitive role for NMDA and AMPA receptor mechanisms has yet to be established, these findings suggest that the two glutamate receptor subtypes contribute in different, perhaps even opposite, ways to the reinstatement of cocaine-seeking behavior.

COCAINE CUES

The neurobiological basis of cue-induced relapse to drug seeking is only now being investigated, but already appears to involve neural systems that are important in the processing of other motivationally relevant stimuli (See, 2002; Shalev et al., 2002). Studies in rats, for example, have demonstrated significant increases in extracellular dopamine in the amygdala in response to environmental stimuli previously paired with or predictive of cocaine self-administration (Tran-Nguyen, Fuchs, Coffey, O'Dell, Baker, & Neisewander, 1998; Weiss, Maldonado-Vlaar, Parsons, Kerr, Smith, & Ben-Shahar, 2000), as well as attenuation of cue-induced reinstatement of cocaine seeking by inactivation of this brain region with tetrodotoxin (Grimm & See, 2000; Kruzich & See, 2001). In addition, Neisewander, Baker, Fuchs, Tran-Nguyen, Palmer, and Marshall (2000) and Ciccocioppo,

Sanna, and Weiss (2001) reported increases in neural activity (as measured by Fos protein expression) in the basolateral amygdala and other regions of the brain, including the anterior cingulate and portions of the frontal cortex, in rats exposed to an environment previously associated with cocaine self-administration. These consistent findings support a potentially important role for the amygdala and regions of the frontal lobe in the reinstatement of drug seeking by drug-associated stimuli (cf. See, 2002). Functional magnetic resonance imaging (fMRI) and positron emission tomography (PET) studies in human cocaine abusers also have begun to explore neural pathways that are activated in response to cocaine-associated stimuli or in conjunction with self-reported craving for cocaine. Although anatomical resolution was necessarily limited in these studies, the results generally confirm the importance of the amygdala, anterior cingulate, and frontal cortical structures in mediating the effects of cocaine cues in humans (Childress et al., 1999; Garavan et al., 2000; London, Bonson, Ernst, & Grant, 1999; Maas et al., 1998; Wexler et al., 2001).

Pharmacological studies of receptor mechanisms underlying cue-induced reinstatement of drug seeking point to a potentially key role for dopamine D_1-like receptor mechanisms. Although much of this research is still preliminary due in part to technical and conceptual challenges in developing sustainable models of cue-induced reinstatement (cf. Meil & See, 1996; Shalev et al., 2002; Weiss et al., 2000), the available data have so far revealed a consistent effect of the D_1-like receptor antagonists SCH 23390 and ecopipam in blocking reinstatement of drug seeking induced by cocaine-associated stimuli in rats (Alleweireldt, Weber, Kirschner, Bullock, & Neisewander, 2002; Ciccocioppo et al., 2001; See et al., 2001; Weiss et al., 2001). We have observed similar effects with ecopipam in a subgroup of monkeys that exhibited sustained increases in drug seeking induced by a cocaine-paired stimulus (unpublished observations). In addition, Alleweireldt et al. (2002) recently found that the D_1-like receptor agonist SKF 81297 inhibited cue-induced reinstatement of cocaine seeking in rats, an effect similar to that seen in the cocaine priming models discussed above. D_2-like receptor antagonists, on the other hand, appear to have less consistent effects on reinstatement of drug seeking induced by drug cues. See et al. (2001), for example, found that raclopride, in contrast to SCH 23390, had little or no effect on cue-induced reinstatement of cocaine seeking when injected into the basolateral amygdala of rats. McFarland and Ettenberg (1997) reported a similar lack of effect with systemically administered haloperidol on cue-induced reinstatement of heroin seeking.

A role for glutamate receptor mechanisms in cue-induced reinstatement of drug seeking also has been difficult to establish. Although Bespalov, Zvartau, Balster, and Beardsley (2000) reported dose-dependent attenuation of cue-induced cocaine seeking in rats by the NMDA receptor antagonist D-CPPene, other studies have observed little or no effect with competitive or noncompetitive NMDA receptor antagonists, such as AP-5 and memantine, or with the AMPA/kainate receptor antagonists CNQX on reinstatement of cocaine seeking induced by drug cues (Bespalov et al., 2000; See et al., 2001). Given the present state of knowledge, it is difficult to gauge the extent to which common neurotransmitter mechanisms might underlie cue-induced and priming-induced reinstatement of drug seeking. The answer to this question, however, could have implications for developing targeted therapeutic interventions for relapse prevention.

STRESS

In contrast to the accumulating body of information on the role of DA in drug priming and cue-induced reinstatement of drug seeking, surprisingly little is known about the contribution of DA mechanisms in stress-induced relapse. In one of the few published studies to address this question directly, Shaham and Stewart (1996) found that whereas flupenthixol inhibited foot-shock-induced reinstatement of heroin seeking in rats, neither SCH 23390 nor raclopride did so at doses that were sufficient to block the effects of drug priming. A possible role for DA mechanisms in stress-induced reinstatement of cocaine seeking has not yet been evaluated, but given the likely impact of stress on mesocorticolimbic DA activity (Finlay & Zigmond, 1997; Piazza & Le Moal, 1996), studies of this type would appear to be of considerable interest.

There is now compelling evidence for a complex relationship between stress, activation of the hypothalamic-pituitary-adrenal (HPA) axis, and the behavioral effects of cocaine related to its abuse (Goeders 2002; Kreek & Koob, 1998; Piazza & Le Moal, 1996). Exposure to many types of stress initiates a cascade of events within the HPA axis sometimes referred to as the "stress hormone cycle." The initial step in this cycle involves release of the neuropeptide corticotropin-releasing factor (CRF) from neurons in the hypothalamus. CRF then stimulates secretion of adrenocorticotropic hormone (ACTH) from the anterior pituitary, which in turn triggers release of glucocorticoids (cortisol in primates, corticosterone in rodents) from the adrenal glands. Glucocorticoids are then carried back to the hypothalamus and pituitary to inhibit further release of CRF and ACTH, thus completing the cycle.

Speculation that activation of the HPA axis and consequent release of glucocorticoids might play a role in stress-induced relapse was encouraged by initial reports that priming with corticosterone partially mimicked the relapse-inducing effects of shock in rats (Deroche, Marinelli, Le Moal, & Piazza, 1997) and that ketoconazole, a mixed-action glucocorticoid synthesis inhibitor/receptor antagonist, attenuated shock-induced reinstatement of cocaine seeking in this species (Mantsch & Goeders, 1999a). Although these findings are consistent with a role for glucocorticoid release in stress-induced relapse, other results have been less supportive. For example, adrenalectomy (in rats with histories of heroin self-administration) or adrenalectomy with replacement of corticosterone to basal levels (in rats with histories of cocaine self-administration) failed to inhibit shock-induced reinstatement of drug seeking even though removal of the adrenal glands prevented glucocorticoid release in both cases (Erb, Shaham, & Stewart, 1998; Shaham, Funk, Erb, Brown, Walker, & Stewart, 1997). Similarly, blockade of glucocorticoid synthesis with metyrapone did not affect shock-induced reinstatement of drug seeking despite blocking shock-induced increases in corticosterone (Shaham et al., 1997). Moreover, in contrast to the relapse-inducing effects of corticosterone reported in rats, systemic injections of cortisol, ACTH or CRF, over a range of relevant doses, failed to induce significant reinstatement of cocaine seeking in squirrel monkeys even though each of these treatments elevated cortisol to levels comparable to or exceeding those typically induced by stress (Lee, Tiefenbacher, Platt, Rowlett, & Spealman, 2001; Lee, Tiefenbacher, Platt, & Spealman, 2003). Thus, although some inconsistencies still exist, the available data do not support a primary role for activation of the HPA axis in stress-induced relapse.

In addition to its function within the HPA axis, CRF binds to at least two major receptor subtypes (CRF_1 and CRF_2) in diverse brain regions, including those implicated in the etiology of addiction and stress disorders (Chalmers, Lovenberg, & De Souza, 1995; Sanchez, Young, Plotsky, & Insel, 1999). Recent studies involving central administration of CRF and CRF antagonists have provided important new insights linking these extrahypothalamic CRF systems to stress-induced relapse in animals. Administration of CRF into the bed nucleus of the stria terminalis (BNST), for example, was found to induce significant reinstatement of cocaine seeking in rats, thus partially mimicking the effects of foot-shock in this model (Erb & Stewart, 1999). These findings, coupled with the observation that CRF does not reinstate cocaine seeking when administered systemically to monkeys (Lee et al., 2001), point to a key role for central CRF mechanisms in stress-induced relapse. Additional support for this possibility comes from studies demonstrating that both intra-BNST administration of D-Phe $CRF_{12–41}$ (a peptide CRF antagonist that does not cross the blood-brain barrier) and systemic administration of CP 154,526 (a nonpeptide CRF_1 antagonist that penetrates the brain) effectively blocked foot-shock-induced reinstatement of cocaine seeking in rats (Erb et al., 1998; Erb & Stewart, 1999; Shaham, Erb, Leung, Buczek, & Stewart, 1998).

There is now an extensive literature linking activation of central NE transmission to the behavioral and physiological consequences of stress (Bremner, Krystal, Southwich, & Charney, 1996; Southwick, Bremner, Rasmusson, Morgan, Arnsten, & Charney, 1999; Stanford, 1995), and recent findings have begun to reveal a potentially important role for these mechanisms in stress-induced reinstatement of drug seeking. As discussed earlier, drugs such as talsupram, which selectively stimulate NE transmission by inhibiting neurotransmitter uptake, induce significant reinstatement of drug seeking in monkeys with histories of i.v. cocaine self-administration. Using this same model, Lee, Tiefenbacher, and Spealman (2002; Figure 6) observed similar reinstatement of cocaine-seeking behavior with yohimbine, an α-2 adrenoceptor antagonist that induces NE release and elicits signs of fear and anxiety in humans (Charney, Woods, Krystal, Nagy, & Heniger, 1992; McDougle et al., 1994). Moreover, the relapse-inducing effects of yohimbine in these experiments could be blocked by the α-2 adrenoceptor agonist clonidine, which inhibits NE release and attenuates behavioral and physiological responses to stress (Bremner et al., 1996). Additional studies in rats have shown that foot-shock-

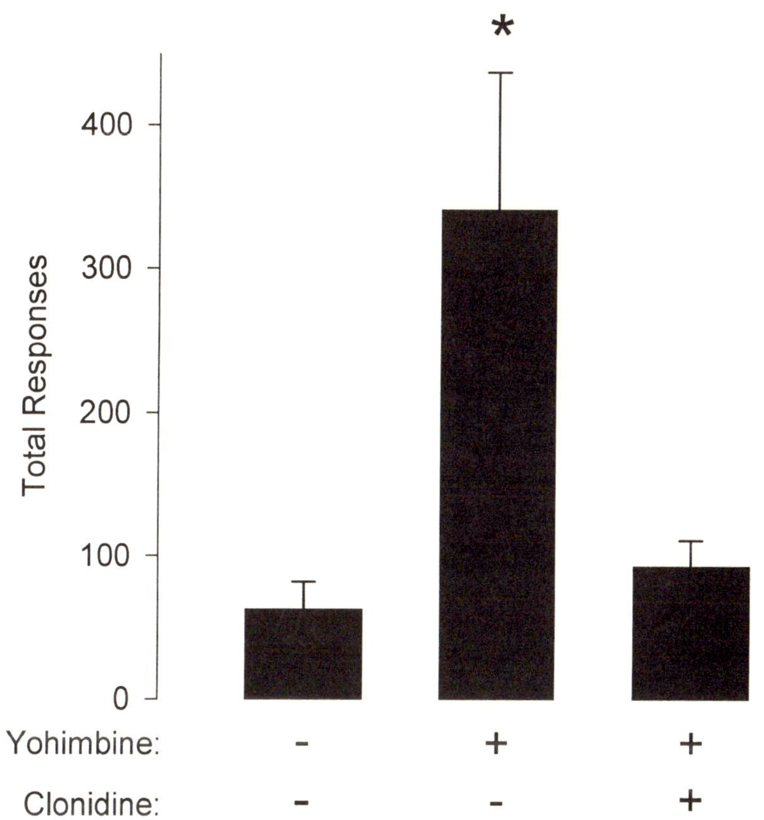

Figure 6. Reinstatement of drug seeking by a maximally effective dose of the α-2 adrenoceptor antagonist yohimbine (0.3–1.0 mg/kg depending on subject) and reversal by the α-2 agonist clonidine (0.3 mg/kg) in monkeys with histories of i.v. cocaine self-administration. Data are means (± SEM, $N = 4$). Asterisks show significant differences from vehicle ($p < 0.05$, Dunnett's test). Adapted from Lee et al. (2002).

induced reinstatement of cocaine seeking can be attenuated by clonidine and other α-2 adrenoceptor agonists at doses that inhibit shock-induced release of NE but do not alter reinstatement of drug seeking induced by cocaine priming (Erb, Hitchcott, Rajabi, Mueller, Shaham, & Stewart, 2000). The effects of the α-2 adrenoceptor agonists in these studies likely reflect their actions on central NE function because systemic treatment with ST-91, an analog of clonidine that does not readily cross the blood-brain barrier, had little effect on shock-induced reinstatement of cocaine seeking (Erb et al., 2000). Furthermore, central (i.c.v.) injections of clonidine were found to be as effective as systemic injections in blocking shock-induced reinstatement of drug seeking in this study. Growing evidence for interactions between central NE and CRF receptor systems in the modulation of stress (Koob, 1999) has prompted speculation that these systems also may interact to promote relapse under stressful conditions (Erb et al., 2000; Shalev et al., 2002).

Conclusions and Implications for Relapse Prevention

Nonhuman primate and rodent models have been developed that simulate relevant features of the drug use and relapse patterns observed in humans. Continued refinement of these models has provided important new insights into the pharmacological and environmental triggers of relapse, underlying neurobiological mechanisms, and potential pharmacotherapies for relapse prevention. As in humans, relapse to cocaine seeking can be triggered by drug priming, drug-associated stimuli, and certain types of stress in animals. Emerging data suggest that these triggers may interact to exacerbate relapse. For example, reinstatement of drug seeking is often greatest when drug cues are combined with drug priming or when exposure to stress occurs in an environment previously associated with drug self-administration.

Pharmacological studies have begun to reveal an unexpectedly complex role for DA receptor mechanisms in both cocaine priming and cue-induced relapse. Drugs that share cocaine's indirect DA agonist effects or that act as direct D_2-like (but not D_3) receptor agonists typically induce robust reinstatement of cocaine-seeking behavior, whereas D_1-like receptor agonists inhibit drug seeking induced by cocaine priming and/or cocaine-associated stimuli. D_1-like receptor antagonists also inhibit cocaine priming and the effects of cocaine-associated stimuli, whereas D_2-like receptor antagonists have different effects depending on receptor subtype and the type of model employed. These findings imply fundamental differences in the contribution of D_1-like and D_2-like receptor mechanisms to the relapse process and suggest that medications capable of modulating D_1-like receptor function might be rational candidates for development as anti-relapse pharmacotherapies. Recent evidence also implicates other monoaminergic as well as glutamatergic mechanisms as modulators of cocaine-induced drug seeking, suggesting additional targets for medication development.

Reinstatement of drug seeking as a result of foot-shock stress is a reproducible finding in rats. Establishing the generality of other types of stressors, especially psychological and social stress, as triggers of drug seeking in animals would appear to be a worthwhile objective because of its potential implications for stress management strategies targeting relapse prevention. Although initial studies in rodents encouraged speculation that glucocorticoid release might be the principal mechanism underlying stress-induced reinstatement of drug seeking, recent findings point to a key role for central CRF and NE mechanisms. Converging lines of evidence in nonhuman primates and rats suggest that modulation of CRF and/or α-2 NE activity in the brain warrant consideration as possible strategies to promote abstinence in individuals subjected to high levels of stress.

It has sometimes been hypothesized that the ability of drug priming, drug-associated stimuli, and stress to reinstate extinguished drug seeking depends on the degree to which these factors mimic the subjective and/or reinforcing effects of the self-administered drug. This view was encouraged initially by findings that many drugs capable of reinstating cocaine-seeking behavior also induced cocaine-like effects in drug discrimination and drug self-administration paradigms. Although conceptually appealing, the hypothesis is not particularly well supported by the available data. For example, drugs such as the D_1-like receptor agonists SKF 81297 and SKF 82958 and the D_3 receptor agonist PD 128,907 do not reinstate cocaine-seeking behavior in monkeys, yet share discriminative stimulus and reinforcing effects with cocaine (Spealman et al., 1999). Conversely, the α-2 adrenoceptor antagonist yohimbine induces significant reinstatement of cocaine seeking in monkeys, but does not share cocaine's discriminative stimulus effects (Spealman, 1995) and does not induce conditioned place preference (File, 1986). Along similar lines, reinstatement of drug seeking induced by cocaine-associated stimuli appears to be blocked more consistently by D_1-like than D_2-like receptor antagonists (See et al., 2001), whereas the discriminative stimulus and reinforcing effects of cocaine are blocked by both drug classes (Spealman, Bergman, Madras, Kamien, & Melia, 1992). Finally, although electric shock has been found to mimic the discriminative stimulus effects of cocaine as well as to reinstate cocaine-seeking behavior, drug treatment that attenuates shock-induced reinstatement of responding (i.e., ketoconazole) does not alter the cocainelike discriminative stimulus effects of shock or the effects of cocaine itself (Mantsch & Goeders, 1999a, 1999b).

Thus, although considerable overlap exists, pharmacological manipulations that modulate the discriminative stimulus and reinforcing effects of cocaine do not invariably affect reinstatement of cocaine-seeking behavior and vice versa. An important conclusion to be drawn from these observations is that the relapse-inducing, subjective, and reinforcing effects of cocaine are pharmacologically dissociable and therefore unlikely to reflect a single neurobiological process. A more comprehensive understanding of similarities and differences in mechanisms underlying the diverse behavioral effects of cocaine might be exploited profitably to develop treatment strategies targeting different phases of the cocaine addiction cycle.

References

Ahmed, S. H., & Koob, G. F. (1997). Cocaine- but not food-seeking behavior is reinstated by stress after prolonged extinction. *Psychopharmacology, 132,* 289–295.

Alleweireldt, A. T., Weber, S. M., Kirschner, K. F., Bullock, B. L., & Neisewander, J. L. (2002). Blockade or stimulation of D_1 dopamine receptors attenuates cue reinstatement of extinguished cocaine-seeking behavior in rats. *Psychopharmacology, 159,* 284–293.

Bespalov, A. Y., Zvartau, E. E., Balster, R. L., & Beardsley, P. M. (2000). Effects of N-methyl-D-aspartate receptor antagonists on reinstatement of cocaine-seeking behavior by priming injections of cocaine or exposures to cocaine-associated cue in rats. *Behavioural Pharmacology, 11,* 37–44.

Bradberry, C. W., Barrett-Larimore, R. L., Jatlow, P., & Rubino, S. R. (2000). Impact of self-administered cocaine and cocaine cues on extracellular dopamine in mesolimbic and sensorimotor striatum in rhesus monkeys. *Journal of Neuroscience, 20,* 3874–3883.

Bremner, J. D., Krystal, J. H., Southwich, S. M., & Charney, D. S. (1996). Noradrenergic mechanisms in stress and anxiety: I. Pre-clinical studies. *Synapse, 23,* 28–38.

Buczek, Y., Lê, A. D., Wang, A., Stewart, J., & Shaham, Y. (1999). Stress reinstates nicotine seeking but not sucrose solution seeking in rats. *Psychopharmacology, 144,* 183–188.

Carroll, M. E. (1985). The role of food deprivation in the maintenance and reinstatement of cocaine-seeking behavior in rats. *Drug and Alcohol Dependence, 16,* 95–109.

Carter, B. L., & Tiffany, S. T. (1999). Meta-analysis of cue-reactivity in addiction research. *Addiction, 94,* 327–340.

Chalmers, D. T., Lovenberg, T. W., & De Souza, E. B. (1995). Localization of novel corticotropin-releasing factor receptor (CRF2) MRNA expression to specific subcortical nuclei in rat brain: Comparison with CRF1 receptor MRNA expression. *Journal of Neuroscience, 15,* 6340–6350.

Charney, D. S., Woods, S. W., Krystal, J. H., Nagy, L. M., & Heniger, G. R. (1992). Noradrenergic neuronal dysregulation in panic disorder: The effects of intravenous yohimbine and clonidine in panic disorder patients. *Acta Psychiatrica Scandinavica, 86,* 273–282.

Childress, A. R., Hole, A. V., Ehrman, R. N., Robbins, S. J., McLellan, A. T., & O'Brien, C. P. (1993). Cue reactivity and cue reactivity interventions in drug dependence. NIDA *Research Monograph, 137,* 73–95.

Childress, A. R., McLellan, A. T., Ehrman, R., & O'Brien, C. P. (1988). Classically conditioned responses in opioid and cocaine dependence: A role in relapse? NIDA *Research Monograph, 84,* 25–43.

Childress, A. R., Mozley, P. D., McElgin, W., Fitzgerald, J., Reivich, M., & O'Brien, C. P. (1999). Limbic activation during cue-induced cocaine craving. *American Journal of Psychiatry, 156,* 11–18.

Ciccocioppo, R., Sanna, P. P., & Weiss, F. (2001). Cocaine-predictive stimulus induces drug-seeking behavior and neural activation in limbic brain regions after multiple months of abstinence: Reversal by D_1 antagonists. *Proceedings of the National Academy of Sciences, 98,* 1976–1981.

Coe, C. L., Franklin, D., Smith, E. R., & Levine, S. (1982). Hormonal responses accompanying fear and agitation in the squirrel monkey. *Physiology and Behavior, 29,* 1051–1057.

Cornish, J. L., Duffy, P., & Kalivas, P. W. (1999). A role for nucleus accumbens glutamate transmission in the relapse to cocaine-seeking behavior. *Neuroscience, 93,* 1359–1367.

Cornish, J. L., & Kalivas, P. W. (2000). Glutamate transmission in the nucleus accumbens mediates relapse in cocaine addiction. *Journal of Neuroscience, 20,* RC89.

Dackis, C. A., & O'Brien, C. P. (2001). Cocaine dependence: A disease of the brain's reward centers. *Journal of Substance Abuse Treatment, 21,* 111–117.

Davis, M. W., & Smith, S. G. (1976). Role of conditioned reinforcers in the initiation, maintenance and extinction of drug-seeking behavior. *Pavlovian Journal of Biological Science, 11,* 222–236.

DeJong, W. (1994). Relapse prevention: An emerging technology for promoting long-term drug abstinence. *International Journal of Addictions, 29,* 681–705.

DeRoche, V., Marinelli, M., Le Moal, M., & Piazza, P. V. (1997). Glucocorticoids and behavioral effects of psychostimulants. II: Cocaine intravenous self-administration and reinstatement depend on glucocorticoid levels. *Journal of Pharmacology and Experimental Therapeutics, 281,* 1401–1407.

De Vries, T. J., Schoffelmeer, A. N. M., Binnekade, A. H., Vanderschuren,

L. J. M. J. (1999). Dopaminergic mechanisms mediating the incentive to seek cocaine and heroin following long-term withdrawal of IV drug self-administration. *Psychopharmacology, 143,* 254–260.

de Wit, H., & Stewart, J. (1981). Reinstatement of cocaine-reinforced responding in the rat. *Psychopharmacology, 75,* 134–143.

Erb, S., Hitchcott, P. K., Rajabi, H., Mueller, D., Shaham, Y., & Stewart, J. (2000). Alpha-2 adrenergic receptor agonists block stress-induced reinstatement of cocaine seeking. *Neuropsychopharmacology, 23,* 138–150.

Erb, S., Shaham, Y., & Stewart, J. (1996). Stress reinstates cocaine-seeking behavior after prolonged extinction and drug-free periods. *Psychopharmacology, 128,* 408–412.

Erb, S., Shaham, Y., & Stewart, J. (1998). The role of corticotropin-releasing factor and corticosterone in stress- and cocaine-induced relapse to cocaine seeking in rats. *Journal of Neuroscience, 18,* 5529–5536.

Erb, S., & Stewart, J. (1999). A role for the bed nucleus of the stria terminalis, but not the amygdala, in the effects of corticotropin-releasing factor on stress-induced reinstatement of cocaine seeking. *Journal of Neuroscience, 19,* RC35.

File, S. E. (1986). Aversive and appetitive properties of anxiogenic and anxiolytic agents. *Behavioural Brain Research, 21,* 189–194.

Finlay, J. M., & Zigmond, M. J. (1997). The effects of stress on central dopaminergic neurons: Possible clinical implications. *Neurochemical Research, 22,* 1387–1394.

Foltin, R. W., & Haney, M. (2000). Conditioned effects of environmental stimuli paired with smoked cocaine in humans. *Psychopharmacology, 149,* 24–33.

Garavan, H., Pankiewicz, J., Bloom, A., Cho, J. K., Sperry, L., Ross, T. J., et al. (2000). Cue-induced cocaine craving: Neuroanatomical specificity for drug users and drug stimuli. *American Journal of Psychiatry, 157,* 1789–1798.

Gawin, F. H., & Kleber, H. D. (1986). Abstinence symptomatology and psychiatric diagnosis in cocaine abusers: Clinical observations. *Archives of General Psychiatry, 43,* 107–113.

Goeders, N. E. (2002). The HPA axis and cocaine reinforcement. *Psychoneuroendocrinology, 27,* 13–33.

Goldberg, S. R., Kelleher, R. T., & Morse, W. H. (1975). Second-order schedules of drug injection. *Federation Proceedings, 34,* 1771–1776.

Grech, D. M., Spealman, R. D., & Bergman, J. (1996). Self-administration of D_1 receptor agonists by squirrel monkeys. *Psychopharmacology, 125,* 97–104.

Grimm, J. W., Hope, B. T., Wise, R. A., & Shaham, Y. (2001). Neuroadaption. Incubation of cocaine craving after withdrawal. *Nature, 412,* 141–142.

Grimm, J. W., & See, R. E. (2000). Dissociation of primary and secondary reward-relevant limbic nuclei in an animal model of relapse. *Neuropsychopharmacology, 22,* 473–479.

Jaffe, J. H. (1990). Trivializing dependence. *British Journal of Addiction, 85,* 1425–1427.

Jaffe, J. H., Cascella, N. G., Kumor, K. M., & Sherer, M. A. (1989). Cocaine-induced cocaine craving. *Psychopharmacology, 97,* 59–64.

Kalivas, P. W., Pierce, R. C., Cornish, J., & Sorg, B. A. (1998). A rolc for sensitization in craving and relapse in cocaine addiction. *Journal of Psychopharmacology, 12,* 49–53.

Kelland, M. D., Freeman, A. S., & Chiodo, L. A. (1990). Serotonergic afferent regulation of the basic physiology and pharmacological responsiveness of nigrostriatal dopamine neurons. *Journal of Pharmacology and Experimental Therapeutics, 253,* 803–811.

Khroyan, T. V., Platt, D. M., Rowlett, J. K., & Spealman, R. D. (2003). Attenuation of relapse to cocaine seeking by dopamine D_1 receptor agonists and antagonists in non-human primates. *Psychopharmacology*, 168, 124–131.

Khroyan, T. V., Rowlett, J. K., & Spealman, R. D. (2001). Dopamine D1-like receptor agonists and antagonists attenuate relapse to cocaine-seeing behavior. *Drug and Alcohol Dependence, 63,* S80.

Koob, G. F. (1999). Corticotropin-releasing factor, norepinephrine, and stress. *Biological Psychiatry, 46,* 1167–1180.

Kreek, M. J., & Koob, G. F. (1998). Drug dependence: Stress and dysregulation of brain reward pathways. *Drug and Alcohol Dependence, 51,* 23–47.

Kruzich, P. J., & See, R. E. (2001). Differential contributions of the basolateral and central amygdala in the acquisition and expression of conditioned relapse to cocaine-seeking behavior. *Journal of Neuroscience, 21,* RC155.

Lê, A. D., Quan, B., Juzystch, W., Fletcher, P. J., Joharchi, N., & Shaham, Y. (1998). Reinstatement of alcohol-seeking by priming injections of alcohol and exposure to stress in rats. *Psychopharmacology, 135,* 169–174.

Lee, B., Tiefenbacher, S., Platt, D. M., Rowlett, J. K., & Spealman, R. D. (2001). Role of HPA axis in relapse to cocaine-seeking behavior. *Society for Neuroscience Abstracts, 27,* Program # 978.4.

Lee, B., Tiefenbacher, S., & Spealman, R. D. (2002). Reinstatement of cocaine-seeking behavior by yohimbine and reversal by clonidine in squirrel monkeys. *Society for Neuroscience Abstracts, 28,* Program # 501.11.

Lee, B., Tiefenbacher, S., Platt, D. M., & Spealman, R. D. (2003). Role of the hypothalamic-pituitary-adrenal axis in reinstatement of cocaine-seeking behavior in squirrel monkeys. *Psychopharmaology, 168,* 177–183.

Leshner, A. L. (1997). Addiction is a brain disease, and it matters. *Science, 278,* 45–47.

London, E. D., Bonson, K. R., Ernst, M., & Grant, S. (1999). Brain imaging studies of cocaine abuse: Implications for medication development. *Critical Reviews in Neurobiology, 13,* 227–242.

Maas, L. C., Lukas, S. E., Kaufman, M. J., Weiss, R. D., Daniels, S. L., Rogers, et al. (1998). Functional magnetic resonance imaging of human brain activation during cue-induced cocaine craving. *American Journal of Psychiatry, 155,* 124–126.

Mantsch, J. R., & Goeders, N. E. (1999a). Ketoconazole blocks the stress-induced reinstatement of cocaine seeking behavior in rats: Relationship to the discriminative stimulus effects of cocaine. *Psychopharmacology, 142,* 399–407.

Mantsch, J. R., & Goeders, N. E. (1999b). Ketoconazole does not block cocaine discrimination or the cocaine-induced reinstatement of cocaine-seeking behavior. *Pharmacology Biochemistry and Behavior, 64,* 65–73.

Marien, M., Lategan, A., & Colpaert, F. (1994). Noradrenergic control of striatal dopamine release. In M. Briley, & M. Marien (Eds.), *Noradrenergic mechanisms in Parkinson's disease* (pp. 127–138). Ann Arbor MI: CRC Press.

McDougle, C., Black, J., Malison, R., Zimmermann, R., Kosten, T., Heniger, et al. (1994). Noradrenergic dysregulation during discontinuation of cocaine use in addicts. *Archives of General Psychiatry, 51,* 713–719.

McFarland, K., & Ettenberg, A. (1997). Reinstatement of drug-seeking behavior produced by heroin-predictive environmental cues. *Psychopharmacology, 131,* 86–92.

Meil, W. M., & See, R. E. (1996). Conditioned cued recovery of responding following prolonged withdrawal from self-administered cocaine in rats: An animal model of relapse. *Behavioural Pharmacology, 7,* 754–763.

Neisewander, J. L., Baker, D. A., Fuchs, R. A., Tran-Nguyen, L. T., Palmer, A., & Marshall, J. F. (2000). Fos protein expression and cocaine-seeking behavior in rats after exposure to a cocaine self-administration environment. *Journal of Neuroscience, 20,* 798–805.

Newman, J. D., & Farley, M. J. (1995). An ethologically based, stimulus and gender-sensitive nonhuman primate model for anxiety. *Progress in Neuropsychopharmacology and Biological Psychiatry, 19,* 677–685.

Norman, A. B., Norman, M. K., Hall, J. F., & Tsibulsky, V. L. (1999). Priming threshold: A novel quantitative measure of the reinstatement of cocaine self-administration. *Brain Research, 831,* 165–174.

O'Brien, C. P., Childress, A. R., Ehrman, R., & Robbins, S. J. (1998). Conditioning factors in drug abuse: Can they explain compulsion? *Journal of Psychopharmacology, 12,* 15–22.

O'Brien, C. P., Childress, A. R., McLellan, A. T., & Ehrman, R. (1992). Classical conditioning in drug-dependent humans. *Annals of the New York Academy of Sciences, 28,* 400–415.

Park, W. K., Bari, A. A., Jey, A. P., Anderson, S. M., Spealman, R. D., Rowlett, J. K., & Pierce, R. C. (2002). Cocaine administered into the medial prefrontal cortex reinstates cocaine-seeking behavior by increasing AMPA receptor-mediated glutamate transmission in the nucleus accumbens. *Journal of Neuroscience, 22,* 2916–2925.

Piazza, P. V., & Le Moal, M. (1996). Pathophysiological basis of vulnerability to drug abuse: Role of an interaction between stress, glucocorticoids, and dopaminergic neurons. *Annual Review of Pharmacology and Toxicology, 36,* 359–378.

Pierce, R. C., Bell, K., Duffy, P., & Kalivas, P. W. (1996). Repeated cocaine augments excitatory amino acid transmission in the nucleus accumbens only in rats having developed behavioral sensitization. *Journal of Neuroscience, 15,* 1550–1560.

Platt, D. M., Rowlett, J. K., & Spealman, R. D. (2001). Monoaminergic transport mechanisms in relapse to cocaine-seeking behavior. *Society of Neuroscience Abstracts, 27,* Program # 788.2.

Preston, K. L., Sullivan, J. T., Strain, E. C., & Bigelow, G. E. (1992). Effects of cocaine alone and in combination with bromocriptine in human cocaine abusers. *Journal of Pharmacology and Experimental Therapeutics, 262,* 279–291.

Robbins, S. J., Ehrman, R. N., Childress, A. R., & O'Brien, C. P. (1997). Relationships among physiological and self-reported responses produced by cocaine-related cues. *Addictive Behaviors, 22,* 157–167.

Rohsenow, D. J., Niaura, R. S., Childress, A. R., Abrams, D. B., & Monti, P. M. (1990–1991). Cue reactivity in addictive behaviors: Theoretical and treatment implications. *International Journal of Addictions, 25,* 957–993.

Sanchez, M. M., Young, L. J., Plotsky, P. M., & Insel, T. R. (1999). Autoradiographic and in situ hybridization localization of corticotropin-releasing factor 1 and 2 receptors in nonhuman primate brain. *Journal of Comparative Neurology, 408,* 365–377.

See, R. E. (2002). Neural substrates of conditioned-cued relapse to drug-seeking behavior. *Pharmacology Biochemistry and Behavior, 71,* 517–529.

See, R. E., Kruzich, P. J., & Grimm, J. W. (2001). Dopamine, but not glutamate, receptor blockade in the basolateral amygdala attenuates conditioned reward in a rat model of relapse to cocaine-seeking behavior. *Psychopharmacology, 154,* 301–310.

Self, D. W., Barnhart, W. T., Lehman, D. A., & Nestler, E. J. (1996). Opposite modulation of cocaine-seeking behavior by D_1 and D_2-like dopamine receptor agonists. *Science, 271,* 1586–1589.

Self, D. W., Genova, L. M., Hope, B. T., Barnhart, W. J., Spencer, J. J., & Nestler, E. J. (1998). Involvement of cAMP-dependent protein kinase in the nucleus accumbens in cocaine self-administration and relapse of cocaine-seeking behavior. *Journal of Neuroscience, 18,* 1848–1859.

Self, D. W., & Nestler, E. J. (1998). Relapse to drug seeking: Neural and molecular mechanisms. *Drug and Alcohol Dependence, 51,* 49–60.

Self, D. W., & Stein, L. (1992). The D_1 agonists SKF 82958 and SKF 77434 are self-administered by rats. *Brain Research, 582,* 349–352.

Shaham, Y., Erb, S., Leung, S., Buczek, Y., & Stewart, J. (1998). CP 154,526, a selective, non-peptide antagonist of the corticotropin-releasing factor 1 receptor attenuates stress-induced relapse to drug seeking in cocaine- and heroin-trained rats. *Psychopharmacology, 137,* 184–190.

Shaham, Y., Erb, S., & Stewart, J. (2000). Stress-induced relapse to heroin and

cocaine seeking in rats: A review. *Brain Research Reviews, 33,* 13–33.
Shaham, Y., Funk, D., Erb, S., Brown, T. J., Walker, C. D., & Stewart, J. (1997). Corticotropin-releasing factor, but not corticosterone, is involved in stress-induced relapse to heroin seeking in rats. *Journal of Neuroscience, 17,* 2605–2614.
Shaham, Y., & Stewart, J. (1996). Effects of opioid and dopamine receptor antagonists on relapse induced by stress and reexposure to heroin in rats. *Psychopharmacology, 125,* 385–391.
Shalev, U., Grimm, J. W., & Shaham, Y. (2002). Neurobiology of relapse to heroin and cocaine seeking: A review. *Pharmacological Reviews, 54,* 1–42.
Shalev, U., Highfield, D., Yap, J., & Shaham, Y. (2000). Stress and relapse to drug seeking in rats: Studies on the generality of the effect. *Psychopharmacology, 150,* 337–346.
Simpson, D. D., Joe, G. W., Fletcher, B. W., Hubbard, R. L., & Anglin, M. D. (1999). A national evaluation of treatment outcomes for cocaine dependence. *Archives of General Psychiatry, 56,* 507–514.
Sinha, R. (2001). How does stress increase risk of drug abuse and relapse? *Psychopharmacology, 158,* 343–359.
Sinha, R., Catapano, D., & O'Malley, S. S. (1999). Stress-induced craving and stress responses in cocaine dependent individuals. *Psychopharmacology, 142,* 343–351.
Sinha, R., Fuse, T., Aubin, L. R., & O'Malley, S. S. (2000). Psychological stress, drug-related cues and cocaine craving. *Psychopharmacology, 152,* 140–148.
Sokoloff, P., & Schwartz, J. C. (1995). Novel dopamine receptors half a decade later. *Trends in Pharmacological Sciences, 16,* 270–275.
Southwick, S., Bremner J., Rasmusson, A., Morgan, C. R., Arnsten, D., & Charney, D. (1999). Role of norepinephrine in the pathophysiology and treatment of post-traumatic stress disorder. *Biological Psychology, 46,* 1192–1204.
Spealman, R. D. (1993). Modification of behavioral effects of cocaine by selective serotonin and dopamine uptake inhibitors in squirrel monkeys. *Psychopharmacology, 112,* 93–99.
Spealman, R. D. (1995). Noradrenergic involvement in the discriminative stimulus effects of cocaine in squirrel monkeys. *Journal of Pharmacology and Experimental Therapeutics, 275,* 53–62.
Spealman, R. D., Barrett-Larimore, R. L., Rowlett, J. K., Platt, D. M., & Khroyan, T. V. (1999). Pharmacological and environmental determinants of relapse to cocaine-seeking behavior. *Pharmacology Biochemistry and Behavior, 64,* 327–336.
Spealman, R. D., Bergman, J., Madras, B .K., Kamien, J. B., & Melia, K. F. (1992). Role of D_1 and D_2 dopamine receptors in the behavioral effects of cocaine. *Neurochemistry International, 20,* 147S-152S.
Spealman, R. D., Bergman, J., Madras, B. K., & Melia, K. C. (1991). Discriminative stimulus effects of cocaine in squirrel monkeys: Involvement of dopamine receptor subtypes. *Journal of Pharmacology and Experimental Therapeutics, 258,* 945–953.

Spealman, R. D., Khroyan, T. V., Barrett-Larimore, R. L., Rowlett, J. K., & Platt, D. M. (2000). Dopaminergic mechanisms in relapse to cocaine-seeking behavior. *Annals of the New York Academy of Sciences, 909,* 273–274.

Spealman, R. D., Kongsamut, S., Wettstein, J. G., & Rowlett, J. K. (2002). Dopamine D2-like receptor mechanisms in the discriminative stimulus and relapse-inducing effects of cocaine: Studies with selective D2, D3, and D4 antagonists. FASEB *Journal, 16,* A194.

Stanford, S. (1995). Central noradrenergic neurons and stress. *Pharmacology and Therapeutics, 68,* 297–342.

Sutton, M. A., Karanian, D. A., & Self, D. W. (2000). Factors that determine a propensity for relapse to cocaine-seeking behavior in rats. *Neuropsychopharmacology, 22,* 626–641.

Tessel, R. E. (1990). Noradrenergic processes in the behavioral actions of psychomotor stimulants. *Drug Development Research, 20,* 359–368.

Tran-Nguyen, L. T., Bellew, J. G., Grote, K. A., & Neisewander, J. L. (2001). Serotonin depletion attenuates cocaine seeking but enhances sucrose seeking and the effects of cocaine priming on reinstatement of cocaine seeking in rats. *Psychopharmacology, 157,* 340–348.

Tran-Nguyen, L. T., Fuchs, R. A., Coffey, G. P., O'Dell, L. E., Baker, D. A., & Neisewander, J. L. (1998). Time-dependent changes in cocaine-seeking behavior and dopamine overflow in the amygdala during cocaine withdrawal. *Neuropsychopharmacology, 19,* 48–59.

Walsh, S. L., & Cunningham, K. A. (1997). Serotonergic mechanisms involved in the discriminative stimulus, reinforcing and subjective effects of cocaine. *Psychopharmacology, 130,* 41–58.

Weed, M. R., & Woolverton, W. L. (1995). The reinforcing effects of D1 receptor agonists in rhesus monkeys. *Journal of Pharmacology and Experimental Therapeutics, 275,* 1367–1374.

Weerts, E. M., & Miczek, K. A. (1996). Primate vocalizations during social separation and aggression: Effects of alcohol and benzodiazepines. *Psychopharmacology, 127,* 255–264.

Weiss, F., Maldonado-Vlaar, C. S., Parsons, L. H., Kerr, T. M., Smith, D. L., & Ben-Shahar, O. (2000). Control of cocaine-seeking behavior by drug-associated stimuli in rats: Effects on recovery of extinguished operant-responding and extracellular dopamine levels in amygdala and nucleus accumbens. *Proceedings of the National Academy of Sciences, 97,* 4321–4326.

Weiss, F., Martin-Fardon, R., Ciccocioppo, R., Kerr, T. M., Smith, D. L., & Ben-Shahar, O. (2001). Enduring resistance to extinction of cocaine-seeking behavior induced by drug-related cues. *Neuropsychopharmacology, 25,* 361–372.

Weissenborn, R., Deroche, V., Koob, G., & Weiss, F. (1996). Effects of dopamine agonists and antagonists on cocaine-induced operant responding for a cocaine-associated stimulus. *Psychopharmacology, 126,* 311–322.

Wexler, B. E., Gottschalk, C. H., Fulbright, R. K., Prohovnik, I., Lacadie, C. M., Rounsaville, B. J., & Gore, J. C. (2001). Functional magnetic resonance imaging of cocaine craving. *American Journal of Psychiatry, 158,* 86–95.

Wise, R. A., Murray, A., & Bozarth, M. A. (1990). Bromocriptine self-administration and bromocriptine-reinstatement of cocaine-trained and heroin-trained lever pressing in rats. *Psychopharmacology, 100,* 355–360.
Witkin, J. M., Nichols, D. E., Terry P., & Katz, J. L. (1991). Behavioral effects of selective dopaminergic compounds in rats discriminating cocaine injections. *Journal of Pharmacology and Experimental Therapeutics, 257,* 706–713.
Wolf, M. E. (1998). The role of excitatory amino acids in behavioral sensitization to psychomotor stimulants. *Progress in Neurobiology, 54,* 669–720.

The Role of Emotional Systems in Addiction: A Neuroethological Perspective

Jaak Panksepp, Christine Nocjar, Jeff Burgdorf, Jules B. Panksepp, and Robert Huber
Bowling Green State University

Modern neuroscience provides a variety of explanatory schemes for understanding drug addiction. These focus to a large extent either on vast molecular complexities of relevant brain systems or their expressions in the form of characteristic and objectively observed behaviors. Regardless of the particular approach used, however, considerations of causal mechanisms commonly neglect the inclusion of psychological and contextual constructs. In the present chapter, we argue that intervening neuro-mental states, such as experienced emotional and motivational forces in all animals, and certainly thoughts in humans, are relevant to a scientific understanding of such issues. Claims about experiential states by themselves, however, provide no novel strategies toward studies of behavioral control in animals. To be useful, such concepts have to be expanded not only by neuroscience perspectives but also with specific predictions and appropriate research paradigms. We aim to share some in this chapter.

To address these issues, we first summarize our general theoretical premises, then proceed to a detailed discussion of one example that underscores the great difficulties conscious feeling states have posed for the experimental analysis of addiction. We will conclude with a review of two new experimental paradigms that may help to address the complex interface between affective states and neural substrates for the study of addiction. Predictions arising from this work can ultimately be confirmed by taking findings from animal models, applying them to human contexts, and advancing successful treatments of psychiatric problems.

Brain-Mind "Docking" in Addiction Research

A set of theoretical premises guides our work into the relations of brain and mind: (1) fundamental psychological concepts (such as basic emotional states) reflect functional neural assemblies that are at least partially accessible to selective forces within an evolutionary context; (2) a key process of the brain is the generation of psychological states that guide behavior toward adaptive responses; (3) thinking, perceiving, feeling, and behaving are not simply properties of molecules, but of integrated sensory-motor and intervening emotion-motivation mediating neural systems.

In order to understand how the brain was shaped by natural selection, we will need to coalesce psychological and neuroscience perspectives into an internally consistent framework. A pure brain-behavior equation, which is still a guiding light for behavioral neuroscience, is not by itself sufficient for such understanding. We also need psychological concepts that provide a testable gateway for conceptualizing the relevant evolved functional systems of the brain. The inclusion of such psychological processes into behavioral neuroscience presents special challenges. Among neuroscientists, three overlapping reasons are commonly advanced for the widespread neglect of such considerations.

(1) *Mental states cannot be measured using objective procedures in any species,* except for weak measurement tools such as Likert-type rating scales in humans. But progress can be made. For instance, it is likely that certain behaviors in animals reflect veridical readouts of their ongoing emotional experiences (Panksepp, 1998). In this chapter, we suggest that ultrasonic vocalizations can be used to index both positive and negative affective states in rats.

(2) *There is a general suspicion among behavioral neuroscientists that consciously experienced mental states are, for the most part, outside the*

scope of scientific investigation. Hence one is forced to deny or to remain agnostic about such issues. We will argue that such mind/brain processes are a reality of mammalian brain organization, and that affective experiences are instantiated largely within the evolutionarily ancient emotional operating systems of the brain. As summarized herein, we have now even found amphetamine-reward in crayfish. Although we are careful not to ascribe affective consciousness to such creatures, we would be even more hesitant to deny them that possibility. There is thus cause for hope if we can make productive predictions across species. For instance, neural homologies in mammalian, subcortical brain circuits may allow us to predict changes in human affect by studying the neural (especially the neurochemical) causes of emotions and affect-related behaviors, which can be measured objectively in other animals.

(3) *It is difficult to imagine how mental states could have any causal role within the materialistic schemes of brain functions that are presently conceptualized.* We will suggest that affective states are not causally inconsequential epiphenomena, because they are thoroughly expressed in the neurobiological domain. The emergence of affective experiences in the evolution of nervous system function may have offered an efficient substrate for encoding biological values, and hence controlling the long-term behavior patterns of animals through the establishment of central experiential states. Such states are reflected directly in certain action tendencies of "simple minded" animals and in the internal cognitive deliberations (i.e., weighing courses of action) of more "complex minded" ones.

The experience of emotional feelings, as a complex neurobiological process, is an integral part of dynamic, hierarchical brain operating systems. For instance, as humans become addicted, their capacity for rational choice is compromised by the internal insistence of ancestral affective urges. By objectively measuring the behavioral expressions of emotional systems in action, we can thus shed light on the internal brain/mind processes of emotional experiences that contribute to the choices confronted by all animals, including humans. Affective states thus are viewed as biases toward long-term, adaptive, psychobehavioral strategies (Kravitz, 1988; Panksepp, 1982, 1998) rather than simply a governing agent for short-term reflexive emotional responses.

Radically positivistic-behaviorists who still shun and discourage discussions about neuro-theoretical mental states, especially in animals, ignore that multiple levels of control exist within all complex systems, such as the mammalian brain/mind. For an early comprehensive theoretical framework, see Tinbergen (1952), and for the nuts and bolts of later neuro-evolutionary constructions see MacLean (1990) and Panksepp (1998). Within such complex adaptive systems, nested levels of control promote the emergence of phenomena that are not intuitively obvious from linear analyses of cause and effect. For instance, there is little in the modern analysis of fear-learning (LeDoux, 1996) that predicts how fear might be experienced in the brain; however, fear is surely experienced. Likewise, the analysis of sensory systems does not necessarily predict in what way perception is elaborated through chaotic attractor patterns of large neural ensembles in the cortex (Freeman, 1999).

With basic emotional rules thoroughly constructed in neural and neurochemical domains, emergent affective processes that are ultimately accessible to selection processes as adaptive psycho-behavioral responses are favored. In our view, evolved instinctual systems of the brain are not simply unconscious output devices, but are mindful attractors, integrating and coordinating action states of the nervous system. Primary-process aspects of consciousness, such as basic feeling states, are fundamentally built upon stable motor-action systems of the brain, including the instinctual neural apparatus for emotional behavioral tendencies (Panksepp, 1998, 2001). Brain systems such as the neocortex are not needed to generate these dynamics, even though they can both strengthen and weaken them in multiple ways.

If one is willing to provisionally accept these admittedly radical points of view (at least for many neuro-behaviorists and pure animal behaviorists), then we might also conclude that biology-alone approaches, even when linked to rigorous behavioral analyses, will not suffice to completely understand changes in brain functions underlying addiction. We are willing to claim that our ability to anthropomorphize about emotional states in scientifically useful ways in animal research (i.e., anchored by neuronal homologies) is important for progress on key psychological issues, namely the various affective functions of the human brain that we still share with the other animals (Panksepp, 2003).

Such state-control functions are basic utilities arising from within the great intermediate net of the brain so that organisms can compete effectively in complex worlds where reflexes simply do not suffice. State-control systems operate at a broad-scale network (i.e., at a "systems doctrine") level, which is not clearly evident at a single-unit level of analysis. We can contrast "state controls" to more information-constrained "channel control" functions in the brain, especially for multiple streams of information converging onto evolved brain operating systems from multiple sensory channels (Mesulam, 2000). The thorough integration of such processes in the brain is undisputed, and higher forms of consciousness may indeed emerge through those interactions. In our view, however, addiction appears to operate largely through changes in affective state-control processes rather than perceptual channel-control functions of the brain. Thus, in our estimation, neither we nor other animals are unconscious zombies, but rather are the inheritors of an emotionally guided neuromental apparatus with psychologically relevant organizational aspects that are very relevant for understanding the motivational aspects of addiction (i.e., the coordinated activities of many brain areas generate internally experienced representations that can sustain and guide behavioral choices that promote positive affect).

A Deconstruction: The Lamb et al. Type of Argument for Unconscious Reinforcement

A classic, methodologically creative study by Lamb et al. (1991) is commonly used to argue against the role of conscious reward processes in drug seeking. Five heroin addicts were allowed to work for one of five doses of morphine (vehicle placebo, 3.75, 7.5, 15, or 30 mg per dose). Under each of the respective dose conditions a cognitively mediated task was presented for a daily, one hour, fixed ratio schedule throughout a continuous workweek. Slowly absorbed, intramuscular injections were administered by the nursing staff, which typically allowed a maximum of four to six infusions per session. Operant response rates were monitored (mean lever-press rates were 4–5/s), in addition to several affective and autonomic responses at the end of each session. Subjects worked vigorously for all doses of morphine but exhibited significant levels of drug-induced liking only with the highest dose. Responding was sustained at high levels even for the first "extinction" day with a rapid decline thereafter, suggesting that intentional cognitive mediation sustained asymptotic behavior for at least one full session. The investigators never tested the obvious mediating role of voluntary intentional behavior in their paradigm, nor did they inquire about the potential consequences of subjects discussing experimental aspects with one another. Thus, the role of "reinforcement" in drug-seeking behavior (at least in a Thorndikian sense of short-term "law of effect" processes helping to shape behavior) was probably not even evaluated by this experimental design.

The widely touted mystery emerged at the three intermediate dose conditions where subjects continued to work quite hard for the morphine, even without reporting subjective drug liking. The suggestion was that with behavior dissociated from conscious experiences of euphoric-reward, some type of unconscious "reinforcement" process was sustaining the operant behavior (e.g., Berridge & Robinson, 1998).

Fair enough? Well, not quite if this was more of a cognitively mediated operant task rather than a "reinforced" self-administration task (since subjects would surely never have "picked up" the behavior with the outrageous fixed ratio 3,000 reinforcement contingency). Perhaps the subjects knew that they were getting some drug, and were aspiring to go even faster to get at least something for their efforts. At these low doses the only thing the addicts might have felt was a slight normalization of mood, but that was not assessed. One should have also evaluated their urge to respond and their current desire for drug reward. The subjects surely should have been asked why they were continuing to respond on this cognitively mediated task. Answers to such questions would have been essential when concluding that the subjects were really behaving unconsciously. Moreover, biased design features predisposed the studies' outcomes against detecting positive affective responses (e.g., negative contrasts in sequence of morphine doses; the ability to share impressions with cohort members concurrently receiving the same drug schedule; subjects with sustained operant output in a situation with nothing else to do for an hour; individuals were accustomed to much higher doses of opiates compared to those used in the study; and perhaps with a general overrepresentation of emotionally unresponsive, perhaps even alexithymic, males in addict populations who might be loath to talk about their feelings). Contrary to the common behavioristic interpretation, this study actually illustrates the existence of an impressive experiential response as subjects reported a perception of the drug 38% of the time even at the lowest 3.75 mg doses compared to 0% for vehicle controls.

In summary, this study should not be used as evidence against consciously experienced consequences of low doses of morphine and it is simply not sufficient to argue for the absence of conscious motivational and emotional contributions to the observed low-dose drug-seeking behaviors. In our estimation, the matter remains as open as it always has, except for the recognition that the amount of perceived "drug reward/euphoria" is certainly not the only psychological factor that plays a role in the maintenance of drug taking.

An alternative and more telling methodology might place individuals in a peaceful setting by themselves (perhaps alone in a "waveless" flotation tank to minimize distractions and other attentional biases that may disrupt the experience of internal feelings), and infuse various doses of drug as individuals give online reports of their experiential states. Such procedures should give us a better "psycho-ethological" perspective on mental processes when neurochemical environments are actually being altered. The time is ripe for the establishment of a psycho-ethological tradition that attempts to capture the ongoing dynamics of the human mind in various emotionally challenging situations (for an extended discussion, see Panksepp, 1999). Without such studies, claims of unconscious information processing may reflect little more than insufficient evaluation of conscious changes or effects of context-dependent distractibility during testing.

We critique this classic experiment in order to argue against further marginalizing affective consciousness in addiction research and to highlight that behavioral psychology must invest more in ethological approaches for human mental processing and states. Without a full consideration of the intrinsic emotional and behavioral tendencies arising from ancestral brain action systems, many paradoxes in the drug-addiction literature may be difficult to resolve, and various important avenues of research will remain unexplored. For instance, certain addictions may be based on consumatory types of pleasure, appetitive types, or rather the alleviation of pain, fear, anger, and other forms of suffering and irritability. Indeed, we believe that neglecting affective consciousness is delaying our understanding of the true nature of addictions.

A Reconstruction: Brain Operating Systems and Affective-Behavioral Processes

Aiming to clarify some of the urges and pleasures that accompany brain addictive processes, we review findings from behavioral neuroscience experiments that address relationships between basic mental and neural functions relevant for addiction. Several distinct emotional state systems probably contribute to the addictive process.

Our approach is both evolutionary and ethological, with a foremost concern for elements of the neuro-mental apparatus that derive, at least partially, from heritable genetic components. The human brain/mind was built upon a distinct set of emotional systems that we share with evolutionary ancestors and that govern certain "instinctual" action tendencies. Characteristic dynamics arising from such systems help generate the corresponding affective experiences within the brain. In common parlance, these dynamics are called basic emotional feelings, and include neuro-mental experiences of anger, fear, grief, joy, and desire on the one hand and the bodily or physical motivational feelings such as hunger, thirst, and the pleasant feelings that accompany return toward homeostasis on the other. These genetically ingrained operating systems contribute to an affective coloring of consciousness. Drug addictions thus represent the ability of certain molecules to take control of these systems by stimulating critical aspects of the underlying brain circuitry (Nesse & Berridge, 1997; Panksepp, Knutson, & Burgdorf, 2002; Wise, 1998). To understand the multidimensional nature of addiction, it is essential that we distinguish different types of drug rewards, including social and homeostatic reward processes (e.g., opioids), arousal of intrinsic emotional desire/action systems of the brain (e.g., dopamine), or those motivated by anxiety or chronic irritability (e.g., the benzodiazepine anxiolytics). Both ethological and behavioristic analyses can work together effectively: ethological analyses for characterizing the tools that evolution provided toward the instigation and guidance of behavior; behavioristic analyses for describing how these tools permit learning of novel behavior patterns. Nevertheless, brain experiential responses, difficult as they are to objectify, should not be minimized or marginalized in either of these analyses.

Approaches in both behaviorism and ethology have traditionally used a reasonable "hands-off" attitude when attributing mental properties to observable behaviors. However, as neuroscience research advances into human psychological issues, such research can now entertain the inner psychological aspects of certain neural processes by focusing on evolutionary homologies (e.g., Panksepp, 1998, 2003). Would individuals exhibit addictive behaviors if there were no affective payoffs? We suspect an answer of "no" for both humans and other species, and hence are willing to provisionally grant a wide range of organisms a similar capacity for neuropsychological processes that make addictive activities compelling for humans. To do otherwise is to sustain the hegemony of a dualistic tradition in mind science that has caused serious mischief in the field for well over a century (Blumberg & Wasserman, 1995; LeDoux, 2000; Skinner, 1987).

Acceptance of widely shared, intrinsic emotional components that contribute to affective experience in humans (Heath, 1996) provides us with a wealth of mental constructs for the study of animal behavior. We now consider two emotional systems of the brain that figure heavily in the study of drug addictions: a system monitoring social support and generating separation-distress/PANIC, and an appetitive/SEEKING system.

THE OPIOID-BASED, SOCIAL AFFECT SYSTEM

Opioids mediate positive feelings and suppress various kinds of negative affect. Our search for the underlying nature of social comfort and hence social bonds led us to consider the importance of opioid systems in the early 1970s. There are remarkable similarities between the dynamics of social dependence and narcotic addiction. Each is characterized by an intense attraction process at the outset (euphoria phase), which diminishes as a function of exposure (the tolerance phase). Following the emergence of tolerance, the system has adapted to a new homeostatic "set point" whereby removal of the object of desire/satisfaction leads to a pattern of affectively negative distress symptoms that are remarkably similar for social loss and opiate withdrawal (Panksepp, 1981a; Panksepp, Herman, Vilberg, Bishop, & DeEskinazi, 1980).

The prediction that social isolation should enhance the rewarding effects of opiates has been supported by numerous studies using self-administration of opiates (Alexander, Coambs, & Hadaway 1978; Alexander, Beyerstein, Hadaway, & Coambs, 1981; Bozarth, Murray,

& Wise, 1989) even though place preference studies do not consistently support such conclusions (Schenk, Hunt, Colle, & Amit, 1983; Wongwitdecha & Marsden, 1996). At a sociocultural level, the incidence of opiate addiction has been highest in circumstances where individuals were isolated from their normal social supports (Panksepp, 1981a). There are a host of convergent findings consistent with this theoretical viewpoint: Feelings associated with opiate withdrawal are similar in characteristics to those experienced during social loss and separation distress (Panksepp, Siviy, & Normansell, 1985); brain mechanisms for separation distress are modulated by endogenous opioids (Herman & Panksepp, 1981; Panksepp, Normansell, Herman, Bishop, & Crepeau, 1988); opioids participate in the contact-comfort animals derive from both somatosensory stimulation (Panksepp, Meeker, & Bean, 1980) and the sexual reward they obtain from copulation (Ågmo & Berenfeld, 1990; Ågmo & Gomez, 1993); opiates diminish the need for social interactions in animals and humans (Panksepp, Najam, & Soares, 1979); and modest doses of opioids facilitate social dominance, potentially through the facilitation of feelings of confidence (Panksepp, Jalowiec, DeEskinazi, & Bishop, 1985).

It thus seems likely that individuals who are not obtaining sufficient support from their social interactions or feel the sting of alienation in other ways, are more tempted to alleviate those feelings of social discomfort with pharmacological rewards. Disassociation of pharmacologically induced social rewards from ongoing social interactions may directly promote addiction as opposed to social relations. These gratifying behaviors may become self-sustaining as the arousal of negative affect during drug absence will exacerbate the feelings that promoted drug consumption in the first place. The addictive process is thus fostered through unconditional positive affective components as well as the alleviation of negative ones.

Beyond the realm of social rewards, endogenous opioids appear to mediate feelings of bodily warmth and even pleasures of food and may constitute a general antistress signal in the body, which indicates that current behavioral activities are supporting homeostasis (Panksepp, 1998). With many distinct pleasures and satisfactions related to opioid activity, it is not yet clear to what extent we should consider all aspects of opioid reward to represent a single harmoniously operating "global pleasure system" and the extent to which distinct pleasures are resolved by opioids operating at different points in the extended neural matrix for motivational processes.

It remains unclear whether opioids are functionally acting at global or local levels and also how such rewards relate to ethologically distinct emotional and motivational processes. Anatomically, however, sites of positive, opioid-mediated reward are distinctly subcortical. Strong place preferences result from intracerebral administration of morphine into the peri-aqueductal gray (PAG) and ventral tegmental area (VTA), but not into higher areas such as the amygdala or prefrontal cortex (PFC) (Olmstead & Franklin, 1997). Also, relief of withdrawal symptoms with injections of opioids seems to rely on different brain systems than those that produce positive affect unconditionally (Delfs, Zhu, Druhan, & Aston-Jones, 2000).

THE DOPAMINE-BASED, REWARD-SEEKING SYSTEM

The long-standing antagonism between ethological and behaviorist views, as symbolized by the Lehrman-Lorenz debate (see Lehrman, 1953), also frames the search for the neural mechanisms that shape learned behaviors of animals. The discovery of self-stimulation of the brain suggested the involvement of dopamine-based hedonic mechanisms as an obvious substrate for behavioral concepts such as reward, reinforcement, and addictive behaviors. There were good reasons to sustain ideas of a general type of reinforcement-based, learned plasticity acting in self-stimulation reward. For instance, many distinct consummatory behavior patterns (feeding, drinking, gnawing, etc.) could be evoked by stimulation of the medial forebrain bundle that seemed more consistent with a nonspecific and plastic learning substrate rather than coherent psychobehavioral operating systems for a variety of specific motivations (Valenstein, Cox, & Kakolewski, 1970).

Unfortunately, investigators had ignored the natural, unconditional behavioral patterns that were evoked by such stimulation. Activation of the medial forebrain bundle evokes appetitive behaviors even in the absence of any potential goal objects. Animals become behaviorally energized, they move forward, vigorously exploring and investigating their environments in a manner that is reminiscent of the behavior patterns evoked by psychomotor stimulants such as amphetamine and cocaine. Despite the existence of many paradoxes with simple reward or reinforcement concepts early on, only a few recognized this brain system as the fundamental substrate for exploration, foraging, and thus the seeking of rewards, as opposed to the essence of the reward itself (Panksepp, 1981b; Robinson & Berridge, 1993). Both behavioral (error-signal hypothesis; Schultz, 2000) and ethological approaches ("incentive salience" and seeking hypotheses; Berridge & Robinson, 1998; Ikemoto & Panksepp, 1999) have now converged on a dopamine mediated "go" signal at the core of a complex system that guides appetitive behaviors. These mechanisms are essential for animals to regulate goal directed behavioral urges partly through focusing attention on potential reward objects. This system is especially active when animals encounter potential rewards and shift into a more intense engagement as they familiarize themselves with potential incentive objects (Bassareo & Di Chiara, 1999; Di Chiara, Loddo, & Tanda, 1999; Fiorino & Phillips, 1999a, 1999b; Ahn & Phillips, 1999; Ikemoto & Panksepp, 1999).

A system, which allows animals to become urgently engaged with reward seeking, has great potential as a core substrate in all addictions. Positive feedback properties are inherent to mechanisms that allow individuals to spontaneously learn about the particular environmental constellations that may guide and energize behavior toward available resources on subsequent occasions. With an affectively positive tone, its overarousal cascades into repetitive compulsive activities of various kinds. Self-stimulation of this circuitry has always had an obsessive-compulsive character to it (Trowill, Panksepp, & Gandelman, 1969), and it is understandable how this type of neuropsychic "energy" would feed into the urgency of both adaptive behaviors and addictions.

When competing for resources, an ability to predict a desired outcome is of great value, potentially explaining the sensitization of appetitive motivational systems as a function of experience and furthermore why animals sensitize more readily when given psychostimulants in novel environments rather than in their home cages (Badiani, Anagnostaras, & Robinson, 1995; Badiani, Browman, & Robinson, 1995). It is intuitive that such a reward-seeking system should up-regulate in novel situations and, when impinged upon by drugs, produces even greater sensitization in unfamiliar locations as opposed to home environments where one may already be familiar with location and value of resources. Sensitization then reflects a higher baseline of responsiveness, no matter where the animal is tested.

Our interpretation of these phenomena is that sensitization reflects a magnification instead of a change in normal behavioral patterns. Referring to this appetitive network as the SEEKING system, we feel that this represents a parsimonious designation of the underlying hypothetical construct. The anatomy of this system is extensive and well documented, with abundant inputs into the meso-diencephalic junction, and abundant in/outputs in the terminal regions of the nucleus accumbens (NAC), the olfactory tubercle ventrally, and the frontal cortex rostrally (for overview see Berridge & Robinson, 1998; Di Chiara, 1995; Ikemoto & Panksepp, 1999; Kalivas & Nakamura, 1999; Wise, 1987).

Psychostimulant Sensitization of SEEKING

The phenomenon of sensitization, where individuals become increasingly responsive to previously experienced doses of various drugs of abuse, is widely believed to be a major indication of the transitions leading to addiction. Repeated intermittent exposure to psychostimulants leads to increased drug-taking behavior, presumably by increasing drug "wanting/seeking" (Berridge & Robinson, 1998; Ikemoto & Panksepp, 1999; Robinson & Berridge, 1993) and drug-experienced rats will more readily learn to self-administer several classes of addicting drugs and will work harder for them (for review see, Nocjar & Panksepp, 2002). They will also develop stronger psychostimulant and opiate place preference conditioning (see Shippenberg, Lefevour, & Thompson, 1998; Nocjar & Panksepp, 2002). Interestingly, appetites for food and sexual reward are similarly enhanced after long-term abstinence from repeated drug exposure in rats (Fiorino & Phillips, 1999a, 1999b; Nocjar & Panksepp, 2002). Characteristic patterns of incentive-sensitization are depicted in Figure 1. This strengthening of reward seeking is evident for sexual incentives even in animals that have never been permitted sexual experiences .

Recent evidence suggests that dysregulation of glutamate and dopamine interactions in the PFC and/or VTA could play an important modulatory role in drug-seeking behaviors of animals. In fact, glutamatergic dysregulation of reward systems is being increasingly entertained as a critical factor in addiction (Wolf, 1998; for review

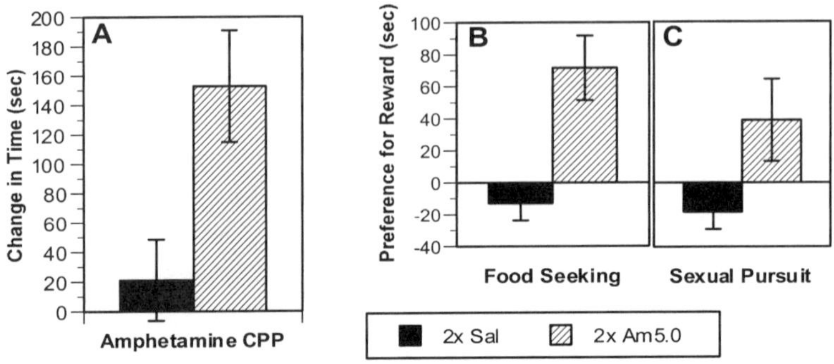

Figure 1. Increased amphetamine place preference conditioning (A), food seeking (B), and sexual pursuit (C) by amphetamine-experienced rats. Note that the hamburger and receptive female rat used as the incentive stimuli in the food seeking and sexual pursuit paradigms were contained behind a screened barrier in the test cage, blocking consumption of the reward. Time spent sniffing and pawing at these screened stimulus barriers was measured and compared to time spent at stimulus barriers respectively containing no food or a nonreceptive female rat. Thus the paradigm assessed appetitive interest rather than consummatory behavior. Adapted from Nocjar and Panksepp (2002).

see Pulvirenti & Diana, 2001). Novelty, which is known to be behaviorally rewarding (see Bardo's chapter in this volume, and Bevins & Bardo, 1999; Bevins, 2001; Bevins, Besheer, Palmatier, Jensen, Pickett, & Eurek, 2002), also facilitates mesocorticolimbic dopamine release (Feenstra & Botterblom, 1996; Feenstra, Botterblom, & Mastenbroek, 2000; Rebec, Grabner, Johnson, Pierce, & Bardo, 1997) as well as glutamate release in prefrontal cortical sites where mesocortical dopamine terminals are concentrated (Figure 2, Nocjar & E. A. Pehek, unpublished data). Novelty also magnifies the development of incentive sensitization (Figure 3, adapted from Nocjar & Panksepp, 2002).

Many factors, including stress, drugs, and drug-associated cues, can reinstate drug-seeking behaviors in animals as is also frequently seen in human drug addicts (Childress, Mozley, McElgin, Fitzgerald, Reivich, & O'Brien, 1999; Everitt, Parkinson, Olmstead, Arroyo, Robledo, & Robbins, 1999; Stewart, 2000). Although these studies indicate that different, yet overlapping, circuitries may trigger relapse by each of these factors (McFarland & Kalivas, 2001; Stewart, 2000), dopaminergic and glutamatergic interactions within the limbic-prefrontal cortex, amygdala, nucleus accumbens, and ventral tegmental area, as well as higher motor regions of the brain, may play an important role

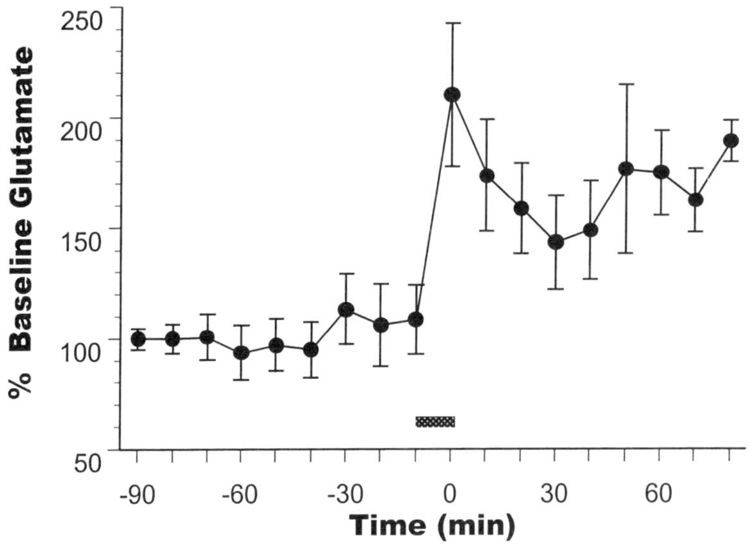

Figure 2. Ten minute exposure to a novel environment (see black bar) increases extracellular glutamate in the PFC of rats. Data were obtained using in vivo microdialysis and HPLC with electrochemical detection.

in their expression (see Cornish & Kalivas, 2000; Everitt et al., 1999; Grimm & See, 2000; McFarland & Kalivas, 2001; Self & Nestler, 1998; Stewart 2000). In fact, dopamine administered directly into PFC (McFarland & Kalivas, 2001) or nucleus accumbens (Cornish & Kalivas, 2000) reinstates drug seeking, suggesting that increased dopamine function may initiate drug-seeking behaviors. However, activation of glutamatergic AMPA receptors in the nucleus accumbens similarly reinstates drug seeking, and AMPA receptor antagonists block this priming effect as well as that induced by accumbens dopamine administration (Cornish & Kalivas, 2000).

These findings suggest that glutamatergic arousals in the nucleus accumbens are important in the facilitation of drug seeking (McFarland & Kalivas, 2001) and that dopaminergic systems function to modulate appetitive behavior (Kalivas & Nakamura, 1999), possibly by enhancing the salience of rewards (Robinson & Berridge, 2000). Since glutamate in the PFC and VTA modulates DA function (Giorgetti, Hotsenpiller, Ward, Teppen, & Wolf, 2001; Takahata & Moghaddam, 2000), dysregulation of glutamatergic interactions with DA could fos-

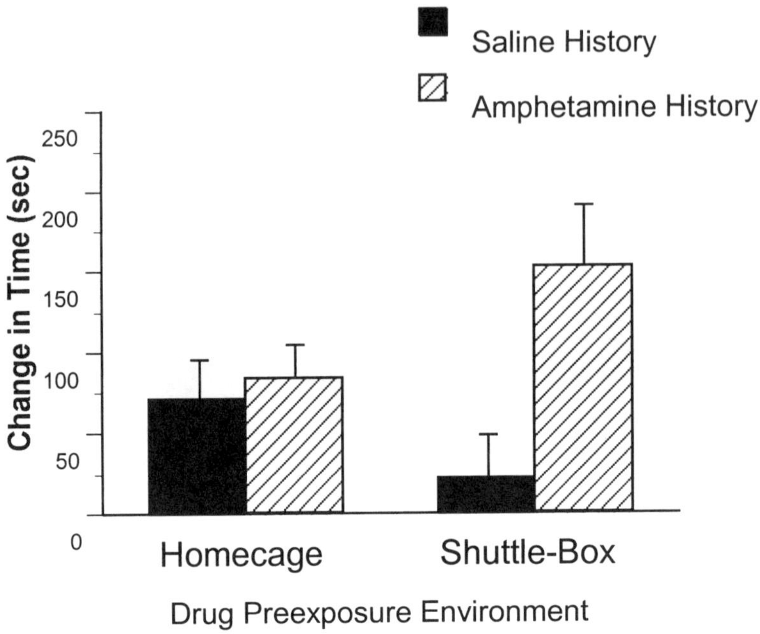

Figure 3. Future amphetamine CPP was magnified in amphetamine-experienced animals if the drug history had been received in an initially novel shuttle-box. An identical amphetamine preexposure in the homecage did not alter future drug-seeking behavior. Adapted from Nocjar and Panksepp (2002).

ter the change of an animal's normal appetitive nature into one that is sensitized to the incentive quality of rewards in its environment. A general neuronal model for these possible interactions is depicted in Figure 4.

The final common neural pathway for sensitization and drug addiction is widely held to be increases of drug or stimulus-induced (rather than basal level) dopamine transmission in the nucleus accumbens (for review see Wise, 1998). Animals will readily self-administer amphetamine and other psychostimulants directly into the accumbens (Hoebel, Monaco, Hernandez, Aulisi, Stanley, & Lenard, 1983; Ikemoto, Glazier, Murphy, & McBride, 1997) leading to increased dopamine levels in this brain structure (Pontieri, Tanda, & Di Chiara, 1995). Moreover, microinjections of dopamine receptor agonists into the accumbens elicits robust increases in locomotor and

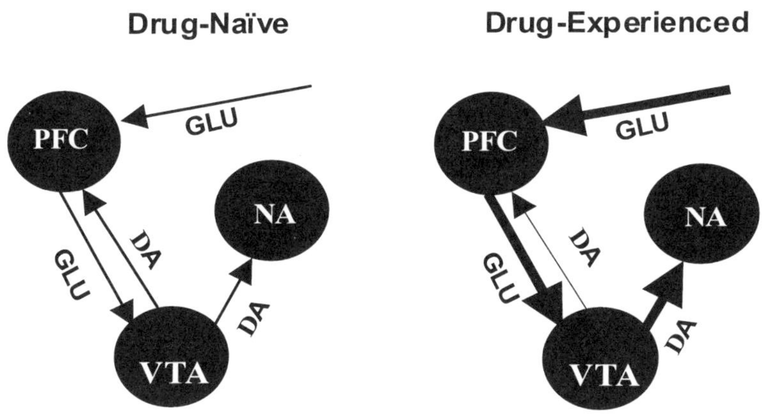

Figure 4. Cartoon representation of hypothesized glutamate and dopamine alterations responsible for magnified reward-seeking behaviors following amphetamine-experience (i.e., enhanced reward-related glutamate function in the PFC corticotegmental pathway). The enlarged circuitry arrows depict enhanced function following drug-experience.

rearing behavior (Kelley, Gauthier, & Lang, 1989; Wang & Rebec, 1998), as well as 50 kHz ultrasonic vocalizations (Burgdorf, Knutson, Panksepp, & Ikemoto, 2001), which are all unconditioned behaviors associated with reward (Knutson, Burgdorf, & Panksepp, 1998; Wise & Bozarth, 1987). Few studies, however, have examined the effect of intra-accumbens microinjections of dopamine receptor agonists on unconditioned appetitive behaviors (Wang & Rebec, 1998).

It appears that dopamine both "pushes" animals out into the environment to seek out rewards as well as "pulls" animals toward specific stimuli that are associated with reward when encountered. On the one hand, stress, which is a common pathway to relapse in recovering drug addicts, also increases dopamine function (Shaham, Erb, & Stewart, 2000), thereby possibly "pushing" recovered addicts back to drug use. On the other hand, elevated cravings from exposure to drug paraphernalia, which can "pull" abstaining human drug addicts back to drug use (O'Brien, Childress, Ehrman, & Robbins, 1998), are at least partially dopamine mediated (Berridge & Robinson, 1998).

Dopamine is implicated in the induction of euphoria, a form of positive affect. Psychostimulant induced positive affect correlated with displaced dopamine D_2 antagonist binding (which presumably reflects increased dopamine release) in the accumbens in humans (Drevets et al., 2001), while euphoric effects of psychostimulants are reduced by dopamine receptor antagonists (Newton, Ling, Kalechstein, Uslaner, & Tervo, 2001; Romach et al., 1999; but see Brauer, Goudie, & de Wit, 1997). As a rule, all drugs that elevate dopamine levels in the nucleus accumbens (i.e., alcohol, amphetamine, cocaine, heroin, nicotine, and marijuana) induce some type of positive affect in humans. In animal models of positive affect, consummatory processes, that presumably evoke sensory pleasure, appear to be dopamine independent (Berridge, 1996; Berridge & Robinson, 1998), while appetitive positive affective states akin to positively valenced excitement and joy appear to be heavily modulated by dopamine (Burgdorf, Knutson, Panksepp, & Ikemoto,, 2001; Wintink & Brudzynski, 2001). fMRI studies of humans working on appetitive tasks exhibit arousal within the accumbens, and the degree of arousal correlates with increases in positive affect (Knutson, Fong, Adams, Varner, & Hommer, 2001).

Sensitized meso-cortical circuitry might be expected to foster elevated levels of positive affect. However, more likely, a sensitized nervous system is simply one that experiences more urgency to indulge in appetitive reward-seeking behaviors, and hence may actually be more susceptible to frustration if rewards are not forthcoming.

A Rodent Model for Affective "Self-report"

Current neuroethological models of drug abuse utilize animals' natural appetitive responses to drugs in order to model addictive states. Glickman and Schiff (1967) were among the first to note that electrical stimulation of the brain, that supported vigorous bar-pressing, could unconditionally elicit appetitive behaviors in rodents as well. For example, electrical brain stimulation that unconditionally elicits sniffing behavior supports self-stimulation, and conversely sites that do not elicit sniffing do not support self-stimulation in rats (Rossi & Panksepp, 1992). The idea that there is a relationship between arousal of this appetitive system and exploratory urges has also been extended to drugs of abuse, since many drugs unconditionally elicit exploratory behavior in a dose-dependent manner (Wise & Bozarth, 1987). A final common neural pathway for most drugs of abuse is thought to involve increases in dopamine levels in the nucleus accumbens, and accumbens dopamine levels have been closely associated with exploratory and other appetitive behaviors (Kalivas & Nakamura, 1999; Wise, 1998).

Recently, our lab has examined another natural appetitive behavior to model drug abuse in rats, the 50 kHz ultrasonic vocalization. Rats exhibited these calls during appetitive aspects of play and sexual behavior (Knutson, Burgdorf, & Panksepp, 1998). We have also shown that these vocalizations are closely tied to both natural and artificial (i.e., drugs of abuse) rewards (Burgdorf, Knutson, Panksepp, & Shippenberg, 2001). Specifically, 50 kHz calls are exhibited to conditioned stimuli that predict a wide range of reinforcers such as amphetamine, morphine, rewarding electrical brain stimulation, play, sexual behavior, and food (Burgdorf, Knutson, & Panksepp, 2000). These vocalizations are also unconditionally elicited by psychostimulant administration (Burgdorf, Knutson, Panksepp, & Ikemoto, 2001; Burgdorf, Knutson, & Panksepp, 2000). 50 kHz vocalization rate has been shown to have a strong positive correlation with the magnitude of reinforcement as measured by the speed of approach behavior (Panksepp & Burgdorf, 2000). In contrast, aversive stimuli such as foot-shock and predator odor reduces 50 kHz ultrasonic vocalization rates (Panksepp & Burgdorf, 1999).

The proximate brain mechanisms for 50 kHz calls involve the activation of dopamine systems in the nucleus accumbens (Burgdorf, Knutson, Panksepp, & Ikemoto, 2001). This finding is especially relevant to drug addiction, since nearly all addictive drugs are associated with this effect (Di Chiara & Imparato, 1988). In addition to dopamine, glutamate levels, particularly in the preoptic area, are involved in 50 kHz calls (Fu & Brudzynski, 1994; Wintink & Brudzynski, 2001). The preoptic area has been implicated consistently in sexual and maternal rewards (Panksepp, 1998).

Whereas 50 kHz calls seem to model a positively valenced, drug-craving state, 20 kHz calls seem to model an aversive drug-craving state in rats (Burgdorf, Knutson, Panksepp, & Shippenberg, 2001). The aversion related 20 kHz calls are heard in rats during both opiate and psychostimulant withdrawal (Mutschler & Miczek, 1998; Vivian & Miczek, 1991), as well as in anticipation of foot-shock and environments associated with aversive drug administration (Burgdorf, Knutson, Panksepp, & Shippenberg, 2001; Cuomo, Cagiano, De

Salvia, Maselli, Renna, & Racagni, 1988). Rats also exhibit these calls during barpressing under extinction for electrical brain stimulation reward (Burgdorf, Knutson, & Panksepp, 2000). From an ethological perspective, 20 kHz calls are mainly heard during aversive natural events such as social defeat and predator presence (Blanchard, Blanchard, Agullana, & Weiss, 1991; Tornatzky & Miczek, 1995). This observation is especially interesting since both social subordination (Kabbaj et al., 2001; Miczek & Mutschler, 1996) and social instability (Lemaire, Deminiere, & Mormede, 1994), as well as social isolation, have been associated with increased drug intake in laboratory animals (Bowling & Bardo, 1994; Boyle, Gill, Smith, & Amit, 1991; Kraemer & McKinney, 1985; Schenk et al., 1987; Wolffgramm & Heyne, 1995; although see Miczek & Mutschler, 1996).

In addition to serving as indicators of drug-craving states, both 50 and 20 kHz calls may also index affective states in rats (Burgdorf et al., 2000; Knutson, Burgdorf, & Panksepp, 2002). The appetitive eagerness related 50 kHz calls is emitted most robustly during tickling and chasing behavior and during rough-and-tumble play (Panksepp & Burgdorf, 1999, 2000). In human children, laughter occurs primarily during the chasing subcomponent of human play, which is similar to 50 kHz calls during rat play (Scott & Panksepp, 2003). Taken together with evidence that 50 kHz calls are principally associated with positive reinforcement and decreased by punishment, we suggest that 50 kHz calls index a positive emotional state akin to excitement or joy. In contrast, 20 kHz calls are associated with negative affective states such as anxiety, since anticipation of aversive outcomes (e.g., foot-shock or predator) elicit these calls and 20 kHz call rate is reduced by anxiolytic compounds (Miczek, Weerts, Vivian, & Barros, 1995).

To evaluate this possibility, we determined whether contextual cues associated with the administration of positive affective drugs such as morphine, and negative affective drugs such as naloxone and lithium chloride, would lead to data congruent with the above assertion. As summarized in Figure 5, environments paired with morphine promoted 50 kHz USVs, and reduced 20 kHz calls. Conversely, the two negative drugs had opposite effects (data adapted from Burgdorf et al., 2001).

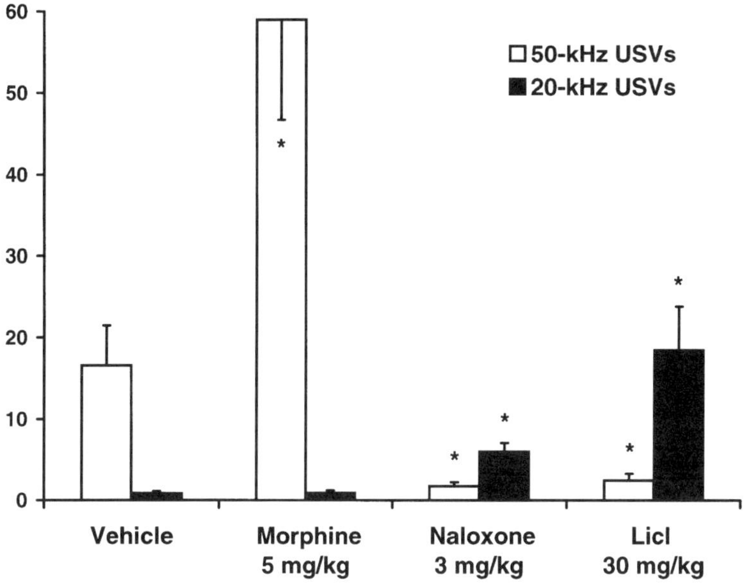

Figure 5. Mean (± SEM) 50 kHz and 20 kHz USVs in a drug free state when rats were placed back in the conditioning compartment where they had been conditioned with vehicle, morphine, naloxone, or lithium chloride (LiCl). *$P < 0.05$ relative to the respective vehicle, two-tailed, Bonferroni corrected. (Adapted from Burgdorf et al., 2001).

Potential Psychostimulant Sensitization in ADHD

Sensitization is of considerable societal importance, not only regarding the obvious circumstances of everyday addictive behaviors, but in potential long-term consequences from medical use of such agents, particularly in childhood disorders like ADHD. Concerns have recently been expressed that treatment with Ritalin (methylphenidate, MPH) may lead to psychostimulant sensitization of brain circuits known to be important for drug reward (Wise, 1998). This effect may foster, later in life, a disposition for and a greater prevalence of addictive behaviors (Panksepp, 1998). MPH is currently the drug treatment of choice for childhood attention deficit/hyperactivity disorder (ADHD), and is now prescribed each year for over 2 million school-aged children in the United States alone (Safer, Zito, & Fine, 1996). This mediation practice is happening despite the fact that MPH has actions very similar to amphetamine and cocaine, widely recognized as major drugs of abuse. This issue is especially relevant since children with ADHD have been shown to be at higher risk for developing substance abuse disorders later in life (Biederman, Wilens, Mick, Faraone, & Spencer, 1998). Even though the role of such pharmacological treatment in promoting future drug use has not been supported by recent work (Biederman, Wilens, Mick, Spencer, & Faraone, 1999), those studies could be questioned on the basis of the fact that the total amount of such prescription medicines freely provided was not computed in the overall levels of drug intake, and the baseline drug abuse rates were much higher in the nonmedicated ADHD group. Also, no study has yet attempted to evaluate the desire for drugs of children that have been on medication, as compared to those who have not.

To provide some insight into these processes, we have conducted preliminary work to evaluate whether a potential measure of "desire" may be a sensitized response in young rats exposed to MPH for a week, just prior to their daily play sessions (Panksepp, Burgdorf, Gordon, &Turner, 2002). As summarized in Figure 6, and as expected from previous work (e.g., Beatty, Dodge, Dodge, White, & Panksepp, 1982), this psychostimulant markedly reduces playfulness in animals as do all drugs that activate the dopamine system. From a perspective that all "psychostimulants" promote locomotor activity, this effect may appear paradoxical but it suggests that these drugs may reduce symptoms of ADHD partly by reducing the natural urge of young children to play. Accordingly, it also forces us to wonder what other long-term consequences in brain development may result from continued treatment with such agents (Panksepp, 1998; Panksepp, Burgdorf, Gordon, & Turner, 2002).

Even more troubling would be any finding suggesting that such regimes of medication might sensitize the minds of children in ways similar to that of young rats during MPH challenges administered following their weeklong drug regime (Figure 7). We interpret this amplification of ultrasonic vocalization to potentially reflect a heightened craving response for rough-and-tumble play engagement, which may be manifested when these children are off drug. This type of sensitization may also establish a central nervous system condition that would be conducive to elevated future seeking and desire for rewards of all kinds. After all, this system was not designed for drug abuse, but for the tendency of animals to eagerly seek

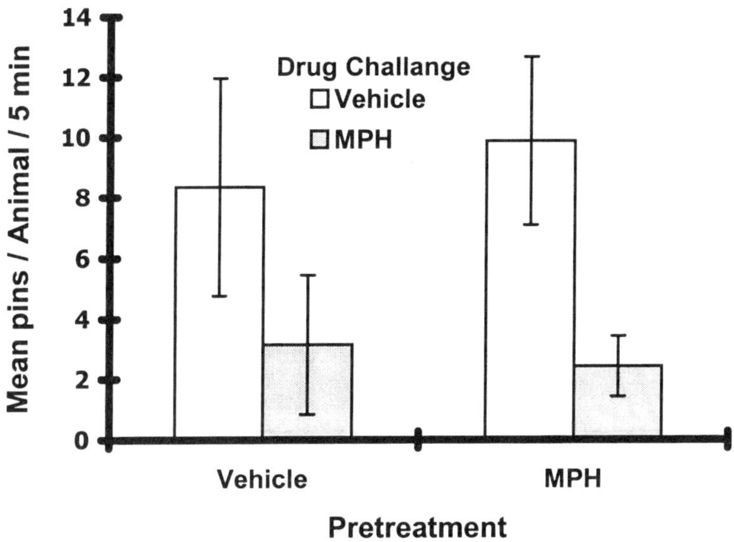

Figure 6. Mean ± SEM pinning scores during a 5-minute rough-and-tumble play session in adolescent rats after receiving a challenge dose of 5.0 mg/kg methylphenidate (MPH). Subjects had either received pretreatment with 5.0 mg/kg MPH or vehicle. MPH challenge was able to reduce play behavior compared to vehicle-challenged rats regardless of pretreatment condition ($F(1,54) = 13.34$, $p < .001$).

out and to develop positive expectancies for resources of all kinds (Panksepp, 1981b, 1982). Moreover, it is extremely troublesome that young mammals treated with MPH in this way exhibit heightened cocaine self-administration (Brandon, Marinelli, Baker, & White, 2001), even when they do not exhibit elevated place preferences for such agents (Andersen, Arvanitogiannis, Pliakas, LeBlanc, & Carlezon, 2002). Nonetheless, our work suggests that the use of novel psychological measures such as ultrasonic vocalizations may provide a sensitive view into the underlying emotional-affective systems of mammals within the context of addiction.

Evidence for Motivational Effects of Drug Rewards in Invertebrates

Virtually all research concerning reward processes in vertebrate species has assumed activity in brain dopamine circuits to be a common neural substrate involved in the expression of reward-related

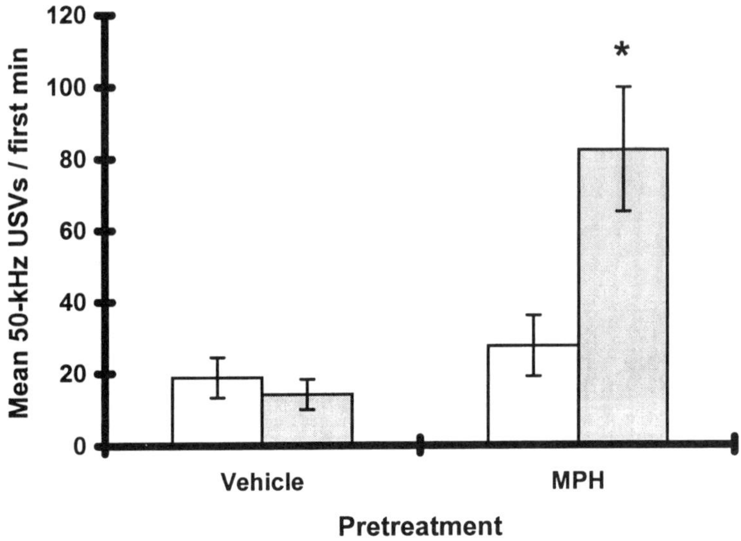

Figure 7. Mean ± SEM 50 kHz USVs "wanting/seeking" vocalizations during the first minute of play behavior in response to MPH challenge. MPH challenge increased 50 kHz USVs in only the MPH pretreated group as compared to vehicle (* $p < .05$, Dunnett's test). This effect declined sharply during the subsequent minutes of testing.

changes in motivated behaviors. It is thus intriguing that recent work in several invertebrate species has revealed similarities in nervous system biochemistry and behavior following exposure to addictive drugs. Some of the first thorough characterizations of the effects of controlled substances on behavior in an invertebrate species were by McClung and Hirsch (1998) and Torres and Horowitz (1998). Both groups found that fruit flies exhibited several conspicuous behavior patterns when exposed to different cocaine derivatives—including grooming, stereotypical locomotion, and eventually akinesia after high doses. These behavioral changes were both dose-dependent and subject to sensitization upon subsequent drug treatment (McClung & Hirsch, 1998). While the mere behavioral resemblance to vertebrates was striking in and of itself, the occurrence of behavioral sensitization in fruit flies has certainly made the most ardent naysayer (to such comparative approaches) intrigued!

As behavioral sensitization is thought to reflect an intensification of drug craving in vertebrates (Robinson & Berridge, 1993), the occurrence of this phenomenon in fruit flies offers the potential for studying its neurobiological underpinnings in a genetically tractable species (Wolf, 1999). Hirsh and colleagues have gone on to carry out a series of elegant experiments examining the neurochemical basis of behavioral sensitization in fruit flies. They have found tyramine to be essential for behavioral sensitization: Genetic mutants with reduced tyramine levels respond normally to initial cocaine exposure, but do not sensitize, and increased levels of tyramine mirror behavioral sensitization in wild-type flies (McClung & Hirsch, 1999). Tyramine is found at trace levels in the vertebrate brain (Durden & Davis, 1993), with a large amount supplied through food intake. In vertebrates its pharmacological profile is "amphetamine-like," as it can augment synaptic catecholemines via inhibition of membrane transporter uptake (Sitte, Huck, Reither, Boehm, Singer, & Pifl, 1998). In mammals, although the role of tyramine in normal brain function has received relatively little attention, the recent cloning of 15 trace amine receptors from rat and human brain tissues (a notable finding being the identification of receptors that bind tyramine in the ventral tegmental area) makes the importance of tyramine in fruit fly behavioral sensitization particularly interesting (Borowsky et al., 2001).

Further studies by the Hirsh group have uncovered important interactions between members of the circadian gene family, tyramine, and behavioral sensitization (Andretic, Chaney, & Hirsh, 1999). Up-regulated transcription of *per,* a circadian gene that is required for sensitization in flies, has recently been demonstrated in dorsal striatal regions that receive input from midbrain dopamine neurons (Nikaido, Akiyama, Moriay, & Shibata, 2001). In contrast to wild-type flies, it was also shown that, following a single cocaine exposure, flies lacking *per* do not exhibit heightened behavioral responsiveness (i.e., sensitization) to postsynaptic stimulation with a vertebrate D_2 agonist (Andretic et al., 1999). Interestingly, in both flies (Li, Chaney, Forte, & Hirsh, 2000) and rats (Kalivas, 1995), repeated postsynaptic exposure with psychostimulants is by itself not sufficient to produce sensitization; only after concurrent exposure of presynaptic sites does behavioral sensitization ensue.

The integral role of postsynaptic dopamine receptors in cocaine-induced fruit fly behavior has been further characterized in strains of mutant flies that exhibit respective, compensatory under- and over-expression of such receptors (Li et al., 2000). Flies that underexpress postsynaptic dopamine receptors display a blunted response to cocaine upon initial exposure, whereas the opposite is true of overexpressing flies. Both types of mutants do not sensitize. Overall, of course with much still to be worked out, there exist intriguing parallels between cocaine-induced alterations in flies and vertebrates. Presynaptic mechanisms seem to be modulating the occurrence of behavioral sensitization, while postsynaptic elements may be subserving such control through the maintenance of senstitization. Further support for behavioral and pharmacological similarities between vertebrates and invertebrates after treatment with addictive substances has come from additional work in fruit flies (Bainton, Tsai, Singh, Moore, Neckameyer, & Heberlein, 2000) and planaria (Palladini, Ruggeri, Stocchi, De Pandis, Venturini, & Margotta, 1996).

The potential influence of addictive drugs on motivational plasticity (e.g., reward) in invertebrate species has however received relatively little attention. A related series of studies was conducted nearly a decade ago, where land snails self-administered electrical current into distinct brain regions (Balaban & Chase, 1993). When delivered to a different brain area, the same electrical stimulus could serve as a negative reinforcer as well. The investigators thus concluded that snails of the genus *Helix* had both positively and negatively "colored" brain regions—anatomical sites that had been previously studied for their respective roles in the organization of sexual behavior and escape. To our knowledge, only one study has been published investigating the relationship between drugs of abuse and motivation in invertebrates. Kusayama and Watanabe (2000) reported that treatment with methamphetamine in planarians reversed an individual's natural substrate preference. In other words, planarians developed a place preference for an environment that had been paired with methamphetamine, an effect that was blocked by pretreatment with several different vertebrate dopamine antagonists.

These findings have led us to conduct one of the first studies evaluating psychostimulant reward in crayfish as a model invertebrate system for studying the role neuromodulatory monoamines in behavior. For several reasons such animals may be suitable for studies of reward in invertebrates: (1) The central nervous system of decapod crustaceans contains several of the amine-modulatory systems that putatively underlie motivational effects in vertebrates for drugs like cocaine and amphetamine. Moreover, the neurons that constitute each respective monoamine system are relatively few (Beltz & Kravitz, 1987; Cournil, Casasnovas, Helluy, & Beltz, 1995; Schneider, Budhiraja, Walter, Beltz, Peckol, & Kravitz, 1996), and their physiological properties are well characterized (Crider & Cooper, 1999; Heinrich, Cromarty, Horner, Edwards, & Kravitz, 1999; Teshiba, Shamsian, Yashar, Yeh, Edwards, & Krasne, 2001). (2) The behavioral repertoire of decapod crustaceans is marked by several conspicuous behavior patterns that contain distinct appetitive components. Reproductive behavior (Ingle & Thomas, 1974), feeding and foraging (Steele, Skinner, Steele, Alberstadt, & Mathewson, 1999), and agonistic behavior (Huber & Kravitz, 1995) are examples that have been studied extensively. (3) Our previous work with serotonin and aggression in crayfish has made use of techniques that allow continuous delivery of pharmacological compounds into freely moving crayfish (see Figure 8a), both acutely (Huber & Delago, 1998) and chronically (Panksepp & Huber, 2002).

We have thus begun examining the possibility that crayfish subjected to conditioning or operant paradigms, where a psychostimulant serves as the respective UCS or reinforcer, exhibit changes in motivation that are indicative of reward. In an initial set of experiments, crayfish *(Orconectes rusticus)* were conditioned using a place preference procedure wherein two distinct visual environments ("white" or "striped") were provided (Figure 8b); one randomly selected environment was randomly paired with a *d*-amphetamine (5g/g bodyweight) infusion directly into the circulation whereas the other environment was associated with a vehicle infusion. Controls received either a vehicle infusion or no infusion in both environments (there were no significant differences between these two control groups). Individual crayfish were isolated and conditioned in each environment for a total of 30 minutes (infusions took place during the first 5 minutes of each session) once a day for 5 successive days (order of conditioning was randomized on each day with 8–12 hours between each conditioning session). Following 5 days of such conditioning, crayfish were allowed to move freely about the entire arena for 60 minutes in a "drug-free" state and their location was monitored with a video tracking system. In the control group, a natural preference was found such that a modest, yet significant, spatial bias for the white visual environment existed. We have replicated this result in two additional experiments and found that this preference is stochas-

A. **B.**

C. *Table of place-preference variables and results*

	Vehicle	Amphetamine
N	13	9
Average Weight	19.6 ± 82g	18.4 ± 94g
Drug Dosage	125 mM NaCl or no infusion	5μg/g body weight
Probability (Striped)	.42 ± .018	.62 ± .047 (46% increase)
ANOVA	$F(1,20) = 20.47$, $p < 0.001$	

Figure 8. Upper left (8A): Crayfish prepared for infusion of amphetamine. *Upper right* (8B) configuration of the place preference test. Infusions were administered on the striped side, which was initially slightly less preferred. *Bottom* (8C): Summary of testing parameters and the 46% shift in place preference toward the amphetamine paired side.

tic (i.e., average) rather than being manifest at the level of individual animals. The experimental data were thus analyzed as a biased design (viz. can the negative preference for the striped environment be reversed by amphetamine conditioning?). Our results demonstrated that crayfish exhibit a 46% shift (relative to controls) in spatial use when the striped environment was paired with amphetamine (Figure 8c).

Whether these effects will generalize to cocaine remain to be tested. However, in our estimation, that seems unlikely based on behavioral observations that indicate crayfish exhibit what appears to be a vigorous flight response to similar injections of cocaine. This difference may reflect the fact that cocaine protects coca plants from insect invaders (Nathanson, Hunnicutt, Kantham, & Scavone, 1993), and crayfish may still exhibit an ancestral aversion to this plant alkaloid.

In summary, despite marked differences in neuroanatomy between vertebrates and invertebrates, these data support the notion that similarities in neurochemistry are sufficient to support motivational changes associated with addictive substances. A simple explanation of our findings is that with amphetamine conditioning, we have altered neuronal function such that the respectively paired environment was perceived with a heightened level of "attraction." Although we do not yet suggest what type of motivational construct might explain such a process in crayfish, it will be of interest to explore such drug effects in more natural contexts, such as those that involve foraging or aggression.

Conclusions

It is now generally accepted that many drugs of abuse may "hijack" the "reward centers" of the brain. Of course, the scientific journey is to unpack the words in quotes in both neuro-behaviorally and psychologically meaningful ways. We do not think that one or the other will alone suffice. In neuroscience the first approach prevails, and in the social sciences the second. Only through the blending of the two will a coherent and comprehensive scheme emerge. We do not think this can be achieved until neuroscientists begin to take affective processes seriously as basic functions of the brain, and psychologists reciprocate with recognition of the absolute need for an integrated neuroscientific approach.

One of the main reasons people take drugs and continue to take drugs is because certain neurochemical agents make one feel better, not only by arousing affectively positive "reward" types of feelings, but also because they can alleviate many forms of emotional suffering. Certain drugs can reduce the affective pain of inadequate social support, persistent feelings of shyness, and the resulting difficulties in relating to others, the violent rages and other irritabilities that people experience because of the apparent "slings and arrows of misfortune."

The reason that the brain dopamine facilitated SEEKING system lies at the heart of every addiction is because "repetition compulsions" are built into the persistent psychomotor features of the emotional system that was designed by evolution to vigorously pursue available resources. This compulsion is especially manifest in the sterotypies that can be provoked in animals with high doses of psychostimulants that put certain ascending dopamine systems (typically the nigrostriatal pathway) into an energized "do-loop."

The affective properties of the various major types of addictive agents probably need to be considered independently of one another to some extent. All may share the persistent seeking and repetition compulsions that dopamine overarousal can produce, but each also induces other psychological properties. For instance, the opioids produce a magnificent calming effect that can take away both the pain of social loss and the not uncommon irritability induced by excessive proximity to too many conspecifics. The psychostimulants can extract one from a state of excruciating boredom and ennui and infuse one with dramatic feeling of positive engagement and power in the world. Alcohol, barbiturates, and benzodiazepines can melt the psychologically agitating tensions of anxiety, and heaven knows why folks smoke cigarettes other than for the mild dopamine release and cognitive facilitation and incentive salience effects of heightened cholinergic activity (Caggiula et al., 2001). Parenthetically, considering the attachment that folks have for their cigarettes, we were really not surprised that nicotine was quite potent in alleviating separation distress in animal models (Sahley, Panksepp, & Zolovick, 1981). From this we would predict that smoking reduces feelings of separation distress in humans.

A key issue to remember is that emotions and motivations are not permanently satiable. Consummatory behaviors do not satisfy for more than a short period of time. The underlying brain systems have evolved to goad organisms into action, to make them restless, to make them seek out resources. To do that well often means they have to be attracted to novelty. All these feelings go into the equation that a human brain, with its vast cognitive resources, has to consider for planning future actions. Once the addictive process has jelled, the intense animalian feelings and urges often prevail.

The brain codes for a large array of positive and negative affects that have never been properly conceptualized in neuroscience research. Although the external common denominator on the behavioral surface of the animal may be approach and avoidance, there are many internally coded reasons—various pleasures and pains that goad them into action. There are many psychological "goods" that can make life more attractive, including in humans, the ability of drugs to reduce perceived personality deficits, deeply experienced, that prevent certain people from experiencing the world as they wish.

Unfortunately, what most people on the path to addiction do not realize is the profound "Catch-22" that is built into the neural matrix from which our emotional experiences arise. In the long run, most of these drugs eventually cause more suffering than they originally alleviated (Koob & LeMoal, 1997, 2001). The opponent-process type, counter-regulatory adjustments in each of these systems as the short-term drug effects wear off, gradually raise the psychological stakes, increasing with each indiscretion. Opioid withdrawal is characterized by an existential pain, suffusing the body and mind, which often feels like the loss of a best friend or a beloved companion. Psychostimulant withdrawal precipitates a depressive lassitude where the psychic landscape is depressively dreary. Withdrawal from the anxiolytics (i.e., alcohol, barbiturates, and benzodiazepines), leads to a wired anxiety where both body and mind tremble in agony, relieved only by the unconsciousness of life-threatening seizures.

These are the ways our neural systems, both of "man" and mouse, have been designed to operate on behalf of evolutionary fitness. If we do not take the diverse psychological aspects of these drugs seriously in the animals we study, then we are also not pursuing a study of the brain as seriously as we should. As William James (1890/1961, pp. 16–17) put the key issues we have been discussing over a century ago: "We are spinning our own fates, good or evil, and never to be undone. . . . The drunken Rip Van Winkle, in Jefferson's play, excuses himself for every fresh dereliction by saying, 'I won't count this time?' Well! He may not count it, and a kind Heaven may not count it; but it is being counted nonetheless. Down among his nerve cells and fibres the molecules are counting it, registering and storing it up to be used against him when the next temptation arises." The way these indiscretions are manifested in the brain is through the global, experiential states of the nervous system.

References

Agmo, A., & Berenfeld, R. (1990). Reinforcing properties of ejaculation in the male rat: Role of opioids and dopamine. *Behavioral Neuroscience, 104,* 177–182.

Agmo, A., & Gomez, M. (1993). Sexual reinforcement is blocked by infusion of naloxone into the medial preoptic area. *Behavioral Neuroscience, 107,* 812–818.

Ahn, S., & Phillips, A. G. (1999). Dopaminergic correlates of sensory-specific satiety in the medial prefrontal cortex and nucleus accumbens of the rat. *Journal of Neuroscience, 19,* 1–5.

Alexander, B. K., Beyerstein, B. L., Hadaway, P. F., & Coambs, R. B. (1981). Effect of early and later colony housing on oral ingestion of morphine in rats. *Pharmacology Biochemistry and Behavior, 15,* 571–576.

Alexander, B. K., Coambs, R. B., & Hadaway, P. F. (1978). The effect of housing and gender on morphine self-administration in rats. *Psychopharmacology, 58,* 175–179.

Andersen, S. L., Arvanitogiannis, A., Pliakas, A. M., LeBlanc, C., & Carlezon, Jr., W. A. (2002). Altered responsiveness to cocaine in rats exposed to methylphenidate during development. *Nature Neuroscience, 5,* 13–14.

Andretic, R., Chaney, S., & Hirsh, J. (1999). Requirement of circadian genes for cocaine sensitization in *Drosophila. Science, 285,* 1066–1068.

Badiani, A., Anagnostaras, S. G., & Robinson, T. E. (1995). The development of sensitization to the psychomotor stimulant effects of amphetamine is enhanced in a novel environment. *Psychopharmacology, 117,* 443–452.

Badiani, A., Browman, K. E., & Robinson, T. E. (1995). Influence of novel versus home environments on sensitization to the psychomotor stimulant effects of cocaine and amphetamine. *Brain Research, 674,* 291–298.

Bainton, R. J., Tsai, L. T.-Y., Singh, C. M., Moore, M. S., Neckameyer, W. S., & Heberlein, U. (2000). Dopamine modulates acute responses to cocaine, nicotine and ethanol in *Drosophila. Current Biology, 10,* 187–194.

Balaban, P. M., & Chase, R. (1991). Interrelationships of the emotionally positive and negative regions of the brain of the edible snail. *Neuroscience and Behavioral Physiology, 21,* 172–180.

Bassareo, V., & Di Chiara, G. (1999). Differential responsiveness of dopamine transmission to food-stimuli in nucleus accumbens shell/core compartments. *Neuroscience, 89,* 637–641.

Beatty, W. W., Dodge, A. M., Dodge, L. J., White, K., & Panksepp, J. (1982). Psychomotor stimulants, social deprivation and play in juvenile rats. *Pharmacology Biochemistry and Behavior, 16,* 417–422.

Beltz, B. S., & Kravitz, E. A. (1987). Physiological identification, morphological analysis, and development of identified serotonin-proctolin containing neurons in the lobster ventral nerve cord. *Journal of Neuroscience, 7,* 533–546.

Berridge, K. C. (1996). Food reward: Brain substrates of wanting and liking. *Neuroscience and Biobehavioral Reviews, 20,* 1–25.

Berridge, K. C., & Robinson, T. E. (1998). What is the role of dopamine in reward: Hedonic impact, reward learning, or incentive salience? *Brain Research Reviews, 28,* 309–369.

Bevins, R. A. (2001). Novelty seeking and reward: Implications for the study of high-risk behavior. *Current Directions in Psychological Science, 10,* 189–193.

Bevins, R. A., & Bardo, M. T. (1999). Conditioned increase in place preference by access to novel objects: Antagonism by MK-801. *Behavioural Brain Research, 99,* 53–60.

Bevins, R. A., Besheer, J., Palmatier, M. I., Jensen, H. C., Pickett, K. S., & Eurek, S. (2002). Novel-object place conditioning: Behavioral and dopaminergic processes in expression of novelty reward. *Behavioural Brain Research, 129,* 41–50.

Biederman, J., Wilens, T. E., Mick, E., Faraone, S. V., & Spencer, T. (1998). Does attention-deficit hyperactivity disorder impact the developmental course of drug and alcohol abuse and dependence? *Biological Psychiatry, 44,* 269–273.

Biederman, J., Wilens, T., Mick, E., Spencer, T., & Faraone, S. V. (1999). Pharmacotherapy of attention-deficit/hyperactivity disorder reduces risk for substance use disorder. *Pediatrics, 104*(e20), 1–5.

Blanchard, R. J., Blanchard D. C., Agullana, R., & Weiss, S. M. (1991). Twenty-two kHz alarm cries to presentation of a predator, by laboratory rats living in visible burrow systems. *Physiology and Behavior, 50,* 967–972.

Blumberg, M. S., & Wasserman, M. S. (1995). Animal minds and the argument from design. *American Psychologist, 50,* 133–144.

Borowsky, B., Adham, N., Jones, K. A., Raddatz, R., Artymyshyn, R., Ogozalek, K. L., et al. (2001). Trace amines: Identification of a family of mammalian G-protein-coupled receptors. *Proceedings of National Academy of Sciences, 98,* 8966–8971.

Bowling, S. L., & Bardo, M. T. (1994). Locomotor and rewarding effects of amphetamine in enriched, social, and isolate reared rats. *Pharmacology Biochemistry and Behavior, 48,* 459–464.

Boyle, A. E., Gill, K., Smith, B. R., & Amit, Z. (1991). Differential effects of an early housing manipulation on cocaine-induced activity and self-administration in laboratory rats. *Pharmacology Biochemistry and Behavior, 39,* 269–274.

Bozarth, M. A., Murray, A., & Wise, R. A. (1989). Influence of housing conditions on the acquisition of intravenous heroin and cocaine self-administration in rats. *Pharmacology Biochemistry and Behavior, 33,* 903–907.

Brandon, C. L., Marinelli, M., Baker, L. K., & White, F. J. (2001). Enhanced reactivity and vulnerability to cocaine following methylphenidate treatment in adolescent rats. *Neuropharmacology, 25,* 651–661.

Brauer, L. H., Goudie, A. J., & de Wit, H. (1997). Dopamine ligands and the stimulus effects of amphetamine: Animal models versus human laboratory data. *Psychopharmacology, 130,* 2–13.

Burgdorf, J., & Panksepp J. (2001). Tickling induces reward in adolescent rats. *Physiology and Behavior, 72,* 167–173.

Burgdorf, J., Knutson, B., & Panksepp, J. (2000). Anticipation of rewarding brain stimulation evokes ultrasonic vocalizations in rats. *Behavioral Neuroscience, 114,* 320–327.

Burgdorf, J., Knutson, B., Panksepp, J., & Ikemoto, S. (2001). Nucleus accumbens amphetamine microinjections unconditionally elicit 50 kHz ultrasonic vocalizations in rats. *Behavioral Neuroscience, 115,* 940–944.

Burgdorf, J., Knutson, B., Panksepp, J., & Shippenberg, T. (2001). Ultrasonic vocalizations index pharmacological aversion in adult rats. *Psychopharmacology, 155,* 35–42.

Caggiula, A. R., Donny, E. C., White, A. R., Chaudhri, N., Booth, S., Gharib, M. A., et al. (2001). Cue dependency of nicotine self-administration and smoking. *Pharmacology Biochemistry and Behavior, 70,* 515–530.

Childress, A. R., Mozley, P. D., McElgin, W., Fitzgerald, J., Reivich, M., & O'Brien, C. P. (1999). Limbic activation during cue-induced cocaine craving. *American Journal of Psychiatry, 156,* 11–18.

Cornish, J. L., Duffy, P., & Kalivas, P. W. (1999). A role for nucleus accumbens glutamate transmission in the relapse to cocaine-seeking behavior. *Neuroscience, 93,* 1359–1367.

Cornish, J. L., & Kalivas, P. W. (2000). Glutamate transmission in the nucleus accumbens mediates relapse in cocaine addiction. *Journal of Neuroscience, 20,* 1–5.

Cuomo, V., Cagiano, R., De Salvia, M. A., Maselli, M. A., Renna, G., & Racagni, G. (1988). Ultrasonic vocalization in response to unavoidable aversive stimuli in rats: Effects of benzodiazepines. *Life Sciences, 43,* 485–491.

Cournil, I., Casasnovas, B., Helluy, S. M., & Beltz, B. S. (1995). Dopamine in the lobster *Homarus-Gammarus.* 2. Dopamine-immunoreactive neurons and development of the nervous system. *Journal of Comparative Neurology, 362,* 1–16.

Crider, M. E., & Cooper, R. L. (1999). Importance of stimulation paradigm in determining facilitation and effects of neuromodulation. *Brain Research, 842,* 324–331.

Delfs, J. M., Zhu Y., Druhan, J. P., & Aston-Jones, G. (2000). Noradrenaline in the ventral forebrain is critical for opiate withdrawal-induced aversion. *Nature, 403,* 430–434.

Di Chiara, G. (1995). The role of dopamine in drug abuse viewed from the perspective of its role in motivation. *Drug Alcohol Dependence, 38,* 95–137.

Di Chiara, G., & Imperato, A. (1988). Drugs abused by humans preferentially increase synaptic dopamine concentrations in the mesolimbic system of freely moving rats. *Proceedings of the National Academy of Sciences, 85,* 5274–5278.

Di Chiara, G., Loddo, P., & Tanda, G. (1999). Reciprocal changes in prefrontal and limbic dopamine responsiveness to aversive and rewarding stimuli after chronic mild stress: Implications for the psychobiology of depression. *Biological Psychiatry, 46,* 1624–1633.

Drevets, W. C., Gautier, C., Price, J. C., Kupfer, D. J., Kinahan, P. E., Grace, A. A., et al. (2001). Amphetamine-induced dopamine release in human ventral striatum correlates with euphoria. *Biological Psychiatry, 49,* 81–96.

Durden, D. A., & Davis, B. A. (1993). Determination of regional distributions of phenylethylamine and meta- and para-tyramine in rat brain regions and presence in human and dog plasma by an ultra-sensitive negative chemical ion gas chromatography-mass spectrometric (NCI-GC-MS) method. *Neurochemical Research, 18,* 995–1002.

Everitt, B. J., Parkinson, J. A., Olmstead, M. C., Arroyo, M., Robledo, P., & Robbins, T. W. (1999). Associative processes in addiction and reward: The role of amygdala-ventral striatal subsystems. *Annals of the New York Academy of Sciences, 877,* 412–438.

Feenstra, M. G. P., & Botterblom, M. H. A. (1996). Rapid sampling of extracellular dopamine in the rat prefrontal cortex during food consumption, handling and exposure to novelty. *Brain Research, 742,* 17–24.

Feenstra, M. G. P., Botterblom, M. H. A., & Mastenbroek, S. (2000). Dopamine and noradrenaline efflux in the prefrontal cortex in the light and dark period: Effects of novelty and handling and comparison to the nucleus accumbens. *Neuroscience, 100,* 741–748.

Fiorino, D. F., & Phillips, A. G. (1999a). Facilitation of sexual behavior and enhanced dopamine efflux in the nucleus accumbens of male rats after *d*-amphetamine-induced behavioral sensitization. *Journal of Neuroscience, 19,* 456–463.

Fiorino, D. F., & Phillips, A. G. (1999b). Facilitation of sexual behavior in male rats following *d*-amphetamine-induced behavioral sensitization. *Psychopharmacology, 142,* 200–208.

Freeman, W. J. (1999). *How brains make up their minds.* London: Weidenfeld and Nicholson.

Fu, X. W., & Brudzynski, S. M. (1994). High-frequency ultrasonic vocalization induced by intracerebral glutamate in rats. *Pharmacology Biochemistry and Behavior, 49,* 835–841.

Giorgetti, M., Hotsenpiller, G., Ward, P., Teppen,T., & Wolf, M. E. (2001). Amphetamine-induced plasticity of AMPA receptors in the ventral tegmental area: Effects on extracellular levels of dopamine and glutamate in freely moving rats. *Journal of Neuroscience, 21,* 6362–6369.

Glickman, S. E., & Schiff, B. B. (1967). A biological theory of reinforcement. *Psychological Review, 74,* 81–109.

Grimm, J., & See, R. (2000). Dissociation of primary and secondary reward-relevant limbic nuclei in an animal model of relapse. *Neuropsychopharmacology, 22,* 473–479.

Heath, R. G. (1996). *Exploring the mind-brain relationship.* Baton Rouge LA: Moran Printing.

Heinrich, R., Cromarty, S. I., Horner, M., Edwards, D. H., & Kravitz, E. A. (1999). Autoinhibition of serotonin cells: An intrinsic regulatory mechanism sensitive to the pattern of usage of cells. *Proceedings of the National Academy of Sciences, 96,* 2473–2478.

Herman, B. H., & Panksepp, J. (1981). Ascending endorphinergic inhibition of distress vocalization. *Science, 211,* 1060–1062.

Hoebel, B. G., Monaco, A. P., Hernandez, L., Aulisi, E. F., Stanley, B. G., & Lenard, L. (1983). Self-injection of amphetamine directly into the brain. *Psychopharmacology, 81,* 158–163.

Huber, R., & Delago, A. (1998). Serotonin alters decisions to withdraw in fighting crayfish, *Astacus astacus:* The motivational concept revisited. *Journal of Comparative Physiology A, 182,* 573–583.

Huber, R., & Kravitz, E. A. (1995). A quantitative analysis of agonistic behavior in juvenile american lobsters (*Homarus americanus L.*). *Brain and Behavioral Evolution, 46,* 72–83.

Ikemoto, S., Glazier, B. S., Murphy, J. M., & McBride, W. J. (1997). Role of dopamine D_1 and D_2 receptors in the nucleus accumbens in mediating reward. *Journal of Neuroscience, 17,* 8580–8587.

Ikemoto, S., & Panksepp, J. (1999). The role of nucleus accumbens dopamine in motivated behavior: A unifying interpretation with special reference to reward seeking. *Brain Research Reviews, 31,* 6–41.

Ingle, R. W., & Thomas, W. (1974). Mating and spawning of the crayfish *Autropotamobius pallipes* (Crustacea: Astacidae). *Journal of Zoology (London), 173,* 525–538.

James, W. (1890/1961). *The principles of psychology.* New York: Harper and Row.

Kabbaj, M., Norton, C. S., Kollack-Walker, S., Watson, S. J., Robinson, T. E, & Akil, H. (2001). Social defeat alters the acquisition of cocaine self-administration in rats: Role of individual differences in cocaine-taking behavior. *Psychopharmacology, 158,* 382–387.

Kalivas, P. W. (1995). Neural basis of sensitization to cocaine. In R. P. Hammer (Ed.), *The Neurobiology of cocaine: Cellular and molecular mechanisms (pp. 81–98).* Boca Raton FL: CRC Press.

Kalivas, P. W., & Nakamura, M. (1999). Neural systems for behavioral activation and reward. *Current Opinion in Neurobiology, 9,* 223–227.

Kelley, A. E., Gauthier, A. M., & Lang, C. G. (1989). Amphetamine microinjections into distinct striatal subregions cause dissociable effects on motor and ingestive behavior. *Behavioral Brain Research, 35,* 27–39.

Knutson, B., Burgdorf, J., & Panksepp, J. (1998). Anticipation of play elicits high-frequency ultrasonic vocalizations in young rats. *Journal of Comparative Psychology, 112,* 65–73.

Knutson, B., Fong, G. W., Adams, C. M., Varner, J. L., & Hommer, D. (2001). Dissociation of reward anticipation and outcome with event-related fMRI. *Neuroreport, 12,* 3683–3687.

Koob, G. F., & Le Moal, M. (1997). Drug abuse: hedonic homeostatic dysregulation. *Science, 278,* 52–58.

Koob, G. F., & Le Moal, M. (2001). Drug addiction, dysregulation of reward, and allostasis. *Neuropsychopharmacology, 24,* 97–129.
Kraemer, G. W., & McKinney, W. T. (1985). Social separation increases alcohol consumption in rhesus monkeys. *Psychopharmacology, 86,* 182–189.
Kravitz, E. A. (1988). Hormonal control of behavior: Amines and the biasing of behavioral output in lobsters. *Science, 241,* 1775–1781.
Kusayama, T., & Watanabe, S. (2000). Reinforcing effects of methamphetamine in planarians. *Neuroreport, 11,* 2511–2513.
Lamb, R. J., Preston, K. L., Schindler, C. W., Meisch, R. A., Davis, F., Katz, J. L., et al. (1991). The reinforcing and subjective effects of morphine in post-addicts: A dose-response study. *Journal of Pharmacology and Experimental Therapeutics, 259,* 165–173.
LeDoux, J. E. (1996). *The emotional brain.* New York: Simon and Schuster.
LeDoux, J. E. (2000). Emotion circuits in the brain. *Annual Review of Neuroscience, 23,* 155–184.
Lemaire, V., Deminiere, J. M., & Mormede, P. (1994). Chronic social stress conditions differentially modify vulnerability to amphetamine self-administration. *Brain Research, 649,* 348–352.
Lehrman, D. S. (1953). Problems raised by instinct theories. *Quarterly Review of Biology, 28,* 337–365.
Li, H., Chaney, S., Forte, M., & Hirsh, J. (2000). Ecotopic G-protein expression in dopamine and serotonin neurons blocks cocaine sensitization in *Drosophila melanogastor. Current Biology, 10,* 211–214.
MacLean, P. D. (1990). *The triune brain in evolution: Role in paleocerebral functions.* New York: Plenum Press.
McClung, C., & Hirsh, J. (1998). Stereotypical behavioral responses to free-base cocaine and the development of behavioral sensitization in *Drosophila. Current Biology, 8,* 109–112.
McClung, C., & Hirsh, J. (1999). The trace amine tyramine is essential for sensitization to cocaine in *Drosophila. Current Biology, 9,* 853–860.
McFarland, K., & Kalivas, P. W. (2001). The circuitry mediating cocaine-induced reinstatement of drug-seeking behavior. *Journal of Neuroscience, 21,* 8655–8663.
Mesulam, M. (2000). Brain, mind, and the evolution of connectivity. *Brain and Cognition, 42,* 4–6.
Miczek, K. A., & Mutschler, N. H. (1996). Activational effects of social stress on IV cocaine self-administration in rats. *Psychopharmacology, 128,* 256–264.
Miczek, K. A., Weerts, E. M., Vivian, J. A., & Barros, H. M. (1995). Aggression, anxiety and vocalizations in animals: GABAA and 5-HT anxiolytics. *Psychopharmacology, 121,* 38–56.
Mutschler, N. H., & Miczek, K. A. (1998). Withdrawal from a self-administered or non-contingent cocaine binge: Differences in ultrasonic distress vocalizations in rats.*Psychopharmacology, 136,* 402–428.

Nathanson, J. A., Hunnicutt, E. J., Kantham, L., & Scavone, C. (1993). Cocaine as a naturally occurring insecticide. *Proceedings of the National Academy of Sciences, 90,* 9645–9648.

Nesse, R. M., & Berridge, K. C. (1997). Psychoactive drug use in evolutionary perspective. *Science, 278,* 63–66.

Newton, T. F., Ling, W., Kalechstein, A. D., Uslaner, J., & Tervo, K. (2001). Risperidone pre-treatment reduces the euphoric effects of experimentally administered cocaine. *Psychiatry Research, 102,* 227–233.

Nikaido, T., Akiyama, M., Moriay, T., & Shibata, S. (2001). Sensitized increase of period gene expression in the mouse caudate/putamen caused by repeated injection of methamphetamine. *Molecular Pharmacology, 59,* 894–900.

Nocjar, C., & Panksepp, J. (2002). Chronic intermittent amphetamine pretreatment enhances future appetitive behavior for drug- and natural-reward: Interaction with environmental variables. *Behavioural Brain Research, 128,* 189–203.

O'Brien, C. P., Childress, A. R., Ehrman, R., & Robbins, S. J. (1998). Conditioning factors in drug abuse: Can they explain compulsion? *Journal of Psychopharmacology, 12,* 15–22.

Olmstead, M. C., & Franklin, K. B. (1997). The development of a conditioned place preference to morphine: Effects of microinjections into various CNS sites. *Behavioral Neuroscience, 111,* 1324–1334.

Palladini, G., Ruggeri, S., Stocchi, F., De Pandis, M. F., Venturini, G., & Margotta, V. (1996). A pharmacological study of cocaine activity in planaria. *Comparative Biochemistry and Physiology, 115C*(1), 41–45.

Panksepp, J. (1981a). Brain opioids: A neurochemical substrate for narcotic and social dependence. In S. Cooper (Ed.), *Progress in theory in psychopharmacology* (pp. 149–175). London: Academic Press.

Panksepp, J. (1981b). Hypothalamic integration of behavior: Rewards, punishments, and related psychobiological process. In P. J. Morgane, & J. Panksepp (Eds.), *Handbook of the hypothalamus: Vol. 3, Part A. Behavioral studies of the hypothalamus* (pp. 289–487). New York: Marcel Dekker.

Panksepp, J. (1982). Toward a general psychobiological theory of emotions. *Behavioral and Brain Sciences, 5,* 407–467.

Panksepp, J. (1998). *Affective neuroscience: The foundations of human and animal emotions.* New York: Oxford University Press.

Panksepp, J. (1999). Emotions as viewed by psychoanalysis and neuroscience: An exercise in consilience. *Neuro-Psychoanalysis, 1,* 15–38.

Panksepp, J. (2001). On the subcortical sources of basic human emotions and the primacy of emotional-affective (action-perception) processes in human consciousness. *Evolution and Cognition, 7,* 134–140.

Panksepp, J. (2003). At the interface of affective, behavioral and cognitive neurosciences: Decoding the emotional feelings of the brain. *Brain and Cognition, 52,* 4–14.

Panksepp, J., & Burgdorf, J. (1999). Laughing rats? Playful tickling arouses high frequency ultrasonic chirping in young rodents. In S. Hameroff, D. Chalmers, & A. Kazniak (Eds.), *Toward a science of consciousness III* (pp. 231–244). Cambridge: MIT Press.

Panksepp, J., & Burgdorf, J. (2000). 50k-Hz chirping (laughter?) in response to conditioned and unconditioned tickle-induced reward in rats: Effects of social housing and genetic variables. *Behavioural Brain Research, 115,* 25–38.

Panksepp, J., Burgdorf, J., & Gordon, N. (2001). Towards a genetics of joy: Breeding rats for "laughter." In A. Kazniak (Ed.), *Emotions, qualia and consciousness* (pp. 124–136). Singapore: World Scientific.

Panksepp, J., Burgdorf, J., Gordon, N., & Turner, C. (2002). Treatment of ADHD with methylphenidate may sensitize brain substrates of desire. *Consciousness and Emotion, 3,* 7–19.

Panksepp, J., Herman, B., Conner, R., Bishop, P., & Scott, J. P. (1978). The biology of social attachments: opiates alleviate separation distress. *Biological Psychiatry, 13,* 607–18.

Panksepp, J., Herman, B. H., Villberg, T., Bishop, P., & DeEskinazi, F. G. (1980). Endogenous opioids and social behavior. *Neuroscience and Biobehavioral Reviews, 4,* 473–487.

Panksepp, J., Jalowiec, J., DeEskinazi, F. G., & Bishop, P. (1985). Opiates and play dominance in juvenile rats. *Behavioral Neuroscience, 99,* 441–453.

Panksepp, J., Knuston, B., & Burgdorf, J. (2002). The role of emotional brain systems in addictions: A neuro-evolutionary perspective. *Addiction, 97,* 459–469.

Panksepp, J., Meeker, R., & Bean, N. J. (1980). The neurochemical control of crying. *Pharmacology Biochemistry and Behavior, 12,* 437–443.

Panksepp, J., Najam, N., & Soares, F. (1979). Morphine reduces social cohesion in rats. *Pharmacology Biochemistry and Behavior, 11,* 131–134.

Panksepp, J., Normansell, L. A., Herman, B., Bishop, P., & Crepeau, L. (1988). Neural and neurochemical control of the separation-distress call. In J. D. Newman (Ed.), *The physiological control of mammalian vocalization* (pp. 263–299). New York: Plenum Press.

Panksepp, J., Siviy, S. M., & Normansell, L. A. (1985). Brain opioids and social emotions. In M. Reite, & T. Fields (Eds.), *The psychobiology of attachment and separation* (pp. 3–49). New York: Academic Press.

Panksepp, J. B., & Huber, R. (2002). Chronic alterations in serotonin function: Dynamic neurochemical properties in agonistic behavior of the crayfish, *Orconectes rusticus. Journal of Neurobiology, 50,* 276–290.

Pontieri, F. E., Tanda, G., & Di Chiara, G. (1995) Intravenous cocaine, morphine, and amphetamine preferentially increase extracellular dopamine in the "shell" as compared with the "core" of the rat nucleus accumbens. *Proceedings of the National Academy of Sciences, 92,* 12304–12308.

Pulvirenti, L., & Diana, M. (2001). Drug dependence as a disorder of neural plasticity: Focus on dopamine and glutamate. *Review of Neuroscience, 12,* 141–215.

Rebec, G. V., Grabner, C. P., Johnson, M., Pierce, R. C., & Bardo, M. T. (1997). Transient increases in catecholaminergic activity in medial prefrontal cortex and nucleus accumbens shell during novelty. *Neuroscience, 76,* 707–714.

Robinson, D. L., Phillips, P. E. M., Budygin, E. A., Trafton, B. J., Garris, P. A., & Wightman, R. M. (2001). Sub-second changes in accumbal dopamine during sexual behavior in male rats. *Neuroreport, 12,* 2549–2552.

Robinson, T. E., & Berridge, K. C. (1993). The neural basis of drug craving: An incentive-sensitization theory of addiction. *Brain Research Reviews, 18,* 247–291.

Robinson, T. E., & Berridge, K. C. (2000). The psychology and neurobiology of addiction: An incentive-sensitization view. *Addiction, 95,* S91–S117.

Romach, M. K., Glue, P., Kampman, K., Kaplan, H. L., Somer, G. R., Poole, S., et al. (1999). Attenuation of the euphoric effects of cocaine by the dopamine D_1/D_5 antagonist ecopipam (SCH 39166). *Archives of General Psychiatry, 56,* 1101–1106.

Rossi, J., III, & Panksepp, J. (1992). Analysis of the relationships between self-stimulation sniffing and brain-stimulation sniffing. *Physiology and Behavior, 51,* 805–813.

Safer, D. J., Zito, J. M., & Fine, E. M. (1996). Increased methylphenidate usage for attention deficit disorder in the 1990s. *Pediatrics, 98,* 1084–1088.

Sahley, T. L., Panksepp, J., & Zolovick, A. J. (1981). Cholinergic modulation of separation distress in the domestic chick. *European Journal of Pharmacology, 72,* 261–264.

Schenk, S., Hunt, T., Colle, L., & Amit, Z. (1983). Isolation versus grouped housing in rats: Differential effects of low doses of heroin in the place preference paradigm. *Life Sciences, 32,* 1129–1134.

Schenk, S., Lacelle, G. Gorman, K., & Amit, Z. (1987). Cocaine self-administration in rats influenced by environmental conditions: Implications for the etiology of drug abuse. *Neuroscience Letters, 81,* 227–231.

Schneider, H., Budhiraja, P., Walter, I., Beltz, B., Peckol, E., & Kravitz, E. A. (1996). Developmental expression of the octopamine phenotype in lobsters, *Homarus americanus. Journal of Comparative Neurology, 371,* 3–14.

Schultz, W. (2000). Multiple reward signals in the brain. *Nature Reviews Neuroscience, 1,* 199–207.

Scott, E., & Panksepp, J. (2003). Rough-and-tumble play in human children. *Aggressive Behavior,* in press.

Self, D. W., & Nestler, E. J. (1998). Relapse to drug seeking: Neural and molecular mechanisms. *Drug and Alcohol Dependence, 51,* 49–60.

Shaham, Y., Erb, S., & Stewart, J. (2000). Stress-induced relapse to heroin and cocaine seeking in rats: A review. *Brain Research Review, 33,* 13–33.

Shippenberg, T. S., Lefevour, A., & Thompson, A. C. (1998). Sensitization to the conditioned rewarding effects of morphine and cocaine: Differential effects of the kappa-opioid receptor agonist U69593. *Behavioural Brain Research, 89,* 99–106.

Sitte, H. H., Huck, S., Reither, H., Boehm, S., Singer, E. A., & Pifl, C. (1998). Carrier-mediated release, transporter rates, and charge transfer induced by amphetamine, tyramine, and dopamine in mammalian cells transfected with the human dopamine transporter. *Journal of Neurochemistry, 71,* 1289–1297.

Skinner, B. F. (1987). Whatever happened to psychology as the science of behavior? *American Psychologist, 42,* 780–786.

Steele, C., Skinner, C., Steele, C., Alberstadt, P., & Mathewson, C. (1999). Organization of chemically activated food search behavior in *Procambarus clarkii* Girard and *Orconectes rusticus* Girard crayfishes. *Biological Bulletin, 196,* 295–302.

Stewart, J. (2000). Pathways to relapse: The neurobiology of drug- and stress-induced relapse to drug taking. *Journal of Psychiatry and Neuroscience, 25,* 125–136.

Takahata, R., & Moghaddam, B. (2000). Target-specific glutamatergic regulation of dopamine neurons in the ventral tegmental area. *Journal of Neurochemistry, 75,* 1775–1778.

Teshiba, T., Shamsian, A., Yashar, B., Yeh, S. R., Edwards, D. H., & Krasne, F. B. (2001). Dual and opposing modulatory effects of serotonin on crayfish lateral and giant escape command neurons. *Journal of Neuroscience, 21,* 4523–4529.

Tinbergen, N. (1952). *The study of instinct.* Oxford: Clarendon Press.

Tornatzky, W., & Miczek, K. A. (1995). Alcohol, anxiolytics and social stress in rats. *Psychopharmacology, 121,* 135–144.

Torres, G., & Horowitz, J. M. (1998). Activating properties of cocaine and cocaethylene in a behavioral preparation of *Drosophila melanogastor. Synapse, 29,* 148–161.

Trowill, J. A., Panksepp, J., & Gandelman, R. (1969). An incentive model of rewarding brain stimulation. *Psychological Review, 76,* 264–281.

Valenstein, E. S., Cox, V. C., & Kakolewski, J. W. (1970). Reexamination of the role of the hypothalamus in motivation. *Psychological Review, 77,* 16–31.

Vivian, J. A., & Miczek, K. A. (1991). Ultrasounds during morphine withdrawal in rats. *Psychopharmacology, 104,* 187–193.

Wang, Z., & Rebec, G. V. (1998). Neuroethological assessment of amphetamine-induced behavioral changes and their reversal by neuroleptics: Focus on the amygdala and nucleus accumbens. *Progress in Neuropsychopharmacology and Biological Psychiatry, 22,* 883–905.

Wintink, A. J., & Brudzynski, S. (2001). Production of 50 kHz ultrasonic calls by adult rats is dependent on dopaminergic transmission. *Pharmacology Biochemistry and Behavior, 70,* 317–323.

Wise, R. A. (1987). The role of reward pathways in the development of drug dependence. *Pharmacology and Therapeutics, 35,* 227–263.

Wise, R. A. (1998). Drug-activation of brain reward pathways. *Drug and Alcohol Dependence, 51,* 13–22.

Wise, R. A., & Bozarth, M. A. (1987). A psychomotor stimulant theory of addiction. *Psychological Review, 94,* 469–492.

Wolf, M. E. (1998). The role of excitatory amino acids in behavioral sensitization to psychomotor stimulants. *Progress in Neurobiology, 54,* 679–720.

Wolf, M. E. (1999). Cocaine addiction: Clues from *Drosophila* on drugs. *Current Biology, 9,* R770–R772.

Wolffgramm, J., & Heyne, A. (1995). From controlled drug intake to loss of control: The irreversible development of drug addiction in the rat. *Behavioural Brain Research, 70,* 77–94.

Wongwitdecha, N., & Marsden, C. A. (1996). Effect of social isolation on the reinforcing properties of morphine in the conditioned place preference test. *Pharmacology Biochemistry and Behavior, 53,* 531–534.

Biological Connection between Novelty- and Drug-seeking Motivational Systems

Michael T. Bardo and
Linda P. Dwoskin
University of Kentucky

There has been considerable emphasis on research aimed at determining the genetic factors responsible for phenotypic expression of increased drug abuse vulnerability (Crabbe, Phillips, Buck, Cunningham, & Belknap, 1999). Identification of the multiple genetic factors that determine vulnerability is critically important and currently feasible with modern molecular technology. However, significant efforts also need to be directed at understanding the impact of intervening environmental factors that modify the trajectory of an individual's genetic vulnerability. In the present chapter, we will attempt to build a case that one of the critical environmental determinants that sets the stage for an individual's motivation to take drugs during adulthood is the amount of stimulus enrichment that is experienced during development.

The overall working hypothesis that we have been investigating in our laboratory is that repeated exposure to novelty during development increases the sensitivity of the mesolimbic dopamine (DA) reward pathway and that this neurochemical change produces a concomitant increase in the rewarding effect of novelty and am-

The authors acknowledge T. Green, J. Klebaur, and J. Zhu for their expert help in the experiments described. This work was supported by USPHS grants P50 DA05312, R01 DA12964, and KO2 DA00399.

phetamine during adulthood. This hypothesis is derived from work showing that both novelty and drugs of abuse activate the mesolimbic DA system. To the extent that these stimuli work via a similar neural substrate, this commonality would suggest that novel stimulation may substitute for drug reward.

In this chapter we will first describe some of the important historical antecedents that provide a background for our working hypothesis. The research on motivational aspects of novelty-seeking and drug-seeking behavior has a long, illustrious history. We will trace some of the more important nodes of information relevant to our current work that were available approximately 50 years ago, when the first Nebraska Symposium on Motivation was held. With this historical backdrop, we will then describe the recent work from our laboratory and others that suggests some modification in our hypothesis is needed. In particular, contrary to our initial hypothesis, we now have clear evidence that rats raised in an enriched condition (EC) show less motivation to self-administer drugs than rats raised in an isolated condition (IC). We will conclude by speculating about the potential application of these findings for the clinical setting.

A Historical Perspective on the Motivation for Novelty

One of the fundamental principles in the field of psychology is that the temporal or spatial arrangement of stimulus events in the environment is a critical determinant of behavior change. Two stimuli that occur together become associated such that occurrence of one leads to an expectation of the second. The impact of these stimuli on behavior is especially important when one or both of the stimuli impact on the survival or general health of the organism. Thus, for example, presentation of a visual stimulus with food produces greater behavior change than presentation of a visual stimulus with an auditory tone. For the most part, psychologists have concentrated on investigating the motivational aspects of stimuli that have obvious survival consequences, including food, water, sex, and painful stimuli.

In addition to natural reinforcers, there is no doubt that drugs of abuse are powerful in activating motivational systems within the brain. While it is generally thought that drug and natural reinforcers activate a common mesolimbic DA reward substrate (Wise, 1989), it has been argued that drug reinforcement is also uniquely different from food reinforcement in several ways (Wise, 1987). First, while responding for food reinforcement is followed by a consummatory act, responding for drug is not. Second, when the amount of food reinforcement per response is varied, responding on a simple fixed ratio (FR) schedule tends to follow a monophasic increase. In contrast, when the unit dose of drug is varied, responding on a FR schedule follows a biphasic inverted U-shaped function. The ascending limb of the dose response curve presumably reflects an increase in reinforcing efficacy that is not readily satiated, whereas the descending limb presumably reflects satiation, as well as potentially aversive or response-suppressant properties of high unit doses. Third, related to the notion of satiety, a single presentation of food reinforcement is not typically sufficient to produce satiety, whereas a single drug injection can produce apparent satiety for a prolonged postreinforcement period.

In discussing the relationship between motivational systems involved in natural and drug reinforcers, it seems appropriate for the 50th annual volume of the Nebraska Symposium on Motivation that some historical perspective be offered. While current motivational theories are often constructed as sophisticated neural circuitry models, they continue to be steeped in the Hullian notion, now more than 50 years old, that tissue needs serve to drive goal-directed behaviors (Hull, 1943). If a goal is obtained, the specific drive is decreased in intensity for some finite period of time. The work of Hebb (1955) has also been influential because it articulated that drives are neurally based in two different sensory systems, one that represents a point-to-point connection between the thalamus and cortex and a second that involves the diffuse reticular activating system. It was postulated that the first system organizes goal-directed behaviors, whereas the second system provides a general arousal to drive the behaviors. While Hebb was not a drive-reductionist in the Hullian sense, his contributions at the neural level had a profound influence on the way we conceptualize the brain as a networked organ that seeks out and interacts with specific environmental stimuli.

One of the early controversies that emerged from the seminal drive-reduction theory espoused by Hull was related to a series of experiments published during the 1950s indicating that organisms were not only motivated by stimuli that restored tissue deficits, but were also motivated by novel environmental stimuli. For example, 9-month-old human infants were found to be attracted to complex visual patterns (Berlyne, 1958), and rhesus monkeys were found to solve discrimination tasks when novel visual and auditory stimuli were presented contingent on correct lever-press responding (Butler, 1953; 1957). In rats, the phenomenon of spontaneous alternation in a T-maze was thought to reflect a need for novelty (Dember, 1961), and exposure to a novel cue light was found to serve as a reinforcer for lever pressing in an operant conditioning box (Barnes & Baron, 1961; Marx, Henderson, & Roberts, 1955). Because exploration of novel stimuli was thought to be a general phenomenon that was conserved across both invertebrate and vertebrate species (Welker, 1961), it was postulated that organisms have a curiosity or exploratory drive. However, this notion did not fit neatly into existing drive-reduction theory at that time because novel stimuli could motivate behavior in the absence of any internal tissue need. Further, in contrast to other types of drives such as hunger, thirst, or sex, novelty seeking is not goal directed, and there is no consummatory response. In this regard, novelty seeking appears to share some attributes with drug seeking. Further, it was recognized that novelty-seeking behavior is not readily satiated, and in this regard it is somewhat analogous to the phenomenon of brain stimulation reward discovered by Olds and Milner (1954).

As discussed by Fiske and Maddi (1961), novelty should not be construed as a physical attribute of a stimulus, but rather the degree to which a stimulus differs from preceding stimulation. Novel stimulation is thought to play a critical role in promoting normal development, as well as maintaining an optimal level of arousal for information processing. Further, Fiske and Maddi (1961) postulated that another function of novelty seeking is to produce positive affect. It is the latter function that may be most relevant for understanding the connection between novelty- and drug-seeking behaviors. Elicitation of approach behavior by a novel object, interaction with a novel object, and the demonstration of choice to spend time in a novel environment rather than a familiar environment suggests positive affect engendered by novelty (Hughes, 1968; Sheldon, 1969).

One line of research that illustrated the importance of novel stimulation in normal functioning was the pioneering work conducted on sensory deprivation in humans (Bexton, Heron, & Scott, 1954; Heron,

Doane, & Scott, 1956). In those studies, subjects were instructed to lie on a bed in a sound-attenuated cubicle. Sensory information was restricted by having the subjects wear goggles and gloves. Prolonged sensory deprivation had a debilitating effect on normal functions, often producing hallucinatory experiences and unpleasant emotional feelings. Immediately upon termination of the sensory deprivation period, significant deficits in performance on various cognitive tasks were also noted. However, not all individuals suffered deleterious effects, and there were large individual differences in the reaction to the sensory deprivation.

Another line of work relevant to this issue was the discovery that providing novel environmental enrichment during development could alter neurochemistry and improve learning performance (Krech, Rosenzweig, & Bennett, 1960; Thompson, 1955). In these studies, EC rats were raised with novel objects (replaced daily) and social cohorts, whereas IC rats were raised without objects or cohorts. Early environmental enrichment was recognized to have a profound influence on learning, as the differences normally observed between genetically bred maze bright and maze dull rats were eliminated when both strains were raised in the enriched environment (Cooper & Zubek, 1958).

Thus, this early work pointed to at least three conclusions. First, environmental novelty provides arousal and positive affect for the organism. Second, unlike drives that are based on tissue needs, novelty does not elicit any consummatory behaviors, and the drive for novelty is not readily satiated. Third, repeated exposure to novelty can affect brain structure and function, as well as alter behavior. We will now present more recent research that suggests one additional conclusion: Exposure to novel stimulation can influence the same brain systems involved in drug reward, and in so doing, can alter the motivation for the drug.

Effect of Novelty on the Neural Systems Involved in Reward

Evidence indicates that exposure to novelty activates the mesolimbic DA system. Similar to the effects of amphetamine, rats exposed to novel environmental stimuli display an increase in locomotor activity (Welker, 1959). Rats also show a conditioned place preference

(CPP) when novel objects are paired with one compartment of a place preference apparatus (Besheer, Jensen, & Bevins, 1999; Bevins & Bardo, 1999; Bevins, Besheer, Palmatier, Jensen, Pickett, & Eurek, 2002). When entering a novel compartment from a familiar compartment, there is a transient and rapid surge in accumbal DA activity recorded by in vivo voltammetry (Rebec, Christensen, Guerra, & Bardo, 1997). Further, injection of the neurotoxin 6-hydroxydopamine (6-OHDA) into the mesolimbic DA system disrupts the increase in locomotion and rearing normally elicited by novel stimuli (Fink & Smith, 1979; Mogenson & Nielson, 1984). Novelty-induced place preference is also blocked by DA antagonist drugs (Bardo, Bowling, Robinet, Rowlett, Lacy, & Mattingly, 1993; Misslin, Ropartz, & Jung, 1984) and by lesioning the nucleus accumbens (Pierce, Crawford, Nonneman, Mattingly, & Bardo, 1990). Even though the 6-OHDA-induced blockade of novelty-induced place preference is reversed after 4 weeks, a deficit in exploratory behavior persists (Weissenborn & Winn, 1992).

In recent reports using electrophysiological techniques, novelty signal detection has been observed in the ventral tegmental area (VTA) of behaving animals. VTA neurons show tonic impulse activity, but respond with short-latency, short-duration bursts of activity to novel stimuli, unpredictable positive rewards, and conditioned stimuli that reliably predict positive rewards (Mirenowicz & Schultz, 1994; Schultz & Dickinson, 2000). VTA neuron burst firing has been described as indicating that the stimulus input is sufficiently novel to warrant a change in behavior (Schultz & Dickinson, 2000; Spanagel & Weiss, 1999). Furthermore, accumulating evidence indicates that the hippocampus also is involved in novelty signal detection (Lisman & Otmakhova, 2001). Although no direct neural connections have been found between the VTA and the hippocampus, most hippocampal targets send efferent projections to the VTA. For example, the hippocampus sends efferents to the medial prefrontal cortex, which sends excitatory input stimuli to the VTA (Carr & Sesack, 2000; Murase, Grenhoff, Chouvet, Gonon, & Svensson, 1993). Exposure to novel environmental stimuli also increases the concentration of extracellular norepinephrine in the frontal cortex assessed by in vivo microdialysis, which presumably reflects an increased response of neurons in the locus coeruleus (Dalley & Stanford, 1995; Vankov, Herve-Minvielle, & Sara, 1995). In any case, these results indicate that the VTA acquires information about stimulus novelty via circuitry involving the prefrontal cortex and hippocampus, sites for memory storage and novelty detection.

Environmental Enrichment Alters the Neural Systems Involved in Reward

Many preclinical studies have shown that, compared to rats raised in social groups, rats raised in isolation during development have different neurochemical and behavioral profiles as adults. Isolation-reared rats exhibit locomotor hyperactivity and reduced habituation to a novel testing environment, such as an open field arena; however, exploration of novel objects is not different between isolation-reared and group-reared rats (Jones, Hernandez, Kendall, Marsden, & Robbins, 1992; Hall, Humby, Wilkinson, & Robbins, 1997). Additionally, social isolation has been reported to produce an anxiogenic behavioral profile in the elevated plus maze test (Bickerdicke, Wright, & Marsden, 1993), as well as deficits in prepulse inhibition to acoustic startle (Geyer, Wilkinson, Humby, & Robbins, 1993; Varty, Paulus, Braff, & Geyer, 2000). Early environmental isolation also produces long-term effects on basal neurotransmitter function in dopaminergic, serotonergic, and noradrenergic systems, as well as the respective neurochemical response to novelty exposure (Bickerdicke, Wright, & Marsden, 1993; Fulford & Marsden, 1997; Miura, Qiao, & Ohta, 2002).

While neurochemical differences may be induced simply by raising rats in isolated or social housing conditions, more profound differences are evident when EC and IC rats are compared. The effect of environmental enrichment is thought to be due to the repeated activation of various neural systems as rats explore and interact with novel objects in the home cage. Exposure to novel stimuli has been reported to produce increased levels of extracellular DA and its metabolites in the medial prefrontal cortex (Beaufour, Le Bihan, Hamon, & Thiebot, 2001; Feenstra & Botterblom, 1996), suggesting a close relationship between dopaminergic activation in the prefrontal cortex and exposure to novelty. Moreover, environmental enrichment during development has been shown to produce neuroanatomical, structural, and neurochemical changes throughout the neocortex, particularly in the occipital visual cortex (Renner & Rosenzweig, 1987; Wallace, Kilman, Withers, & Greenough, 1992). Compared to IC rats, EC rats have greater neocortical weight and thickness, primarily due to an increased density of glial and capillary endothelial cells (Diamond et al., 1966; Sirevaag & Greenough, 1988). Environmental enrichment also increases cholinesterase activity in the neocortex (Rosenzweig, Krech, Bennett, & Diamond, 1962) and increases cortical levels of norepinephrine and DA (Reige & Morimoto, 1970).

In addition to neocortical changes, environmental enrichment has also been shown to induce neuroanatomical and neurochemical changes in subcortical regions. In the hippocampus, enrichment-induced structural changes include increases in thickness and density of glial cells, increased hippocampal dendritic arborizations, as well as increased survival and total granule cell count in the dentate gyrus (Fiala, Joyce, & Greenough, 1978; Kempermann, Kuhn, & Gage, 1997; Walsh, Budtz-Olsen, Penny, & Cummings, 1969). Environmental enrichment also enhances baseline synaptic strength in both the dentate gyrus and pyramidal cells of the CA1 region of the hippocampal slice preparation, suggesting an increased number or efficacy of receptors on hippocampal neurons (Foster & Dumas, 2001; Green & Greenough, 1986). In behavioral studies, environmental enrichment has been shown to improve spatial memory and performance in the Morris water maze task (Williams et al., 2001). Neurochemical analyses revealed increased immunoreactivity to CAMP response element (CREB) binding in hippocampus protein (Nilsson, Perfilieva, Johansson, Orwar, & Eriksson, 1999; Williams et al., 2001) and increased nerve growth factor in the hippocampus and cortex, as well as increased nerve growth factor receptors (p75 and trkA) in the medial septal area (Pham, Ickes, Albeck, Soderstrom, Granholm, & Mohammed, 1999; Pham, Soderstrom, Winblad, & Mohammed, 1999). Such structural reorganization and modulation of neurochemical function in hippocampus in response to environmental enrichment may augment memory storage, that is, the formation and consolidation of long-term reference memories, and thus novelty signal detection in hippocampus.

Despite the various changes noted in the cortex and hippocampus, relatively little is known about the effect of environmental enrichment on the mesolimbic DA system. In one study, no difference in DA D_1 or D_2 receptor levels was found between EC and IC rats (Bardo & Hammer, 1991). More recently, it has been shown that EC rats have greater glucose utilization in the nucleus accumbens following exposure to a novel environment relative to IC rats (Gonzalez-Lima, Ferchmin, Eterovic, & Gonzalez-Lima, 1994). However, it is not known if this increase in metabolic activity reflects a specific activation of mesolimbic DA neurons.

In vitro neurochemical analyses of DA function have also been used to determine the underlying cellular mechanisms mediating alterations in behavior following environmental enrichment. Such in vitro studies offer control over drug concentration and duration of drug exposure, as well as allowing for the selection of specific DA terminal fields to be isolated from the influence of other components of the neurochemical circuitry present in vivo. Differences were not found between EC and IC rats with regard to electrical field-stimulation (15, 60, or 300 pulses, 1 Hz stimulation)-evoked DA release from superfused striatal or nucleus accumbens slices (Bardo, Bowling, Rowlett, Manderscheid, Buxton, & Dwoskin, 1995). Additionally, no differences were detected with respect to amphetamine (1.0–10 æM)-evoked DA release from striatal or nucleus accumbens slices, or with respect to D_2 DA autoreceptor modulation of evoked DA release. These negative in vitro findings call attention to the potential importance of using an intact neural circuitry in vivo in order to identify the modulatory effects of environmental enrichment on neurotransmitter function.

The dopamine transporter (DAT) is another presynaptic target that has been investigated for enrichment-induced alterations in function. DAT may be a particularly important target site because psychostimulant drugs interact with this presynaptic site to alter dopaminergic function, thus setting the stage for abuse. For example, cocaine inhibits DAT directly and amphetamine releases DA into the synaptic cleft *via* reversal of DAT (Liang & Rutledge, 1982; Sulzer, Chen, Lau, Kristensen, Rayport, & Ewing, 1995). The net effect of such actions on DAT protein is an increase in the concentration of DA in the synaptic cleft and the promotion of dopaminergic neurotransmission. However, behavioral effects of drugs are determined both by their intrinsic pharmacological properties and by the environmental context in which they are administered (Falk & Feingold, 1987). In this respect, environmental novelty has been shown to modulate the response to amphetamine and cocaine in rats with respect to stimulation of locomotor activity and *c-fos* mRNA expression in cortex, caudate, and nucleus accumbens, as well as in subregions of the bed nucleus of the stria terminalis and amygdala (Badiani, Oates, Day,

Watson, Akil, & Robinson, 1998; Day et al. 2001). Interestingly, this previous work has also shown that amphetamine-induced DA release in striatum or nucleus accumbens determined by in vivo microdialysis is not modulated by environmental novelty (Badiani et al., 2001). Thus, while the patterns of immediate early gene expression in specific neural circuits following psychostimulant drug administration are modulated by environmental context, the specific neurotransmitters involved in this circuitry still requires elucidation. In any case, the pattern of *c-fos* expression in frontal cortex in response to drugs from other pharmacological classes (e.g., haloperidol) have been shown to be similarly dependent on the relative novelty of the stimulus context under which drug is administered (Murphy & Feldon, 2001).

To begin investigating the effect of environmental enrichment and the consequent exposure to novelty during development on DAT function, we initially used striatal tissue due to the high density of DAT protein in this brain region. Potential alterations in kinetic parameters (K_m and V_{max}) of DAT function were determined using substrate saturation analysis. No differences were observed between EC and IC rats with respect to the kinetic parameters of DA uptake, indicating that DAT in striatum functions similarly in the two groups of rats (Bardo et al., 1999). More recently, these data were replicated and extended to other DA terminal regions, including nucleus accumbens and medial prefrontal cortex (Zhu, Green, Bardo, & Dwoskin, in press). Although K_m and V_{max} values in striatum and nucleus accumbens did not differ between EC and IC rats, a significant decrease (36%) in V_{max} in medial prefrontal cortex was found for EC relative to IC rats (V_{max}, 4.9 ± 0.06 and 7.7 ± 0.06 pmol/min/mg, respectively), with no change in observed K_m. Furthermore, DA metabolism to dihydroxyphenylacetic acid was lower in medial prefrontal cortex in EC rats compared to IC rats, whereas differences were not observed in either striatum or nucleus accumbens. These results indicate decreased DA uptake and subsequently decreased DA metabolism in presynaptic terminals in medial prefrontal cortex in EC rats relative to IC rats.

Consistent with the in vitro studies, recent evidence from our laboratory has shown that DA clearance in medial prefrontal cortex assessed in vivo is also lower in EC rats compared to IC rats (Figure 1). In these studies using anesthetized EC and IC rats, DA clearance

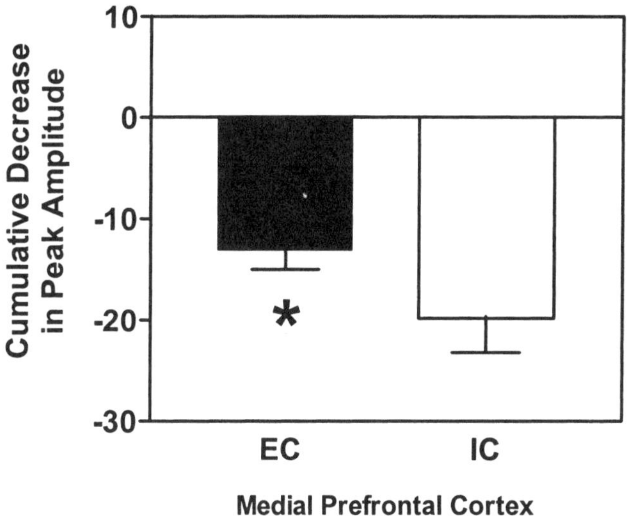

Figure 1. DA clearance in medial prefrontal cortex in anesthetized EC and IC rats using in vivo voltammetry. Each bar represents the mean (± *SEM*) cumulative decrease in DA peak amplitude such that greater negative values represent greater DA clearance rate. Chronoamperometric recordings of DA peak amplitude were made continuously at 5 Hz and averaged to 1 Hz with a nafion-coated carbon fiber electrode, attached to a micropipette filled with DA (200 μM). The electrode/micropipette assembly was lowered into the medial prefrontal cortex (2.9 mm anterior to Bregma, 1.0 mm lateral from midline, 2.5–5.0 mm below the cortical surface). DA (200 μM) was pressure ejected at 5 minute intervals until a reproducible baseline signal was obtained. DA peak amplitude was determined at 5 minute intervals for 60 minutes following saline injection (s.c.). Asterisk (*) indicates significant difference from IC rats, $p < 0.05$. $N = 8$ rats per group.

in medial prefrontal cortex was determined during a 60 minute period by exogenous application of DA via micropipette at 5 minute intervals and continuous amperometric detection of the applied DA and its clearance via a nafion-coated carbon fiber electrode using in vivo voltammetry. Differences in DAT function in medial prefrontal cortex of EC and IC rats suggest that this presynaptic protein may be important as an underlying determinant of the modulation of the observed behavioral effects of environmental enrichment. The medial prefrontal cortex has been suggested to be an important DA terminal region playing a significant role in drug abuse (Goeders & Smith, 1983; McGregor & Roberts, 1995). Alterations in the function of the dopaminergic system in medial prefrontal cortex may be an important link to a better understanding of the effects of environmental enrichment on behavior.

Potential alterations in the ability of several drugs (amphetamine, cocaine, BTCP, and GBR12935) to inhibit DA transport into the presynaptic terminal have also been investigated in EC and IC rats. No differences in cocaine or BTCP-induced inhibition of DAT function were observed (Bardo et al., 1999). In more recent studies, no differences were also observed between amphetamine-induced inhibition of DA uptake in striatal and nucleus accumbens synaptosomes (unpublished results). It will be important to determine the effects of amphetamine in medial prefrontal cortex from EC and IC rats. Interestingly, GBR12935 more potently inhibited DA uptake in striatum from EC rats compared to IC rats, potentially reflecting a specific molecular site on DAT protein in striatum that is modified by environmental enrichment (Bardo et al., 1999). GBR12935 is a highly selective DAT inhibitor; however, GBR12935 has also been reported to inhibit DA uptake into synaptic vesicles and interact with the vesicular monoamine transporter (VMAT2; Reith, Coffey, Xu, & Chen, 1994). Importantly, EC rats showed greater GBR12935-induced increases in locomotor activity compared to IC rats, although baseline activity levels for EC rats were lower than that for IC rats (Zhu, Green, Bardo, & Dwoskin, in press). Moreover, after repeated GBR12935 administration, only EC rats exhibited behavioral sensitization. Thus, differences between EC and IC rats with respect to GBR12935-induced inhibition of DA uptake and behavioral effects may be the result of an enhancement in VMAT2 function by environmental enrichment. This enhancement in VMAT2 function would be expected to redistribute the presynaptic DA from the cytosolic pool to the readily releasable vesicular storage pool. Such a redistribution of presynaptic DA may be an adaptive response to maintain the vesicular pool as a result of the enhanced bursting impulse flow from the VTA that occurs during environmental enrichment.

Environmental Enrichment Alters Novelty Seeking

Given the extensive neuroanatomical and neurochemical alterations produced by environmental enrichment, it is not surprising that a host of studies have shown that EC animals display a wide range of neurobehavioral changes relative to IC animals (Renner & Rosenzweig, 1987). These enrichment-induced changes are not bound by the species examined, as neurobehavioral differences have been observed with rats, mice, monkeys, cats, hamsters, gerbils, and pigs (Renner & Rosenzweig, 1987; Wemelsfelder, Haskell, Mendl, Calvert, & Lawrence, 2000). While a full description of the various neurobehavioral changes are beyond the scope of the present chapter, some relevant findings will be highlighted.

One notable enrichment-induced change in behavior relates to the interaction with novel places and objects. In general, EC animals find novelty to be less stressful and more rewarding than IC animals. For example, EC rats display less activity than IC rats in an inescapable novel environment (Bowling, Rowlett, & Bardo, 1993; Lore & Levowitz, 1966). In a free-choice situation, however, EC rats enter a novel compartment and manipulate novel objects more than IC rats (Renner & Rosenzweig, 1986; Widman & Rosellini, 1990). Thus, while an individual's response to novelty is partially under genetic control (Oliverio & Messeri, 1973; Peeler & Nowakowski, 1987), it is also clearly influenced by environmental factors.

In a recent study by Zimmermann, Stauffacher, Langhans, and Würbel (2001), 22-day-old male rats were raised in one of four different conditions varying in stimulus novelty. At adulthood, these rats were then assessed for entry into an open field arena and interaction with novel objects. As found previously by others, EC rats entered the novel arena and contacted the novel objects more quickly than IC rats. More important, in the novel object test, not only did EC rats approach the novel stimulus more quickly, they also showed a more rapid loss of response to the novel stimulus. This suggests that EC rats are less motivated to interact with the attractive features of a novel stimulus for extended periods, or alternatively that the novelty signal was not maintained in EC rats relative to IC rats. Consistent with this notion, isolated rats show an increased number of exploratory bouts to a single novel object and a greater preference for a novel context (Sahakian, Robbins, & Iversen, 1977).

Other work has shown that environmental enrichment can affect the ability of animals to learn various behavioral tasks. Correlated with the neocortical changes discussed previously, EC rats are superior to IC rats in various learning tasks using either appetitive or aversive stimuli. Although some inconsistencies in the literature exist, it has been generally concluded that the most reliable differences between EC and IC rats are observed in studies using complex spatial tasks (Renner & Rosenzweig, 1987). In particular, successful navigation of a complex maze is reliably enhanced by environmental enrichment (Freeman & Ray, 1972; Greenough, Madden, & Fleischman, 1972).

Interestingly, there is less of an impact of enrichment, if any at all, on simple learning tasks. For example, environmental enrichment does not appear to impact the ability of animals to acquire a classically conditioned taste aversion (Domjan, Schorr, & Best, 1977). In a recent study from our laboratory (Bardo, Klebaur, Valone, & Deaton, 2001), we examined the ability of environmental enrichment to alter acquisition of a lever-press response for sucrose on a simple FR5 schedule of reinforcement in male and female rats. Early in acquisition, EC rats showed an enhanced performance over IC rats in the number of sucrose pellets earned. However, when stable responding was evident on the FR5 schedule after five sessions, differences between EC and IC rats were no longer evident, regardless of sex. One possible explanation for the enhanced initial performance of EC rats is that these animals may have been less distracted when first placed into the novel operant conditioning chamber. However, as both groups acclimated to the chamber, the superiority of EC rats on simple FR responding may have been lost.

We have recently examined if environmental enrichment alters the reinforcing effect of novel visual stimuli. EC and IC rats were placed into an operant conditioning chamber with two levers present and a white cue light located directly above each lever. Across six daily 1-hour sessions, pressing on either lever was recorded, but there was no programmed consequence. Following this baseline period, rats were given four more daily sessions in which one of the cue lights provided blinking illumination contingent on each lever press. To maximize visual novelty, the position of the light (left or right) that was illuminated was randomly determined for each lever press, with the blinking duration varying from 2–8 seconds and the flash rate varying between 0.2–0.75 seconds. Finally, after assessing responding in the presence of the contingent light, four more baseline sessions (no cue light) were conducted as described previously. Results from this study suggest that environmental enrichment decreases the motivation for visual novelty (Figure 2). In the initial baseline phase without any cue lights, IC rats made significantly more responses

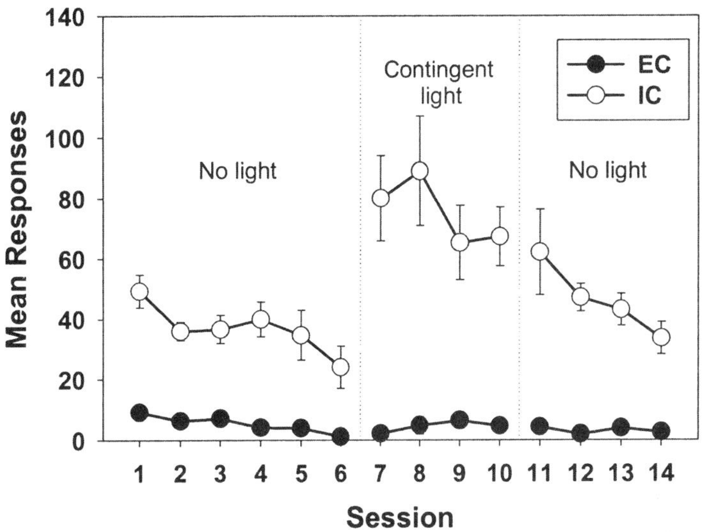

Figure 2. Responding for visual novelty in EC and IC rats. Each point represents the mean (± *SEM*) number of responses made by EC and IC rats before, during, and after contingent presentations of a novel blinking light during 1-hour daily sessions. Baseline responding was higher in IC rats than EC rats prior to presentation of the light (left panel). The contingent novel light significantly increased responding in IC rats, but not in EC rats (middle panel), and this increase was extinguished to the baseline rate when the light was omitted (right panel). *N* = 6 rats per group.

than EC rats. This finding parallels the increase in activity typically seen with IC rats compared to EC rats when exposed to novelty in an inescapable context. More important, however, when the contingent light novelty was imposed, IC rats increased their responding significantly, whereas EC rats did not. Removal of the contingency extinguished responding comparable to the level of responding observed prior to presentation of the visual novelty. These results are important because they suggest that, in addition to decreasing the motivation for amphetamine, environmental enrichment decreases the motivation for novelty. Alternatively, EC rats may have perceived the stimulus as a lower novelty value or may have responded less to visual novelty due to a lower baseline rate of responding prior to the introduction of the contingent light. In any case, it appears that, relative to EC rats, IC rats might be classified as high novelty seekers that are prone to self-administer drugs. As discussed in the next section, these preclinical results may have important implications for the prevention and treatment of drug abuse in a clinical setting.

Environmental Enrichment Alters Drug Seeking

Most relevant to the topic of the current chapter, a number of studies have examined the effect of environmental enrichment on the neurobehavioral effects of drugs of abuse. In one of the first studies to examine this issue, Juraska, Greenough, and Conlee (1983) examined the sensitivity of EC and IC rats to the behavioral effects of phenobarbital. Following acute phenobarbital, EC rats lost the righting reflex and became unconscious more rapidly than IC rats. One interpretation of this finding is that IC rats were more aroused by the injection and test procedure, and thus were more resistant to the anesthetic. Alternatively, because IC rats have more adipose tissue compared to EC rats, it is possible that the high solubility of phenobarbital in adipose tissue might have reduced the bioavailability of drug to the IC brain.

Our laboratory has conducted a series of experiments to determine the effect of environmental enrichment on the psychostimulant effect of amphetamine. When amphetamine was administered acutely, EC rats showed greater amphetamine-induced hyperactivity compared to IC rats (Bowling et al., 1993; Bowling & Bardo, 1994). This enrichment-induced difference was not likely related to pharmacokinetic differences, since injection of ^{3}H-amphetamine in EC and IC rats produced an equivalent uptake of radiolabel into the brain of both groups (Bardo et al., 1999). Nonetheless, interpretation of the enrichment-induced difference in amphetamine-stimulated locomotor activity is complicated somewhat because baseline (no drug) levels of activity were less in EC rats compared to IC rats. However, in at least one study, when tested under conditions in which baseline differences between groups were not obtained, EC rats still showed greater amphetamine-induced hyperactivity compared to IC rats (Bardo et al., 1999), indicating that EC rats are more sensitive to the psychostimulant effect of amphetamine. This conclusion is supported by evidence showing that acute amphetamine stimulates DA release and metabolism in nucleus accumbens to a greater extent in EC rats than IC rats (Bardo et al., 1999).

Using the CPP paradigm, differences in amphetamine reward between EC and IC rats have also been identified (Bardo et al., 1995; Bowling & Bardo, 1994). In these studies, 4-trial CPP was assessed using varying doses of amphetamine (0.1–2.0 mg/kg). No baseline differences in preference for the two end compartments of the CPP apparatus were observed for EC, social-housed condition (SC) or IC saline control rats. However, EC rats showed greater amphetamine CPP compared to IC rats; SC rats were intermediate between EC and IC rats. These results corroborate the conclusion drawn from the locomotor activity studies, namely that environmental enrichment enhances the psychoactive effect of amphetamine.

It is important to point out that environmental enrichment does not enhance all effects of amphetamine. In particular, when amphetamine is given repeatedly, it appears that environmental enrichment can actually retard the development of sensitization. This phenomenon has been shown with locomotor activity, as EC rats show an attenuation of locomotor sensitization relative to IC rats across repeated injections (Bardo et al., 1995; Smith, Neill, & Costall, 1997). In the drug discrimination paradigm, in which training involves repeated amphetamine injections, EC rats show a reduction in the discriminative stimulus effects of amphetamine compared to IC rats (Fowler, Johnson, Kallman, Liou, Wilson, & Hikal, 1993). Thus, while EC rats may be initially more sensitive than IC rats to the psychostimulant effect of amphetamine, IC rats catch up to and surpass EC rats in sensitivity to amphetamine across repeated injections.

Several studies have examined the effect of environmental enrichment on self-administration of stimulant, opiate, and sedative drugs. Male EC rats given a choice between oral amphetamine and barbital showed an increase in barbital consumption, but not amphetamine consumption, relative to IC rats (Zimmerberg & Brett, 1992). This difference was sex-dependent, as female EC rats decreased barbital consumption relative to IC female rats. In other studies, compared to IC male rats, EC males consume significantly more cocaine (Hill & Powell, 1976) and ethanol (Rockman, Hall, Markert, & Glavin, 1988). While these results suggest that enrichment may enhance the reinforcing effect of drugs, this conclusion is tempered because the route of drug administration was oral. This is, the oral route does not allow one to determine if the effects of enrichment reflect differences in drug reinforcement or neophobia related to the taste of the drug.

To assess more directly the effect of environmental enrichment on the abuse liability of amphetamine, we have used the intravenous drug self-administration paradigm (Bardo et al., 2001). EC and IC rats were first trained briefly to lever press for a sucrose pellet reinforcer. They were then trained to self-administer amphetamine intravenously on a continuous reinforcement schedule using a training dose of either 0.03 or 0.1 mg/kg/infusion. Across five daily 3-hour sessions, IC rats consistently earned about 50 self-infusions of the low unit dose (0.03 mg/kg/infusion) and 30 infusions of the high unit dose (0.1 mg/kg/infusion). EC rats initially earned about the same number of self-infusions as IC rats; this initial high rate of responding was due to the prior experience with sucrose-reinforced responding. However, across five daily sessions, the number of self-infusions dropped dramatically in EC rats, such that by the fifth session, EC rats earned less than half the number of amphetamine self-infusions (0.03 mg/kg/infusion) as the IC rats (Figure 3). Interestingly, the enrichment-induced decrease in amphetamine self-administration evident at the low unit dose was not obtained at the high unit dose. These results are important because they confirm that environmental factors alter drug-taking behavior and that environmental enrichment may reduce this behavior.

At the present time, it is not known if the enrichment-induced decrease in amphetamine self-administration reflects a specific alteration in the reinforcing efficacy of amphetamine. Since EC rats are more sensitive to the locomotor stimulant effect of acute amphetamine and to amphetamine CPP (Bowling & Bardo, 1994), it is tempting to speculate that EC rats are more sensitive to the reinforcing effect of amphetamine, and thus they reduce their intake because less drug is needed to reach an optimal level of positive hedonic state. This explanation would be cogent if EC rats showed a leftward shift in the amphetamine self-administration dose response curve relative to IC rats. However, since no difference between EC and IC rats was obtained at the higher unit dose of amphetamine (0.1 mg/kg/infusion), alternative explanations must also be considered. For example, it is possible that EC rats show a reduction in reinforcement threshold, an effect that may only be evident at low unit doses. In addition, enrichment-induced changes in either the aversive or direct response-altering effects of amphetamine, independent of reinforcement, should be considered.

It will be important to determine if the effect of environmental

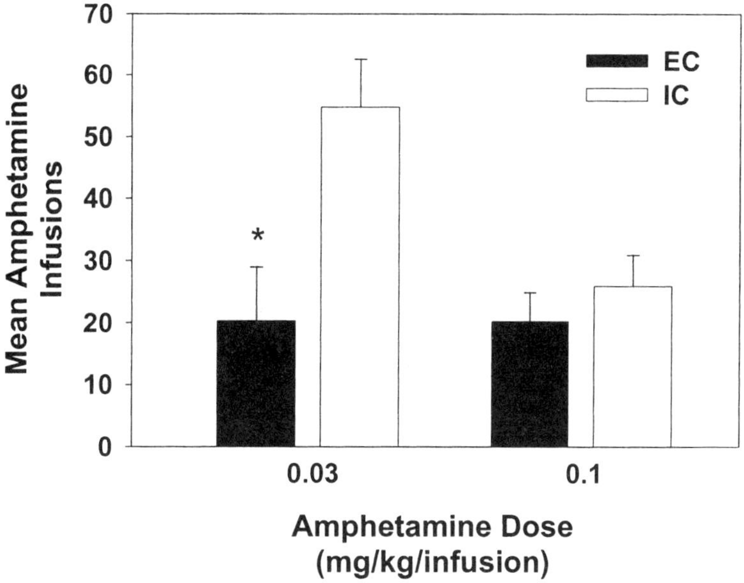

Figure 3. Responding for intravenous amphetamine in EC and IC rats. Each bar represents the mean (± *SEM*) number of intravenous amphetamine infusions earned by EC and IC rats at a unit dose of either 0.03 or 0.1 mg/kg/infusion using a continuous reinforcement schedule during a 3-hour session. EC rats earned significantly fewer infusions than IC rats at 0.03 mg/kg/infusion, but not at 0.1 mg/kg/infusion (results adapted from Bardo et al., 2001). Asterisk (*) indicates significant difference from IC rats, $p < 0.05$. N = 12–17 rats per group.

enrichment is unique to amphetamine or if it generalizes to other drugs that are self-administered intravenously. While this issue has not been examined in EC rats, some work has examined intravenous self-administration of drugs other than amphetamine in group-housed and isolated rats. In one study, Schenk, Lacelle, Gorman, and Amit (1987) trained group-housed and isolated rats to self-administer cocaine (0.1–1.0 mg/kg/infusion). Group-housed rats self-administered less cocaine than isolated rats, an effect that paralleled the reduced amphetamine self-administration in EC rats compared to IC rats reported by Bardo et al. (2001). However, in contrast to Bardo et al. (2001), the environmentally induced difference in cocaine intake was greatest with high training doses (0.5 and 1.0 mg/kg/infusion), rather than the lowest training dose (0.1 mg/kg/infusion). Importantly, yoked-control isolated rats did not reliably self-administer cocaine, indicating the environment-induced difference was not related to a direct response-activating effect of cocaine, but more likely reflected the reinforcing effect of cocaine. In any case, definitive conclusions must be tempered at this time because the results of Schenk et al. (1987) were not replicated in another laboratory (Phillips, Howes, Whitelaw, Wilkinson, Robbins, & Everitt, 1994).

Potential influences of environmental enrichment on intravenous drug self-administration beyond the stimulant class have been largely unexplored. Other than the studies using oral drug self-administration cited earlier, one study has examined morphine CPP in EC and IC rats using the subcutaneous route (Bardo, Robinet, & Hammer, 1997). This study found an enrichment-induced increase in morphine CPP, which parallels the increase observed with amphetamine CPP (Bowling & Bardo, 1994). These initial findings suggest that enrichment may enhance the rewarding effect of various drugs of abuse, an effect that could lead to a reduction in drug intake using a simple FR schedule in the intravenous drug self-administration paradigm.

One approach to determine if the enrichment-induced alteration in amphetamine self-administration is due to a change in drug reinforcement is to use a progressive ratio (PR) schedule. PR schedules increment the response requirement following presentation of each reinforcer within the session until the animal stops responding for a prolonged (e.g., 60 minute) interval, with the total number of infusions earned being defined as the break point (Richardson & Roberts, 1996). An increase in the break point presumably reflects an increase in reinforcing efficacy. Initial results with this method indicated that EC rats have a lower break point than IC rats on a PR schedule for amphetamine reinforcement, although this finding was limited to a single session determination using a low training dose (Bardo et al., 2001). This initial finding has been corroborated by recent results showing that EC rats have a lower break point than IC rats when tested at a low unit dose of amphetamine (0.006 mg/kg/infusion) across multiple sessions (Green, Gehrke, & Bardo, 2002). These findings lead us to conclude that environmental enrichment decreases the ability of a low unit dose of amphetamine to serve as an effective reinforcer.

A somewhat puzzling aspect about the current results lies in the apparent discrepancy between the findings obtained with amphetamine CPP and self-administration. That is, EC rats show greater amphetamine CPP than their IC counterparts, yet they show reduced self-administration and lower break points on a PR schedule. This discrepancy may simply reflect an inherent difference between these two behavioral preparations, as they are thought to represent different processes being mediated, at least in part, by dissociable neuropharmacologic mechanisms (Bardo & Bevins, 2000). Alternatively, these discrepant results may be reconciled when viewed within the context of the evidence discussed previously showing that, when compared to IC rats, EC rats are more sensitive to the acute locomotor stimulant effect of amphetamine, but are less sensitive to locomotor sensitization across repeated injections. Perhaps EC rats are also more sensitive to the rewarding effect of amphetamine following acute administration, but become less sensitive across repeated administrations. In the case of amphetamine CPP, since only four injections are given, one might expect that EC rats would initially show more robust amphetamine CPP compared to IC counterparts. In contrast, with amphetamine self-administration, many self-injections are given over a prolonged period of acquisition and maintenance sessions. This extensive training history is thought to induce sensitization to the rewarding effect of the stimulant that is self-administered (Schenk & Partridge, 1997). If EC rats are less prone to develop sensitization compared to IC rats, then the rewarding effect of amphetamine may become relatively less pronounced in EC rats compared to IC rats across repeated injections. Such differential sensitization could explain why EC rats eventually self-administered less amphetamine than IC rats, at least at a low unit dose.

Regardless of the discrepancy between the CPP and self-administration results, the enrichment-induced decrease in amphetamine self-administration is generally congruent with previous work assessing individual differences in response to novelty (Piazza, Deminiere, Le Moal, & Simon, 1989). In the latter work, a random population of rats was categorized as either high or low responders based on the amount of locomotor activity exhibited in an inescapable novel environment. High responders were more sensitive than low responders to amphetamine self-administration (Piazza et al., 1989; Pierre & Vezina, 1997) and this effect appears to be specific to low unit doses (Klebaur, Bevins, Segar, & Bardo, 2001). In the current work,

IC rats appear similar to high responder rats because they display increased activity in an inescapable novel environment and greater amphetamine self-administration at low unit doses compared to EC rats. These findings indicate that response to novelty, whether it is inherent within a random population or induced directly by an environmental manipulation during development, is a useful predictor of liability for stimulant abuse.

Clinical Implications

Can exposure to novel environmental stimuli protect against drug abuse? It would be wonderful to answer this question with a simple "yes," but such an affirmation would be premature. Nonetheless, we would like to construct an optimistic view about this possibility. We have considerable evidence that novelty can function as a positive reinforcer, dependent at least in part, upon activation of the mesolimbic DA system (Bardo, Donohew, & Harrington, 1996; Bevins, 2001). The next step in answering the question posed will be to obtain direct evidence that presentation of novel stimuli can effectively compete with or substitute for drug reinforcers.

While there is currently scant evidence that would directly support the notion that novel stimulation substitutes for the reinforcing effect of drugs, there is clear evidence that other nondrug reinforcers have this capacity. For example, the notion of substitution is supported by the observation that abstinent drug addicts and alcoholics consume large amounts of sweet foods and beverages (Morabia, Fabre, Chee, Zeger, Orsat, & Robert, 1989; Yamamoto, Block, & Ishii, 1991). In addition, nondrug reinforcers such as food and sweet drinking solutions are known to decrease drug taking in laboratory animals (Carroll & Lac, 1993; Nader & Woolverton, 1991). However, one potential limitation of appetitive nondrug reinforcers such as food is that they produce satiation after repeated presentation at regular intervals. Thus, in addition to activation of the reward substrates of the brain, nondrug reinforcers ultimately recruit opponent brain systems that inhibit the continued consumption of food or sweet solutions, thus limiting their ability to decrease drug intake over prolonged intervals. One exception of a nondrug reinforcer that may not satiate readily is the presentation of money or merchandise vouchers in humans, which have some clinical efficacy in reducing drug intake

(Budney, Higgins, Radonovich, & Novy, 2000; Hart, Haney, Foltin, & Fischman, 2000). Presentation of novel stimulus materials may be another exception, since evidence suggests that the motivation to seek novelty is not readily sated.

We have also learned, as outlined in this chapter, that novelty not only has an immediate reinforcing effect, but that repeated exposure to novelty during development produces long-lasting neurobehavioral changes. Enriched stimulus environments appear to foster the development of individuals that are not highly motivated to work for either novelty or a low dose of amphetamine. Perhaps enrichment activates the mesolimbic DA system repeatedly, leading to a need for greater stimulus salience in order to motivate novelty-seeking or drug-seeking behaviors. Conversely, isolated environments appear to foster the development of individuals that are highly motivated to work for either novelty or a low dose of amphetamine. While this conceptual framework is braced by empirical support, it is important to note that the results to date have been derived from highly controlled studies using laboratory animals. In humans, other than perhaps a few tragic psychiatric case reports, there is no equivalent to the type of extreme isolation that is endured by IC rats in the laboratory. Nonetheless, the preclinical data indicate that the neural systems that underlie motivated behaviors for both drug and nondrug reinforcers are malleable during development.

One area for potential application of the present work to humans concerns the relationship between novelty or sensation seeking and drug abuse liability. Novelty or sensation seeking has been defined as a biologically based personality trait characterized by the general need for novel and complex experiences, including a willingness to take risks to obtain those experiences (Zuckerman, 1994). Using Cloninger's novelty-seeking scale or Zuckerman's sensation-seeking scale, high novelty seekers have been shown to use drugs more frequently than low novelty seekers (Donohew, Lorch, & Palmgreen, 1991; Wills, Windle, & Cleary, 1998). High novelty seekers also relapse out of clinical treatment programs more frequently than low novelty seekers (Helmus, Downey, Arfken, Henderson, & Schuster, 2001). The apparent link between novelty seeking and drug use has led some investigators to develop more effective drug abuse prevention messages that specifically target high risk novelty seekers (Palmgreen, Donohew, Lorch, Hoyle, & Stephenson, 2001). Work has also been conducted to identify potential leisure activities with high sensation value that would encourage high novelty seekers to participate in nondrug alternative activities (D'Silva, Harrington, Palmgreen, Donohew, & Lorch, 2001). Combined with the current preclinical work on novelty and drug seeking in environmentally enriched and impoverished rats, it seems reasonable to predict that, to the extent that novelty may substitute for drug reward, high novelty seekers may be most affected by such prevention and treatment interventions.

References

Badiani, A., Oates, M. M., Day H. E. W., Watson, S. J., Akil, H., & Robinson, T. E. (1998). Amphetamine-induced behavior, dopamine release, and *c-fos* mRNA expression: Modulation by environmental novelty. *Journal of Neuroscience, 18,* 10579–10593.

Bardo, M. T., & Bevins, R. A. (2000). Conditioned place preference: What does it add to our preclinical understanding of drug reward? *Psychopharmacology, 153,* 31–43.

Bardo, M. T., Bowling, S. L., Robinet, P. M., Rowlett, J. K., Lacy, M., & Mattingly, B. A. (1993). Role of D_1 and D_2 receptors in novelty-maintained place preference. *Experimental and Clinical Psychopharmacology, 1,* 101–109.

Bardo, M. T., Bowling, S. L., Rowlett, J. K., Manderscheid, P., Buxton, S. T., & Dwoskin, L. P. (1995). Environmental enrichment attenuates locomotor sensitization, but not in vitro dopamine release, induced by amphetamine. *Pharmacology Biochemistry and Behavior, 51,* 397–405.

Bardo, M. T., Donohew, R. L., & Harrington, N. G. (1996). Psychobiology of novelty-seeking and drug-seeking behavior. *Behavioural Brain Research, 77,* 23–43.

Bardo, M. T., & Hammer, R. P. (1991). Autoradiographic localization of dopamine D_1 and D_2 receptors in rat nucleus accumbens: Resistance to differential rearing conditions. *Neuroscience, 45,* 281–290.

Bardo, M. T., Klebaur, J. E., Valone, J. M., & Deaton, C. (2001). Environmental enrichment decreases intravenous self-administration of amphetamine in female and male rats. *Psychopharmacology, 155,* 278–284.

Bardo, M. T., Robinet, P. M., & Hammer, R. P. (1997). Effect of differential rearing environments on morphine induced behaviors, opioid receptors and dopamine neurotransmission. *Neuropharmacology, 36,* 251–259.

Bardo, M. T., Valone, J., Robinet, P. M., Buxton, S., Shaw, W., & Dwoskin, L. P. (1999). Environmental enrichment enhances the stimulant effect of intravenous amphetamine: Search for a cellular mechanism in the nucleus accumbens. *Psychobiology, 27,* 292–299.

Barnes, G. W., & Baron, A. (1961). Stimulus complexity and sensory reinforcement. *Journal of Comparative and Physiological Psychology, 54,* 466–469.

Beaufour, C. C., Le Bihan, C., Hamon, M., & Thiebot M. H. (2001). Extracellular dopamine in the rat prefrontal cortex during reward-, punishment- and novelty-associated behavior: Effects of diazepam. *Pharmacology Biochemistry and Behavior, 69,* 133–142.

Berlyne, D. E. (1958). The influence of the albedo and complexity of stimuli on visual fixation in the human infant. *British Journal of Psychology, 49,* 315–318.

Besheer, J., Jensen, H. C., & Bevins, R. A. (1999). Dopamine antagonism in a novel-object recognition and a novel-object place conditioning preparation in rats. *Behavioural Brain Research, 103,* 35–44.

Bevins, R. A. (2001). Novelty seeking and reward: Implications for the study of high-risk behaviors. *Current Directions in Psychological Science, 10,* 189–193.

Bevins, R. A., & Bardo, M. T. (1999). Conditioned increase in place preference by access to novel objects: Antagonism by MK-801. *Behavioural Brain Research, 99,* 53–60.

Bevins, R. A., Besheer, J., Palmatier, M. I., Jensen, H. C., Pickett, K. S., & Eurek, S. (2002). Novel-object place conditioning: behavioral and dopaminergic processes in expression of novelty reward. *Behavioural Brain Research, 129,* 41–50.

Bexton, W. H., Heron, W., & Scott, T. H. (1954). Effects of decreased variation in the sensory environment. *Canadian Journal of Psychology, 8,* 70–76.

Bickerdicke, M. J., Wright, I. K., & Marsden, C. A. (1993). Social isolation attenuates rat forebrain 5-HT release induced by KCl stimulation and exposure to a novel environment. *Behavioural Pharmacology, 4,* 231–236.

Bowling, S. L., & Bardo, M. T. (1994). Locomotor and rewarding effects of amphetamine in enriched, social and isolate reared rats. *Pharmacology Biochemistry and Behavior, 48,* 459–464.

Bowling, S. L., Rowlett, J. K., & Bardo, M. T. (1993). The effect of environmental enrichment on amphetamine-stimulated locomotor activity, dopamine synthesis and dopamine release. *Neuropharmacology, 32,* 885–893.

Budney, A. J., Higgins, S. T., Radonovich, K. J., & Novy, P. L. (2000). Adding voucher-based incentives to coping skills and motivational enhancement improves outcomes during treatment for marijuana dependence. *Journal of Consulting and Clinical Psychology, 68,* 1051–1061.

Butler, R. A. (1953). Discrimination learning by rhesus monkeys to visual exploration motivation. *Journal of Comparative and Physiological Psychology, 46,* 95–98.

Butler, R. A. (1957). Discrimination learning by rhesus monkeys to auditory incentives. *Journal of Comparative and Physiological Psychology, 50,* 239–241.

Carr, D. B., & Sesack, S. R. (2000). Projections from the rat prefrontal cortex to the ventral tegmental area: Target specificity in the synaptic associations with mesoaccumbens and mesocortical neurons. *Journal of Neuroscience, 20,* 3864–3873.

Carroll, M. E., & Lac, S. T. (1993). Autoshaping i.v. cocaine self-administration in rats: Effects of nondrug alternative reinforcers on acquisition. *Psychopharmacology, 110,* 5–12.

Cooper, R. M., & Zubek, J. P. (1958). Effects of enriched and restricted early environment on the learning ability of bright and dull rats. *Canadian Journal of Psychology, 12,* 159–164.

Crabbe J. C., Phillips, T. J., Buck, K. J., Cunningham, C. L., & Belknap, J. K. (1999). Identifying genes for alcohol and drug sensitivity: Recent progress and future directions. *Trends in Neuroscience, 22,* 173–179.

Dalley, J. W., & Stanford, S. C. (1995). Incremental changes in extracellular noradrenaline availability in the frontal cortex induced by naturalistic environmental stimuli: A microdialysis study in the freely moving rat. *Journal of Neurochemistry, 65,* 2644–2651.

Day, H. E. W., Badiani, A., Uslaner, J. M., Oates, M. M., Vittoz, N. M., Robinson, T. E., Watson, S. J., & Akil, H. (2001). Environmental novelty differentially affects *c-fos* mRNA expression induced by amphetamine or cocaine in subregions of the bed nucleus of the stria terminalis and amygdala. *Journal of Neuroscience, 21,* 732–740.

Dember, W. N. (1961). Alternation behavior. In D. W. Fiske, & S. R. Maddi (Eds.), *Functions of varied experience* (pp. 227–252). Homewood IL: Dorsey.

Diamond, M. C., Law, F., Rhodes, H., Linder, B., Rosenzweig, M. R., Krech, D., et al. (1966). Increases in cortical depth and glia numbers in rats subjected to enriched environments. *Journal of Comparative Neurology, 128,* 117–126.

Domjan, M., Schorr, R., & Best, M. (1977). Early environmental influences on conditioned and unconditioned ingestional and locomotor behavior. *Developmental Psychobiology, 10,* 499–506.

Donohew, R. L., Lorch, E. P., & Palmgreen, P. (1991). Sensation seeking and targeting of televised anti-drug PSAs. In L. Donohew, H. Sypher, & W. Bukoski (Eds.), *Persuasive communication and drug abuse prevention* (pp. 209–226). Hillsdale NJ: Erlbaum.

D'Silva, M. U., Harrington, N. G., Palmgreen, P., Donohew, L., & Lorch, E. P. (2001). Drug use prevention for the high sensation seeker: The role of alternative activities. *Substance Use and Misuse, 36,* 373–385.

Falk, J. L., & Feingold, D. A. (1987). Environmental and cultural factors in the behavioral actions of drugs. In H. Y. Meltzer (Ed.), *Psychopharmacology: The third generation of progress* (pp. 1503–1510). New York: Raven.

Feenstra, M. G., & Botterblom, M. H. (1996). Rapid sampling of extracellular dopamine in the rat prefrontal cortex during food consumption, handling and exposure to novelty. *Brain Research, 742,* 17–24.

Fiala, B. A., Joyce, J. N., & Greenough, W. T. (1978). Environmental complexity modulates growth of granule cell dendrites in developing but not adult hippocampus of rats. *Experimental Neurology, 59,* 372–389.

Fink, J. S., & Smith, G. P. (1979). Decreased locomotor and investigatory exploration after denervation of catecholamine terminal fields in the forebrain of rats. *Journal of Comparative and Physiological Psychology, 93,* 34–65.

Fiske, D. W., & Maddi, S. R. (1961). A conceptual framework. In D. W. Fiske,

& S. R. Maddi (Eds.), *Functions of varied experience* (pp. 11–56). Homewood IL: Dorsey.

Foster, T. C., & Dumas, T. C. (2001). Mechanism for increased hippocampal synaptic strength following differential experience. *Journal of Neurophysiology, 85,* 1377–1383.

Fowler, S. C., Johnson, J. S., Kallman, M. J., Liou, J. R., Wilson, M. C., & Hikal, A. H. (1993). In a drug discrimination procedure isolation-reared rats generalized to lower doses of cocaine and amphetamine than rats reared in an enriched environment. *Psychopharmacology, 110,* 115–118.

Freeman, B. J., & Ray, O. S. (1972). Strain, sex, and environmental effects on appetitively and aversively motivated learning tasks. *Developmental Psychobiology, 5,* 101–109.

Fulford, A. J., & Marsden, C. A. (1997). Effect of isolation-rearing on noradrenaline release in rat hypothalamus and hippocampus in vitro. *Brain Research, 748,* 93–99.

Geyer, M. A., Wilkinson, L. S., Humby, T., & Robbins, T. W. (1993). Isolation rearing of rats produces a deficit in prepulse inhibition of the acoustic startle similar to that of schizophrenia. *Biological Psychiatry, 34,* 361–372.

Goeders, N. E., & Smith, J. E. (1983). Cortical dopaminergic involvement in cocaine reinforcement. *Science, 221,* 773–775.

Gonzalez-Lima, F., Ferchmin, P. A., Eterovic, V. A., & Gonzalez-Lima, E. M. (1994). Metabolic activation of the brain of young rats after exposure to environmental complexity. *Developmental Psychobiology, 27,* 343–351.

Green, E. J., & Greenough, W. T. (1986). Altered synaptic transmission in dentate gyrus of rats reared in complex environments: Evidence from hippocampal slices maintained in vitro. *Journal of Neurophysiology, 55,* 739–750.

Green, T. A., Gehrke, B. J., & Bardo, M. T. (2002). Environmental enrichment decreases intravenous amphetamine self-administration: Dose response functions for fixed- and progressive-ratio schedules. *Psychopharmacology, 162,* 373–378.

Greenough, W. T., Madden, T. C., & Fleischman, T. B. (1972). Effects of isolation, daily handling, and enriched rearing on maze learning. *Psychonomic Science, 27,* 279–280.

Hall, F. S., Humby, T., Wilkinson, L. S., & Robbins, T. W. (1997). The effects of isolation-rearing of rats on behavioral responses to food and environmental novelty. *Physiology and Behavior, 62,* 281–290.

Hart, C. L., Haney, M., Foltin, R. W., & Fischman, M. W. (2000). Alternative reinforcers differentially modify cocaine self-administration by humans. *Behavioural Pharmacology, 11,* 87–91.

Hebb, D. O. (1955). Drives and the C.N.S. (conceptual nervous system). *Psychological Review, 62,* 243–254.

Helmus, T. C., Downey, K. K., Arfken, C. L., Henderson, M. J., & Schuster, C. R. (2001). Novelty seeking as a predictor of treatment retention for heroin dependent cocaine users. *Drug and Alcohol Dependence, 61,* 287–295.

Heron, W., Doane, B. K., & Scott, T. H. (1956). Visual disturbances after prolonged perceptual isolation. *Canadian Journal of Psychology, 10,* 13–18.

Hill, S. Y., & Powell, B. J. (1976). Cocaine and morphine self-administration: Effects of differential rearing. *Pharmacology Biochemistry and Behavior, 5,* 701–704.

Hughes, R. N. (1968). Behavior of male and female rats with free choice of two environments differing in novelty. *Animal Behaviour, 16,* 92–96.

Hull, C. L. (1943). *Principles of behavior.* New York: Appleton-Century-Crofts.

Jones, G. H., Hernandez, T. D., Kendall, D. A., Marsden, C. A., & Robbins, T. W. (1992). Dopaminergic and serotonergic function following isolation rearing in rats: A study of behavioral responses and postmortem and in vivo neurochemistry. *Pharmacology Biochemistry and Behavior, 43,* 17–35.

Juraska, J. M., Greenough, W. T., & Conlee, J. W. (1983). Differential rearing affects responsiveness of rats to depressant and convulsant drugs. *Physiology and Behavior, 31,* 711–715.

Kempermann, G., Kuhn, H. G., & Gage, F. H. (1997). More hippocampal neurons in adult mice living in an enriched environment. *Nature, 386,* 493–495.

Klebaur, J. E., Bevins, R. A., Segar, T. M., & Bardo, M. T. (2001). Individual differences in behavioral responses to novelty and amphetamine self-administration in female and male rats. *Behavioural Pharmacology, 12,* 267–275.

Krech, D., Rosenzweig, M. R., & Bennett, E. L. (1960). Effects of environmental complexity and training on brain chemistry. *Journal of Comparative and Physiological Psychology, 53,* 509–519.

Liang, N. Y., & Rutledge, C. O. (1984). Comparison of the release of [^{3}H]dopamine from isolated corpus striatum by amphetamine, fenfluramine and unlabeled dopamine. *Biochemical Pharmacology, 31,* 983–992.

Lisman, J. E., & Otmakhova, N. A. (2001). Storage, recall, and novelty detection of sequences by the hippocampus: Elaborating on the SOCRATIC model to account for normal and aberrant effects of dopamine. *Hippocampus, 11,* 551–568.

Lore, R. K., & Levowitz, A. (1966). Differential rearing and free versus forced exploration. *Psychonomic Science, 5,* 21–422.

Marx, M. H., Henderson, R. L., & Roberts, C. L. (1955). Positive reinforcement of the bar-pressing response by a light stimulus following dark operant pretests with no aftereffect. *Journal of Comparative and Physiological Psychology, 48,* 73–75.

McGregor, A., & Roberts, D. C. S. (1995). Effect of medial prefrontal cortex injections of SCH 23390 on intravenous cocaine self-administration under both a fixed and progressive ratio schedule of reinforcement. *Behavioural Brain Research, 67,* 75–80.

Mirenowicz, J., & Schultz, W. (1994). Importance of unpredictability for reward responses in primate dopamine neurons. *Journal of Neurophysiology, 72,* 1024–1027.

Misslin, R., Ropartz, P., & Jung, L. (1984). Impairment of responses to novelty by apomorphine and its antagonism by neuroleptics in mice. *Psychopharmacology, 82,* 113–117.

Miura, H., Qiao, H., & Ohta, T. (2002). Attenuating effects of the isolated rearing condition on increased brain serotonin and dopamine turnover elicited by novelty stress. *Brain Research, 926,* 10–17.

Mogenson, G. J., & Nielsen, M. (1984). Neuropharmacological evidence to suggest that the nucleus accumbens and subpallidal region contribute to exploratory locomotion. *Behavioral and Neural Biology, 42,* 52–60.

Morabia, A., Fabre, J., Chee, E., Zeger, S., Orsat, E., & Robert, A. (1989). Diet and opiate addiction: A quantitative assessment of the diet of non-institutionalized opiate addicts. *British Journal of Addiction, 84,* 173–180.

Murase, S., Grenhoff, J., Chouvet, G., Gonon, F. G., & Svensson, T. H. (1993). Prefrontal cortex regulates burst firing and transmitter release in rat mesolimbic dopamine neurons studied in vivo. *Neuroscience Letters, 157,* 53–56.

Murphy, C. A., & Feldon, J. (2001). Interactions between environmental stimulation and antipsychotic drug effects on forebrain *c-fos* activation. *Neuroscience, 104,* 717–730.

Nader, M. A., & Woolverton, W. L. (1991). Effects of increasing the magnitude of an alternative reinforcer on drug choice in a discrete-trials choice procedure. *Psychopharmacology, 105,* 169–174.

Nilsson, M., Perfilieva, E., Johansson, U., Orwar, O., & Eriksson, P. S. (1999). Enriched environment increases neurogenesis in the adult rat dentate gyrus and improves spatial memory. *Journal of Neurobiology, 39,* 569–578.

Olds, J., & Milner, P. (1954). Positive reinforcement produced by electrical stimulation of septal area and other regions of the brain. *Journal of Comparative and Physiological Psychology, 47,* 419–427.

Oliverio, A., & Messeri, P. (1973). An analysis of single-gene effects on avoidance, maze, wheel running and exploratory behavior in the mouse. *Behavioral Biology, 8,* 771–783.

Palmgreen, P., Donohew, L., Lorch, E. P., Hoyle, R. H., & Stephenson, M. T. (2001). Television campaigns and adolescent marijuana use: Tests of sensation seeking targeting. *American Journal of Public Health, 91,* 292–296.

Peeler, D. F., & Nowakowski, R. S. (1987). Genetic factors and the measurement of exploratory activity. *Behavioral and Neural Biology, 48,* 90–103.

Pham, T. M., Ickes, B., Albeck, D., Soderstrom, S., Granholm, A. C., & Mohammed, A. H. (1999). Changes in brain nerve growth factor levels and nerve growth factor receptors in rats exposed to environmental enrichment for one year. *Neuroscience, 94,* 279–286.

Pham, T. M., Soderstrom, S., Winblad, B., & Mohammed, A. H. (1999). Effects of environmental enrichment on cognitive function and hippocampal NGF in the non-handled rat. *Behavioural Brain Research, 103,* 63–70.

Phillips, G. D., Howes, S. R., Whitelaw, R. B., Wilkinson, L. S. Robbins, T. W.,

& Everitt, B. J. (1994). Isolation rearing enhances the locomotor response to cocaine and a novel environment, but impairs the intravenous self-administration of cocaine. *Psychopharmacology, 115,* 407–418.

Piazza, P. V., Deminiere, J. M., Le Moal, M., & Simon, H. (1989). Factors that predict individual vulnerability to amphetamine self-administration. *Science, 245,* 1511–1513.

Pierce, R. C., Crawford, C. A., Nonneman, A. J., Mattingly, B. A., & Bardo, M. T. (1990). Effect of forebrain dopamine depletion on novelty-induced place preference behavior in rats. *Pharmacology Biochemistry and Behavior, 36,* 321–325.

Pierre, P. J., & Vezina, P. (1997). Predisposition to self-administer amphetamine: The contribution of response to novelty and prior exposure to the drug. *Psychopharmacology, 129,* 277–284.

Rebec, G. V., Christensen, J. R. C., Guerra, C., & Bardo, M. T. (1997). Regional and temporal differences in dopamine efflux in the nucleus accumbens during free-choice novelty.*Brain Research, 776,* 61–67.

Reige, W. H., & Morimoto, H. (1970). Effects of chronic stress and differential environments upon brain weights and biogenic amine levels in rats. *Journal of Comparative and Physiological Psychology, 71,* 396–404.

Reith, M. E., Coffey, L. L., Xu, C., & Chen, N. H. (1994). GBR12909 and 12935 block dopamine uptake into brain synaptic vesicles as well as nerve endings. *European Journal of Pharmacology, 253,* 175–178.

Renner, M. J., & Rosenzweig, M. R. (1986). Object interactions in juvenile rats *(rattus norvegicus):* Effects of different experiential histories. *Journal of Comparative Psychology, 100,* 229–236.

Renner, M. J., & Rosenzweig, M. R. (1987). *Enriched and impoverished environments: Effects on brain and behavior.* New York: Springer-Verlag.

Richardson, N. R., & Roberts, D. C. S. (1996). Progressive ratio schedules in drug self-administration studies in rats: A method to evaluate reinforcing efficacy. *Journal of Neuroscience Methods, 66,* 1–11.

Rockman, G. E., Hall, A. M., Markert, L. E., & Glavin, G. B. (1988). Influence of rearing conditions on voluntary ethanol intake and response to stress in rats. *Behavioral and Neural Biology, 49,* 184–191.

Rosenzweig, M. R., Krech, D., Bennett, E. L., & Diamond, M. C. (1962). Effects of environmental complexity and training on brain chemistry and anatomy: A replication and extension. *Journal of Comparative and Physiological Psychology, 55,* 429–437.

Sahakian, B. J., Robbins, T. W., & Iversen, S. D. (1977). The effects of isolation on exploration in the rat. *Animal Learning and Behavior, 5,* 193–198.

Schenk, S., Lacelle, G, Gorman, K., & Amit, Z. (1987). Cocaine self-administration in rats influenced by environmental conditions: Implications for the etiology of drug abuse. *Neuroscience Letters, 81,* 227–231.

Schenk S., & Partridge, B. (1997). Sensitization and tolerance in psychostimulant self-administration. *Pharmacology Biochemistry and Behavior, 57,* 543–550.

Schultz, W., & Dickinson, A. (2000). Neuronal coding of prediction errors. *Annual Review of Neuroscience, 23,* 473–500.
Sheldon, A. B. (1969). Preference for familiar versus novel stimuli as a function of the familiarity of the environment. *Journal of Comparative Physiology and Psychology, 67,* 516–521.
Sirevaag, A. M., & Greenough, W. T. (1988). A multivariate statistical summary of synaptic plasticity measures in rats exposed to complex, social and individual environments. *Brain Research, 441,* 386–392.
Smith, J. K., Neill, J. C., & Costall, B. (1997). Post-weaning housing conditions influence the behavioral effects of cocaine and *d*-amphetamine. *Psychopharmacology, 131,* 23–33.
Spanagel, R., & Weiss, F. (1999). The dopamine hypothesis of reward: Past and current status. *Trends in Neuroscience, 22,* 521–527.
Sulzer, D., Chen, T. K., Lau, Y. Y., Kristensen, H., Rayport, S., & Ewing, A. (1995). Amphetamine redistributes dopamine from synaptic vesicles to the cytosol and promotes reverse transport. *Journal of Neuroscience, 15,* 4102–4108.
Thompson, W. R. (1955). Early development—its importance for later behavior. In P. H. Hoch, & J. Zubin (Eds.), *Psychopathology of childhood* (pp. 120–139). New York: Gurne and Stratton.
Vankov, A., Herve-Minvielle, A., & Sara, S. J. (1995). Response to novelty and its rapid habituation in locus coeruleus of the freely exploring rat. *European Journal of Neuroscience, 7,* 1180–1187.
Varty, G. B., Paulus, M. P., Braff, D. L., & Geyer, M. A. (2000). Environmental enrichment and isolation rearing in the rat: Effects on locomotor behavior and startle response plasticity. *Biological Psychiatry, 47,* 864–873.
Wallace, C. S., Kilman, V. L., Withers, G. S., & Greenough, W. T. (1992). Increases in dendritic length in occipital cortex after 4 days of differential housing in weanling rats. *Behavioral and Neural Biology, 58,* 64–68.
Walsh, R. N., Budtz-Olsen, O. E., Penny, J. E., & Cummings, R. A. (1969). The effects of environmental complexity on the histology of the rat hippocampus. *Journal of Comparative Neurology, 137,* 361–366.
Weissenborn, R., & Winn, P. (1992). Regulatory behaviour, exploration and locomotion following NMDA or 6-OHDA lesions in the rat nucleus accumbens. *Behavioural Brain Research, 51,* 127–137.
Welker, W. I. (1959). Escape, exploratory, and food-seeking responses of rats in a novel situation. *Journal of Comparative and Physiological Psychology, 52,* 106–111.
Welker, W. I. (1961). An analysis of exploratory and play behavior in animals. In D. W. Fiske, & S. R. Maddi (Eds.), *Functions of varied experience* (pp. 175–226). Homewood IL: Dorsey.
Wemelsfelder, F., Haskell, M., Mendl, M. T., Calvert, S., & Lawrence, A. B. (2000). Diversity of behaviour during novel object tests is reduced in pigs housed in substrate-impoverished conditions. *Animal Behaviour, 60,* 385–394.

Widman, D. R., & Rosellini, R. A. (1990). Restricted daily exposure to environmental enrichment increases the diversity of exploration. *Physiology and Behavior, 47,* 57–62.

Williams, B. M., Luo, Y., Ward, C., Redd, K., Gibson, R., Kuczaj, S. A., & McCoy, J. G. (2001). Environmental enrichment: Effects on spatial memory and hippocampal CREB immunoreactivity. *Physiology and Behavior, 73,* 649–658.

Wills, T. A., Windle, M., & Cleary, S. D. (1998). Temperament and novelty seeking in adolescent substance use: Convergence of dimensions of temperament with constructs from Cloninger's theory. *Journal of Personality and Social Psychology, 74,* 387–406.

Wise, R. A. (1987). Intravenous drug self-administration: A special case of positive reinforcement. In M. A. Bozarth (Ed.), *Methods of assessing the reinforcing properties of abused drugs* (pp. 117–141). New York: Springer-Verlag.

Wise, R. A. (1989). The brain and reward. In J. M. Liebman, & S. J. Cooper (Eds.), *The neuropharmacological basis of reward* (pp. 377–424). New York: Oxford.

Yamamoto, M. E., Block, G. D., & Ishii, E. (1991). Food patterns among adolescents: Influence of alcohol consumption. *Alcoholism: Clinical and Experimental Research, 15,* 359.

Zhu, J., Green, T., Bardo, M. T., & Dwoskin, L. P. (In press). Environmental enrichment enhances sensitization to GBR12935-induced activity and decreases dopamine transporter function. *Behavioural Brain Research.*

Zimmerberg, B., & Brett, M. B. (1992). Effects of early environmental experience on self-administration of amphetamine and barbital. *Psychopharmacology, 106,* 474–478.

Zimmermann, A., Stauffacher, M., Langhans, W., & Würbel, H. (2001). Enrichment-dependent differences in novelty exploration in rats can be explained by habituation. *Behavioural Brain Research, 121,* 11–20.

Zuckerman, M. (1994). *Behavioral expressions and biosocial bases of sensation seeking.* Cambridge, England: Cambridge.

Drive, Incentive, and Reinforcement: The Antecedents and Consequences of Motivation

Roy A. Wise
National Institute on Drug Abuse, NIH

The aim of scientific explanation is to characterize the important antecedents of observable (or at least objectively confirmable) events. Explanations of behavior in terms of motivational states are appeals to unobservable, internal events for interpretations of behavior that is variable under apparently constant external stimulus conditions (see, e.g., Brown, 1953; Hinde, 1960). To be identified as the cause of a behavior, the unobservable event or condition must preexist the behavioral event to be explained. A behavior cannot be explained by its consequences, though it may be explained as a consequence of similar events in the animal's history. Scientific explanation involves the sequential identification of what comes first and what follows. To understand correctly what comes first and what follows is to achieve the primary goal of science.

While the teleology of Aristotle's notion of "final causes" encouraged the explanation of what comes first by what comes *after*, the major advance of the scientific revolution was to substitute mechanical causes—necessary and sufficient conditions (the "efficient causes" of Aristotle)—for the "final causes" previously legitimized by Aristotle's teachings (see Aristotle, Physics, in Barnes, 1984). Galileo precip-

I thank Leon Brown, Satoshi Ikemoto, Yavin Shaham, and Abraham Zangen for insightful comments on earlier versions of this chapter.

itated the culling of Aristotelean teleology from physics; we no longer accept Aristotle's notion that heavy things fall faster than light ones or his teleological suggestion that they do so "in order to reach their natural place." Two centuries after Galileo, Darwin (1859) offered a nonteleological explanation for human evolution; his principles of random mutation and natural selection offered a mechanistic alternative to the Aristotelean notion that human evolution was partly determined by the goal or intention of a creator. Skinner's (1966) parallel suggestion that behavior is generated randomly and selected by its consequences was an attempt to go beyond the rigidity of reflexes while avoiding the teleology inherent in the notion of goal direction. The apparent goal direction of motivated behavior explains nothing; it is the mystery that remains to be explained.

The problem of teleology is the problem of suggesting a consequence—something that follows—as the explanation of its cause—something that came first. A major challenge for psychology is to find mechanistic alternatives to teleological explanations of behavior. For psychology to advance our understanding of behavior within the scientific paradigm it must find the efficient causes—the necessary and sufficient antedating conditions—for behaviors that appear to be controlled by their consequences. This was really the quest of Skinner: the explanation of a given act in terms of its reinforcement history rather than in terms of the animal's presumed intentions. In no sphere of psychology is the temptation to explain an act by its intended consequences stronger than in the field of motivation. Eating is "explained" with the notion that it satisfies the bodily need for energy repletion; sexual behavior is "explained" with the notion that it satisfies the need of the species (or the "need" of the gene) for reproduction. The implication is that sex is initiated in order to reproduce the species and that eating is initiated in order to replenish energy reserves. These are Aristotelian—teleological—explanations. They do not advance our understanding. The task is to impose the step-by-step analysis of linear thinking—the efficient causes of Aristotle (what comes first and what follows)—on the cycles of hunger and satiety that offer our dominant model of motivation.

The Problem of Definition

As can be seen from a survey of articles from the Nebraska Symposia of years past, there has never been an adequate scientific definition of motivation. As Beach (1956) once noted on a related topic, "Most writers are satisfied to begin with the uncritical assumption of a mutual understanding between their readers and themselves"(p. 1). Not even in undergraduate textbooks can we find a definition that clearly differentiates motivational from nonmotivational phenomena. Jones, in introducing this symposium in 1955, identified the problem of motivation as the problem of "how behavior gets started, is energized, is sustained, is directed, is stopped, and what kind of subjective reaction is present in the organism while all this is going on" (p. vii). Jones has reserved the whole field of psychology for the motivational specialist. His statement gives us little insight as to an exclusionary rule; what does not fall under the rubric of motivation? In Beck's (1978) text the following was offered in place of a definition: "Motivation is broadly concerned with the contemporary determinants of choice (direction), persistence, and vigor of goal-directed behavior" (p. 24). Beck acknowledged that this is not a definition, apologizing that we cannot "just define motivation; we define a set of variables that are called motivational" (p. 25). The problem, not solved by Beck, is to define the set of such variables in such a way as to define equally the set of nonmotivational variables. Petri's (1981) popular textbook suggests that motivation is "the concept we use when we describe the forces acting on or within an organism to initiate and direct behavior" (p. 3). None of these distinguishes motivation as a subcategory of behavior; none distinguishes motivational theory as distinct from general behavior theory. Most writers have not come to grips with the problem of differentiating motivation from everything else.

Given this serious problem of definition, motivational theory rests on lists rather than principles. The traditional list includes three main motivational variables: drive, incentive, and reinforcement. There is no consensus as to whether these variables are to be invoked merely to explain the intensity of behavior, as argued by some authors (e.g., Brown, 1953; Hebb, 1955; Hull, 1943; Woodworth, 1918), or to explain both the intensity and the direction of behavior as suggested by others (e.g., Bindra, 1974; Teitelbaum, 1966; Toates, 1986; Young, 1949).

The Variables of Motivation

DRIVE

Early attempts to explain behavior involved inflexible reflexes and instincts as their basic elements. Reflexes and instincts were too rigid to accommodate instrumental behavior (e.g., Skinner, 1931, 1932), and instincts proved unpalatable because of the conceit that what applied to other animals did not apply to humans. While the instincts that figure in the theories of James and McDougall were not carried forward into more modern theories of behavior, the concept of drive, introduced by Woodworth in 1918, took their place. Woodworth posited multiple drives, the prototypes being hunger and thirst. Woodworth's notion was influenced by Sherrington's (1906) distinction between "preparatory" and "consummatory" (referring to consummation rather than consumption) behaviors. Preparatory or "anticipatory" reactions were seen by Sherrington as responses to distant stimuli that constituted the "attempt either to obtain actual contact or to avoid actual contact with the object" (p. 326). The basic tendencies to approach or withdraw from environmental stimuli were fundamental to Pavlov's early notions of orienting or investigatory reflexes on the one hand and defensive reflexes on the other (see, e.g., Sokolov, 1963). Craig's (1918) Sherrington-like distinction between "appetitive" and consummatory behaviors linked the root of the word "appetite" to the approach behaviors of investigation and manipulation. The tendency to approach or withdraw that was common to Pavlov's and Sherrington's basic reflexes would become the cornerstone of the important theory of motivation developed by Schneirla (1939, 1959) and extended by Glickman and Schiff (1967).

Woodworth characterized the preparatory stage of a reaction as being marked by a state of tension, the strength of which was proportional to the strength of the drive that would see the action through to its consummatory stage (completion). The drive theory first articulated by Woodworth was expanded on by later behaviorists, such as Hull (1943) and Hebb (1955). Inherent in Woodworth's view (as in Hull's and Hebb's) was the postulate that drive was directly responsible for the intensity of behavior but not, directly, for the direction or selection of behavior. By intensifying the responsiveness to food (by making food-related incentives more salient), however, hunger could indirectly increase the probability of feeding at the cost of play, sex, or some other alternative. The analogy of Hebb (1955) was to the automobile. In his model drive is like the gas pedal, determining how fast the car will go (or whether it will move at all), whereas environmental cues govern the steering function, determining the direction the car will take (when and if it moves). While this distinction has generally not been made in social or personality theory, it has played a major role in behaviorist theories.

Hull attempted to tie his drive concept closely to tissue needs. It was easy to accept that hunger was a response to caloric needs and thirst a response to hydrational needs. By tying drive states to physiological need, he offered a definition of drive that was not based on the behavior it was used to explain. By suggesting that the reduction of a need state was the necessary and sufficient condition for reinforcement of learning, he offered a plausible and noncircular theory of how adaptive behavior is learned. However, like many simple, elegant, and testable ideas, his was quickly shown to have major shortcomings. First, rats learn to lever press not only for glucose, which replenishes the energy reserves of the body, but also for saccharin, which is useless as a bodily fuel (Sheffield & Roby, 1950). Second, most drinking in laboratory rats is ancillary to the eating of dry food rather than dictated by dehydration (Kissileff, 1969). Third, and perhaps more fatal than each of these flaws, eating and drinking anticipate (develop prior to) need; we usually eat and drink long before we develop states of tissue need (Fitzsimons, 1972; Le Magnen, 1969). The growing problem of obesity in modern society should make it clear that the feeding behavior can be robust and compulsive in the absence of any serious threat of tissue need. Fourth, Hull's notion that drive is a general state, something akin to an arousal state, and that it energizes all motivated behaviors under a common guiding principle was unworkable. While it sidestepped the triviality of Woodworth's multiple drives (each with its own rules and hence each with little generality), it offered an unsuitable model for sex, play, or even the avoidance of pain (see, e.g. Fiske & Maddi, 1961; Harlow, 1953). As pointed out by Beach (1956, p. 3) "Sexual activity is not, in the biological sense, essential to the well-being of the individual. Despite the fact that arguments to the contrary often provide a convenient rationalization during certain stages of life, no one ever died for the lack of sex." The argument that, just as hunger and thirst were essential to the survival of the individual, sex was essential to the survival of the species was specious; it is difficult to imagine that a copulating rat has the survival of its species on its mind.

INCENTIVE MOTIVATION

The attempt to define motivation in terms of needs and drives failed for a variety of additional reasons. While it is easy to imagine that hunger and thirst are controlled by internal factors reflecting need states, it is difficult to exclude a role for external factors in these—and a dominating role for external factors in other—motivations. Male sexual arousal, for example, is often excited by purely visual or olfactory stimuli. The sight of an attractive female can quickly turn a male's thoughts away from other matters. The smell of a receptive female can awaken a male rodent from sleep, elevate its brain temperature 1° or 1.5° C, and channel its behavior from other activities to the vigorous pursuit of social interaction (E. A. Kiyatkin & R. A. Wise, unpublished observations). While it might be suggested that sexual arousal is controlled by hormones—particularly in lower species—Lehrman's (1965) elegant studies of the reproductive cycles of ring doves illustrate how the hormonal levels that dominate the motivational states of the dove are themselves triggered by external stimulus displays. The feedback from one behavior triggers release of the hormones that induce sensitivity to the stimuli that, in turn, elicit the next behavior in the reproductive sequence. Indeed, even in the case of feeding it proved necessary to modify Hull's model to include what Spence (1956) labeled as "incentive motivation": the energizing of the animal by the food incentive and the otherwise neutral stimuli that become associated with food in the development of food-seeking habits.

Incentive motivation, a drivelike state-variable, was formulated as a contribution to the energizing of behavior rather than to the selection of behavior. A familiar example is the motivational state that results from the tasting of a salted peanut. A weak impulse—arguably elicited by the sight of available nuts—to eat a peanut accounts for the tasting of the first nut. The tasting of the first nut, however—the "sampling" of the incentive—arouses much stronger responsiveness to the remaining nuts. The person will now pursue with more force the nuts that, at first, elicited a weak attraction. The difference in response strength between reaching for the first nut and reaching for the second is the portion of response strength attributed to the initial contact with the incentive. The subject now has stronger arousal and stronger responsiveness to nuts than existed on the strength of either the physiological state or the stimulus situation that existed a moment earlier. The enhanced arousal and responsiveness is incentive motivation (meaning incentive-induced motivation or arousal rather than incentive-directed motivation or arousal). The increased responsiveness to the second nut suggests that the salience of the stimulus (Robinson & Berridge, 1993; Stewart, de Wit, & Eikelboom, 1984) has been increased by the tasting of the first nut. It is as if the second nut—as a result of increased appetite induced by the taste of the first nut—is brighter and more fragrant than the first nut. The construct of incentive motivation is normally invoked to explain the arousal associated with conditioned incentive stimuli rather than with the primary incentives themselves.

Bolles (1975) explains how the motivational state—presumably contributing to the strength and not the selection of a response—has what appears to be a response-eliciting power in a food reinforcement task: "when the hungry rat looks to the water side, nothing happens; but when it looks to the food side, it gets excited; thus it is more likely to go to the food side" (p. 294). Thus it is the sight, smell, taste, touch, or sound of the incentive that determines the direction of the behavior, and the combination of any internal drive state plus any incentive-motivational state that determines how strongly the subject is attracted in that direction.

REINFORCEMENT

Reinforcement, as a motivational topic, is in some ways an unlikely bedfellow for drive and incentive motivation. Reinforcement is more easily related to topics of learning and memory than to the topic of motivation. Reinforcement comes after motivated behavior whereas drive and incentive motivation precede the behavior and energize it. Reinforcement is defined as a mechanism for strengthening the relations between conditioned and unconditioned stimuli (Pavlov, 1928) or for stamping in the associations between stimuli and responses (Thorndike, 1898), not as a mechanism for changing the momentary state of mind of the animal. The fluctuations in response probability that accompany fluctuations in motivation are phasic, reversible changes like the waxing and waning of hunger and satiety or of sexual arousal and refractoriness. The effects of reinforcement, on the other hand, cause relatively permanent changes in response probability, acting to modify, it is thought, the long-term relations between synapses in the brain rather than the short-term levels of nutrients or hormones in the blood. Nonetheless, reinforcement is part and parcel of the topic of motivation. There are several reasons.

First, the incentives that are primary to incentive motivation are, or lead to, reinforcers (Schnierla, 1939, 1959). The things approached are the things that reinforce exploratory approach patterns, converting them, gradually, into approach habits. The primary reinforcers are things that confer incentive value on the otherwise neutral stimuli that mark the path to food sources, fluid sources, and places of shelter from the elements. It is association with the primary reinforcer—the loved one—that makes special the "street where she lives."

Second, the reinforcers that stamp in memory traces do so variably as a function of motivational states. Food is ineffective as a reinforcer when the animal is sated; indeed, lever pressing for food progressively extinguishes if the animal is tested when sated (Morgan, 1974). Similarly, the tendency to lever press for intravenous drugs extinguishes under conditions of intoxication. Thus it is not just ongoing behavior that waxes and wanes with motivational state, so too does the reinforcing efficacy of various incentives.

The Correlates of Motivation

There is a strong movement to identify the subjective states of motivation, particularly within the field of addiction (see, e.g., Hetherington, 2001; Pickens & Johanson 1992; Tiffany, 1990). While many have argued that they are unknowable, speculations about the subjective states of even the laboratory rat generate considerable interest (Acquas, Carboni, Leone, & Di Chiara, 1989; Koob 1996; Robinson & Berridge, 1993, 2001; Rossetti, Lai, Hmaidan, & Gessa, 1993; Wise, 1982, 2001).

The subjective correlates of drive are craving, hunger, and desire. To illustrate a point about what comes first and what follows, Robinson and Berridge (1993) have introduced "wanting" as a synonym for craving. Unlike terms like hunger, thirst, and withdrawal distress, which tend to focus on antecedent conditions, such terms focus attention on the subject's state of mind prior to the behavior of interest. For those who posit that we work to reduce drive states (e.g., Dackis & Gold, 1985; Hull 1943; Koob, Stinus, Le Moal, & Bloom, 1989), it is generally assumed that these are, to one degree or another, unpleasant states. Indeed, it is clear that, if they have the choice, animals will avoid the places where they have experienced the conditions associated with such states (Bechara, Nader, & van der Kooy, 1995).

The subjective correlates of incentive motivation—wanting, craving, desire, and the like—are common to the subjective correlates of drive. Lust is perhaps the most obvious model here; for the males of most species lust (inferred craving or desire for sexual interaction) is associated more clearly with external arousing stimuli than with internal hormonal levels or conditions of privation.

The subjective correlates of reinforcement can be identified with much less confidence than the subjective correlates of drive or incentive motivation. The widespread assumption is that reinforcement has positive affective correlates. Pleasure and euphoria are the most frequently suggested correlates of reward (McAuliffe & Gordon, 1974, 1980; Olds, 1956); "liking" has been more recently suggested (Robinson & Berridge, 1993). However, it is not at all clear that pleasure is associated with all rewards; monkeys can be trained to work for aversive shock (Kelleher & Morse, 1968) and various compulsive human activities—such as competitive sports and various forms of thrill seeking—are stressful if not painful. Anecdotal evidence would suggest that even addictive drugs can serve as effective reinforcers in the absence of any associated pleasure or euphoria. First-time heroin users, for example, often report that the drug produces nausea and discomfort (Haertzen, 1966); it is, nonetheless, strongly habit forming. After long exposure to heroin, addicts frequently report that the drug continues to control them despite having lost any ability to cause pleasure or euphoria (Chein, Gerard, Lee, & Rosenfeld, 1964). Thus pleasure is clearly not a necessary correlate of reinforcement. Moreover, animals consistently avoid flavors that have been associated with addictive drugs (Cappell & LeBlanc, 1971; Cappell, LeBlanc, & Endrenyi, 1973) despite the fact that they self-administered those drugs (Wise, Yokel, & de Wit, 1976).

The subjective correlates of the absence of pleasure are dysphoria and anhedonia. While it has been suggested that blocking the synaptic action of brain dopamine causes a state of anhedonia or dysphoria—blunting the hedonic impact of food, water, rewarding brain stimulation, and several drugs of abuse (Wise, 1982)—this suggestion was based on evidence that reinforcement function, not hedonic function per se, was attenuated by dopamine blockers (Wise, 1985). While it is clear that dopaminergic blockade attenuates the rewarding effects of amphetamine (Risner & Jones, 1976; Yokel & Wise, 1975, 1976), it has been reported not to block amphetamine-induced euphoria in humans (Brauer & de Wit, 1997, but see Gunne, Änggard, & Jönsson, 1972; Jönsson, Änggard, & Gunne, 1971). Thus, again, pleasure does not appear to be a necessary correlate of the behavioral control exerted by reinforcers.

The Etiology of Addiction

The phenomenon of addiction and the animal models used to study it offer heuristic insights into more conventional motivational states. There are two important features of addiction that differentiate it from more traditional motivations. First, to the degree that drugs come to satisfy bodily needs, it is largely acquired bodily needs that they satisfy (Hebb, 1949; Malmo, 1975); thus in addiction we can study the acquisition of need states that parallel the innate need states associated with hunger and thirst. Second, whereas the incentives of food and water are sensed (we can see, hear, taste, touch, or smell them), the incentives of drugs of abuse are unsensed, at least by laboratory animals that are unable to examine the contents of their remote syringes and protected infusion lines. The animal working for intravenous cocaine or heroin detects the drug by only one of its five peripheral senses (taste), and then only after the drug has been consumed and has diffused into the saliva. The traditional definition of an incentive is that of a thing approached; the animal can never approach an intravenous drug injection or a rewarding brain stimulation event in the way that it can approach a food pellet or a sexual partner. Thus animal models of addiction can reveal aspects of drive and incentive motivation that are not evident with more natural rewards like food, water, or potential mates.

Unlike the cases of hunger and thirst, the case of addiction offers no deficit-driven need for drug at the time of the initial drug reinforcement. What comes first is the first drink, the first puff, the first snort, the first injection. If what is known about reinforcement is valid, the motivation for the second ingestion of a reinforcing dose will be stronger than the motivation for the first. Whatever it is that is stamped in by reinforcers will presumably start strengthening from the very first ingestion. This will include the stamping in of the memory traces of the proprioceptive feedback from the specific responses that led up to the injection, and it will include the stamping in of memory traces associating the drug experience with the various stimuli in the surrounding environment. In some way the reinforcing experience will also decrease the fear of repeating the act. The concerns that accompanied the first ingestion will be weaker with successive ingestions.

What *is* the motivation for the first self-administration of a drug of abuse? This is not easily answered. There are many different motivations—social conformation, peer pressure, status seeking, thrill seeking, relief of boredom, curiosity—so many that we might almost consider the first use of a given drug something akin to the first lever press in an operant chamber: if not an accident, at least not a response that is dependent on any identifiable reinforcement history. However, the motivation for subsequent self-administrations gradually comes under the control of the reinforcement history. Just as natural selection narrows the possibilities for evolution, so does reinforcement narrow the possibilities for future behavior. With each subsequent administration of a reinforcing drug, the freedom of choice—the freedom to accept or decline another administration—is, at least according to reinforcement theory, reduced. In the end, there will be very little freedom of choice for an addict who may have assumed complete freedom during the early stages of drug use; reinforcement is one of the powerful factors that eventually restricts freedom of choice.

Two things change as a subject continues to self-administer a drug. First, there are adaptations of the brain and the gut that occur in the same way and to the same degree whether the subject takes the drug actively or receives it passively. These include adaptations in the autonomic nervous system and changes in the brain circuitry through which the drugs have their rewarding effects. While many of the neuroadaptations—particularly the adaptations of the autonomic nervous system—are unique to the drug or drug class (Kalant, 1977), some of the neuroadaptations of reward circuitry resulting from repeated treatment are common to such different drug classes as the stimulants and the opiates (Beitner-Johnson & Nestler, 1991; Beitner-Johnson, Guitart, & Nestler, 1992; Berhow et al., 1995). It is widely held that some subset of these neuroadaptations must contribute to the fact that drug taking becomes progressively more compulsive with repeated drug self-administration.

Neuroadaptations that are simple and direct consequences of the pharmacological action of the drug cannot, however, explain the rituals of drug procurement, drug preparation, and drug taking that form the habit structure of addiction. Nor can the fact that such drug-induced neuroadaptations involve the brain mechanisms responsible for learning and memory (Berke & Hyman, 2000; Nestler, 2001) explain the critical memory traces that distinguish the brains of self-inflicted addicts from the brains of drug-experienced individuals that do not self-administer the drug. The memory traces that are formed uniquely by the specific acts of drug self-administration thus form a second class of neuroadaptation that clearly plays a central role in the increasingly compulsive nature of drug taking. Indeed, the fact that passive receipt of drug injections can result in neuroadaptations within the brain mechanisms of learning and memory creates a special problem for the addiction theorist: How do we differentiate the neuroadaptations that are associated with a drug-taking habit from the neuroadaptations that are associated with a passive drug-receiving history? Woods (1990) has estimated that fewer than 0.01% of those receiving opiates passively go on to become opiate addicts. Another problem for the theorist is how to distinguish neuroadaptations associated with drug-seeking habits from neuroadaptations associated with food-seeking, sex-seeking, thrill-seeking, or other compulsive habits that depend on shared or parallel motivational circuitry (see Bardo & Dwoskin, this volume).

It is the neuroadaptations associated with the drug-seeking habit and drug-associated memories that are most central to the understanding of the compulsive nature of addiction. This is perhaps most clearly evident from animal models of intracranial self-stimulation and intravenous drug self-administration, where the animals never have direct sensory contact with the stimulation or the drug. Whereas the human addict eventually sees, fondles, smells, and perhaps tastes the drug that is ingested, the animal with a brain stimulation reward habit or an intravenous drug habit has never seen, never touched, never smelled, never tasted its reinforcer. The reinforcer is delivered directly to the brain or to the heart, through wires or infusion catheters that are opaque and ever present. Thus in these cases the reinforcer itself is not the incentive that is approached; only learned incentives—conditioned incentive stimuli—are approached. The things approached are the walls, lights, levers, or nose-poke holes where the animal is able to trigger the hidden mechanisms that deliver the stimulation or the drug. The levers, lights, and holes become learned incentives and secondary reinforcers, as their manipulation or their display becomes associated with time-locked drug delivery. The street corner where drug is purchased (Simon & Burns, 1997), the seller, the pipe or syringe—these are things that become objects of compulsive search and approach. Along with the laying down of learned associations and memories of how to remove the hubcap quietly, how to approach the seller surreptitiously, how to keep the cash safe until the transaction is made, how to slip into the safe house without being noticed by the police or by local freeloaders—along with all these memory traces there accrue, with drug experience, the neuroadaptations associated with the unlearning of various fears. In the case of the laboratory animal, these involve fear of the strange testing situation: the apparatus itself, the handling, the drag of connected stimulating cables or drug lines, the sudden clicks and intravenous pressure or neuronal activation associated with responding. None of these specific memories can be stamped in by the doctor- or experimenter-administered drug injections that produce the neuroadaptations that have been identified to date.

A strong case has been argued for consideration of addiction as a "brain disease" (Leshner, 1997; McLellan, Lewis, O'Brien, & Kleber, 2000). Inasmuch as some drugs of abuse are neurotoxic (Carlson 1977; Schmidt, 1987; Wagner, Ricaurte, Seiden, Schuster, Miller, & Westley, 1980), it is clear that addiction can cause brain disease. What is not yet equally clear, however, is the degree to which brain disease causes addiction. Here we come up against the thorny question of which comes first and which follows. It is often suggested in recent years that mere self-administration of drugs—the self-administration, for example, demonstrated over the last several decades in limited-access animal models—is not tantamount to addiction (e.g., Ahmed & Koob, 1998; Robinson & Berridge, 2000; Tornatzky & Miczek, 2000). With increasing attempts and increasing failure to find an objective, noncircular definition for addiction (Wise, 1987), it has become fashionable to characterize addiction as compulsive drug self-administration, and to look for the event or events that explain the transition from casual to compulsive drug self-administration. The operant psychologist can only wonder how reinforcement itself has come to be seen as insufficient to explain addiction without further postulates. Positive reinforcement is the only explanation sought or offered for the compulsive self-administration of direct electrical stimulation to the lateral hypothalamus, and this is a behavior sufficiently compulsive to lead, like self-administration of cocaine, to self-starvation and death. It has never been suggested that some form of brain disease is required to explain the happy, healthy, long-living (if allowed access to stimulation for only a limited portion of each day), compulsively self-stimulating rat.

The possibility that has status of place in the history of addiction theory is that adaptations to the repeated pharmacological actions of the drug bias the brain and body to such a degree that self-medication becomes necessary for normal mood, function, and homeostasis. Often referred to as dependence theory, this "medical model," or "self-medication hypothesis," is best characterized as an opponent-process view of motivation (Solomon & Corbit, 1974) and addiction (Solomon & Corbit, 1973). In early incarnations, dependence models focused on compensatory responses identified largely with the autonomic nervous system (Wei, Tseng, Loh, & Way, 1974) and the withdrawal distress—sweating, cramps, diarrhea, thermoregulatory disturbance—that is experienced when opiate or alcohol use is discontinued. As evidence accumulated against the view that withdrawal distress was a necessary condition for addiction (Deneau, Yanagita, & Seevers, 1969; Jaffe, 1985; McAuliffe & Gordon, 1980; Wise, 1987; Woods & Schuster, 1971), attention shifted from the adaptations of the autonomic nervous system to adaptations within the brain mechanisms of reward themselves, which might desensitize the subjects to various forms of pleasure and reinforcement (Dackis & Gold, 1985; Frank, Martz, & Pommering, 1988; Kokkinidis, Zacharko, & Predy, 1980; Leith & Barrett, 1976; Markou & Koob, 1991; Nestler, 1992). It is clear that there are many neuroadaptations that result from repeated drug use (Nestler, 2001; White & Kalivas, 1998), and that in the neuroadapted state the drug itself can oppose the effects of at least some of those neuroadaptations: the drug effect, for the moment, shifts the animal back in the direction of normalcy. That is, the drug does "medicate," by opposing them, some of the neuroadaptations induced by past use of the drug. To what degree such neuroadaptations are causes rather than consequences of addiction, however, is only beginning to be examined in depth (Carlezon et al., 1998; Kelz et al., 1999). The answer depends fundamentally on a very simple issue: which comes first and which after? In addition, it is not clear to what effect the known neuroadaptations are drug-opposite in nature; indeed, most of the known neuroadaptations have been found to result from drug treatments that cause sensitization, not tolerance, to the drug in question.

Our own studies of drug self-administration in rodents have led me to suspect that drug self-administration becomes compulsive long before the significant development of most of the recently characterized neuroadaptations. We have no scientific standards for the word "compulsive," but dictionary definitions involve such terms as being compelled, forced, coerced, or constrained: "in psychopathology, an irresistible impulse to perform some irrational act." One measure of compulsion is the domination of the compelling behavior over less compelling alternatives. Rats or monkeys allowed to lever press for unlimited intravenous amphetamine or cocaine injections will do so to the point of death (Bozarth & Wise, 1985; Johanson, Balster, & Bonese, 1976). Thus we normally do not allow our animals unlimited drug access, but restrict them to sessions of 4 hours or less per day.

A second criterion for compulsion is invariance and predictability. Once a habit is established to the point of no return, the most critical transition toward addiction has already occurred. So long as reinforcement continues, the habit will only become more strongly stamped in. Our experienced animals respond for intravenous cocaine at very constant rates, suggesting strongly established habits; the standard deviation of their inter-response times is close to 20% of their mean inter-response time. When their inter-response intervals reach this level of regularity we can predict with great certainty that they would continue to self-administer the drug compulsively to the point of death if given the opportunity. This level of control is evident in some animals within a single day of training; in 90% of our animals it is reached within five days of training in 4-hour daily sessions. In the absence of catheter or vein failures, such a habit will always become progressively more compulsive—that is, the standard deviation of the inter-response times will invariably continue to decrease—over the next few weeks. Thus, after as little as one or two days of training it is often clear that a given animal has already reached the stage of compulsive responding. While drug self-administration during 4-hour periods of drug access per day may not establish the escalated (Ahmed & Koob, 1998) or dysregulated (Tornatzky & Miczek, 2000) intake patterns that become typical of animals tested for longer periods with higher doses or unlimited access, testing animals under conditions of limited access is sufficient to establish self-administration habits that are compulsive enough to irrevocably lead, under unrestricted access, to such escalation and dysregulation. Studies of the neuroadaptations to addictive drugs have, for the most part, been based on much longer and stronger drug exposure than is required to establish the point of no return.

I would not argue this for all drugs, nor would I argue it for all doses or routes of administration of even the psychomotor stimulants. However, in the case of intravenous cocaine, amphetamine, and heroin, I think compulsive habits—irrevocably compulsive habits when drug is freely available—are established very early in the animal's exposure, long before we see signs of escalated or dysregulated intake. Most of the neuroadaptations we are currently studying are established after much more severe regimens of repeated drug administration than are necessary to establish sensitized behavioral responses to the drug.

Whatever the strength of the treatments required to produce them, most of the neuroadaptations we are currently studying are not the neuroadaptations associated with the memory traces of the response habit itself. Continued opportunity for drug self-administration extends the stamping in of the response habit and the stimulus associations that sustain the behavior. Inasmuch as the peripheral senses of the animal are exposed to the manipulandum and surrounding stimuli but not the drug itself, the things the animal learns to approach are the features of the test box that, until associated with reinforcement, have only the appeal of novelty. In our paradigm, the most obvious learned incentives are the lever and the light above the lever. We see a form of autoshaping as the habit becomes established. Our light is illuminated whenever the pump is delivering drug; it gives the signal that the animal has made the required response and that the drug effect will soon be felt. At first the rat just appears to notice the light, glancing at it briefly after each response. In time the animal begins to approach the light, sniff it, lick it, and eventually bite it after each lever press. The approach to the light, like the approach to the lever, becomes highly driven, and the drive is clearly due to the conditioned association between the reinforcing injection and the manipulandum and cue light. As the regularity of approach to the lever increases with each reinforced trial, the incentive value and salience of other environmental stimuli—for example, an identical but ineffective ("inactive") manipulandum—presumably decrease.

As the animal is repeatedly reinforced for the investigatory reflexes that result in the initial lever presses, the behavior comes under increasing stimulus control. The strong stimulus control that can be established within the first hour of testing results in invigorated approach, sniffing, and facial poking at the lever. In the early stages of this learning, the animal may make several responses during the time-out period when the pump is already delivering an injection. It may also earn two or more injections in rapid succession. This is a learned response pattern, clearly resulting from prior reinforcement. The excitement at the lever is a manifestation of incentive motivation: activation due to the experience of the incentives in the situation. Prior to the first response of the day, the incentives are the learned incentives, the environmental stimuli that, through learning, have become associated with the primary reinforcer. After the first response, the decaying signal from the last reinforcement is a second source of incentive motivation.

The incentive motivation caused by the unconditioned reinforcer itself is often termed a "priming effect." It is an unlearned response that decays rapidly as soon as the reinforcer is no longer felt. The rapid decay of the priming effect is most obvious with the reward of direct electrical stimulation of the brain, where the reinforcer usually lasts a half-second or less and decays as rapidly as it appears. The running speed of a brain-stimulation-rewarded animal, reinforced at the end of a runway, varies with both the strength of reinforcement in the goal box and also the strength of any "priming" stimulation that is given in the start box. However, it is only the memory of the last reinforcement, not the memory of the last priming stimulation, that is effective after a minute or two delay (Gallistel, Stellar, & Bubis,

1974). Thus the priming that energizes responding leaves no lasting memory trace, whereas the memory of the most recent reinforced trials lasts and can influence subsequent running speed despite the passage of a week or more. Priming stimuli are the effective terminators of periods of abstinence; they are among the most potent stimuli for reinstating temporarily disrupted self-administration habits (de Wit & Stewart, 1981, 1983; Gerber & Stretch, 1975; Stretch & Gerber, 1973).

Priming stimulation is used a good deal by workers in the field of brain stimulation reward and intravenous stimulant self-administration. In an untrained animal, priming stimulation or priming stimulant injections cause the heightened state of arousal that is the hallmark of incentive motivation and psychomotor activation. Even in the untrained animal, priming stimulation is an energizer of behavior. The forward locomotion it induces is initially aimless, increasing the probability of movement but not of any particular movement. Priming stimulation is used in its simplest form to wake or activate the animal. In the trained animal, however, priming stimulation and priming injections selectively energize approach to the reinforcement-associated stimuli in the environment: the side of the cage containing the manipulandum and the manipulandum itself. In experienced animals, priming appears to be a very effective stimulus for craving. Indeed, I believe this is why 12-point rehabilitation programs set total abstinence as their goal; in the wake of the priming effect of a first cigarette, a first drink, or a first snort it becomes much more difficult to resist a second.

Priming injections are often given to animals at the beginning of cocaine self-administration sessions where drug-free animals are more reluctant to initiate cocaine self-administration than might be expected by nonspecialists. The memory of yesterday's cocaine reinforcement apparently carries an ambivalent memory, one tinged, it would seem, with some form of anxiety; when treated with anxiolytic drugs trained rats are much quicker to initiate cocaine self-administration (Ettenberg & Geist, 1991). Priming overcomes this anxiety and shifts the animal's responsiveness to the incentive (approach-inducing) properties of the drug-associated cues.

Priming is confounded with reinforcement in lever-pressing tasks where no time-out is imposed. When time-outs or low-density reinforcement schedules are used, the inter-response time can exceed the period of effective priming that is established by the previous reinforcement. When animals are allowed to earn reinforcement at their own preferred frequency, the varying strength of the priming effect largely determines when craving will again arise and when the next response will be made. I will return to this topic in the section on regulation of drug intake.

With sufficient drug experience, animals undergo a number of the neuroadaptive changes mentioned earlier (Nestler & Aghajanian, 1997; White & Kalivas, 1998). Many of these known adaptations are within the circuitry of the brain that is essential for the reinforcing actions of drugs of abuse. While most of the known neuroadaptations last less than a week or two, they may prove important in the development of more long-lasting changes. The craving-associated memory traces of the addict are themselves long-lasting; thus it is the long-lasting neuroadaptations—probably most importantly those associated with learning and memory for past drug experience—that offer the possibility of an explanation for the problems of relapse and compulsion that plague the addict. The most interesting long-lasting changes are perhaps the dendritic branching of neurons in the reward pathway (Robinson & Kolb, 1997, 1999). Such changes can be produced by self-administered cocaine experience of as little as 1 hour per day (although such exposure has been maintained for many days in the work thus far: Robinson, Gorny, Mitton, & Kolb, 2001).

It is clear that some changes in the brain must distinguish the addicted brain from the nonaddicted brain. One thing that remains to be determined is whether any of the known changes—changes induced, for the most part, by high doses of experimenter-administered drugs—is a significant contributing cause of addiction and not just a consequence of addiction. That is, must any of these known neuroadaptations occur prior to the transition from voluntary to compulsive drug self-administration? Or must there already be compulsive drug self-administration before there is sufficient drug exposure to produce the known neuroadaptations and make them stand out from the everyday neuroadaptations that result from the various stresses and pleasures of normal life? A second thing to be determined is the relative importance of differences between the drug-naive and the drug-addicted brain and differences between the brains of experienced subjects that have self-administered the drug and experienced subjects that have received the drug passively.

The Regulation of Drug Intake

Hunger and thirst are the prototypical drive states of motivational theory. Motivation for food and water wax and wane, and behavior makes a major contribution to the maintenance of homeostatic balance. Fluctuations in water seeking and food seeking are periodic and periods of satiety determine when water and food will be ineffective as reinforcers (Smith, 1982). The behavioral contribution to fluid and energy balance has been termed "behavioral homeostasis."

Thirst is the simplest model because the category of water is well defined while the category of food includes a wide variety of substances and varies between cultures and environments. Fluid balance is controlled in part by the function of the kidney, which extracts water from the blood when blood pressure is high and ceases to do so when pressure (and its usual correlate, extracellular fluid volume) is low. Fluid balance is also influenced by body temperature; the evaporation of perspiration and saliva are major sources of cooling in a hot environment and after exertion. Finally, fluid balance is controlled by behavior; when blood pressure is low or when salt concentration in cells of the hypothalamus is high thirst is experienced and the probability of water seeking and drinking is increased.

It is of interest to inquire just how water seeking and drinking are triggered. The traditional view is the drive hypothesis. Epstein (1973) summarized the thirst literature of the time with the suggestion that "(a) thirst goes on in the brain, (b) the neurological machine for thirst integrates multiple inputs, and (c) from these inputs a specific motivational state arises and drives the animal to seek water and ingest it" (p. 316). This summary is useful for those who are interested in the sensation and perception of thirst, but it offers no explanation of the motivational consequences of thirst. Rather, the research has focused on the sensing of deficit, not the control of behavior by deficit. The research, valuable as it has been in identifying the sources of thirst, deals with the sensory physiology, not the motivation, of drinking behavior. The drive hypothesis always fails to suggest a mechanism for the initiation and energizing of the seeking and ingesting acts. An incentive-motivational hypothesis, in contrast, offers at least the outline of a mechanism. It suggests that the state of dehydration increases probability of water seeking and drinking by increasing the salience—the Siren Cry[1]—of water-associated incentives in the environment, and that these learned incentives—with their stronger valences the closer they are to the goal—lead the animal from point to point along the learned path to water. The drive hypothesis suggests that it is the reduction of the need state or reduction of the associated drive that accounts for the reinforcing effects of water for a thirsty animal, whereas incentive-oriented studies suggest it is enhanced responsiveness to the lure of the incentive that is critical. The issue is whether the drive causes a push stimulus to action or rather the environmental cue causes a pull to action. The latter hypothesis is the stronger one, because it can account for the direction the animal takes; the animal that is responsive to drive and ignores the environment has little chance of getting on the right path, whereas the animal that is more and more strongly attracted to water-associated environmental stimuli is very likely to be drawn to water once thirst makes the animal sufficiently sensitive to such cues.

Drive states clearly modulate the motivational effectiveness of environmental stimuli. Studies of air licking in thirsty rats suggest that it is the cooling sensation in the oral cavity that accounts for the reinforcing effects of ingested fluids, and that such cooling sensations are reinforcing only if the animal is dehydrated (Freed & Mendelson, 1974; Mendelson & Chillag, 1970; Ramsauer, Mendelson, & Freed, 1974). Thirsty animals will not only drink water; they will lick at air streams that cool the oral cavity. They will lick at cool airstreams and they will lick at warm airstreams if the warm air is dry enough to evaporate saliva from the oral cavity (Freed & Mendelson, 1974). Air licking is an act that becomes compulsive in fluid-deprived rodents despite the fact that this behavior increases, through evaporation, the bodily need for water. The incentive motivational hypothesis is that behavior of the thirsty animal becomes controlled by the thirst-enhanced salience of stimuli that have, in the animal's reinforcement history, been associated with oral cooling. The reinforcing action of oral cooling in thirsty rodents is a sufficient mechanism to guarantee that few individuals fail to meet their hydrational needs except under conditions of extreme drought, since few rodents outside the laboratory ever find means of oral cooling that fail to involve the ingestion of fluids.

In a similar way, the reinforcing property of sweet taste is a sufficiently powerful stimulus to guarantee that animals do not starve to death in the presence of fruit. That sweet things become more attractive during states of privation (Cabanac, 1971) guarantees consumption of sweet things, which, except in laboratory conditions (Sheffield & Roby, 1950), tend to provide for much of an animal's nutrient need. Reinforcement by sweet taste provides a mechanism that makes intake of caloric foods highly probable in the wild. Drive-induced modulation of the salience of sweetness makes such intake more probable during states of privation. Control by sweetness usually accomplishes these things without the direct intervention of actual need reduction. However, the more an animal needs glucose, the more it can be seduced by the sweet taste of a non-nutritive substance (Jacobs & Sharma, 1969). Thus drive reduction is a seemingly inadequate and, indeed, seemingly incorrect explanation of why food and water are reinforcing.

It remains possible, however, that sweet taste becomes reinforcing through experience with need reduction. Le Magnen (1959) has shown that rats adjust their intake of a given food, after four or five days, on the basis of the caloric value of the food but also the caloric value of intragastric glucose that is given as a supplement. The animal's approach to the food is adjusted to compensate for the amount of glucose in the associated stomach load. Thus it is possible that even sweet taste is an acquired incentive, one that is reinforcing because of prior conditioning, prior need reduction, associated with sweet tastes in the past (Le Magnen, 1959; Myers and Sclafani, 2001a, 2001b). Mammals gain experience with sweet taste—and, indeed, have their needs met in association with the sweet taste of mothers' milk—from the time of birth; such experience results from the consequences of the expression of the neonatal suckling reflex. Sweet taste is an instrumental reinforcer very early in life; rats can learn on the first day of life to lever press for intra-oral milk infusions (Johanson & Hall, 1979). However, rats do not show deprivation-enhanced approach to either food or water stimuli until much later in life (Changizi, McGehee, & Hall, 2002). Thus the modulation of ingestive reflexes may itself be learned. In any case, whether or not need reduction contributes to the reinforcing effects of such things as oral cooling or sweet taste, it is the sensory events of oral cooling and sweet taste that come to control motivated behavior. They do so to the point that oral cooling or sweet taste in the absence of need reduction can become compulsive and dominate other behaviors (Jacobs & Sharma, 1967).

Just as drinking and eating are cyclic behaviors, characterized by periods of drive and satiety, so is drug seeking a cyclic behavior in animal models of intravenous drug self-administration. Well-trained animals respond about once every five minutes for 1 mg/kg injections of cocaine (Wise, Newton, Leeb, Burnette, Pocock, & Justice, 1995), about once every 20 minutes for 0.1 mg/kg injections of heroin (Gerber & Wise, 1989), and about once every 30 minutes for 0.25 mg/kg injections of amphetamine (Yokel & Pickens, 1973, 1974). Such injections cause, each by its own pharmacological mechanism, elevations of brain dopamine in nucleus accumbens. This elevation is essential to the reinforcing effects of amphetamine (Lyness, Friedle, & Moore, 1979; Yokel & Wise, 1975) and cocaine (de Wit & Wise, 1977; Roberts, Corcoran, & Fibiger, 1977) and, arguably, heroin (Bozarth & Wise, 1986; Wise, 1989). At the beginning of each test session, the trained animal responds frequently; this phase of the session is termed the "loading phase" and is seen as a period when the behavior of the animal is establishing some level of drug satiety. After a pause in which much of the previous injection is metabolized, the animal then settles down to slower and more regular responding termed the "maintenance phase" of the session. It is in the maintenance phase that the animal appears to regulate its drug intake with some kind of homeostatic precision.

In the maintenance phase of responding, the animal makes each response for additional cocaine (Wise, Newton, Leeb, Burnette, Pocock, & Justice, 1995), amphetamine (Ranaldi, Pocock, Zereik, & Wise, 1999), or heroin (Wise, Leone, Rivest, & Leeb, 1995) long before dopamine levels return to normal baseline. The dopamine level at the time of response may differ somewhat between animals, ranging between two and three times the normal basal level of nucleus accumbens dopamine. While there is variability of trigger level between animals, the level within a given animal is quite consistent. It is as if the animal is "hungry" for drug whenever dopamine levels fall below about 200% of normal and as if they are sated whenever dopamine levels surge above about 300% of normal. One may question whether this is a true case of homeostatic regulation, but it is not really clear what constitutes "true" regulation even in the case of food or fluid intake. We know that many humans take in more food than they need to maintain body weight, and they do so despite significant penalties, gradually increasing their weight and their health risks over the course of their lifetime. Similarly, we know that there is little penalty for taking in more fluid than we need, as, for example, when drinking beer on a hot day; excess is simply excreted. Thus the term "regulation" has wide application and is descriptive rather than explanatory; the appearance of regulation is evident in many things and is always a phenomenon to be understood rather than to be used as an explanation. Whether apparent regulation depends on reward in states of depletion or penalties or nonreward during states of satiety must be determined individually for each incentive that is capable of establishing compulsive behavior.

The apparent regulation of drug intake involves a rate of intake that matches, reasonably well, the rate of metabolism. Once the animals have loaded their system with drug, each subsequent injection is taken when the drug level in blood (Yokel & Pickens, 1973, 1974) and the dopamine level in nucleus accumbens (Ranaldi et al., 1999; Wise, Newton, Leeb, Burnette, Pocock, & Justice, 1995; Wise, Leone, Rivest, & Leeb, 1995) have been metabolized to within 10% or so of the levels at which the last injection was taken. The hypothesis that the drug intake is somehow regulated by drug level in the blood, dopamine level in the brain, or some correlate of the two is self-evident and confirmed by the finding that supplemental experimenter-administered infusions of the drug postpone the animal's next response by just enough to compensate for the supplement (Gerber & Wise, 1989; Tsibulsky & Norman, 1999). The mechanics of how this level of regulation is achieved remain to be determined.

The issue of regulation revolves around the question of why, if the drug is powerfully reinforcing, the animals do not take drug more frequently than they do. Why, if food is powerfully reinforcing, do we not overeat? Of course we often do, but food loses at least some of its reinforcing efficacy—its incentive salience—in periods of satiety (Cabanac, 1971). Is the same true for cocaine? The control of subsequent drug intake by drug in the blood, dopamine in the brain, or some correlate of the two could reflect either active or passive regulation. That is, the animals might be conjoined against taking more drug, just as a full stomach and its hormonal consequences is one of the factors that actively inhibits food intake (Smith & Gibbs, 1994), by some performance impairing or aversive effects of high drug or transmitter levels. Neither of these possibilities would seem to be the case. First, we know from two-lever tests offering the choice between drug and brain stimulation reinforcement that rats remain capable of lever pressing at high rates between normal responses for amphetamine (Wise, Yokel, Hansson, & Gerber, 1977) or heroin (Gerber, Bozarth, Spindler, & Wise, 1985). Second, we know that the animals do not find higher levels of drug or dopamine to become, on balance, aversive. If they did, they would choose between two levers the one associated with smaller doses, keeping low the peak drug and dopamine levels resulting from each injection (but compensating by taking the low dose more frequently). Instead, if anything, rats and monkeys, while taking them less frequently, prefer the higher of two doses offered concurrently (Iglauer, Llewellyn, & Woods, 1976; Manzardo, Del Rio, Stein, & Belluzzi, 2001; Yokel, 1987).

It appears most likely that the intake of stimulants, at least, is passively regulated; as in the case of water intake, there is apparently no significant penalty for taking more than satiating levels of drug, but neither, it appears, is there any significant benefit. Thus, the tendency of animals to respond soon after the previous injection, which is seen in the first few days of training, appears to gradually disappear because there is no added reward value of drug once dopamine levels are elevated. As the animal learns this fact there is decreased incentive salience associated with the response lever—the animal stops responding to it—when dopamine levels are above about 300% normal. The gradual extinction of the tendency to respond before the last injection has been metabolized suggests a model of cycles of incentive motivation (induced by the priming effects of the last injection) and satiety (induced by *d*-amphetamine concentrations above 0.2 g/ml of blood or dopamine concentrations higher than 300% of normal).

What is the mechanism by which drug intake becomes regulated? Our examination of the progression from investigatory lever pressing to regulated lever pressing within binges of limited-access drug self-administration suggest an incentive motivational view rather than a drive interpretation. It is clearly the place cues in the environment that are the determinants of the left turn or the right turn that takes the animal to the lever. It is clearly the spatially localized lever, not the spatially ambiguous drug, that the animal approaches. Once the animal is away from the lever, it is only environmental cues that give information as to which way to turn. The behavior is clearly dependent in some way or another on a correlate of drug concentration in the body. Our working hypothesis is that dopamine levels influence behavior as occasion-setters, not as eliciting stimuli, determining on a moment-to-moment basis the incentive salience—the drawing power—of the lever.

In this view, drug-associated environmental stimuli have maximum incentive salience when dopamine levels are somewhere between normal and twice normal. Elevating dopamine levels by giving a priming injection will increase the probability that the animal in a lever-pressing task will notice, approach, and manipulate the lever. In a two-lever task, the words of Bolles (1975), slightly modified, best illustrate the point: when the rat with slightly elevated dopamine levels happens to look to the "inactive" lever side, nothing happens; but when it happens to look to the "active" lever side, it gets excited; thus it is more likely to notice the active lever, approach it, and press it. When it does so, the drug will serve as a reinforcer just as food does when the animal is food deprived. However, when the dopamine level is elevated, the animal is unresponsive to the active lever, unmoved by it just as is the sated animal that looks at a food-associated lever. Now, the dopamine level is out of the optimal range and does not serve as an occasion-setter. Should the animal occasionally press the lever in this condition the drug injection and its associated dopamine bolus will not be reinforcing. High dopamine levels signal to the investigator, and presumably to the animal, that while another drug injection may prolong the rewarding effects of the previous injection, the second injection will not intensify the reward resulting from the previous injection, and will thus not serve as an effective reinforcer; high dopamine levels reduce the incentive value of the drug-associated cues so that the animal learns to no longer respond.

Dysregulation of Intake

If drug intake is maintained for prolonged periods at high doses, the apparent regulation that is typical of limited access experiments deteriorates. The point of dysregulation suggests yet another transition in the etiology of addiction that should be associated with neuroadaptations of one sort or another, and in this case neuroadaptations in the brain mechanisms of drug reward are suggested. Animals given unlimited access to intravenous cocaine or amphetamine come to take the drugs erratically and to the point of death (Bozarth & Wise,

1985; Johanson et al., 1976). The most obvious result is weight loss; most deaths occur when the animals approach death by starvation (Bozarth & Wise, 1985). Loss of sleep is also evident. In the initial opportunity for unlimited drug access, the animals frequently respond regularly for one to three days without interruption (Pickens & Harris, 1968). The behavior then becomes sporadic, with binges and abstinence periods of irregular length (Pickens & Harris, 1968) that give the appearance of periodicity to group averages (Bozarth & Wise, 1985). If, instead of continuous drug access, animals are given intermittent access in long (6 hour or longer) sessions, dysregulation can take another form. In such circumstances the animals tend to respond more and more strongly during the initial, "loading," phase of each session (prior to establishing the elevated drug or transmitter levels that provide regulatory feedback), thus increasing their total drug intake for each session (Ahmed & Koob, 1998). The fact that the animals return to escalated intake even after long periods of withdrawal is reminiscent of the way that obese humans, once they have undergone a period of overfeeding, tend to return to a pattern of excess following periods of diet and weight loss (Levin, 2000). The degree to which these dysregulations depend on known neuroadaptations is unclear, however. The irregular intake that develops after prolonged continuous intoxication (Bozarth & Wise, 1985; Tornatzky & Miczek, 2000) is associated with a dosing regimen that should be associated with the development of drug tolerance (Emmett-Oglesby & Lane, 1992; Li, Depoortere, & Emmett-Oglesby, 1994), whereas the escalated early intake that develops after repeated periodic intoxication is associated with a regimen associated with drug sensitization or "reverse tolerance" (Downs & Eddy, 1932; Kilbey & Ellinwood, 1977; Segal & Mandell, 1974). Thus the two forms of dysregulation are probable consequences of independent mechanisms and opposite neuroadaptations.

Contrasts between Sensed and Unsensed Incentives

What unique insights can be gained from comparing the motivations for sensed and unsensed rewarding incentives? Perhaps the most obvious has to do with the role of learning in the control of behavior by sensed incentives. In the case of drug reward and brain stimulation reward, the sensed incentives are the cues and manipulanda that have learned motivational significance and cue value and are the objects of attention at or just prior to the time of drug delivery. In these cases the click of the relay or the flash of the cue light is the sensory message of receipt of reward. Similarly, in a well-trained animal the click of the latch on the door hiding the food may simply be the sound of receipt of reward. Consider the person who wins a lottery: Is not the moment of the receipt of reward—the moment of celebration, of motivational excitation—the moment the winning number is announced? Don't the subsequent events of the receiving of the check, the cashing of the check, the trading of the cash for food, and the eating of the food constitute progressively weaker rewarding events than the first message announcing the inevitability of reward? Separating the motivational importance of the sensory information that predicts reward from the sensory information that constitutes reward is not so straightforward as might first be assumed.

Another important insight is that in addition to behavior controlled by drugs or brain stimulation, behavior controlled by rewards of sweet taste or oral cooling can become compulsive. In the case of air-licking or compulsive saccharin drinking there seems no obvious reason to invoke neuroadaptations or brain disease to explain compulsive behavior. It seems self-evident that the variety of compulsive behaviors forms a continuum, differing more in degree than in kind, and from this perspective it seems more heuristic to look for commonalities between the habits established by various incentives than to look for unique properties that set addiction, for example, apart from the rest. Inasmuch as drug seeking and food seeking appear to be controlled by the same motivational substrates (see, e.g., Ettenberg & Camp, 1986; Wise, 1982), it might well prove to be the case that drug-induced brain pathology is a consequence, rather than the precipitating cause, of compulsive behavior. It seems unlikely that brain pathology plays a significant role in the variety of nondrug compulsions—such as compulsive self-stimulation—that accompany a wide range of motivated behaviors.

Note

1. I use here a metaphor from C. R. Gallistel, likening the attraction of an incentive to the seductive come-hither songs of the sea nymphs of Greek and Roman myth. The idea is that each object in the animal's environment

has a degree of allure that sometimes exceeds and sometimes fails to exceed the animal's threshold for approach responses. A given drive state is seen to increase the probability that an individual is responsive to the appropriate incentive stimuli, enhancing their allure (their salience as attractants).

References

Acquas, E., Carboni, E., Leone, P., & Di Chiara, G. (1989). SCH 23390 blocks drug-conditioned place-preferences and place aversion: Anhedonia (lack of reward) or apathy (lack of motivation) after dopamine-receptor blockade? *Psychopharmacology, 99,* 151–155.

Ahmed, S. H., & Koob, G. F. (1998). Transition from moderate to excessive drug intake: Change in hedonic set point. *Science, 282,* 298–300.

Barnes, J. (Ed.). (1984). *The complete works of Aristotle* (Vol. 1). Princeton: Princeton University Press.

Beach, F. A. (1956). Characteristics of masculine "sex drive." In M. R. Jones (Ed.), *Nebraska symposium on motivation* (pp. 1–32). Lincoln: University of Nebraska Press.

Bechara, A., Nader, K., & van der Kooy, D. (1995). Neurobiology of withdrawal motivation: Evidence for two separate aversive effects produced in morphine-naive versus morphine-dependent rats by both naloxone and spontaneous withdrawal. *Behavioral Neuroscience, 109,* 91–105.

Beck, R. C. (1978). *Motivation.* New York: Prentice-Hall.

Beitner-Johnson, D., Guitart, X., & Nestler, E. J. (1992). Neurofilament proteins and the mesolimbic dopamine system: Common regulation by chronic morphine and chronic cocaine in the rat ventral tegmental area. *Journal of Neuroscience, 12,* 2165–2176.

Beitner-Johnson, D., & Nestler, E. J. (1991). Morphine and cocaine exert common chronic actions on tyrosine hydroxylase in dopaminergic brain reward regions. *Journal of Neurochemistry, 57,* 344–347.

Berhow, M., Russell, D. S., Terwilliger, R. Z., Beitner-Johnson, D., Self, D. S., Lindsay, R. M., et al. (1995). Influence of neurotrophic factors on morphine- and cocaine-induced biochemical changes in the mesolimbic dopamine system. *Neuroscience, 68,* 969–979.

Berke, J. D., & Hyman, S. E. (2000). Addiction, dopamine, and the molecular mechanisms of memory. *Neuron, 25,* 515–532.

Bindra, D. (1974). A motivational view of learning, performance, and behavior modification. *Psychological Review, 81,* 199–213.

Bolles, R. C. (1975). *Theory of motivation* (2nd ed.). New York: Harper and Row.

Bozarth, M. A., & Wise, R. A. (1985). Toxicity associated with long-term intravenous heroin and cocaine self-administration in the rat. *Journal of the American Medical Association, 254,* 81–83.

Bozarth, M. A., & Wise, R. A. (1986). Involvement of the ventral tegmental dopamine system in opioid and psychomotor stimulant reinforcement. In

L. S. Harris (Ed.), *Problems of drug dependence 1985* (Vol. 67, pp. 190–196). Washington DC: U.S. Government Printing Office.

Brauer, L. H., & de Wit, H. (1997). High dose pimozide does not block amphetamine-induced euphoria in normal volunteers. *Pharmacology Biochemistry and Behavior, 56,* 265–272.

Brown, J. S. (1953). Problems presented by the concept of acquired drives. In M. R. Jones (Ed.), *Nebraska symposium on motivation* (pp. 1–21). Lincoln: University of Nebraska Press.

Cabanac, M. (1971). Physiological role of pleasure. *Science, 173,* 1103–1107.

Cappell, H., & LeBlanc, A. E. (1971). Conditioned aversion to saccharin by single administrations of mescaline and *d*-amphetamine. *Psychopharmacologia, 22,* 352–356.

Cappell, H., LeBlanc, A. E., & Endrenyi, L. (1973). Aversive conditioning by psychoactive drugs: Effects of morphine, alcohol and chlordiazepoxide. *Psychopharmacologia, 29,* 239–246.

Carlezon, W. A. J., Thome, J., Olson, V. G., Lane-Ladd, S. B., Brodkin, E. S., Hiroi, N., et al. (1998). Regulation of cocaine reward by CREB. *Science, 282,* 2272–2275.

Carlson, K. R. (1977). Supersensitivity to apomorphine and stress two years after chronic methadone treatment. *Neuropharmacology, 16,* 795–798.

Changizi, M. A., McGehee, R. M., & Hall, W. G. (2002). Evidence that appetitive responses for dehydration and food-deprivation are learned. *Physiology and Behavior, 75,* 295–304.

Chein, I., Gerard, D. L., Lee, R. S., & Rosenfeld, E. (1964). *The road to H: Narcotics, delinquency, and social policy.* New York: Basic Books.

Craig, W. (1918). Appetites and aversions as constituents of instincts. *Biological Bulletin, 34,* 91–107.

Dackis, C. A., & Gold, M. S. (1985). New concepts in cocaine addiction: The dopamine depletion hypothesis. *Neuroscience and Biobehavioral Reviews, 9,* 469–477.

Darwin, C. (1859). *On the origin of species.* London: John Murray.

Deneau, G., Yanagita, T., & Seevers, M. H. (1969). Self-administration of psychoactive substances by the monkey: A measure of psychological dependence. *Psychopharmacologia, 16,* 30–48.

de Wit, H., & Stewart, J. (1981). Reinstatement of cocaine-reinforced responding in the rat. *Psychopharmacology, 75,* 134–143.

de Wit, H., & Stewart, J. (1983). Drug reinstatement of heroin-reinforced responding in the rat. *Psychopharmacology, 79,* 29–31.

de Wit, H., & Wise, R. A. (1977). Blockade of cocaine reinforcement in rats with the dopamine receptor blocker pimozide, but not with the noradrenergic blockers phentolamine or phenoxybenzamine. *Canadian Journal of Psychology, 31,* 195–203.

Downs, A. W., & Eddy, N. B. (1932). The effect of repeated doses of cocaine on the dog. *Journal of Pharmacology and Experimental Therapeutics, 46,* 195–198.

Emmett-Oglesby, M. W., & Lane, J. D. (1992). Tolerance to the reinforcing effects of cocaine. *Behavioural Pharmacology, 3,* 193–200.

Epstein, A. N. (1973). Epilogue: Retrospect and prognosis. In A. N. Epstein, H. R. Kissileff, & E. Stellar (Eds.), *The neuropsychology of thirst: New findings and advances in concepts* (pp. 315–332). Washington: Winston.

Ettenberg, A., & Camp, C. H. (1986). Haloperidol induces a partial reinforcement extinction effect in rats: Implications for a dopamine involvement in food reward. *Pharmacology Biochemistry and Behavior, 25,* 813–821.

Ettenberg, A., & Geist, T. D. (1991). Animal model for investigating the anxiogenic effects of self-administered cocaine. *Psychopharmacology, 103,* 455–461.

Fiske, D. W., & Maddi, S. R. (Eds.). (1961). *Functions of varied experience.* Homewood IL: Dorsey.

Fitzsimons, J. T. (1972). Thirst. *Physiological Reviews, 52,* 468–561.

Frank, R. A., Martz, S., & Pommering, T. (1988). The effect of chronic cocaine on self-stimulation train-duration thresholds. *Pharmacology Biochemistry and Behavior, 29,* 755–758.

Freed, W. J., & Mendelson, J. (1974). Airlicking: Thirsty rats prefer a warm dry airstream to a warm humid airstream. *Physiology and Behavior, 12,* 557–561.

Gallistel, C. R., Stellar, J. R., & Bubis, E. (1974). Parametric analysis of brain stimulation reward in the rat: I. The transient process and the memory-containing process. *Journal of Comparative and Physiological Psychology, 87,* 848–859.

Gerber, G. J., Bozarth, M. A., Spindler, J., & Wise, R. A. (1985). Concurrent heroin self-administration and intracranial self-stimulation in rats. *Pharmacology Biochemistry and Behavior, 23,* 837–842.

Gerber, G. J., & Stretch, R. (1975). Drug-induced reinstatement of extinguished self-administration behavior in monkeys. *Pharmacology Biochemistry and Behavior, 3,* 1055–1061.

Gerber, G. J., & Wise, R. A. (1989). Pharmacological regulation of intravenous cocaine and heroin self- administration in rats: A variable dose paradigm. *Pharmacology Biochemistry and Behavior, 32,* 527–531.

Glickman, S. E., & Schiff, B. B. (1967). A biological theory of reinforcement. *Psychological Review, 74,* 81–109.

Gunne, L. M., Änggard, E., & Jönsson, L. E. (1972). Clinical trials with amphetamine-blocking drugs. *Psychiatria Neurologia Neurochirurgia, 75,* 225–226.

Haertzen, C. A. (1966). Development of scales based on patterns of drug effects, using the Addiction Research Center Inventory. *Psychological Reports, 18,* 163–194.

Harlow, H. F. (1953). Mice, monkeys, men and motives. *Psychological Review, 60,* 23–32.

Hebb, D. O. (1949). *The organization of behavior.* New York: Wiley.

Hebb, D. O. (1955). Drives and the C.N.S. (conceptual nervous system). *Psychological Review, 62,* 243–254.

Hetherington, M. (Ed.). (2001). *Food cravings and addiction.* London: Leatherhead Press.

Hinde, R. A. (1960). Energy models of motivation. *Symposia of the Society for Experimental Biology, 14,* 199–213.

Hull, C. L. (1943). *Principles of behavior.* New York: Appleton-Century-Crofts.

Iglauer, C., Llewellyn, M. E., & Woods, J. H. (1976). Concurrent schedules of cocaine injection in rhesus monkeys: Dose variations under independent and non-independent variable-interval procedures. *Pharmacological Reviews, 27,* 367–383.

Jacobs, H. L., & Sharma, K. N. (1969). Taste versus calories: Sensory and metabolic signals in the control of food intake. *Annals of the New York Academy of Sciences, 157,* 1084–1125.

Jaffe, J. H. (1985). Drug addiction and drug abuse. In A. G. Gilman, L. S. Goodman, & A. Gilman (Eds.), *The pharmacological basis of therapeutics* (pp. 532–581). New York: Macmillan.

Johanson, C. E., Balster, R. L., & Bonese, K. (1976). Self-administration of psychomotor stimulant drugs: The effects of unlimited access. *Pharmacology Biochemistry and Behavior, 4,* 45–51.

Johanson, I. B., & Hall, W. G. (1979). Appetitive learning in 1-day-old rat pups. *Science, 205,* 419–421.

Jones, M. R. (1955). Introduction. In M. R. Jones (Ed.), *Nebraska symposium on motivation* (p. vii). Lincoln: University of Nebraska Press.

Jönsson, L., Änggard, E., & Gunne, L. (1971). Blockade of intravenous amphetamine euphoria in man. *Clinical Pharmacology and Therapeutics, 12,* 889–896.

Kalant, H. (1977). Comparative aspects of tolerance to, and dependence on, alcohol, barbiturates, and opiates. In M. M. Gross (Ed.), *Alcohol intoxication and withdrawal* (pp. 169–186). New York: Plenum.

Kelleher, R. T., & Morse, W. H. (1968). Schedules using noxious stimuli. 3. Responding maintained with response produced electric shocks. *Journal of the Experimental Analysis of Behavior, 11,* 819–838.

Kelz, M. B., Chen, J., Carlezon, W. A., Whisler, K., Gilden, L., Bechmann, A. M., et al. (1999). Expression of the transcription factor FosB in the brain controls sensitivity to cocaine. *Nature, 401,* 272–276.

Kilbey, M. M., & Ellinwood, E. H., Jr. (1977). Reverse tolerance to stimulant-induced abnormal behavior. *Life Sciences, 20,* 1063–1076.

Kissileff, H. R. (1969). Food-associated drinking in the rat. *Journal of Comparative and Physiological Psychology, 67,* 284–300.

Kokkinidis, L., Zacharko, R. M., & Predy, P. A. (1980). Post-amphetamine depression of self-stimulation responding from the substantia nigra: Reversal by tricyclic antidepressants. *Pharmacology Biochemistry and Behavior, 13,* 379–383.

Koob, G. F. (1996). Drug addiction: The yin and yang of hedonic homeostasis. *Neuron, 16,* 893–896.

Koob, G. F., Stinus, L., Le Moal, M., & Bloom, F. E. (1989). Opponent process theory of motivation: Neurobiological evidence from studies of opiate dependence. *Neuroscience and Biobehavioral Reviews, 13,* 135–140.

Lehrman, D. S. (1965). Interaction between internal and external environments in the regulation of the reproductive cycle of the ring dove. In F. A. Beach (Ed.), *Sex and behavior.* New York: Wiley.

Leith, N. J., & Barrett, R. J. (1976). Amphetamine and the reward system: Evidence for tolerance and post-drug depression. *Psychopharmacologia, 46,* 19–25.

Le Magnen, J. (1959). Effets des administrations post-prandiales de glucose sur l'etablissement des appétits. *Comptes rendus des seances de la Societe de biologie et de ses filiales, 158,* 212–215.

Le Magnen, J. (1969). Peripheral and systemic actions of food in the caloric regulation of intake. *Annals of the New York Academy of Sciences, 157,* 1127–1157.

Leshner, A. I. (1997). Addiction is a brain disease, and it matters. *Science, 278,* 45–47.

Levin, B. (2000). Metabolic imprinting on genetically predisposed neural circuits perpetuates obesity. *Nutrition, 16,* 909–915.

Li, D. H., Depoortere, R. Y., & Emmett-Oglesby, M. W. (1994). Tolerance to the reinforcing effects of cocaine in a progressive ratio paradigm. *Psychopharmacology, 116,* 326–332.

Lyness, W. H., Friedle, N. M., & Moore, K. E. (1979). Destruction of dopaminergic nerve terminals in nucleus accumbens: effect on *d*-amphetamine self-administration. *Pharmacology Biochemistry and Behavior, 11,* 553–556.

Malmo, R. B. (1975). *On emotions, needs, and our archaic brain.* New York: Holt, Rinehart and Winston.

Manzardo, A. M., Del Rio, J. A., Stein, L., & Belluzzi, J. D. (2001). Rats choose cocaine over dopamine agonists in a two-lever self-administration preference test. *Pharmacology Biochemistry and Behavior, 70,* 257–265.

Markou, A., & Koob, G. F. (1991). Postcocaine anhedonia: An animal model of cocaine withdrawal. *Neuropsychopharmacology, 4,* 17–26.

McAuliffe, W. E., & Gordon, R. A. (1974). A test of Lindesmith's theory of addiction: The frequency of euphoria among long-term addicts. *American Journal of Sociology, 79,* 795–840.

McAuliffe, W. E., & Gordon, R. A. (1980). Reinforcement and the combination of effects: Summary of a theory of opiate addiction. In D. J. Lettieri, M. Sayers, & H. W. Pearson (Eds.), *Theories of drug abuse* (pp. 137–141). Washington DC: National Institute on Drug Abuse.

McLellan, A. T., Lewis, D. C., O'Brien, C. P., & Kleber, H. D. (2000). Drug dependence, a chronic medical illness: Implications for treatment, insurance, and outcomes evaluation. *Journal of the American Medical Association, 284,* 1689–1695.

Mendelson, J., & Chillag, D. (1970). Tongue cooling: A new reward for thirsty rodents. *Science, 170,* 1418–1421.

Morgan, M. J. (1974). Resistance to satiation. *Animal Behaviour, 22,* 449–466.

Myers, K. P., & Sclafani, A. (2001a). Conditioned enhancement of flavor evaluation reinforced by intragastric glucose. II. Taste reactivity analysis. *Physiology and Behavior, 74,* 495–505.

Myers, K. P., & Sclafani, A. (2001b). Conditioned enhancement of flavor evaluation reinforced by intragastric glucose: I. Intake acceptance and preference analysis. *Physiology and Behavior, 74,* 481–493.

Nestler, E. J. (1992). Molecular mechanisms of drug addiction. *Journal of Neuroscience, 12,* 2439–2450.

Nestler, E. J. (2001). Molecular basis of long-term plasticity underlying addiction. *Nature Reviews Neuroscience, 2,* 119–128.

Nestler, E. J., & Aghajanian, G. K. (1997). Molecular and cellular basis of addiction. *Science, 278,* 58–63.

Olds, J. (1956). Pleasure centers in the brain. *Scientific American, 195,* 105–116.

Pavlov, I. P. (1928). *Lectures on conditioned reflexes.* New York: International Publishers.

Petri, H. L. (1981). *Motivation theory and research.* Belmont CA: Wadsworth.

Pickens, R., & Harris, W. C. (1968). Self-administration of *d*-amphetamine by rats. *Psychopharmacologia, 12,* 158–163.

Pickens, R. W., & Johanson, C. E. (1992). Craving: Consensus of status and agenda for future research. *Drug and Alcohol Dependence, 30,* 127–131.

Ramsauer, S., Mendelson, J., & Freed, W. J. (1974). Effects of water temperature on the reward value and satiating capacity of water in water-deprived rats. *Behavioral Biology, 11,* 381–393.

Ranaldi, R., Pocock, D., Zereik, R., & Wise, R. A. (1999). Dopamine fluctuations in the nucleus accumbens during maintenance, extinction, and reinstatement of intravenous D-amphetamine self-administration. *Journal of Neuroscience, 19,* 4102–4109.

Risner, M. E., & Jones, B. E. (1976). Role of noradrenergic and dopaminergic processes in amphetamine self-administration. *Pharmacology Biochemistry and Behavior, 5,* 477–482.

Roberts, D. C. S., Corcoran, M. E., & Fibiger, H. C. (1977). On the role of ascending catecholaminergic systems in intravenous self-administration of cocaine. *Pharmacology Biochemistry and Behavior, 6,* 615–620.

Robinson, T. E., & Berridge, K. C. (1993). The neural basis of drug craving: An incentive-sensitization theory of addiction. *Brain Research Reviews, 18,* 247–292.

Robinson, T. E., & Berridge, K. C. (2000). The psychology and neurobiology of addiction: An incentive-sensitization view. *Addiction*(Suppl. 2), S91–S117.

Robinson, T. E., & Berridge, K. C. (2001). Incentive-sensitization and addiction. *Addiction, 96,* 103–114.

Robinson, T. E., Gorny, G., Mitton, E., & Kolb, B. (2001). Cocaine self-administration alters the morphology of dendrites and dendritic spines in the nucleus accumbens and neocortex. *Synapse, 39,* 257–266.

Robinson, T. E., & Kolb, B. (1997). Persistent structural modifications in nucleus accumbens and prefrontal cortex neurons produced by previous experience with amphetamine. *Journal of Neuroscience, 17,* 8491–8497.

Robinson, T. E., & Kolb, B. (1999). Morphine alters the structure of neurons in the nucleus accumbens and neocortex of rats. *Synapse, 33,* 160–162.

Rossetti, Z. L., Lai, M., Hmaidan, Y., & Gessa, G. L. (1993). Depletion of mesolimbic dopamine during behavioral despair: Partial reversal by chronic imipramine. *European Journal of Pharmacology, 242,* 313–315.

Schmidt, C. J. (1987). Neurotoxicity of the psychedelic amphetamine, methylenedioxymethamphetamine. *Journal of Pharmacology and Experimental Therapeutics, 240,* 1–7.

Schneirla, T. C. (1939). A theoretical consideration of the basis for approach-withdrawal adjustments in behavior. *Psychological Bulletin, 37,* 501–502.

Schneirla, T. C. (1959). An evolutionary and developmental theory of biphasic processes underlying approach and withdrawal. In M. R. Jones (Ed.), *Nebraska symposium on motivation* (pp. 1–42). Lincoln: University of Nebraska Press.

Segal, D. S., & Mandell, A. J. (1974). Long-term administration of *d*-amphetamine: Progressive augmentation of motor activity and stereotypy. *Pharmacology Biochemistry and Behavior, 2,* 249–255.

Sheffield, F. D., & Roby, T. B. (1950). Reward value of a non-nutritive sweet taste. *Journal of Comparative and Physiological Psychology, 43,* 471–481.

Sherrington, C. S. (1906). *The integrative action of the nervous system.* New Haven CT: Yale University Press.

Simon, D., & Burns, E. (1997). *The corner: A year in the life of an inner-city neighborhood.* New York: Broadway Books.

Skinner, B. F. (1931). The concept of the reflex in the description of behavior. *Journal of General Psychology,5,* 427–458.

Skinner, B. F. (1932). On the rate of formation of a conditioned reflex. *Journal of General Psychology, 7,* 274–286.

Skinner, B. F. (1966). The phylogeny and ontogeny of behavior: Contingencies of reinforcement throw light on contingencies of survival in the evolution of behavior. *Science, 153,* 1205–1213.

Smith, G. P. (1982). Satiety and the problem of motivation. In D. W. Pfaff (Ed.), *The physiological mechanisms of motivation* (pp. 133–143). New York: Springer-Verlag.

Smith, G. P., & Gibbs, J. (1994). Satiating effect of cholecystokinin. *Annals of the New York Academy of Sciences, 713,* 236–241.

Sokolov, Y. N. (1963). *Perception and the conditioned reflex.* Oxford: Pergamon.

Solomon, R. L., & Corbit, J. D. (1973). An opponent-process theory of motivation: II. Cigarette addiction. *Journal of Abnormal Psychology, 81,* 158–171.

Solomon, R. L., & Corbit, J. D. (1974). An opponent-process theory of motivation: I. Temporal dynamics of affect. *Psychological Review, 81,* 119–145.

Spence, K. W. (1956). *Behavior theory and conditioning.* New Haven CT: Yale University Press.

Stretch, R., & Gerber, G. J. (1973). Drug-induced reinstatement of amphetamine self-administration behaviour in monkeys. *Canadian Journal of Psychology, 27,* 168–177.

Stewart, J., de Wit, H., & Eikelboom, R. (1984). Role of unconditioned and conditioned drug effects in the self-administration of opiates and stimulants. *Psychological Review, 91,* 251–268.

Teitelbaum, P. (1966). The use of operant methods in the assessment and control of motivational states. In W. K. Honig (Ed.), *Operant behaviour: Areas of research and application* (pp. 565–608). New York: Appleton-Century-Crofts.

Thorndike, E. L. (1898). Animal intelligence: An experimental study of the associative processes in animals. *Psychological Monographs, 8,* 1–109.

Tiffany, S. T. (1990). A cognitive model of drug urges and drug-use behavior: Role of automatic and nonautomatic processes. *Psychological Review, 97,* 147–168.

Toates, F. (1986). *Motivational systems.* Cambridge: Cambridge University Press.

Tornatzky, W., & Miczek, K. (2000). Cocaine self-administration "binges": Transition from behavioral and autonomic regulation toward hymeostatic dysregulation in rats. *Psychopharmacology, 148,* 289–298.

Tsibulsky, V. L., & Norman, A. B. (1999). Satiety threshold: A quantitative model of maintained cocaine self-administration. *Brain Research, 839,* 85–93.

Wagner, G. C., Ricaurte, G. A., Seiden, L. S., Schuster, C. R., Miller, R. J., & Westley, L. (1980). Long-lasting depletion of striatal dopamine and loss of dopamine uptake sites following repeated administration of methamphetamine. *Brain Research, 181,* 151–160.

Wei, E. T., Tseng, L. F., Loh, H. H., & Way, E. L. (1974). Similarity of morphine abstinence signs to thermoregulatory behaviour. *Nature, 247,* 398–399.

White, F. J., & Kalivas, P. W. (1998). Neuroadaptations involved in amphetamine and cocaine addiction. *Drug and Alcohol Dependence, 51,* 141–153.

Wise, R. A. (1982). Neuroleptics and operant behavior: The anhedonia hypothesis. *Behavioral and Brain Sciences, 5,* 39–87.

Wise, R. A. (1985). The anhedonia hypothesis: Mark III. *Behavioral and Brain Sciences, 8,* 178–186.

Wise, R. A. (1987). The role of reward pathways in the development of drug dependence. *Pharmacology and Therapeutics, 35,* 227–263.

Wise, R. A. (1989). Opiate reward: Sites and substrates. *Neuroscience and Biobehavioral Reviews, 13,* 129–133.

Wise, R. A. (2001). Neural circuitry of desire. In M. Hetherington (Ed.), *Food cravings and addiction* (pp. 33–58). London: Leatherhead Press.

Wise, R. A., Yokel, R. A., & de Wit, H. (1976). Both positive reinforcement and conditioned taste aversion from amphetamine and from apomorphine in rats. *Science, 191,* 1273–1275.

Wise, R. A., Yokel, R. A., Hansson, P., & Gerber, G. J. (1977). Concurrent intracranial self-stimulation and amphetamine self-administration in rats. *Pharmacology Biochemistry and Behavior, 7,* 459–461.

Wise, R. A., Newton, P., Leeb, K., Burnette, B., Pocock, P., & Justice, J. B. (1995). Fluctuations in nucleus accumbens dopamine concentration during intravenous cocaine self-administration in rats. *Psychopharmacology, 120,* 10–20.

Wise, R. A., Leone, P., Rivest, R., & Leeb, K. (1995). Elevations of nucleus accumbens dopamine and DOPAC levels during intravenous heroin self-administration. *Synapse, 21,* 140–148.

Woods, J. H. (1990). Abuse liability and the regulatory control of therapeutic drugs: Untested assumptions. *Drug and Alcohol Dependence, 25,* 229–233.

Woods, J. H., & Schuster, C. R. (1971). Opiates as reinforcing stimuli. In T. Thompson, & R. Pickens (Eds.), *Stimulus properties of drugs* (pp. 163–175). New York: Appleton-Century-Crofts.

Woodworth, R. S. (1918). *Dynamic psychology.* New York: Columbia University Press.

Yokel, R. A. (1987). Intravenous self-administration: Response rates, the effects of pharmacological challenges, and drug preferences. In M. A. Bozarth (Ed.), *Methods of assessing the reinforcing properties of abused drugs* (pp. 1–33). New York: Springer-Verlag.

Yokel, R. A., & Pickens, R. (1973). Self-administration of optical isomers of amphetamine and methylamphetamine by rats. *Journal of Pharmacology and Experimental Therapeutics, 187,* 27–33.

Yokel, R. A., & Pickens, R. (1974). Drug level of *d*- and l-amphetamine during intravenous self-administration. *Psychopharmacologia, 34,* 255–264.

Yokel, R. A., & Wise, R. A. (1975). Increased lever pressing for amphetamine after pimozide in rats: Implications for a dopamine theory of reward. *Science, 187,* 547–549.

Yokel, R. A., & Wise, R. A. (1976). Attenuation of intravenous amphetamine reinforcement by central dopamine blockade in rats. *Psychopharmacology, 48,* 311–318.

Young, P. T. (1949). Emotion as disorganized response—a reply to Professor Leeper. *Psychological Review, 56,* 184–191.

Pathways to Relapse: Factors Controlling the Reinitiation of Drug Seeking after Abstinence

Jane Stewart

Concordia University, Montreal, Quebec, Canada

Although considerable knowledge has accumulated over the past 50 years concerning the systems of the brain that support the reinforcing effects of drugs of abuse, this knowledge has not been easily translated into effective treatment. The primary problem for treatment of drug abuse remains the reinitiation of drug craving and seeking after abstinence (relapse). It is not understood why, for example, when drugs are unavailable for long periods of time or when users are successful in curbing their own drug use for extended periods, individuals remain vulnerable to relapse. Studies carried out in rats over the last several years have demonstrated clearly that reinitiation of drug seeking can be induced by reexposure to cues previously associated with drug exposure, by reexposure to the drug itself, and by acute exposure to certain stressors. Thus, when rats are trained to self-administer drugs such as cocaine or heroin, and are then subjected to a period of extinction training, the presentation of cues that have been explicitly paired with drug delivery, an experimenter-delivered

Supported by grants from National Institute on Drug Abuse (NIDA, USA), Canadian Institutes of Health Research (CIHR) and Fonds pour la Formation de Chercheurs et l'Aide la Recherche (FCAR, Quebec). I thank Shimon Amir, Michael Bardo, Francesco Leri, Yavin Shaham, and Barbara Woodside for their helpful readings of the manuscript.

injection of the drug, or acute exposure to foot-shock stress all result in an increase in pressing on lever previously associated with drug delivery; the amount of responding during the period of extinction and during the test for relapse can be considered to reflect the magnitude of drug seeking or the level of motivation to obtain the drug.

Studies carried out in a number of laboratories have provided evidence that the brain systems mediating the effects of conditioned stimuli, priming injections of drugs, and stress on the reinitiation of drug seeking are to some degree dissociable (Erb, Shaham, & Stewart, 2001; McFarland & Kalivas, 2001; Shaham, Erb, & Stewart, 2000; Shalev, Grimm, & Shaham, 2002; Stewart, 2000). Nonetheless, new evidence is beginning to emerge suggesting that the motivation underlying drug seeking induced by all of these manipulations is influenced by two factors, the duration and intensity of preexposure to a drug, and the time since withdrawal of the drug. In this chapter I will discuss how these two factors could act to increase the motivation to take drugs that is observed in the experienced drug user even after long periods of abstinence.[1] Before doing this, however, I will review the evidence showing that repeated exposure to some drugs of abuse does induce changes in the circuitry relevant for reinstatement of drug seeking and will discuss possible mechanisms for the induction of these changes. I will then review evidence showing that preexposure to stimulant and opioid drugs affects both appetitive and aversive motivational processes.

Motivational Processes

The term motivation is invoked by the observation that a particular goal-directed behavior, such as food seeking, occurs at some times and not others, with more or less vigor and persistence. The ease with which a behavior is engaged by environmental stimuli, its persistence, and the energy expended to obtain the goal all appear to depend on internal changes that alter stimulus effectiveness and readiness to act. I will argue here that such altered sensitivity can result from temporary changes in the state of the neural circuitry mediating motivational effects, as well as from long-lasting experience-dependent changes that involve modifications in connectivity and effectiveness of the circuitry.

TEMPORARY STATE CHANGES

Changes in the state of motivational circuits such as those induced by food deprivation and satiety have long been the primary focus of studies in motivation. Such changes can serve to augment or suppress a range of responses to food stimuli and to conditioned stimuli previously paired with food. Similarly, as mentioned above, in rats trained to self-administer a drug such as cocaine, an experimenter-delivered "priming" injection of the drug serves to augment responding to drug-related stimuli (for discussion, see Mueller & Stewart, 2000). Such effects are relatively short-lived and can be turned on and off in the same rat repeatedly.

LONG-LASTING CHANGES IN MOTIVATIONAL SYSTEMS

The second form of altered sensitivity of the brain systems mediating motivational effects is induced by intense or chronic activation of the system and can result in lasting increases in the effects of particular classes of stimuli. Although, traditionally, those interested in motivation have paid less attention to this form of altered sensitivity; in recent years its importance has been recognized, even if its basis is not fully understood.

One area of research that has begun to be concerned with the issue of experience-dependent long-term changes in motivational systems is that of pathological fear and anxiety. Long-lasting hyperexcitability of neural circuitry mediating fear and anxiety has been proposed to underlie the increased response to conditioned fear stimuli and the greater sensitivity to stressful stimuli, in general, seen in posttraumatic stress disorder. It has been recognized that the process of conditioning, in itself, cannot explain the development of pathological anxiety disorders (see Rosen & Schulkin, 1998; Shalev, Peri, Brandes, Freedman, Orr, & Pitman, 2000). In fact, sensitization of the circuitry activated during fear and anxiety states is now considered to provide the best explanation for individual differences in the acquisition and expression of conditioned fears and in the development of pathological fear and anxiety following trauma (see Adamec, Kent, Anisman, Shallow, & Merali, 1998; Adamec, Shallow, & Budgell, 1997). The particular brain circuitry implicated involves the noradrenergic (NE) and corticotropin-releasing factor (CRF) pathways in regions of the amygdala and bed nucleus of the stria terminalis (BNST) (see, for example, Davis, Walker, & Lee, 1997). The recognition that sensitization of this circuitry may develop over time with repeated exposure to stress or following trauma has led to comparisons with the induction of other forms of neural plasticity such as those involved in long-term potentiation (LTP) and kindling that induce synaptic facilitation. Kindling refers to the slow development of seizure activity following repeated subthreshold stimulation and can be compared in its early stages to a nonassociative form of LTP (Sutula & Steward, 1987). Interestingly, it has been found that partial kindling of the amygdala, but not hippocampus, leads to an exaggeration of fear potentiated startle, suggesting sensitization within the circuitry mediating conditioned fear (Rosen, Hamerman, Sitcoske, Glowa, & Schulkin, 1996), and it has been found that fear conditioning, itself, induces LTP in the amygdala (see Bauer, LeDoux, & Nader, 2001; Rogan, Staubli, & LeDoux, 1997). Both kindling and LTP induce lasting changes in the morphology of neurons and synapses, and both involve the recruitment of neurotrophic factors (Kokaia, Kelly, Elmer, Kokaia, McIntyre, & Lindvall, 1996; Simonato et al., 1998) that play a role in the enduring changes in the circuitry. Although originally considered important for their role in neuronal development, it is now recognized that neurotrophic factors play a critical role in the survival, maintenance, and morphological plasticity of neurons in adult animals (see Hefti, Denton, Knusel, & Lapchak, 1993).

LONG-LASTING CHANGES IN MOTIVATIONAL SYSTEMS—THE CIRCUITRY MEDIATING THE STIMULANT EFFECTS OF DRUGS

The idea that long-term changes within specific circuitry might alter the motivational effects of drugs has received considerable attention within the field of drug abuse (see for example Nestler, Barrot, & Self, 2001; Piazza, Deminiere, Le Moal, & Simon, 1990; Robinson & Berridge, 2000). The circuitry best studied and found to undergo lasting changes as a result of repeated exposure to stimulant drugs is the mesocorticolimbic dopaminergic system and its targets in striatum, amygdala, and medial prefrontal cortex (MPFC). Stimulant and opioid drugs induce increases in extracellular dopamine in all of these regions, as well as in the BNST (see Di Chiara et al., 1999)

Repeated exposure to stimulant drugs, such as amphetamine and cocaine, results in enhancement of their behavioral activating effects. This phenomenon, known as behavioral sensitization, develops over time and has been observed months and even years after termination of drug treatment (Castner & Goldman-Rakic, 1999; Paulson, Camp, & Robinson, 1991). Behavioral sensitization is accompanied by increased responsiveness of the mesolimbic dopaminergic system (see Kalivas & Stewart, 1991; Robinson & Becker, 1986). It has been found in numerous experiments that the increase in extracellular dopamine in striatal terminal regions after acute systemic injections of amphetamine or cocaine is enhanced following repeated exposure to these drugs (e.g., Heidbreder, Thompson, & Shippenberg, 1996; Paulson & Robinson, 1995). This enhancement in dopaminergic function develops gradually after termination of drug treatment and is long lasting (Heidbreder, Thompson, & Shippenberg, 1996; Kalivas & Duffy, 1993; Kolta, Shreve, De Souza, & Uretsky, 1985; Paulson et al., 1991; Paulson & Robinson, 1995; Robinson, Jurson, Bennett, & Bentgen, 1988; Vezina, 1993; Wolf, White, Nassar, Brooderson, & Khansa, 1993). Enhancement of function appears to result from a series of changes within the dopaminergic system and its targets that occur over time after termination of drug treatment. Electrophysiological studies have shown that initially there is reduced D2 dopamine autoreceptor sensitivity that results in reduced suppression of dopamine cell firing by dopamine and other agonists lasting about one week; this is followed by a period of enhanced sensitivity of D1 dopamine receptors on nucleus accumbens (NAC) neurons lasting about one month; after about 10–20 days depending on the pretreatment regimen, there are increased extracellular levels of dopamine in NAC in response to drug challenge (Henry, Greene, & White, 1989; Henry & White, 1991; Wolf, White, & Hu, 1994). Importantly, it has been found that in addition to behavioral sensitization (Kalivas & Weber, 1988; Vezina, 1993; Vezina & Stewart, 1990), these changes in dopaminergic function and their time course can be mimicked by direct application of amphetamine in the VTA (Hu, Koeltzow, Cooper, Robertson, White, & Vezina, 2002), demonstrating that processes initiated in the cell body region of dopamine neurons are responsible for sensitized functioning within the system. The relevance of such drug-induced sensitization within the mesolimbic dopaminergic system to the motivational effects of drugs and drug-related stimuli has been pointed out by several investigators over the years (De Vries, Schoffelmeer, Binnekade, & Vanderschuren, 1999; Hu et al., 2002; Kalivas, Pierce, Cornish, & Sorg, 1998; Piazza et al., 1990; Piazza & Le Moal, 1996; Robinson & Berridge, 1993; Stewart, de Wit, & Eikelboom, 1984; Vezina, Lorrain, Arnold, Austin, & Suto, 2002), and this issue is being studied using a number of approaches that are discussed later in this chapter.

The long-lasting changes induced by repeated administration of stimulant drugs suggest structural modifications in neuronal circuitry. In fact, changes in dopaminergic cell size, neurofilament proteins, and glial fibrillary acidic protein (GFAP, an astrocytic-specific intermediate filament protein) have all been observed in the cell body region of mesocorticolimbic neurons in the ventral tegmental area (VTA) immediately after repeated injections of morphine or cocaine (Beitner-Johnson, Guitart, & Nestler, 1992; Beitner-Johnson, Guitart, & Nestler, 1993; Sklair-Tavron, Shi, Lane, Harris, Bunney, & Nestler, 1996) and recent studies have shown selective and persistent changes in transcription factors known to be involved in neuroplasticity (Chen et al., 1995; Nestler et al., 2001; Nestler, Kelz, & Chen, 1999), drug-induced changes in synaptic facilitation and long-term potentiation in dopamine neurons in the VTA (Bonci & Williams, 1996; Ungless, Whistler, Malenka, & Bonci, 2001), as well as structural changes in NAC and mPFC neurons following repeated exposure to these drugs (Robinson & Kolb, 1997; Robinson & Kolb, 1999). Although not yet known, it is likely that such structural modifications are brought about by the operation of neurotrophic factors.

NEUROTROPHIC FACTORS IN DRUG-INDUCED SENSITIZATION

In a set of studies done to determine whether neurotrophic factors play a role in the development of enduring changes in dopaminergic functioning seen after repeated exposure to amphetamine, we found that amphetamine induces increases in the neurotrophic and neuroprotective factor, basic fibroblast growth factor (bFGF or FGF-2), in astrocytes in the cell body region of the midbrain dopaminergic neurons. These increases are seen early after termination of drug treatment and last for at least one month (Flores, Rodaros, & Stewart, 1998). We found as well that, as is the case for the development of behavioral sensitization to amphetamine (see Wolf, 1998), the induction of bFGF by amphetamine is prevented by the co-administration of glutamate antagonists (Flores et al., 1998), and, importantly, that inactivation of bFGF in the VTA prevents the development of behavioral sensitization to amphetamine (Flores, Samaha, & Stewart, 2000). These data led us to propose that repeated exposure to stimulant drugs increases the demands on dopaminergic cell functioning, and by stimulating glutamate release recruits neurotrophic and neuroprotective substances such as bFGF. This sequence of events could provide a mechanism for the initiation and maintenance of the long-lasting neuronal adaptations that underlie sensitized responding to further drug exposure (Flores & Stewart, 2000).

Although few studies have been done to explore the induction by stimulant drugs of other neurotrophic factors known to be expressed within the mesolimbic pathway, there is evidence that repeated exposure to amphetamine induces expression of brain-derived neurotrophic factor (BDNF) both within this system and in the amygdala and BNST (Meredith, Callen, & Scheuer, 2002). In addition, Pierce, Pierce-Bancroft, and Prasad (1999) have reported a transient increase in the expression of neurotrophic factor, NT-3, in the VTA following an acute injection of cocaine. Interestingly, short-term treatment with a dopaminergic receptor antagonist, haloperidol, caused a dramatic decrease in BDNF expression in these same regions (Dawson, Hamid, Egan, & Meredith, 2001), suggesting that there is a positive feedback from activation of dopamine receptors on BDNF activity. In other studies of the effects of BDNF on dopaminergic functioning, it has been found that following continuous local infusion of BDNF into the cell body and terminal regions of midbrain dopaminergic neurons the firing rate of these neurons increases (Shen, Altar, & Chiodo, 1994) and the behavioral activating effects of cocaine and the motivational effects of conditioned reinforcers are enhanced (Horger, Iyasere, Berhow, Messer, Nestler, & Taylor, 1999). These results suggest that the activation of such neurotrophic factors can induce long-lasting changes in the sensitivity of this pathway to motivationally significant stimuli, as reflected in, among other things, enhanced behavioral responses to stimuli known to activate dopaminergic systems, enhanced dopamine release in terminal regions in responses to significant stimuli, and enlargement of the dendritic arbor of postsynaptic cells in NAC and mPFC.

Changes in Motivational Systems Relevant to Drug Abuse and Relapse

WHAT DO CHANGES IN MOTIVATIONAL SYSTEMS DO?

Before discussing the relevance of changes in the motivational systems of the brain for craving, drug seeking, and relapse, it is important to remind ourselves that motivational states, as such, do not induce behaviors; rather they change sensitivity to stimuli. Also it is important to note that unconditioned incentive stimuli activate motivational systems directly, leading, in turn, to temporary changes in behavior in response to other stimuli in the environment. Conditioned stimuli, through their association with unconditioned stimuli, can also induce temporary changes in motivational systems that, in turn, modulate responses to the unconditioned stimulus and to other stimuli in the environment. Thus, there is no question that through associative learning processes, stimuli that are paired with incentive events gain the ability to alter motivational processes.

A surprising finding has been that conditioned stimuli (environmental contexts) can also control the expression of the long-lasting sensitization within the neural circuitry mediating motivational effects (Anagnostaras & Robinson, 1996; Vezina & Stewart, 1984). For example, if stimulant drug injections are paired with one environment and saline injections with another, sensitization as measured by enhanced responding to a subsequent injection of the drug is evident only in the drug-paired environment. This does not mean, however, that sensitization is itself a conditioned response; rather, it means that conditioned stimuli (or context) can gate the expression of the underlying sensitization (see Stewart, 1992). Studies showing sensitization of mesolimbic dopaminergic system functioning that is independent of environmental context provide evidence for the separation between the two processes—sensitization and conditioned stimulus control of sensitization. For example, sensitization that is independent of environmental context results from repeated application of amphetamine into the cell body region of dopaminergic neurons in the VTA (Kalivas & Weber, 1988; Vezina, 1993; Vezina & Stewart, 1990). Rats so treated show higher levels of behavioral activation and greater dopamine release in NAC in response to systemic injections of amphetamine regardless of the environment where they are tested.

Other evidence that sensitization occurs to the behavioral activating effects of amphetamine independent of conditioned stimulus control comes from a study by Stewart and Vezina (1991) in which rats experienced injections of amphetamine in one environment and saline in another. Following this training they showed enhanced behavioral activation in response to amphetamine that was evident only in the environment with which the drug had been paired. However, after a period of extinction training, during which the rats were given saline injections repeatedly in both environments (and following which rats showed no evidence for conditioned activity in the "drug-paired" environment), behavioral sensitization was expressed in both environments following an injection of amphetamine. This finding suggested to us that the expression of sensitization in the previously unpaired environment was released from inhibition after extinction of the conditioned stimulus control (Stewart & Vezina, 1991). A similar conclusion was drawn in a study by Anagnostaras, Schallert, and Robinson (2002) in which rats were given pairings of amphetamine with one environment and saline with another. After demonstrating that sensitization to amphetamine was subsequently expressed only in the paired environment, an attempt was made to disrupt the association between the environment and amphetamine by giving electroconvulsive shock (ECS) following the reactivation of the original learning in either the paired or unpaired environments. Those given ECS in the previously unpaired environment showed sensitized responding to amphetamine when subsequently tested in that environment. The effect of ECS was to reveal sensitization in the unpaired environment, again suggesting that the unpaired environment normally exerts inhibitory control over the expression of underlying sensitization (Anagnostaras et al., 2002). It seems clear from these findings and others that enduring enhancement of the functioning of the midbrain dopaminergic systems can exist independently from conditioned stimulus control of the expression of sensitization, and, as was discussed in the case of fear circuitry, this enduring enhancement of functioning would serve to enhance the effectiveness of unconditioned stimuli as well as those of conditioned stimuli.

Evidence That Preexposure to Stimulant Drugs Enhances Subsequent Responses to Appetitive Stimuli

One question that can be asked about the long-lasting consequences of preexposure to drugs is whether they are expressed only as enhanced behavioral activation in response to the drugs themselves, as is seen in studies of behavioral sensitization, or whether they are reflected in motivational properties of drugs and of other natural incentive stimuli. In the following section studies addressing this issue will be reviewed.

THE INCENTIVE MOTIVATIONAL PROPERTIES OF DRUGS

A number of researchers have studied the effects of experimenter-delivered injections of drugs on their subsequent ability to act as reinforcing stimuli. For example, it has been shown that preexposure to stimulant drugs facilitates the subsequent acquisition of a conditioned place preference (CPP), suggesting that the drugs serve as more effective rewards following repeated exposure (Lett, 1989; Shippenberg & Heidbreder, 1995). Similarly, preexposure to stimulant drugs facilitates the subsequent acquisition of responding for intravenous injections of low doses of the drug (Horger, Giles, & Schenk, 1992; Horger, Shelton, & Schenk, 1990; Piazza, Deminiere, Le Moal, & Simon, 1989; Valadez & Schenk, 1994; Vezina, Pierre, & Lorrain, 1999), again suggesting that rats are more sensitive to the reinforcing properties of the drug after preexposure. Interestingly, manipulations that normally block the development of sensitization to these drugs also block the facilitating effects on acquisition of drug taking when they are given concurrently with the drug during the preexposure period (Pierre & Vezina, 1998; Schenk et al., 1993)

More recently, it has been shown that preexposure to amphetamine by experimenter-delivered injections enhances subsequent responding for relatively high doses of amphetamine in rats working on a progressive ratio schedule (Lorrain, Arnold, & Vezina, 2000; Mendrek, Blaha, & Phillips, 1998). Vezina et al. (2002) have found that this increased willingness to work for amphetamine injections is associated with increased levels of extracellular dopamine in NAC following earned injections. It is important to note that in none of these studies was preexposure to the drug given in the environment where the rats were subsequently tested, demonstrating that the changes in functioning of the motivational systems involved were not under the control of conditioned contextual stimuli.

In studies done to model more directly the effects of long-term exposure to self-administration of drugs on subsequent motivation to take them, Deroche, Le Moal, and Piazza (1999) found that rats given an extended period of cocaine self-administration (29 days) subsequently showed greater intake of all doses of cocaine tested, and ran faster in a runway to obtain cocaine injections at all doses, than rats given a short period (6 days). Similarly, it was found that cocaine-trained rats given long daily periods of access subsequently administered twice as much cocaine at all doses as did rats given short daily access (Ahmed & Koob, 1998; Ahmed & Koob, 1999). The upward shift in the dose response curve found in these studies suggests that extended self-administration of cocaine increased the incentive value of all doses of the drug.

BEHAVIORAL AND NEUROCHEMICAL RESPONSES TO SEXUALLY RELEVANT STIMULI IN RATS

Several studies have found that preexposure to opioid or stimulant drugs in rats facilitates sexual responding in tests given later in the absence of drugs. For example, male rats given morphine repeatedly in one environment, and saline in another, were found subsequently to display more pursuit of the female, anogenital exploration, and partial mounts, and to initiate copulation more rapidly when tested in the environment previously paired with morphine than in the saline paired environment (Mitchell & Stewart, 1990). Experiments done in males three weeks after repeated injections of amphetamine revealed enhanced sexual behavior accompanied by enhanced release of dopamine in the NAC in response to the female (Fiorino & Phillips, 1999a; Fiorino & Phillips, 1999b). It is interesting that in these studies with amphetamine, drug preexposure led to facilitation of sexual behaviors that was not dependent on the rats being tested in the drug-paired environment.

APPETITIVE CONDITIONING

There are several studies suggesting that preexposure to stimulant drugs facilitates subsequent learning based on food or water rewards. For example, it was found that rats preexposed to amphetamine showed more rapid appetitive conditioning to a stimulus paired with a sucrose reward (Harmer & Phillips, 1998), and those previously exposed to amphetamine or cocaine, more rapid acquisition of approach behavior to a stimulus paired with water (Taylor & Jentsch, 2001). Furthermore, following training, the conditioned stimulus was found to elicit increases in dopamine in the amygdala that were greater in rats preexposed to amphetamine than in those preexposed to saline (Harmer & Phillips, 1999).

Together these studies support the idea that preexposure to stimulant drugs enhances responding to both unconditioned and conditioned appetitive events including drug, sexual, food, and water stimuli, making it appear that preexposure to stimulant drugs can have long-lasting effects on the neural circuitry subserving appetitive motivation in general (see also Wyvell & Berridge, 2001).

Evidence That Preexposure to Stimulant Drugs Enhances Subsequent Responses to Aversive Stimuli

Acute injections of stimulant and opioid drugs activate the hypothalamic-pituitary-adrenal axis in a manner similar to an acute stressor (Borowsky & Kuhn, 1991; Buckingham & Cooper, 1984; Torres & Rivier, 1992). Furthermore, it has been known for some time that repeated exposure to stimulant drugs enhances behavioral activation induced by stressful stimuli, and vice versa (Antelman & Chiodo, 1983). Acute injections of amphetamine or cocaine have been found to activate cells in the nuclei of the amygdala and BNST as assessed by *c-fos* mRNA expression in these regions. Interestingly, *c-fos* expression is seen in the basolateral amygdala (BLA), and in the central amygdala (CeA) and the oval nucleus of the BNST (BNSTOV) after drug injections, but the effects are differentially affected by novel environmental stimuli. BLA expression is greatly enhanced by a novel environment, whereas CeA and BNSTOV is greatest when injections are given in the home cage (Day et al., 2001). It appears that different circuits are activated by the drugs given in the home cage (a drug effect) than are activated when the drugs are given in the presence of novel stimuli (see also Badiani, Oates, Day, Watson, Akil, & Robinson, 1998). It would be interesting to determine whether these different pathways can be manipulated independently by long-term exposure to cocaine or amphetamine.

Repeated exposure to amphetamine has been shown to enhance stress-induced release of dopamine in prefrontal cortex (Hamamura & Fibiger, 1993), and enhanced activation of limbic regions as measured by *c-fos* expression in response to a conditioned fear stimulus (Hamamura, Ichimaru, & Fibiger, 1997). It has also been shown recently that rats preexposed to amphetamine exhibit higher levels of corticosterone and adrenocorticotropic hormone (ACTH) in response to 30 minutes of restraint stress when tested two weeks after the last injection of amphetamine (Barr, Hofmann, Weinberg, & Phillips, 2002; see also Schmidt, Tilders, Binnekade, Schoffelmeer, & De Vries, 1999). Considerable work has been done to explore changes in the functioning of the CRF systems of the brain following long-term exposure to drugs of abuse (see Koob, 1999; Sarnyai, Shaham, & Heinrichs, 2001). CRF MRNA in amygdala and BNST, regions considered to form part of the fear circuitry, has been found to be upregulated by exposure to corticosterone, unlike what has been found in the hypothalamic pituitary systems (Makino, Gold, & Schulkin, 1994a; Makino, Gold, & Schulkin, 1994b) and chronic exposure to corticosterone augments the enhancement of startle induced by ICV infusions of CRF (Lee, Schulkin, & Davis, 1994). This implies that exposure to treatments that lead to excessive release of corticosterone would have the effect of increasing CRF expression in these regions and possibly the effectiveness of the central actions of CRF. An analysis of studies on the effects of acute and chronic exposure to drugs of abuse on CRF MRNA and protein expression in extrahypothalamic has yield mixed results. Although demonstrating that CRF systems are affected by drug exposure, no clear picture of the short- and long-term effects has emerged (see Sarnyai et al., 2001). CRF1 receptor binding is decreased after cocaine preexposure, but this effect is short-lived (Ambrosia, Sharpe, & Pilotte, 1997). Most interestingly, levels of CRF measured in the amygdala using microdialysis have been found to be increased in the period immediately after withdrawal of a number of drugs including alcohol (Merlo Pich et al., 1995) and cocaine (Richter, Merlo Pich, Koob, & Weiss, 1995). It is not known whether preexposure to such drugs alters the response of these CRF systems to stressors presented long after withdrawal. Interestingly, however, it was found recently that foot-shock stress increases CRF MRNA in the CeA and the dorsal BNST following 1 or 6 days of withdrawal from heroin, but not sucrose, self-administration (Shalev, Hope, Clements, Morales, & Shaham, 2001), suggesting that drug preexposure enhances the response of extrahypothalamic CRF systems to stress.

Evidence from Studies of Relapse to Drug Seeking in Rats

In the previous sections I reviewed results pointing to long-term changes in neural circuitry induced by repeated exposure to stimulant drugs. These changes define the substrates that have been found critical to reinstatement of drug seeking by cues, drugs, and stressors. In this section I will briefly review the evidence for this latter statement and will then turn to the question of whether preexposure to drugs augments reinstatement by cues, drugs, and stressors, and whether time since last exposure to drugs plays a significant role in the magnitude of the response to these events.

Cue-Induced Reinstatement

SYSTEMS OF THE BRAIN MEDIATING CUE-INDUCED REINSTATEMENT

It has long been recognized that stimuli that have been associated with drugs of abuse are powerful instigators of drug craving, seeking, and taking even after long periods of extinction of drug-taking behavior or drug abstinence (Childress, Ehrman, Rohsenow, Robbins, & O'Brien, 1992; Siegel, 1983; Stewart et al., 1984; Wikler & Pescor, 1967). Only recently, however, have studies been done to identify the brain systems mediating the ability of conditioned cues to reinitiate and maintain drug seeking after a period of extinction training during which these cues are not presented (see Figure 1, left panel). Several studies using either permanent or reversible (tetrodotoxin, TTX) lesions have identified the basolateral amygdala (BLA) as a primary site for the actions of conditioned cues previously paired with cocaine (Grimm & See, 2000; Kantak, Black, Valencia, Green-Jordan, & Eichenbaum, 2002; Meil & See, 1996. For additional support for a role of the BLA in cue-induced reinstatement see Cicco-

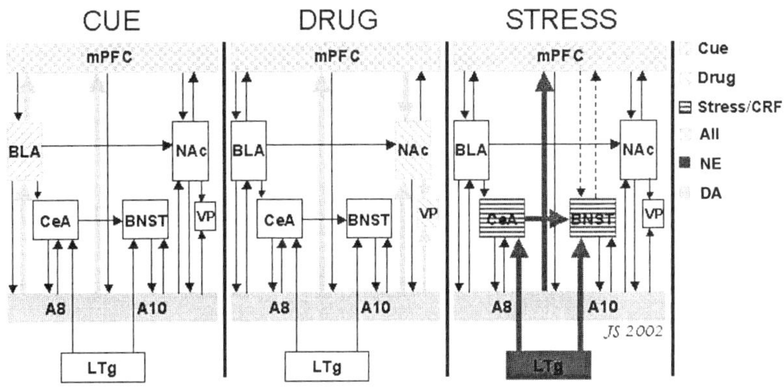

Figure 1. Diagram representing present knowledge of the systems of the brain critical for the induction of reinstatement by cues, drugs, and foot-shock stressor, respectively. In each case, *fat arrows* indicate pathways implicated in reinstatement; *thin arrows* indicate some of the existing direct anatomical connections and *dashed arrows*, indirect connections. Abbreviations: MPFC (medial prefrontal cortex), BLA (basolateral amygdala), CeA (central amygdala), BNST (bed nucleus of the stria terminalis), NAC (nucleus accumbens), A8 and A10 (dopaminergic [DA] cell groups), LTg (noradrenergic [NE] cell groups of the lateral tegmental nuclei), VP (ventral pallidum), CRF (corticotropin-releasing hormone).

cioppo, 1999; Weiss, Maldonado-Vlaar, Parsons, Kerr, Smith, & Ben-Shahar, 2000). Using lesions, Grimm and See (2000) have been able to dissociate the systems responsible for responding controlled by conditioned cues and responding for cocaine itself. TTX lesions of the BLA block the effects of conditioned cues, but have no effect on cocaine self-administration; whereas TTX lesions of the NAC interfere with drug taking without affecting responding controlled by cues alone. Recently, this same group compared reinstatement induced by conditioned cues and by priming injections in heroin-trained rats and found that TTX inactivation of the BLA blocked both cue- and heroin priming-induced responding (Fuchs & See, 2002). It is to be noted however, that the BLA has not been found to be necessary for drug-induced reinstatement in cocaine-trained animals (McFarland & Kalivas, 2001).

There is evidence that the effects of cocaine cues are mediated, at least in part, by dopaminergic mechanisms in the amygdala. D1 dopamine receptor antagonists attenuate cue-induced reinstatement of cocaine seeking whether given systemically or directly into the amygdala (See, Kruzich, & Grimm, 2001). In addition, there is evidence that cocaine cue-induced reinstatement is accompanied by increased release of dopamine in the amygdala (Weiss et al., 2000) and an increased number of Fos-positive cells in both amygdala and mPFC that can be blocked by a D1 dopamine receptor antagonist (Ciccocioppo, Sanna, & Weiss, 2001). Interestingly, imaging studies in human addicts have shown the amygdala and mPFC-cingulate cortex to respond selectively to cues associated with drug taking (Childress, Mozley, McElgin, Fitzgerald, Reivich, & O'Brien, 1999; Grant et al., 1996).

EFFECTS OF DRUG PREEXPOSURE ON CUE-INDUCED REINSTATEMENT

The effectiveness of cues previously paired with drugs in the reinstatement of drug seeking would be expected to depend on learning variables, such as the number of times the cues were paired with drug and the doses of the drugs used. There is some evidence from studies of drug-induced CPP that the effectiveness of cues is increased by the number of training trials (see, for example, Shippenberg & Heidbreder, 1995; Shippenberg, Heidbreder, & Lefevour, 1996). Such studies also address the issue of the effects of drug preexposure on cue-induced reinstatement. For example, as mentioned earlier, Lett (1989) and Shippenberg and Heidbreder (1995) and Shippenberg et al. (1996) showed that preexposure to stimulant drugs facilitates the subsequent expression of the CPP, as measured by approaching and maintaining contact with contextual cues. Interestingly, there is a recent study showing enhanced dopamine release in the amygdala in response to a conditioned stimulus in rats preexposed to amphetamine (Harmer & Phillips, 1999), suggesting that preexposure to drugs could enhance the effectiveness of cues in reinstatement.

EFFECTS OF TIME SINCE TERMINATION OF DRUG EXPOSURE

There is a recent finding that is of particular importance for the idea that long-term changes in the systems mediating the effects of conditioned cues in relapse occur after the period of cue-drug pairing, and following drug withdrawal. Different groups of cocaine-trained rats were tested for extinction and cue-induced relapse at a number of time points, 1–60 days, following the termination of drug self-administration sessions. A progressive and dramatic increase was observed in the number of responses made during extinction and on the test for reinstatement as a function of time since drug termination, suggesting an enhanced motivational effect of cues as a function of time (Grimm, Hope, Wise, & Shaham, 2001). Most interesting for the present discussion is this group's recent finding that in rats trained in a similar manner to self-administer cocaine and then killed at different time points after drug termination, there were significant time-dependent increases in BDNF protein that were apparent in the VTA (at 30 and 90 days), and that increased between 30 and 90 days in both the NAC and the amygdala. No such time-dependent changes were seen in rats trained to self-administer sucrose (Grimm, Lu, Hayashi, Hope, Su, & Shaham, 2003).

There is, interestingly, one study of the expression of fear in response to conditioned cues as a function of the passage of time that parallels these findings of Grimm, Hope, Wise, and Shaham (2001) in a striking manner. Groups of rats were exposed to two CS-foot-shock sessions and were then tested for fear after 1, 20, 40, 60, or 80 days. It was found that freezing in response to contexts and cues previously associated with foot-shock increased as a function of time (Houston, Stevenson, McNaughton, & Barnes, 1999). It can be noted as well that although the authors originally conceived the study to be about consolidation of the associative learning, they postulate that the results may "reflect a generalized increase in the gain of the circuitry mediating the fear response itself" (p. 111). It is important to note that whatever the silent processes are that mediate such effects, they are changes that occur with the passage of time and that develop in the absence of further learning or experience with the unconditioned stimuli.

Drug-induced Reinstatement

Reinstatement of drug seeking by experimenter-delivered priming injections of the drug is a well-established phenomenon (Carroll & Comer, 1996; de Wit, 1996). It has been studied in drug self-administration and in CPP experiments. In the later case, rats are given pairings of one compartment of a choice box apparatus with drug and of another compartment with vehicle. On a test to determine the existence of a condition preference, the rats are allowed to choose freely between the compartments; if rats spend a significantly greater amount of time in the compartment previously paired with drug, they are said to have developed a CPP. It has been found that following the extinction of the preference by repeated trials without drug, the former preference can be completely reinstated by giving the rats a single injection of the drug before the test (Mueller & Stewart, 2000; Parker & McDonald, 2000).

SYSTEMS OF THE BRAIN MEDIATING DRUG-INDUCED REINSTATEMENT

Studies using intracranial injections, lesions, and pharmacological manipulations all point to the importance of activity in the mesolimbic dopamine system and its terminal regions in priming drug-induced reinstatement of lever pressing in rats trained to self-administer opioid and stimulant drugs (see McFarland & Kalivas, 2001; Shalev et al., 2002; Stewart, 2000) (see Figure 1, middle panel). It should also be noted that the neurochemical systems mediating these effects are, in large part, dissociable from those mediating relapse induced by stressors (Shaham, Erb, & Stewart, 2000).

EFFECTS OF DRUG PREEXPOSURE ON DRUG-INDUCED REINSTATEMENT

The possible long-term effects of preexposure to drugs on the effectiveness of priming injections during reinstatement has not been studied systematically, but there are a few pieces of evidence showing that drug-induced reinstatement is enhanced by preexposure to the drug. In the simplest case, there is evidence that priming injections of drugs, such as cocaine and amphetamine, do not reinstate extinguished behavior based on nondrug reinforcers. For example, in a recent unpublished study we found that rats trained to self-administer sucrose pellets and then given extinction training did not show reinstatement of lever pressing following a priming injection of cocaine (see also de Wit & Stewart, 1981). It would be interesting to determine whether a priming injection of cocaine would reinstate lever pressing for sucrose pellets, if rats were preexposed to cocaine before training and extinction.

In a study of the long-lasting consequences of experimenter-administered preexposure to amphetamine on subsequent reinstatement by priming injections of amphetamine, Vezina et al. (2002) showed that rats preexposed to amphetamine made a greater number of lever presses and displayed enhanced levels of dopamine in the NAC following the priming injection of amphetamine. Furthermore, Deroche et al. (1999) found that extended sessions of cocaine self-administration led to a shift to the left of the dose response curve for reinstatement by cocaine; similarly there are two reports that the amount of drug intake during self-administration training correlates with amphetamine- or cocaine-seeking behavior following priming injections (Baker, Tran-Nguyen, Fuchs, & Neisewander, 2001; Sutton, Karanian, & Self, 2000). Thus, the amount of preexposure to drug, whether experimenter-delivered or self-administered, appears to enhance the effectiveness of priming injections as measured in tests for reinstatement.

EFFECTS OF TIME SINCE TERMINATION OF DRUG EXPOSURE

There is only one published study of the effects of priming injections as a function of time since withdrawal of the drug. It was found that cocaine priming injections led to considerably more responding when rats were tested for the first time 30 days after withdrawal than when rats were tested 1 or 7 days after withdrawal (Tran-Nguyen, Fuchs, Coffey, Baker, O'Dell, & Neisewander, 1998). More recently, Shaham et al. (personal communication) studied the time-course of cocaine priming effects using a similar methodology. In one study, cocaine priming tests (5 and 15 mg/kg) were given 1, 30, and 90 days after training in different groups of rats, and in another study (2.5 and 5 mg/kg), 1 and 30 days after; in neither case were there significant differences in the amount of responding as a function of time since withdrawal. One possible explanation for these different results is that in the Shaham study rats took about 45 mg/kg of cocaine per day as opposed to about 7 mg/kg/per day in the study by Tran-Nguyen et al., pointing to an effect of increased drug exposure on drug-induced reinstatement. It is interesting, however, to compare the effects of priming injections of drugs on reinstatement with the behavioral activating effects of drugs (sensitization) seen after termination of drug treatment. It has been found in many studies that enhanced behavioral activation induced by drugs such as cocaine and amphetamine is evident in tests given within 3 days after withdrawal, whereas enhanced dopaminergic levels to drug challenges are not seen until much later. This discrepancy has been troubling for some individuals, but in view of the changes in D1 and D2 dopamine receptor sensitivity seen early after withdrawal, the increased effectiveness of drugs on behavioral activation should not be surprising. In an interesting set of experiments deVries and colleagues (1998; 1999) have shown that the effectiveness of a drug in tests of reinstatement is correlated with the expression of sensitization of the behavioral activating effects.

Another finding from the study by Tran-Nguyen et al. (1998) was that dopamine levels in the amygdala in response to the priming injection were significantly higher 30 days after withdrawal than at earlier time points. Again, this finding is similar to that seen in the NAC after injections of cocaine (Kalivas & Duffy, 1993) or amphetamine (Wolf et al., 1993) in studies of sensitization in which rats are preexposed to repeated injections of these drugs.

Stress-induced Reinstatement

Over the last several years, we have been studying the neural systems mediating stress-induced reinstatement of drug seeking. Most of this work has been carried out in cocaine, heroin, or ethanol self-administering rats that are exposed to a brief period (15 minutes) of intermittent foot-shock after extinction. This kind of manipulation is extremely effective in inducing relapse even after a long period of abstinence. Because this work has been reviewed a number of times in the last two years (Erb, Shaham, & Stewart, J. 2001; Shaham, Erb, & Stewart, 2000; Shalev et al., 2002; Stewart, 2000), I will be selective in my discussion of it, emphasizing aspects that relate to the issues addressed in this chapter. After outlining our studies of the neural circuitry involved, I will, as in the case of cue- and drug-induced reinstatement, explore the evidence to suggest that preexposure to drugs of abuse and the passage of time contribute to the vulnerability of individuals to relapse induced by exposure to stress. Clearly this matter is not settled and much work needs to be done. I think, however, that we are now in a position to tackle the issue, knowing what we do about the systems involved in the mediation of stress-induced reinstatement.

SYSTEM OF THE BRAIN MEDIATING STRESS-INDUCED REINSTATEMENT

We found early on in our studies that pharmacological manipulations, such as opioid and dopamine receptor antagonists, that effectively blocked heroin-induced reinstatement have no effect on stress-induced reinstatement in heroin-trained rats (Shaham, Rajabi, & Stewart, 1996; Shaham & Stewart, 1996). Furthermore, we found that stress-induced corticosterone release was not responsible for the effect in either cocaine- or heroin-trained rats (Erb, Shaham, & Stewart, 1998; Shaham, Funk, Erb, Brown, Walker, & Stewart, 1997). This latter finding led us to explore the role of CRF systems of the brain, and indeed we found that central CRF systems are important. Infusions of CRF given intracerebroventricularly (ICV) or into the ventrolateral BNST induce reinstatement in the absence of an external stressor, whereas infusions into the CRF containing regions of the amygdala have no effect. Infusions of CRF receptor antagonists block foot-shock-induced reinstatement when given ICV or into the ventrolateral BNST, but have no effect in the amygdala (Erb & Stewart, 1999; Shaham et al., 1997).

We have also found that activation of central NE systems is critically involved in stress-induced relapse. Systemic injections of agents that reduce cell firing and release of NE in the brain (Aghajanian, 1982; Carter, 1997), such as the alpha-2 adrenoceptor agonists clonidine and lofexidine, block stress-induced reinstatement in cocaine- (Erb, Hitchcott, Rajabi, Mueller, Shaham, & Stewart, 2000) and in heroin-trained rats (Shaham, Highfield, Delfs, Leung, & Stewart, 2000). The two major NE systems of the brain arise from the locus coeruleus (LC), origin of NE projections to cortex, hippocampus, and other forebrain structures, and from the lateral tegmental nuclei (LTg) projecting via the ventral bundle to the CeA, the septum, and the BNST (Aston-Jones, Delfs, Druhan, & Zhu, 1999). Using infusions of clonidine or ST-91 (a charged analog of clonidine with reduced lipophilic properties) and selective 6-hydroxdopamine lesions, we determined that the ventral NE bundle neurons were of primary importance in stress-induced reinstatement (Shaham, Highfield, Delfs, Leung, & Stewart, 2000). These findings, combined with those showing the importance of CRF activity in the BNST in stress-induced reinstatement (Erb, Salmaso, Rodaros, & Stewart, 2001; Erb & Stewart, 1999) and those showing that temporary inactivation of the BNST or amygdala also blocks foot-shock-induced heroin seeking (Shaham, Erb, & Stewart, 2000), led us to study the role of NE activity in the BNST and CeA region in stress-induced reinstatement. To block NE activity in these regions, different groups of rats were given bilateral infusions of one of four doses of a cocktail of the beta-1 and beta-2 receptor antagonists betaxolol and ICI 181,555 (vehicle, 0.25, 0.5, and 1 nmol of each compound in 0.5 æl) either into the BNST or CeA. We found a dose-dependent reduction of stress-induced reinstatement after infusions into the BNST and a complete blockade of stress-induced reinstatement after infusions into the CeA at all doses tested. The same treatments did not block cocaine-induced reinstatement at either site (Leri, Flores, Rodaros, & Stewart, 2002). In summary, these data suggest that a potential mechanism for the mediation of the effects of foot-shock on reinstatement of drug seeking is via the release of NE in the amygdala and BNST (see Figure 1, right panel). Through effects at beta NE receptors, NE may activate CRF containing cells in both regions. Some of these CRF-neurons project from the CeA to the BNST and others are intrinsic to the BNST itself. This idea, of course, does not rule out other actions of NE in these regions, but it does suggest that the critical event for the initiation of reinstatement induced by stress is the release of CRF in the BNST. Interference in this circuit has no effect on cocaine-induced relapse.

EFFECTS OF DRUG PREEXPOSURE ON STRESS-INDUCED REINSTATEMENT

Again we can ask whether preexposure to drugs of abuse makes animals more vulnerable to stress-induced reinstatement of responding. Interestingly, it was found in several experiments that foot-shock does not reinstate responding after extinction in rats trained to lever press for food or sucrose reinforcers (Ahmed & Koob, 1997; Buczek, Lê, Stewart, & Shaham, 1999; Lê, Quan, Juzytsch, Fletcher, Joharchi, & Shaham, 1998). There are two studies showing that the effects of foot-shock stress on reinstatement are enhanced in animals given greater amount and duration of exposure to drugs. It was found in one study that rats given 11 hours of heroin self-administration daily during training compared to those given 1 hour showed enhanced responding following foot-shock in tests for reinstatement (Ahmed, Walker, & Koob, 2000). Similarly, it was found that in rats trained to lever press for ethanol, an extended period of exposure to ethanol vapor led to enhanced sensitivity to foot-shock-induced reinstatement (Liu & Weiss, 2002). Interestingly, it was found that foot-shock stress reinstates lever pressing in rats trained to self-administer rewarding electrical brain stimulation in the septal area (Shalev, Highfield, Yap, & Shaham, 2000). Although the basis for the susceptibility to stress-induced relapse in these rats is not known, it is interesting to speculate about the possibility that the repeated electrical brain stimulation sensitizes circuits activated by the stressor. This suggestion is based on a study showing that electrical stimulation of the VTA enhances fear potentiated startle (Borowski & Kokkinidis, 1996), provokes afterdischarge in the CeA, and enhances the rate of amygdala kindling (Gelowitz & Kokkinidis, 1999).

EFFECTS OF TIME SINCE TERMINATION OF DRUG EXPOSURE

There is only one study of the effects of time since drug termination on relapse induced by foot-shock stress. In this study rats were trained to self-administer heroin (not cocaine as in the study of cue-induced reinstatement) after termination of drug taking, and different groups were then tested in extinction and, following that, for foot-shock-induced reinstatement of responding at different time points after training (Shalev et al., 2001). It was found that responding in extinction and in tests for foot-shock-induced reinstatement peaked around 12 days after termination of drug treatment.As in the study in cocaine-trained rats, extinction responding and reinstatement was low 24 hours after drug taking and increased over days. The fact that extinction responding did not continue to increase after that as it had in cocaine-trained rats is likely due to differences in the long-lasting effects of opioids and stimulants on specific systems, but further work is needed to determine the source of these differences.

Summary

Studies of cue-, drug-, and stress-induced relapse to cocaine and heroin seeking have provided evidence for a role for drug-experience and time-dependent increases in the sensitivity of systems mediating relapse. Although these data are at this time fragmentary, in combination with the evidence reviewed here showing that repeated exposure to stimulant drugs leads to enhanced responding to motivationally significant stimuli (both positive and negative), as well as to lasting changes in neural systems mediating motivational effects, they provide a basis for future studies. It is likely, simply on the basis of their different pharmacological effects, that different drugs will produce different types of effects on these motivational systems and that there will be differences in the time course of onset and duration of these effects. The challenge will be to sort out the commonalities and differences in the processes that underlie the long-lasting changes induced by different drugs.

The Systems and Their Interactions

There is no doubt that the different systems preferentially mediating reinstatement of drug seeking by cues, drugs, and stressors are intimately connected (see Figure 1). And it is likely, therefore, that activation within one subsystem can affect other subsystems. Thus, long-term exposure to drugs of abuse could have effects on motivational systems either directly or indirectly. For example, if enduring changes in the functioning of the midbrain dopaminergic systems are induced by exposure to drug, these changes would presumably affect drug-induced reinstatement directly and, perhaps, stress-induced reinstatement indirectly though its modulation of the amygdala and BNST system. As discussed earlier, the BLA, found to be critical in cue-induced reinstatement, projects to the CeA, the NAC and MPFC. The mesocorticolimbic system found to play a primary role in relapse induced by priming injections of opioid and stimulant drugs sends it projections from the VTA to NAC, MPFC, amygdala, and BNST and, in turn, receives projections from each of these areas. The CeA and BNST, regions found to play a critical role in stress-induced reinstatement, receive NE inputs from the LTg nuclei. Both the amygdala and BNST have intrinsic CRF-containing neurons, but in addition the CeA sends a CRF projection to the BNST. Both the CeA and BNST send projections to the paraventricular nucleus of the hypothalamus (PVN), which in turn affect the hypothalamic-pituitary-adrenal (HPA)-axis control of release of corticosterone by stimulant drugs and stressors (Herman & Cullinan, 1997; Herman, Cullinan, & Watson, 1994; Prewitt & Herman, 1998). In addition there is evidence that the projection from the BNST to the PVN is CRF containing (Champagne, Beaulieu, & Drolet, 1998). Stimulation of the BNST activates dopaminergic neurons in the VTA (Georges & Aston-Jones, 2001; Marcangione, Stewart, & Rompré, 2000), suggesting a pathway that could be involved in the activation of behavior by manipulations in the BNST.

Because of the potential for interaction between systems, it is likely that activation within one subsystem can affect other subsystems and may lead finally to the engagement of a common pathway that controls the reinitiation of responding in all these circumstances. Interestingly, a series of recent papers has pointed to the importance of the MPFC in reinstatement by cues (See, 2002), drugs (McFarland & Kalivas, 2001; Park et al., 2002) and stressors (Capriles, Rodaros, Sorge, & Stewart, 2003), suggesting that this region of the brain may serve as a common pathway for reinstatement of drug seeking by stressors, priming injections of drugs, and drug-related cues.

Much is yet to be understood about the role of these systems and their interactions in motivated behaviors, in general, and, more specifically, in the motivational changes observed in studies of relapse to drug seeking. From the perspective of the present chapter, the challenge will be to determine how exposure to drugs of abuse changes these systems, and whether and how these changes determine the time-dependent behavioral and neurochemical changes that are seen following termination of drug exposure.

Note

1. Although there is considerable evidence that repeated exposure to stimulant drugs is associated with enduring increases in the incentive properties of drugs, resistance to the idea remains strong. This may arise from the belief that conditioning and learning mechanisms are sufficient to account for the increasing control over behavior that drugs of abuse gain with repeated use and that drugs of abuse are just particularly potent reinforcers (see Di Chiara et al. (1999); Everitt, B. J., Dickinson, A., & Robbins, T. W. (2001); White, N. M. (1996). It may also be, however, that because homeostatic adaptations play an important role in tolerance, dependence, and withdrawal, there is a tendency to invoke them as explanations for escalated use and persistent relapse (see Koob, G. F., & Le Moal, M. (1997). For commentary

on this issue see (Berke, J. D., & Hyman, S. E. (2000); Stewart, J., de Wit, H., & Eikelboom, R. (1984); Wise, R. A. (1996).

References

Adamec, R., Kent, P., Anisman, H., Shallow, T., & Merali, Z. (1998). Neural plasticity, neuropeptides and anxiety in animals—implications for understanding and treating affective disorder following traumatic stress in humans. *Neuroscience and Biobehavioral Reviews, 23,* 301–318.

Adamec, R. E., Shallow, T., & Budgell, J. (1997). Blockade of CCK(B) but not CCK(A) receptors before and after the stress of predator exposure prevents lasting increases in anxiety-like behavior: Implications for anxiety associated with posttraumatic stress disorder. *Behavioral Neuroscience, 111,* 435–449.

Aghajanian, G. K. V., VanderMaelen, C. P. (1982). alpha-2 adrenoceptor-mediated hyperpolarization of locus coeruleus neurons: Intracellular studies in vivo. *Science, 215,* 1394–1396.

Ahmed, S. H., & Koob, G. F. (1997). Cocaine—but not food—seeking behavior is reinstated by stress after extinction. *Psychopharmacology, 132,* 289–295.

Ahmed, S. H., & Koob, G. F. (1998). Transition from moderate to excessive drug intake: Change in hedonic set point. *Science, 282,* 298–300.

Ahmed, S. H., & Koob, G. F. (1999). Long-lasting increase in the set point for cocaine self-administration after escalation in rats. *Psychopharmacology, 146,* 303–312.

Ahmed, S. H., Walker, J. R., & Koob, G. F. (2000). Persistent increase in the motivation to take heroin in rats with a history of drug escalation. *Neuropsychopharmacology, 22*(4), 413–421.

Ambrosia, E., Sharpe, L. G., & Pilotte, N. S. (1997). Regional binding to corticotropin releasing factor receptors in brain of rats exposed to chronic cocaine and cocaine withdrawal. *Synapse, 25,* 272–276.

Anagnostaras, S. G., & Robinson, T. E. (1996). Sensitization to the psychomotor stimulant effects of amphetamine: Modulation by associative learning. *Behavioral Neuroscience, 110,* 1397–1414.

Anagnostaras, S. G., Schallert, T., & Robinson, T. E. (2002). Memory processes governing amphetamine-induced psychomotor sensitization. *Neuropsychopharmacology, 26,* 703–715.

Antelman, S. M., & Chiodo, L. A. (1983). Amphetamine as a stressor. In I. Creese (Ed.), *Stimulants: Neurochemical, behavioral, and clinical perspectives* (pp. 269–299). New York: Raven Press.

Aston-Jones, G., Delfs, J. M., Druhan, J., & Zhu, Y. (1999). The bed nucleus of the stria terminalis. A target site for noradrenergic actions in opiate withdrawal. *Annals of the New York Academy of Sciences, 877,* 486–498.

Badiani, A., Oates, M. M., Day, H. E. W., Watson, S. J., Akil, H., & Robinson, T. E. (1998). Amphetamine-induced behavior, dopamine release, and *c-fos* MRNA expression: Modulation by environmental novelty. *Journal of Neuroscience, 18,* 10579–10593.

Baker, D. A., Tran-Nguyen, T. L., Fuchs, R. A., & Neisewander, J. L. (2001). Influence of individual differences and chronic fluoxetine treatment on cocaine-seeking behavior in rats. *Psychopharmacology, 155,* 18–26.

Barr, A. M., Hofmann, B. A., Weinberg, J., & Phillips, A. G. (2002). Exposure to repeated, intermittent *d*-amphetamine induces sensitization of HPA axis to a subsequent stressor. *Neuropsychopharmacology, 26,* 286–294.

Bauer, E. P., LeDoux, J. E., & Nader, K. (2001). Fear conditioning and LTP in the lateral amygdala are sensitive to the same stimulus contingencies. *Nature Neuroscience, 4,* 687–688.

Beitner-Johnson, D., Guitart, X., & Nestler, E. J. (1992). Neurofilament proteins and the mesolimbic dopamine system: Common regulation by chronic morphine and chronic cocaine in the rat ventral tegmental area. *Journal of Neuroscience, 12,* 2165–2176.

Beitner-Johnson, D., Guitart, X., & Nestler, E. J. (1993). Glial fibrillary acidic protein and the mesolimbic dopamine system: Regulation by chronic morphine and Lewis-Fischer strain differences in the rat ventral tegmental area. *Journal of Neurochemistry, 61,* 1766–1773.

Berke, J. D., & Hyman, S. E. (2000). Addiction, dopamine, and the molecular mechanisms of memory. *Neuron, 25,* 515–532.

Bonci, A., & Williams, J. T. (1996). A common mechanism mediates long-term changes in synaptic transmission after chronic cocaine and morphine. *Neuron, 16,* 631–639.

Borowski, T. B., & Kokkinidis, L. (1996). Contribution of ventral tegmental area dopamine neurons to expression of conditional fear: Effects of electrical stimulation, excitotoxin lesions, and quinpirole infusion on potentiated startle in rats. *Behavioral Neuroscience, 110,* 1349–1364.

Borowsky, B., & Kuhn, C. M. (1991). Monoamine mediation of cocaine-induced hypothalamo-pituitary-adrenal activation. *Journal of Pharmacology and Experimental Therapeutics, 256,* 204–210.

Buckingham, J. C., & Cooper, T. A. (1984). Differences in hypothalamic-pituitary-adrenocortical activity in the rat after acute and prolonged treatment with morphine. *Neuroendocrinology, 38,* 411–417.

Buczek, Y., Lê, A. D., Stewart, J., & Shaham, Y. (1999). Stress reinstates nicotine seeking but not sucrose solution seeking in rats. *Psychopharmacology, 144,* 183–188.

Capriles, N., Rodaros, D., Sorge, R. E., & Stewart, J. (2003). A role for the prefrontal cortex in stress-induced reinstatement of cocaine seeking in rats. *Psychopharmacology, 168,* 66–74.

Carroll, M. E., & Comer, S. D. (1996). Animal models of relapse. *Experimental and Clinical Psychopharmacology, 4,* 11–18.

Carter, A. J. (1997). Hippocampal noradrenaline release in awake, freely moving rats is regulated by alpha-2 adrenoceptors but not by adenosine receptors. *Journal of Pharmacology and Experimental Therapeutics, 281,* 648–654.

Castner, S. A., & Goldman-Rakic, P. S. (1999). Long-lasting psychotomimetic consequences of repeated low-dose amphetamine exposure in rhesus monkeys. *Neuropsychopharmacology, 20,* 10–28.

Champagne, D., Beaulieu, J., & Drolet, G. (1998). CRFergic innervation of the paraventricular nucleus of the rat hypothalamus: A tract-tracing study. *Journal of Neuroendocrinology, 10,* 119–131.

Chen, J., Nye, H. E., Kelz, M. B., Hiroi, N., Nakabeppu, Y., Hope, B. T., et al. (1995). Regulation of delta FosB and FosB-like proteins by electroconvulsive seizure and cocaine treatments. *Molecular Pharmacology, 48,* 880–889.

Childress, A. R., Ehrman, R., Rohsenow, D. J., Robbins, S. J., & O'Brien, C. P. (1992). Classically conditioned factors in drug dependence. In J. W. Lowinson, P. Luiz, R. B. Millman, & G. Langard (Eds.), *Substance abuse: A comprehensive textbook* (pp. 56–69). Baltimore MD: Williams and Wilkins.

Childress, A. R., Mozley, P. D., McElgin, W., Fitzgerald, J., Reivich, M., & O'Brien, C. P. (1999). Limbic activation during cue-induced cocaine craving. *American Journal of Psychiatry, 156,* 11–18.

Ciccocioppo, R. (1999). The role of serotonin in craving: From basic research to human studies. *Alcohol, 34,* 244–253.

Ciccocioppo, R., Sanna, P. P., & Weiss, F. (2001). Cocaine-predictive stimulus induces drug-seeking behavior and neural activation in limbic brain regions after multiple months of abstinence: Reversal by D(1) antagonists. *Proceedings of the National Academy of Sciences, 98,* 1976–1981.

Davis, M., Walker, D. L., & Lee, Y. (1997). Roles of the amygdala and bed nucleus of the stria terminalis in fear and anxiety measured with the acoustic startle reflex. Possible relevance to PTSD. *Annals of the New York Academy of Sciences, 821,* 305–331.

Dawson, N. M., Hamid, E. H., Egan, M. F., & Meredith, G. E. (2001). Changes in the pattern of brain-derived neurotrophic factor immunoreactivity in the rat brain after acute and subchronic haloperidol treatment. *Synapse, 39,* 70–81.

Day, H. E., Badiani, A., Uslaner, J. M., Oates, M. M., Vittoz, N. M., Robinson, et al. (2001). Environmental novelty differentially affects *c-fos* mRNA expression induced by amphetamine or cocaine in subregions of the bed nucleus of the stria terminalis and amygdala. *Journal of Neuroscience, 21,* 732–740.

De Vries, T. J., Schoffelmeer, A. N., Binnekade, R., Mulder, A. H., & Vanderschuren, L. J. (1998). Drug-induced reinstatement of heroin- and cocaine-seeking behaviour following long-term extinction is associated with expression of behavioural sensitization. *European Journal of Neuroscience, 10,* 3565–3571.

De Vries, T. J., Schoffelmeer, A. N., Binnekade, R., & Vanderschuren, L. J. (1999). Dopaminergic mechanisms mediating the incentive to seek cocaine and heroin following long-term withdrawal of IV drug self-administration. *Psychopharmacology, 143,* 254–260.

de Wit, H. (1996). Priming effects with drugs and other reinforcers. *Experimental and Clinical Psychopharmacology, 4,* 5–10.

de Wit, H., & Stewart, J. (1981). Reinstatement of cocaine-reinforced responding in the rat. *Psychopharmacology, 75*, 134–143.

Deroche, V., Le Moal, M., & Piazza, P. (1999). Cocaine self-administration increases the incentive motivational properties of the drug in rats. *European Journal of Neuroscience, 11*, 2731–2736.

Di Chiara, G., Tanda, G., Bassareo, V., Pontieri, F., Acquas, E., Fenu, et al. (1999). Drug addiction as a disorder of associative learning. Role of nucleus accumbens shell/extended amygdala dopamine. *Annals of the New York Academy of Sciences, 877*, 461–485.

Erb, S., Hitchcott, P. K., Rajabi, H., Mueller, D., Shaham, Y., & Stewart, J. (2000). Alpha-2 adrenergic receptor agonists block stress-induced reinstatement of cocaine seeking. *Neuropsychopharmacology, 23*, 138–150.

Erb, S., Salmaso, N., Rodaros, D., & Stewart, J. (2001). A role for the CRF-containing pathway from central nucleus of the amygdala to the bed nucleus of the stria terminalis in stress-induced relapse to cocaine seeking in rats. *Psychopharmacology, 158*, 360–365.

Erb, S., Shaham, Y., & Stewart, J. (1998). The role of corticotropin-releasing factor and corticosterone in stress- and cocaine-induced relapse to cocaine seeking in rats. *Journal of Neuroscience, 18*, 5529–5536.

Erb, S., Shaham, Y., & Stewart, J. (2001). Stress-induced relapse to drug seeking in the rat: Role of the bed nucleus of the stria terminalis and amygdala. *Stress, 4*, 289–303.

Erb, S., & Stewart, J. (1999). A role for the bed nucleus of the stria terminalis, but not the amygdala, in the effects of corticotropin-releasing factor on stress-induced reinstatement of cocaine seeking. *Journal of Neuroscience, 19*, RC35.

Everitt, B. J., Dickinson, A., & Robbins, T. W. (2001). The neuropsychological basis of addictive behaviour. *Brain Research Reviews, 36*, 129–138.

Fiorino, D. F., & Phillips, A. G. (1999a). Facilitation of sexual behavior and enhanced dopamine efflux in the nucleus accumbens of male rats after D-amphetamine-induced behavioral sensitization. *Journal of Neuroscience, 19*, 456–463.

Fiorino, D. F., & Phillips, A. G. (1999b). Facilitation of sexual behavior in male rats following *d*-amphetamine-induced behavioral sensitization. *Psychopharmacology, 142*, 200–208.

Flores, C., Rodaros, D., & Stewart, J. (1998). Long-lasting induction of astrocytic basic fibroblast growth factor by repeated injections of amphetamine: Blockade by concurrent treatment with a glutamate antagonist. *Journal of Neuroscience, 18*, 9547–9555.

Flores, C., Samaha, A. N., & Stewart, J. (2000). Requirement of endogenous basic fibroblast growth factor for sensitization to amphetamine. *Journal of Neuroscience, 20*, RC55.

Flores, C., & Stewart, J. (2000). Basic fibroblast growth factor as a mediator of the effects of glutamate in the development of long-lasting sensitization to stimulant drugs: Studies in the rat. *Psychopharmacology, 151*, 152–165.

Fuchs, R. A., & See, R. E. (2002). Basolateral amygdala inactivation abolishes conditioned stimulus- and heroin-induced reinstatement of extinguished heroin-seeking behavior in rats. *Psychopharmacology, 160,* 425–433.

Gelowitz, D. L., & Kokkinidis, L. (1999). Enhanced amygdala kindling after electrical stimulation of the ventral tegmental area: Implications for fear and anxiety. *Journal of Neuroscience, 19,* RC41.

Georges, F., & Aston-Jones, G. (2001). Potent regulation of midbrain dopamine neurons by the bed nucleus of the stria terminalis. *Journal of Neuroscience, 21,* RC160.

Grant, S., London, E. D., Newlin, D. B., Villemagne, V. L., Liu, X., Contoreggi, C., et al. (1996). Activation of memory circuits during cue-elicited cocaine craving. *Proceedings of the National Academy of Sciences, 93,* 12040–12045.

Grimm, J. W., Hope, B., Wise, R. A., & Shaham, Y. (2001). Incubation of cocaine craving after withdrawal. *Nature, 412,* 141–142.

Grimm, J. W., Lu, L., Hayashi, T., Hope, B. T., Su, T. P., & Shaham, Y. (2003). Time-dependent increases in brain-derived neurotrophic factor protein levels within the mesolimbic dopamine system after withdrawal from cocaine: Implications for incubation of cocaine craving. *Journal of Neuroscience, 23,* 742–747.

Grimm, J. W., & See, R. E. (2000). Dissociation of primary and secondary reward-relevant limbic nuclei in an animal model of relapse. *Neuropsychopharmacology, 22,* 473–479.

Hamamura, T., & Fibiger, H. C. (1993). Enhanced stress-induced dopamine release in the prefrontal cortex of amphetamine-sensitized rats. *European Journal of Pharmacology, 237,* 65–71.

Hamamura, T., Ichimaru, Y., & Fibiger, H. C. (1997). Amphetamine sensitization enhances regional *c-fos* expression produced by conditioned fear. *Neuroscience, 76,* 1097–1103.

Harmer, C. J., & Phillips, G. D. (1998). Enhanced appetitive conditioning following repeated pretreatment with *d*-amphetamine. *Behavioral Pharmacology, 9,* 299–308.

Harmer, C. J., & Phillips, G. D. (1999). Enhanced dopamine efflux in the amygdala by a predictive, but not a non-predictive, stimulus: Facilitation by prior repeated D-amphetamine. *Neuroscience, 90,* 119–130.

Hefti, F., Denton, T. L., Knusel, B., & Lapchak, P. A. (1993). Neurotrophic factors: What are they and what are they doing? In S. Loughlin, & J. Fallon (Eds.), *Neurotrophic factors* (pp. 25–49). San Diego CA: Academic Press.

Heidbreder, C. A., Thompson, A. C., & Shippenberg, T. S. (1996). Role of extracellular dopamine in the initiation and long-term expression of behavioral sensitization to cocaine. *Journal of Pharmacology and Experimental Therapeutics, 278,* 490–502.

Henry, D. J., Greene, M. A., & White, F. J. (1989). Electrophysiological effects of cocaine in the mesoaccumbens dopamine system: Repeated administration. *Journal of Pharmacology and Experimental Therapeutics, 251,* 833–839.

Henry, D. J., & White, F. J. (1991). Repeated cocaine administration causes persistent enhancement of D1 dopamine receptor sensitivity within the rat nucleus accumbens. *Journal of Pharmacology and Experimental Therapeutics, 258,* 882–890.

Herman, J. P., & Cullinan, W. E. (1997). Neurocircuitry of stress: Central control of the hypothalamo-pituitary-adrenocortical axis. *Trends in Neuroscience, 20,* 78–84.

Herman, J. P., Cullinan, W. E., & Watson, S. J. (1994). Involvement of the bed nucleus of the stria terminalis in tonic regulation of paraventricular hypothalamic CRH and AVP MRNA expression. *Journal of Neuroendocrinology, 6,* 433–442.

Horger, B. A., Giles, M. K., & Schenk, S. (1992). Preexposure to amphetamine and nicotine predisposes rats to self-administer a low dose of cocaine. *Psychopharmacology, 107,* 271–276.

Horger, B. A., Iyasere, C. A., Berhow, M. T., Messer, C. J., Nestler, E. J., & Taylor, J. R. (1999). Enhancement of locomotor activity and conditioned reward to cocaine by brain-derived neurotrophic factor. *Journal of Neuroscience, 19,* 4110–4122.

Horger, B. A., Shelton, K., & Schenk, S. (1990). Preexposure sensitizes rats to the rewarding effects of cocaine. *Pharmacology Biochemistry and Behavior, 37,* 707–711.

Houston, F. P., Stevenson, G. D., McNaughton, B. L., & Barnes, C. A. (1999). Effects of age on the generalization and incubation of memory in the F344 rat. *Learning and Memory, 6,* 111–119.

Hu, X.-T., Koeltzow, T. E., Cooper, D. C., Robertson, G. S., White, F. J., & Vezina, P. (2002). Repeated ventral tegmental area amphetamine administration alters dopamine D1 receptor signaling in the nucleus accumbens. *Synapse, 45,* 159–170.

Kalivas, P. W., & Duffy, P. (1993). Time course of extracellular dopamine and behavioral sensitization to cocaine I. Dopamine axon terminals. *Journal of Neuroscience, 13,* 266–275.

Kalivas, P. W., Pierce, R. C., Cornish, J., & Sorg, B. A. (1998). A role for sensitization in craving and relapse in cocaine addiction. *Journal of Psychopharmacology, 12,* 49–53.

Kalivas, P. W., & Stewart, J. (1991). Dopamine transmission in the initiation and expression of drug- and stress-induced sensitization of motor activity. *Brain Research Reviews, 16,* 223–244.

Kalivas, P. W., & Weber, B. (1988). Amphetamine injection into the A10 dopamine region sensitizes rats to peripheral amphetamine and cocaine. *Journal of Pharmacology and Experimental Therapeutics, 245,* 1095–1102.

Kantak, K. M., Black, Y., Valencia, E., Green-Jordan, K., & Eichenbaum, H. B. (2002). Dissociable effects of lidocaine inactivation of the rostral and caudal basolateral amygdala on the maintenance and reinstatement of cocaine-seeking behavior in rats. *Journal of Neuroscience, 22,* 1126–1136.

Kokaia, Z., Kelly, M. E., Elmer, E., Kokaia, M., McIntyre, D. C., & Lindvall, O. (1996). Seizure-induced differential expression of messenger RNAS for neurotrophins and their receptors in genetically fast and slow kindling rats. *Neuroscience, 75,* 197–207.

Kolta, M. G., Shreve, P., De Souza, V., & Uretsky, N. J. (1985). Time course of the development of the enhanced behavioral and biochemical responses to amphetamine after pretreatment with amphetamine. *Neuropharmacology, 24,* 823–829.

Koob, G. F. (1999). Stress, corticotropin-releasing factor, and drug addiction. *Annals of the New York Academy of Sciences, 897,* 27–45.

Koob, G. F., & Le Moal, M. (1997). Drug abuse: Hedonic homeostatic dysregulation. *Science, 278,* 52–58.

Lê, A. D., Quan, B., Juzytsch, W., Fletcher, P. J., Joharchi, N., & Shaham, Y. (1998). Reinstatement of alcohol-seeking by priming injections of alcohol and exposure to stress in rats. *Psychopharmacology, 135,* 169–174.

Lee, Y., Schulkin, J., & Davis, M. (1994). Effect of corticosterone on the enhancement of the acoustic startle reflex by corticotropin releasing factor (CRF). *Brain Research, 666,* 93–98.

Leri, F., Flores, J., Rodaros, D., & Stewart, J. (2002). Blockade of stress-induced, but not cocaine-induced reinstatement, by infusion of noradrenergic antagonists into the bed nucleus of the stria terminalis or the central nucleus of the amygdala. *Journal of Neuroscience, 22,* 5713–5718.

Lett, B. T. (1989). Repeated exposures intensify rather than diminish the rewarding effects of amphetamine, morphine, and cocaine. *Psychopharmacology, 98,* 357–362.

Liu, X., & Weiss, F. (2002). Additive effect of stress and drug cues on reinstatement of ethanol seeking: Exacerbation by history of dependence and role of concurrent activation of corticotropin-releasing factor and opioid mechanisms. *Journal of Neuroscience, 22,* 7856–7861.

Lorrain, D., Arnold, G., & Vezina, P. (2000). Previous exposure to amphetamine increases incentive to obtain the drug: Long lasting effects revealed by the progressive ratio schedule. *Behavioural Brain Research, 107,* 9–19.

Makino, S., Gold, P. W., & Schulkin, J. (1994a). Corticosterone effects on corticotropin-releasing hormone mRNA in the central nucleus of the amygdala and the parvocellular region of the paraventricular nucleus of the hypothalamus. *Brain Research, 640,* 105–112.

Makino, S., Gold, P. W., & Schulkin, J. (1994b). Effects of corticosterone on CRH mRNA and content in the bed nucleus of the stria terminalis; comparison with the effects in the central nucleus of the amygdala and the paraventricular nucleus of the hypothalamus. *Brain Research, 657,* 141–149.

Marcangione, C., Stewart, J., & Rompré, P.-P. (2000). Electrical stimulation of the bed nucleus of the stria terminalis produces opposite effects on midbrain dopamine and non-dopamine cell firing. *Abstract, Society for Neuroscience, 26,* #477.

McFarland, K., & Kalivas, P. W. (2001). The circuitry mediating cocaine-induced reinstatement of drug-seeking behavior. *Journal of Neuroscience, 21,* 8655–8663.

Meil, W. M., & See, R. E. (1996). Conditioned cued recovery of responding following prolonged withdrawal from self-administered cocaine in rats: An animal model of relapse. *Behavioural Pharmacology, 7,* 754–763.

Mendrek, A., Blaha, C. D., & Phillips, A. G. (1998). Pre-exposure of rats to amphetamine sensitizes self-administration of this drug under a progressive ratio schedule. *Psychopharmacology, 135,* 416–422.

Meredith, G., Callen, S., & Scheuer, D. (2002). Brain-derived neurotrophic factor expression is increased in the rat amygdala, piriform cortex and hypothalamus following repeated amphetamine administration. *Brain Research, 949,* 218–227.

Merlo Pich, E., Lorang, M., Yeganeh, M., Rodriguez de Fonseca, F., Raber, J., Koob, G. F., et al. (1995). Increase of extracellular corticotropin-releasing factor-like immunoreactivity levels in the amygdala of awake rats during restraint stress and ethanol withdrawal as measured by microdialysis. *Journal of Neuroscience, 15,* 5439–5447.

Mitchell, J. B., & Stewart, J. (1990). Facilitation of sexual behaviors in the male rat in the presence of stimuli previously paired with systemic injections of morphine. *Pharmacology Biochemistry and Behavior, 35,* 367–372.

Mueller, D., & Stewart, J. (2000). Cocaine-induced conditioned place preference: Reinstatement by priming injections of cocaine after extinction. *Behavioural Brain Research, 115,* 39–47.

Nestler, E. J., Barrot, M., & Self, D. W. (2001). DeltaFosB: A sustained molecular switch for addiction. *Proceedings of the National Academy of Sciences, 98,* 11042–11046.

Nestler, E. J., Kelz, M. B., & Chen, J. (1999). DeltaFosB: A molecular mediator of long-term neural and behavioral plasticity. *Brain Research, 835,* 10–17.

Park, W. K., Bari, A. A., Jey, A. R., Anderson, S. M., Spealman, R. D., Rowlett, J. K., et al. (2002). Cocaine administered into the medial prefrontal cortex reinstates cocaine-seeking behavior by increasing AMPA receptor-mediated glutamate transmission in the nucleus accumbens. *Journal of Neuroscience, 22,* 2916–2925.

Parker, L. A., & McDonald, R. V. (2000). Reinstatement of both a conditioned place preference and a conditioned place aversion with drug primes. *Pharmacology Biochemistry and Behavior, 66,* 559–561.

Paulson, P. E., Camp, D. M., & Robinson, T. E. (1991). Time course of transient behavioral depression and persistent behavioral sensitization in relation to regional brain monoamine concentrations during amphetamine withdrawal in rats. *Psychopharmacology, 103,* 480–492.

Paulson, P. E., & Robinson, T. E. (1995). Amphetamine-induced time-dependent sensitization of dopamine neurotransmission in the dorsal and ventral striatum: A microdialysis study in behaving rats. *Synapse, 19,* 56–65.

Piazza, P. V., Deminere, J. M., Le Moal, M., & Simon, H. (1990). Stress- and pharmacologically induced behavioral sensitization increases vulnerability to acquisition of amphetamine self-administration. *Brain Research, 514,* 22–26.

Piazza, P. V., Deminiere, J. M., Le Moal, M., & Simon, H. (1989). Factors that predict individual vulnerability to amphetamine self-administration. *Science, 245,* 1511–1513.

Piazza, P. V., & Le Moal, M. (1996). Pathophysiological basis of vulnerability to drug abuse: Interaction between stress, glucocorticoids, and dopaminergic neurons. *Annual Review of Pharmacology and Toxicology, 36,* 359–378.

Pierce, R. C., Pierce-Bancroft, A. F., & Prasad, B. M. (1999). Neurotrophin-3 contributes to the initiation of behavioral sensitization to cocaine by activating the Ras/Mitogen-activated protein kinase signal transduction cascade. *Journal of Neuroscience, 19,* 8685–8695.

Pierre, P. J., & Vezina, P. (1998). D1 dopamine receptor blockade prevents the facilitation of amphetamine self-administration induced by prior exposure to the drug. *Psychopharmacology, 138,* 159–166.

Prewitt, C. M., & Herman, J. P. (1998). Anatomical interactions between the central amygdaloid nucleus and the hypothalamic paraventricular nucleus of the rat: A dual tract-tracing analysis. *Journal of Chemical Neuroanatomy, 15,* 173–85.

Richter, R. M., Merlo Pich, E., Koob, G. F., & Weiss, F. (1995). Sensitization of cocaine-stimulated increase in extracellular levels of corticotropin-releasing factor from the rat amygdala after repeated administration as determine by intracranial microdialysis. *Neuroscience Letters, 187,* 169–172.

Robinson, T. E., & Becker, J. B. (1986). Enduring changes in brain and behavior produced by chronic amphetamine administration: A review and evaluation of animal models of amphetamine psychosis. *Brain Research Reviews, 396,* 157–198.

Robinson, T. E., & Berridge, K. C. (1993). The neural basis of drug craving: An incentive-sensitization theory of addiction. *Brain Research Reviews, 18,* 247–291.

Robinson, T. E., & Berridge, K. C. (2000). The psychology and neurobiology of addiction: An incentive-sensitization view. *Addiction, 95,* S91–S117.

Robinson, T. E., Jurson, P. A., Bennett, J. A., & Bentgen, K. M. (1988). Persistent sensitization of dopamine neurotransmission in ventral striatum nucleus accumbens produced by prior experience with (+)-amphetamine: A microdialysis study in freely moving rats. *Brain Research, 462,* 211–222.

Robinson, T. E., & Kolb, B. (1997). Persistent structural modifications in nucleus accumbens and prefrontal cortex neurons produced by previous experience with amphetamine. *Journal of Neuroscience, 17,* 8491–8497.

Robinson, T. E., & Kolb, B. (1999). Alterations in the morphology of dendrites and dendritic spines in the nucleus accumbens and prefrontal cortex following repeated treatment with amphetamine or cocaine. *European Journal of Neuroscience, 11,* 1598–1604.

Rogan, M. T., Staubli, U. V., & LeDoux, J. E. (1997). Fear conditioning induces associative long-term potentiation in the amygdala. *Nature, 390,* 604–607.

Rosen, J. B., Hamerman, E., Sitcoske, M., Glowa, J. R., & Schulkin, J. (1996).

Hyperexcitability: exaggerated fear-potentiated startle produced by partial amygdala kindling. *Behavioral Neuroscience, 110,* 43–50.
Rosen, J. B., & Schulkin, J. (1998). From normal fear to pathological anxiety. *Psychological Review, 105,* 325–350.
Sarnyai, Z., Shaham, Y., & Heinrichs, S. C. (2001). The role of corticotropin-releasing factor in drug addiction. *Pharmacological Reviews, 53,* 209–243.
Schenk, S., Valadez, A., McNamara, C., House, D. T., Higley, D., Bankson, M. G., et al. (1993). Development and expression of sensitization to cocaine's reinforcing properties: Role of NMDA receptors. *Psychopharmacology, 111,* 332–338.
Schmidt, E. D., Tilders, F. J., Binnekade, R., Schoffelmeer, A. N., & De Vries, T. J. (1999). Stressor- or drug-induced sensitization of the corticosterone response is not critically involved in the long-term expression of behavioural sensitization to amphetamine. *Neuroscience, 92,* 343–352.
See, R. E. (2002). Neural substrates of conditioned-cued relapse to drug-seeking behavior. *Pharmacology Biochemistry and Behavior, 71,* 517–529.
See, R. E., Kruzich, P. J., & Grimm, J. W. (2001). Dopamine, but not glutamate, receptor blockade in the basolateral amygdala attenuates conditioned reward in a rat model of relapse to cocaine-seeking behavior. *Psychopharmacology, 154,* 301–310.
Shaham, Y., Erb, S., & Stewart, J. (2000). Stress-induced relapse to heroin and cocaine seeking in rats: A review. *Brain Research Reviews, 33,* 13–33.
Shaham, Y., Funk, D., Erb, S., Brown, T. J., Walker, C.-D., & Stewart, J. (1997). Corticotropin-releasing factor, but not corticosterone, is involved in stress-induced relapse to heroin seeking in rats. *Journal of Neuroscience, 17,* 2605–2614.
Shaham, Y., Highfield, D., Delfs, J., Leung, S., & Stewart, J. (2000). Clonidine blocks stress-induced reinstatement of heroin seeking in rats: An effect independent of the locus coeruleus noradrenergic neurons. *European Journal of Neuroscience, 12,* 292–302.
Shaham, Y., Rajabi, H., & Stewart, J. (1996). Relapse to heroin-seeking under opioid maintenance: The effects of opioid withdrawal, heroin priming and stress. *Journal of Neuroscience, 16,* 1957–1963.
Shaham, Y., & Stewart, J. (1996). Effects of opioid and dopamine receptor antagonists on relapse induced by stress and re-exposure to heroin in rats. *Psychopharmacology, 125,* 385–391.
Shalev, A. Y., Peri, T., Brandes, D., Freedman, S., Orr, S. P., & Pitman, R. K. (2000). Auditory startle response in trauma survivors with posttraumatic stress disorder: A prospective study. *American Journal of Psychiatry, 157,* 255–261.
Shalev, U., Grimm, J. W., & Shaham, Y. (2002). Neurobiology of relapse to heroin and cocaine seeking: A review. *Pharmacological Reviews, 54,* 1–42.
Shalev, U., Highfield, D., Yap, J., & Shaham, Y. (2000). Stress and relapse to drug seeking in rats: Studies on the generality of the effect. *Psychopharmacology, 150,* 337–346.

Shalev, U., Hope, B., Clements, A., Morales, M., & Shaham, Y. (2001). Time-dependent changes in extinction behavior and stress-induced reinstatement of drug seeking following withdrawal from heroin in rats. *Psychopharmacology, 156,* 98–107.

Shen, R.-Y., Altar, C. A., & Chiodo, L. A. (1994). Brain-derived neurotrophic factor increases the electrical activity of pars compacta dopamine neurons in vivo. *Proceedings of the National Academy of Sciences, 91,* 8920–8924.

Shippenberg, T. S., & Heidbreder, C. (1995). Sensitization to the conditioned rewarding effects of cocaine: Pharmacological and temporal characteristics. *Journal of Pharmacology and Experimental Therapeutics, 273,* 808–815.

Shippenberg, T. S., Heidbreder, C., & Lefevour, A. (1996). Sensitization to the conditioned rewarding effects of morphine: Pharmacology and temporal characteristics. *European Journal of Pharmacology, 299,* 33–39.

Siegel, S. (1983). Classical conditioning, drug tolerance and drug dependence. In Y. Israel, F. B. Glaser, H. Kalant, R. E. Popham, W. Schmidt, & R. G. Smart (Eds.), *Research advances in alcohol and drug problems: Vol. 7* (pp. 207–245). New York: Plenum.

Simonato, M., Molteni, R., Bregola, G., Muzzolini, A., Piffanelli, M., Beani, L., et al. (1998). Different patterns of induction of FGF-2, FGF-1, and BDNF mRNAs during kindling epileptogenesis in the rat. *European Journal of Neuroscience, 10,* 955–963.

Sklair-Tavron, L., Shi, W.-X., Lane, S. B., Harris, H. W., Bunney, B. S., & Nestler, E. J. (1996). Chronic morphine induces visible changes in the morphology of mesolimbic dopamine neurons. *Proceedings of the National Academy of Sciences, 93,* 11202–11207.

Stewart, J. (1992). Conditioned stimulus control of the expression of sensitization of the behavioral activating effects of opiate and stimulant drugs. In I. Gormezano, & E. A. Wasserman (Eds.), *Learning and memory: Behavioral and biological substrates* (pp. 129–151). Hillsdale NJ: Erlbaum.

Stewart, J. (2000). Pathways to relapse: The neurobiology of drug- and stress-induced relapse to drug-taking. *Journal of Psychiatry and Neuroscience, 25,* 125–136.

Stewart, J., de Wit, H., & Eikelboom, R. (1984). Role of unconditioned and conditioned drug effects in the self-administration of opiates and stimulants. *Psychological Review, 91,* 251–268.

Stewart, J., & Vezina, P. (1991). Extinction procedures abolish conditioned stimulus control but spare sensitized responding to amphetamine. *Behavioural Pharmacology, 2,* 65–71.

Sutton, M. A., Karanian, D. A., & Self, D. W. (2000). Factors that determine a propensity for cocaine-seeking behavior during abstinence in rats. *Neuropsychopharmacology, 22,* 626–641.

Sutula, T., & Steward, O. (1987). Facilitation of kindling by prior induction of long-term potentiation in the perforant path. *Brain Research, 420*(1), 109–117.

Taylor, J. R., & Jentsch, J. D. (2001). Repeated intermittent administration of psychomotor stimulant drugs alters the acquisition of Pavlovian approach behavior in rats: Differential effects of cocaine, *d*-amphetamine and 3,4-methylenedioxymethamphetamine ("Ecstasy"). *Biological Psychiatry, 50,* 137–143.

Torres, G., & Rivier, C. (1992). Cocaine-induced stimulation of the rat hypothalamic-pituitary-adrenal axis is progressively attenuated following hourly interval regimens of the drug. *Life Sciences, 51,* 1041–1048.

Tran-Nguyen, L. T., Fuchs, R. A., Coffey, G. P., Baker, D. A., O'Dell, L. E., & Neisewander, J. L. (1998). Time-dependent changes in cocaine-seeking behavior and extracellular dopamine levels in the amygdala during cocaine withdrawal. *Neuropsychopharmacology, 19,* 48–59.

Ungless, M. A., Whistler, J. L., Malenka, R. C., & Bonci, A. (2001). Single cocaine exposure in vivo induces long-term potentiation in dopamine neurons. *Nature, 411,* 583–587.

Valadez, A., & Schenk, S. (1994). Persistence of the ability of amphetamine preexposure to facilitate acquisition of cocaine self-administration. *Pharmacology Biochemistry and Behavior, 47,* 203–205.

Vezina, P. (1993). Amphetamine injected into the ventral tegmental area sensitizes the nucleus accumbens dopaminergic response to systemic amphetamine: An in vivo microdialysis study in the rat. *Brain Research, 605,* 332–337.

Vezina, P., Lorrain, D. S., Arnold, G. M., Austin, J. D., & Suto, N. (2002). Sensitization of midbrain dopamine neuron reactivity promotes the pursuit of amphetamine. *Journal of Neuroscience, 22,* 4654–4662.

Vezina, P., Pierre, P., & Lorrain, D. (1999). The effects of previous exposure to amphetamine on drug-induced locomotion and self-administration of a low dose of the drug. *Psychopharmacology, 147,* 125–134.

Vezina, P., & Stewart, J. (1984). Conditioning and place-specific sensitization of increases in activity induced by morphine in the VTA. *Pharmacology Biochemistry and Behavior, 20,* 925–934.

Vezina, P., & Stewart, J. (1990). Amphetamine administered to the ventral tegmental area but not to the nucleus accumbens sensitizes rats to systemic morphine: Lack of conditioned effects. *Brain Research, 516,* 99–106.

Weiss, F., Maldonado-Vlaar, C. S., Parsons, L. H., Kerr, T. M., Smith, D. L., & Ben-Shahar, O. (2000). Control of cocaine-seeking behavior by drug-associated stimuli in rats: Effects on recovery of extinguished operant-responding and extracellular dopamine levels in amygdala and nucleus accumbens. *Proceedings of the National Academy of Sciences,* 4321–4326.

White, N. M. (1996). Addictive drugs as reinforcers: Multiple partial actions on memory systems. *Addiction, 91,* 921–949; discussion 951–965.

Wikler, A., & Pescor, F. T. (1967). Classical conditioning of a morphine abstinence phenomenon, reinforcement of opioid-drinking behavior and "relapse" in morphine-addicted rats. *Psychopharmacologia, 20,* 255–284.

Wise, R. A. (1996). Neurobiology of addiction. *Current Opinion in Neurobiology, 6,* 243–251.

Wolf, M. E. (1998). The role of excitatory amino acids in behavioral sensitization to psychomotor stimulants. *Progress in Neurobiology, 54,* 679–720.
Wolf, M. E., White, F. J., & Hu, X.-T. (1994). MK-801 prevents alterations in the mesoaccumbens dopamine system associated with behavioral sensitization to amphetamine. *Journal of Neuroscience, 14,* 1735–1745.
Wolf, M. E., White, F. J., Nassar, R. N., Brooderson, R. J., & Khansa, M. R. (1993). Differential development of autoreceptor supersensitivity and enhanced dopamine release during amphetamine sensitization. *Journal of Pharmacology and Experimental Therapeutics, 264,* 249–255.
Wyvell, C. L., & Berridge, K. C. (2001). Incentive sensitization by previous amphetamine exposure: Increased cue-triggered "wanting" for sucrose reward. *Journal of Neuroscience, 21,* 7831–7840.

Drugs, Behavior, and Environmental Sources of Motivation: Bridging a Gap

M. Vogel-Sprott
University of Waterloo

> *Given the powerful interaction between neurobiological mechanisms and drug exposure, a question that came up repeatedly . . . was why we do not all become addicts.*—(Altman et al., 1996, p. 319).

> *Individuals differ substantially in how easily and quickly they become addicted.*—(Leshner, 2001, p. 3).

> *. . . alcohol affects different people in different ways and it affects the same person differently on separate occasions.*—(Kerr & Hindmarch, 1998, p. 1).

The above quotations identify an important gap in knowledge. Individual differences in the behavioral effects of an addicting drug, and in susceptibility to addictive behavior, are major puzzles. Motivating and incentive properties are attributed to "natural" reinforcers, like food and addictive drugs, because they energize behavior and activate the dopamine system in the brain. The ability of addicting drugs to function like a reinforcer may contribute to their abuse potential. But evidence that such drugs activate a basic biological process common to all individuals does not explain why there are individual differences in the behavioral effects of addicting drugs, or why only some persons abuse drugs.

Constitutional and personal traits of an individual may provide some answers to these questions. However, these are static attributes.

They would not explain why a drug is used excessively on some occasions but not on others, or why the effect of a drug on an individual varies on different occasions or suddenly changes within an individual on a given occasion. Impaired drivers provide a good example (Goldberg & Harvard, 1968). Before the breathalyser was used to define impairment by blood alcohol levels, police had to substantiate the charge of impairment by a behavioral assessment of the suspect. Unfortunately, it was not uncommon for the symptoms of intoxication to subside during this examination, so that suspects succeeded in passing all the tests and no charge could be laid. However, as soon as these individuals were told that they were free to leave, the symptoms of intoxication frequently reemerged, often to such an extent that they had to be assisted from the police station and escorted home. Similar findings have been obtained in studies showing that skilled behavioral assessments of drivers during police spot checks cannot reliably identify drivers with high blood alcohol levels (Jones & Lund, 1986; Langenbucher & Nathan, 1983; Wells, Greene, Foss, Ferguson, & Williams, 1997). Symptoms of intoxication appear to be very difficult to detect when sobriety is advantageous. It seems that an expected reward for behavior influences the effects of a drug.

The term "expectancy" is generally understood to refer to the anticipation of some type of future event. The expectancy concept has a long history in the psychology of learning (Tolman, 1932). The view of learning as a process of acquiring information about relationships between events introduces expectancies as intervening cognitive variables that represent this information (e.g., Bolles, 1972, 1979; Rescorla, 1987, 1990). If one event (a stimulus or a response) reliably follows another, the occurrence of one leads to the expectation of the other. Animal research has shown that when events in a given situation are arranged to permit the acquisition of an expectancy, the expectancy predictably mediates behavior in that situation (Colwill & Rescorla, 1986). In a situation where two events are related, information about this association also is related to the contextual setting. The background stimuli offer an additional source of learned associations that provide situational specificity to an expectancy. When expectancies are learned, they are retained and function to guide behavior on other occasions in the same situation, and where the environmental context is perceived to be similar.

The influence of expectancies on behavior and shaping experience is receiving considerable attention in psychology (e.g., Kirsch, 1999). Interest in self-reports of drug-related expectancies reflects this general trend. Research has shown that individuals differ in their expectancies about receiving drugs, the types of effects they exert, and the consequence of these effects (Brown, 1993). A particularly interesting finding is that self-reported favorable expectancies about many types of drugs are correlated with the level of drug use (e.g., Goldman, Brown, & Christiansen, 1987; Schafer & Brown, 1991). The majority of this research has examined alcohol-related expectancies. Those who report more pleasant expectancies about alcohol also drink more heavily. Such observations are consistent with the proposition that alcohol-related expectancies may contribute to the risk of drug abuse and relapse after treatment (Marlatt & Gordon, 1985; Miller & Heather, 1986). The more general implication is that individual differences in alcohol expectancies should affect behavior under the drug, as well as drug consumption.

The link between drug use and individual differences in expectancies about a drug indicates the importance of understanding the conditions that give rise to these expectancies. This chapter considers the proposal that events in a drug-taking situation lead to particular types of expectancies, and individual differences in these expectancies influence drug-related behavior in general. A model of events that could regularly occur when humans use a drug, like alcohol, is described to show how individual differences in particular expectancies about these events can be acquired. To date, most research guided by the model has tested the impact of these expectancies on individual differences in the behavioral effects of alcohol. A review of these findings and implications are presented. The review is followed by a discussion of the potential role of these expectancies in alcohol use and abuse.

Learning Drug-related Expectancies

A learning analysis of a drug-taking situation can be applied to identify associations between specific events that give rise to particular expectancies. For the purposes of this analysis, the model of a drug-taking situation involves four events that could occur regularly when an individual uses a drug. These events are shown in Figure 1, and

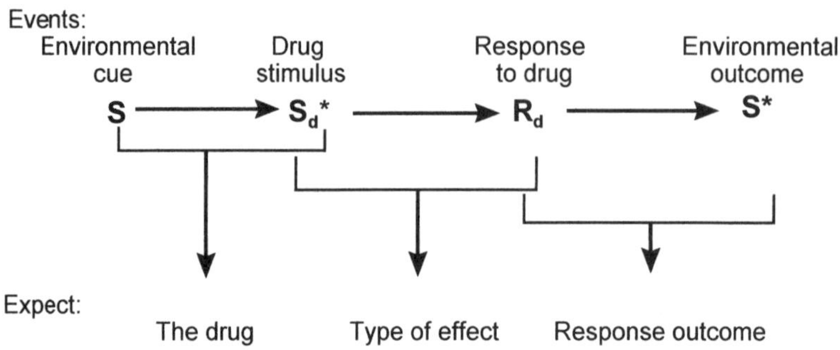

Figure 1. A model of events in a drug-taking situation consisting of some environmental stimulus cue (S) preceding the drug stimulus (S_d*). The drug is followed in turn by a behavioral response (R_d), and some environmental outcome (S*). The temporal association between each successive pair of events leads to the acquisition of three different expectancies.

identified as an environmental stimulus cue for the drug (S), the drug stimulus (S_d*), a response to the drug (R_d), and an environmental outcome (S*).[1] The events occur in temporal order. Their repetition in a drug-taking situation provides an opportunity to associate three successive pairs of events, yielding three different expectancies.

The first expectancy is based on the pair of events consisting of the stimulus (S) and the drug stimulus (S_d*). This association provides an opportunity to learn what stimulus event predicts the drug. When this relationship is reliable, the stimulus functions as a cue to signal the administration of the drug, and the individual expects the drug when this cue is presented. For example, the scent of alcohol in a beverage could lead a drinker to expect alcohol.

The second expectancy is based on the association between a drug stimulus, (S_d*), and the response to the drug, (R_d).[2] The widespread action of a drug allows it to affect many different types of reactions. In the case of overt activity, the particular type of response depends on the drinking situation. The repeated experience of the drug effect on a given activity provides an opportunity to learn the type of effect the drug exerts on this activity. For example, better performance in a game of pool after drinking should lead to the expectation that the drug improves this activity.

The third expectancy depends on the relationship between the last pair of events, the response to the drug, (R_d), and its environmental outcome (S*). When this association is reliable, it conveys information that leads to the expected consequence of the response to a drug. The outcome depends on the environmental context. Thus, a person can learn to expect that a given response leads to a particular outcome in one situation, and an entirely different one in another situation. The expected outcome of dancing at a party would certainly differ from the expected outcome of dancing during a church sermon. In theory, the expected consequence should affect the occurrence of the response, making it more likely to be displayed when the expected outcome is desirable. Thus, the expected consequence of behavior under a drug may function adaptively to modify its behavioral effects in order to maximize a favorable outcome.

Figure 1 shows that the expectation of receiving a drug is a prerequisite, setting the occasion for expectancies about the type of drug effect and the outcome of the response to a drug. Although a person's response to cues for a drug has commonly been attributed to expecting the drug, the model indicates that the response also can be influenced by the other two expectancies. When expectancies are learned, the presentation of a placebo with cues for a drug creates the situation that gives rise to these other expectancies. Their occurrence should affect the response to a placebo in a fashion similar to that shown under the drug. For example, if alcohol is expected to impair behavior, performance under a placebo should become poorer. However, if resisting impairment is expected to yield a favorable outcome, performance under a placebo should improve.

In summary, the sequence of events in this model of a drug-taking situation shows how three different expectancies may be acquired, and how the last event in one expectancy provides the basis for the next expectation. Considerable research has examined the contribution of particular expectancies to individual differences in the behavioral effects of alcohol. The next section reviews some results of these experiments and discusses their implications.

Behavioral Effects of Alcohol

EXPECTING TO RECEIVE THE DRUG

Studies of the effects of a drug commonly administer a placebo with cues for the drug to separate the actual effect of the drug from the influence of expecting it. Experiments testing the impairing effect of alcohol on the cognitive and motor skill tasks performed by social drinkers typically administer alcohol or a placebo to different groups of social drinkers. Participants are tested in a situation that provides no environmental outcome for task performance, and treatment effects are measured by the degree to which performance differs from predrinking levels. Reviews of this research indicate that the degree of impairment may bear some relation to the dose, but individual differences in the intensity of the effects are marked (Holloway, 1995; Wallgren & Barry, 1971). These types of experiments exclude the influence of an expected outcome by providing no environmental consequence for performance. They also control the expectation of receiving the drug by presenting cues for alcohol. But Figure 1 shows that expecting the drug leads to an expected type of effect. This expectancy is uncontrolled, and may influence the response to the drug.

EXPECTED TYPE OF EFFECT

During the normal course of social drinking, people are likely to have many opportunities to experience some alcohol-induced disturbance in their behavior that could lead them to expect some impairment in their performance. However, the particular activities performed, and the doses, are unlikely to be identical for all individuals. As a result, drinkers may differ in the type of effect they expect alcohol to induce on a given activity. In the absence of any environmental outcome of behavior, differences among individuals in the expected intensity of impairment on a given task should predict their change in performance under alcohol.

A number of different tasks have been used to test the relation between social drinkers' expected and actual impairment under alcohol (Fillmore, Carscadden, & Vogel-Sprott, 1998; Fillmore & Vogel-Sprott, 1994, 1995b). Participants in these experiments performed a task alone in a room where no environmental consequence was associated with task performance. After they had learned the task, they rated the expected effect of a moderate dose of alcohol on their performance, using a scale that ranged from extreme impairment to extreme improvement. Although the drinking habits of the participants did not differ, their ratings of the expected effect varied considerably, ranging from slight improvement to moderate impairment.

Participants subsequently performed the task under a moderate dose of alcohol, and the relationship between measures of expectancies and task impairment was tested. This research showed that an individual's expected degree of impairment under alcohol predicted the amount of impairment displayed under the drug. Individual differences in the expected type of effect also affected the response to a placebo when alcohol was expected; those who expected greater impairment from alcohol performed more poorly under a placebo. The influence of the expected type of effect does not appear to be unique to alcohol. This expectancy has been found to influence the response to caffeine and to antidepressants such as Prozac (Fillmore & Vogel-Sprott, 1994; Kirsch & Sapirstein, 1999).

More practice drinking socially should strengthen the precision of the relationship between the expected and actual behavioral effect of alcohol on a given task. This prediction has been confirmed by testing "novice" and "experienced" social drinkers (i.e., drinking alcohol regularly for one year or less, versus two years or more). Although the groups did not differ in age or in drinking habits, a comparison of the groups showed the degree of impairment expected by experienced drinkers more accurately predicted the amount of behavioral impairment they displayed (Fillmore & Vogel-Sprott, 1995a).

The results of this research indicate that social drinkers' susceptibility to alcohol impairment is related to the degree of impairment they expect. In order to demonstrate the separate influence of the expected type of effect, the studies eliminated the influence of an expected outcome of performance by providing no environmental consequence for behavior under the drug. However, this is a rather artificial drug-taking situation because people usually engage in a variety of activities after using a drug, some of which may have important environmental consequences.

EXPECTED OUTCOME OF BEHAVIOR

A desirable outcome of a response, such as food for animals, or money for people, is known to function as a reinforcer. The frequency of a response increases when it is associated with a reinforcer, and decreases when the reinforcer is absent. The information conveyed by these relationships provides the basis for the expected outcome of the response. In the model drug-taking situation, any particular response to the drug (R_d) should increase and decrease as a function of the expected presence or absence of a favorable outcome (S*). This hypothesis has been tested by examining individual differences in behavioral tolerance to repeated doses, and resistance to the impairing effect of a single dose.

Tolerance. Tolerance is identified by a reduction in the intensity of the initial effect of a drug. Drug tolerance is an important concept in the area of addiction. It is commonly attributed to the effects of drug exposures and is considered to contribute to physical dependence (e.g., Kalant, 1975). A drinker's tolerance to alcohol is also used clinically as an indicator of alcohol abuse, and the risk of developing physical dependence.

Research on classically conditioned tolerance to a variety of addicting drugs has shown that tolerance can be elicited by cues for the drug (e.g., Siegel, 1989). Greater tolerance (i.e., a weaker drug effect) is displayed when the drug is expected (i.e., administered in the same environmental context with the usual predrug cues), and less tolerance is shown when the drug is not expected (i.e., administered in a novel environment without these cues). The experimental situations used to investigate conditioned tolerance include stimulus cues for the drug, the drug, and a response, but there is no outcome for the response. The potential influence of the expected outcome on behavioral tolerance is excluded.

Experiments testing the effect of the expected outcome of the response to alcohol only manipulate the environmental outcome of the response. All other events (i.e., the environmental context, cues for the drug, doses, and the activity) are held constant. Reviews of research adopting this procedure to test behavioral tolerance in social drinkers have been presented elsewhere (Vogel-Sprott, 1992, 1997; Vogel-Sprott & Fillmore, 1999a, 1999b). In brief, this research has used simple and complex psychomotor tasks to investigate the development of tolerance to a repeated moderate dose of alcohol (0.62 g/kg) that yields peak blood alcohol levels close to the legal definition of impairment (80 mg/100 ml) in many jurisdictions. In these experiments, groups of drinkers are trained on a task and then attend a series of weekly drinking sessions. During each session they perform the task drug-free to provide a baseline measure of sober performance. Then they receive the dose of alcohol and perform the task at intervals while their blood alcohol concentrations (BACs) rise and decline. The average effect of the dose on each session is measured by the degree to which drinkers' test scores on a task differs from their drug-free baseline scores. The development of tolerance is identified by the reduction in impairment as sessions are repeated. The groups are treated differently only with respect to the outcome of task performance. In order to train the expectation of a desirable outcome for resisting impairment, one group of drinkers receives a reward (i.e., money or verbal approval) whenever their test scores under alcohol are comparable to their drug-free baselines. Other groups receive either equivalent rewards unrelated to their performance, or no rewards.

The results of these motor skill experiments show that all groups tend to show a comparable degree of impairment under the first dose. With repetitions of the dose on each session, only the group expecting a reward for resisting impairment shows a progressive development of tolerance. By the fourth dose, this group displays little impairment whereas the initial intensity of impairment in other groups is undiminished as doses are repeated. These results indicate that behavioral tolerance to alcohol is readily acquired when social drinkers are motivated by the expectation of an immediate reward for resisting impairment (e.g., Sdao-Jarvie & Vogel-Sprott, 1991).

When tolerance is rewarded for the performance of one motor skill task, this tolerance can transfer to another similar task if the situation also provides the expectation of a rewarding outcome for resisting impairment (Rawana & Vogel-Sprott, 1985). After tolerance has been developed by this reward treatment, the influence of the expected outcome also affects placebo responses, and is evident in improved performance when alcohol is expected but a placebo is received (Beirness & Vogel-Sprott, 1984). Studies have demonstrated that when tolerance is expected to yield an immediate reward, it readily extinguishes during subsequent drinking sessions that withhold the reward (Mann & Vogel-Sprott, 1981). This extinction would be predicted because eliminating the reward for resisting the drug effect creates an obvious change in the situation that fails to confirm and maintain the expected reward that motivates tolerance.

However, an immediate reward each time a particular response is displayed is unlikely to occur in the natural environment, or in social drinking situations. In these circumstances, it is deviant or unacceptable behavior that is likely to yield an immediate aversive outcome in the form of social disapproval, criticism, or worse. Responses that conform to the norm are unlikely to have any particular outcome. Rather, such responses are rewarded by the avoidance of a negative outcome. This is referred to as a negative reinforcement procedure. Tolerance trained under negative reinforcement should be highly resistant to extinction because the aversive outcome is absent when tolerance is displayed during training, and when it is actually withheld during extinction tests. With no obvious change in the situation, the expectation of a reward for resisting the drug effect remains unchallenged, and tolerance may not extinguish.

In principle, the expectation of a reward for any particular response to alcohol should increase its occurrence. And when negative reinforcement is used to train the expectation of a reward, the response to alcohol should be resistant to extinction. Some research has used negative reinforcement in the form of verbal disapproval to train the expectation of a reward (i.e., avoiding a negative consequence) for different types of responses to alcohol, and tested their resistance to extinction (Zack & Vogel-Sprott, 1995, 1997). In these experiments, the effect of repeated doses of alcohol was compared in groups of drinkers who were trained to expect a reward for either tolerant or grossly impaired performance. Although the groups did not differ in drinking habits or the doses received, those trained to expect a reward for flagrant impairment showed intense psychomotor impairment under alcohol, whereas those expecting a reward for resisting impairment displayed tolerance. Withholding negative reinforcement on subsequent extinction sessions showed that these two different behaviors persisted unchanged under alcohol and under a placebo. Experiments commonly test the effect of alcohol or a placebo on the performance of social drinkers whose prior expectancies about the type of response that will be rewarded are not known. In the absence of this information, differences among individuals in the degree of impairment or tolerance to a dose might be misleadingly attributed to differences in personality or constitutional traits. The results of these negative reinforcement experiments clearly show that whether behavioral tolerance or impairment is displayed under alcohol depends on which type of response a drinker expects will be rewarded.

Training drinkers to expect a rewarding outcome for drug-tolerant performance of a motor skill task typically results in a progressive increase in tolerance as doses are repeated. This gradual reduction in impairment is unlikely to be due to a weakening drug effect because individuals with no expected outcome of performance continue to show a fairly stable level of impairment under these doses. Another possibility is suggested by the resemblance between the progressive recovery from impairment as doses are repeated, and the gradual improvement that characterizes the learning of a new motor skill. Research has demonstrated that tolerance in motor skills requires the learning of some new behavioral strategy to overcome impairment before the motivating impact of the expected reward becomes evident (Easdon & Vogel-Sprott, 1996; Zinatelli & Vogel-Sprott, 1993). In these experiments, two groups learned a task, and then received additional drug-free practice. An experimental group learned to overcome environmentally induced impairment on the task by practicing under conditions that induced impairment resembling the effect of alcohol. The control group continued with equivalent practice in the standard environment under which the task had been learned. When groups subsequently received a dose of alcohol and performed the task in the standard environment, the control group showed considerable impairment, but the experimental group displayed immediate tolerance. A reward for resisting impairment (i.e., maintaining their drug-free baseline level of performance) was provided to drinkers in both groups in order to ensure that they were motivated to perform as well as they could under alcohol. The experimental group only differed by having a prior history of drug-free training to overcome environmentally induced impairment. It seems that motivation to perform well, coupled with the skill to do so, results in immediate tolerance to the behavioral effects of a dose of alcohol. If these skills have not been acquired in advance, the gradual emergence of tolerance when a motor skill task is performed under repeated doses of alcohol may reflect the development of this learning.

Impairment Following a Single Dose. Research on alcohol tolerance based on psychomotor tasks indicates that repeated doses of alcohol might only be needed to provide task practice to learn some new motor skills to overcome impairment. Another way of assessing this conclusion is to examine cognitive processes, using mental tasks that involve no learned motor skills, merely a button press or a verbal response. Repeated doses providing task practice should not be needed to develop resistance to impairment in such tasks. The expectation of a rewarding outcome, alone, should diminish the impairing effect of alcohol the first time cognitive tasks are performed under a dose of alcohol.

The effect of alcohol on cognitive control of behavior is of considerable interest because some antisocial and hazardous behavior is thought to result from the disrupting effect of alcohol on mental processes. Impaired information processing, reduced intentional control, and behavioral disinhibition are some examples. Basic research on cognitive control of behavior has developed tasks to assess particular cognitive processes. Several of these have been used to show that the expected outcome of cognitive performance alters the impairing effect of a single dose of alcohol (Fillmore & Vogel-Sprott, 1997, 2000; Fillmore, Vogel-Sprott, & Gavrilescu, 1999; Grattan & Vogel-Sprott, 2001; Mulvihill, Skilling, & Vogel-Sprott, 1997). In these experiments, performance was measured when the tasks were performed for the first time under a moderate dose of alcohol. When no environmental outcome was expected, alcohol impaired performance on tasks of information processing, intentional control of behavior, and inhibition of inappropriate responses. In contrast, when drinkers expected a reward for maintaining their sober baseline standard of performance, they displayed immediate resistance to impairment on these tasks. Although the dose of alcohol yielded peak blood alcohol levels close to 80 mg/100 ml, information processing, intentional control, and inhibitory behavior showed no change from the drug-free level of performance.

SUMMARY AND IMPLICATIONS

Research with single and with repeated moderate doses of alcohol shows that the expected type of effect and the expected outcome of behavior can each influence the effect of the drug. When there is no outcome for performance, differences among social drinkers' expected types of effect predict the intensity of alcohol impairment shown in cognitive and motor skills. Individual differences in the expected outcome of performance under alcohol predict the degree of impairment, or tolerance to repeated doses, that will be displayed. These findings have some important implications.

Susceptibility to a dose of alcohol has often been investigated in relation to constitutional or personal attributes that are linked to the risk of alcohol abuse (e.g., Schuckit, 1994). These studies commonly test individuals when their performance has no consequence. This procedure leaves expectations about the type of drug effect uncontrolled. Persons with or without a particular attribute are also likely to have different drinking experiences and information about alcohol that lead to differences in the expected type of effect and its outcome.

When studies of the correlation between drinkers' personal traits and the effect of alcohol are conducted in a setting that provides no consequence for performance, drinkers' various expectancies about the type of effect the drug exerts could influence their response to the dose of alcohol. The use of a placebo in such experiments serves to distinguish the pharmacological effects of a drug from the effects of expecting to receive it. A placebo does standardize this expectancy, but the expectation of receiving a drug leads to the expectations about the type of drug effect, and its outcome. These uncontrolled influences can contaminate placebo responses. The influence of expectancies on the response to a placebo has also been emphasized by others who question the use of placebos as adequate controls in studies that test the efficacy of drug treatments in psychiatry (Kirsch & Sapirstein, 1999).

When performance has no consequence, a moderate dose of alcohol impairs cognitive and motor skills. But the expectation of some favorable outcome for resisting impairment immediately counteracts these drug effects on cognitive processes that are involved in information processing, intentional control of behavior, and inhibition of inappropriate behavior. Efforts to understand the occurrence of inappropriate or antisocial behavior under alcohol have tended to focus on the actions of the drug and personal attributes of the drinker. While these factors may play a role, environmental conditions giving rise to different expectancies about the outcome of performance under alcohol generate reliable differences among drinkers in their cognitive control of behavior. It seems that when drinkers claim that their inappropriate or unacceptable conduct was unintentional and due to the effect of alcohol, an evaluation of the claim should consider whether their behavior yielded some reward.

Behavioral tolerance to alcohol is widely assumed to increase with greater use of the drug, and is commonly considered to be a clinical symptom of alcohol abuse. However, research with social drinkers indicates that only a few doses are needed for the acquisition and display of tolerance in a situation where it is expected to yield a rewarding outcome. These findings indicate that factors responsible for initiating tolerance likely differ from those that sustain tolerance after physical dependence has developed. Others also have commented on the need to consider possible "multiple forms" of tolerance (Altman et al., 1996). Research reviewed in this chapter has been based on social drinkers, and does not address the possibility that alcohol abusers under high doses of alcohol also display less symptoms of behavioral intoxication when it is expected to yield a rewarding outcome. However, some studies of alcoholics indicate that the expected consequence of behavior under the drug continues to influence the display of tolerance when BACs are in excess of 250 mg/100 ml (Mendelson & Mello, 1966; Nathan, Lowenstein, Solomon, & Rossi, 1970).

Drug Use and Abuse

The influence of particular expectancies on the behavioral effects of alcohol should be instances of the effect of these expectancies on individual differences in alcohol-related behavior in general, including alcohol consumption. Research on drug use has concentrated on its relation to favorable drug expectancies in general, with little investigation of specific types of expectancies. However other research on alcohol consumption contains findings that suggest these expectancies have the potential to influence drug use and abuse.

COMBINING THE EXPECTED TYPE OF EFFECT AND ITS OUTCOME

The model of expectancies in a drug-taking situation would predict that a drinker should consume less alcohol when the drug is expected to induce considerable impairment on an activity that is expected to yield a reward for good performance. Some information relevant to this hypothesis has been provided in an experiment by Sharkansky and Finn (1998). Participants in this study were allowed to drink ad lib for a period of time before performing a task on which they could earn money for correct performance. This situation provided the expectation of a reward for resisting the drug effect by performing well on the task. The expected type of behavioral effect of alcohol was manipulated at the outset of the drinking session. Some individuals received information leading them to expect that alcohol would cause intense impairment on the task; others were led to expect slight impairment. The results showed that the expected type of effect altered the amount of alcohol consumed in the ad lib drinking situation. Those who expected little impairment on the task drank significantly more alcohol than those who expected great impairment. Although a more comprehensive investigation of the impact of these expectancies on alcohol consumption is needed, these findings are important. They indicate that a particular combination of these two expectancies can moderate drinking and create sizeable differences among social drinkers in their alcohol consumption.

ALCOHOL AND AFFECT

One approach to understanding drug use and abuse has explored the possibility that alcohol consumption relieves negative emotional states, reducing tension or dampening a stress response (e.g., Sher, 1987; Young, Oei, & Knight, 1990). Reviews of this research find equivocal support for tension-reducing or stress-response dampening effects of alcohol. Whether alcohol changes the general level of affective arousal, or specifically alters either pleasant or unpleasant emotions remains unclear (e.g., Greeley & Oei, 1999).

Some research on affect using the eye blink startle response to sudden stimuli promises to answer these questions. Under drug-free conditions, higher levels of arousal increase the overall magnitude of the startle response, and the ongoing emotional state modulates the startle reaction, revealing a pattern of attenuated startle reactions during pleasant, and augmented startle during negative emotions. Experiments comparing the startle reactions of social drinkers under alcohol and under a placebo have shown that alcohol reduces general arousal (overall magnitude of the startle response), but the same pattern of attenuated startle reaction during pleasant, and augmented startle during negative emotional states is observed under alcohol and under a placebo (Curtin, Lang, Patrick, & Stritzke, 1998; Stritzke, Patrick, & Lang, 1995). A review of the findings indicates that the effect of alcohol is characterized by nonspecific changes in arousal at the subcortical level, and that its emotional interpretation stems from its effects on higher brain processes, such as information processing, learning, and memory (Lang, Patrick, & Stritzke, 1999). These processes provide the basis for the acquisition and retention of expectancies. Research on affect has not manipulated expectancies about the expected type of effect, or its outcome. However, the association between drug-induced affective arousal and the interpretation of emotion-provoking events in a given situation should lead to the expected type of emotional effect of the drug. In the absence of any expected outcome, the expectation of a desirable emotional state should increase the likelihood of alcohol use in the situation.

Research on alcohol and affect suggests that the emotional state attributed to affective arousal depends on the interpretation of events in a given situation. The numerous possible positive and negative events that could occur in various drinking situations suggest that the emotional effects of alcohol and ensuing expectancies of a drinker should vary with the environmental context. This possibility has been examined in recent research using a within-subject design to obtain self-reports of expected effects of alcohol when questionnaires were completed in a laboratory and in a bar (Wall, McKee, & Hinson, 2001; Wall, McKee, Hinson, & Goldstein, 2001). The results indicated that the context in which expectancies were reported altered the intensity and number of expected pleasant effects of alcohol. Whether individual differences in these expectancies are consistent across situations is unknown. This information will be helpful in evaluating the assumption that a preponderance of pleasant expectations about alcohol reported by a drinker in one context is sufficiently stable over situations to play a pivotal role in determining characteristic drinking habits (e.g., Goldman, Del Boca, & Darkes, 1999).

INHERENT REINFORCING EFFECTS OF ALCOHOL

Research investigating the reinforcing properties of addicting drugs has tested the ability of an initial dose to prime further drug consumption. Drug priming experiments represent an instance of the general observation that the presentation of a reinforcing stimulus activates the dopamine system and tends to facilitate behavior related to the reinforcer (Baker, Steinwald, & Bouton, 1991). The dopamine system has been characterized as "a seeking system . . . a goad without a goal" that drives and energizes feelings of intense interest and eager anticipation (Panksepp, 1998, p. 144).

Several early studies of the priming effect of alcohol administered a dose of alcohol to abstinent alcoholics and measured their desire for more alcohol. The results of this research have been mixed. Some experiments have found that a priming dose of alcohol increases self-reports of desire for alcohol and alcohol consumption (e.g., Bigelow, Griffiths, & Liebson, 1977). Others have failed to corroborate these findings (Mello & Mendelson, 1970, 1972; Nathan, O'Brien, & Lowenstein, 1971). Notably, just the belief that alcohol was received has been found to increase alcoholics' desire and consumption of a placebo drink (Engle & Williams, 1972; Marlatt, Demming, & Reid, 1973).

Given that the drug acts on neurobiological processes common to all humans, tests of priming have also been performed with social drinkers. Compared with a placebo, a priming dose of alcohol has been shown to increase self-reported desire for alcohol (de Wit & Chutuape, 1993). Other priming experiments have allowed social drinkers to perform a task for their choice of alcohol or alternative monetary reinforcers that differ in value or probability of occurrence (Chutuape, Mitchell, & de Wit, 1994; Fillmore & Rush, 2001). These studies indicate that alcohol choice responses depend on the relative desirability and availability of alternative environmental rewards in the situation. A priming dose of the drug increases the choice of alcohol, but only when the alternative money reward is of little value, or unlikely to occur. These results bear some resemblance to the findings on behavioral tolerance and impairment reviewed in an earlier section. That research was conducted in a setting that provided one reinforcer for one particular response and showed that its occurrence depended on the expectation that this response yielded the desirable outcome. The situation in priming studies is more complex because it provides alternative reinforcers for different choice responses. Despite this complexity, the results on priming appear to point to the same conclusion: The response an individual chooses to display depends on which one is expected to yield the more desirable outcome.

Research with social drinkers shows that alcohol priming effects on the choice of alcohol are characterized by marked individual differences (de Wit, 1996). Although little is known about the sources of these individual differences, research with animals that measured drug seeking (i.e., bar presses to make alcohol available) and drug taking (i.e., consumption when alcohol was available) indicates that a priming dose of alcohol increases alcohol seeking but does not predict alcohol consumption (Sampson, Slawecki, Sharpe, & Chappell, 1998). These two behaviors apparently are affected by different processes. The activation of the dopamine system by a priming dose can promote drug seeking, but drug taking may depend on expectancies about the effect of the drug and the outcome of consumption. Variations among drinkers in these expectancies should contribute to differences in the choice of alcohol under a priming dose. Those who expect alcohol to induce pleasant effects and desirable outcomes should be most susceptible to priming effects.

DRUG-TAKING AND ENVIRONMENTAL OUTCOMES

Initiating Drug Use. Some investigators have noted that the onset of drug use by adolescents is correlated with drug-using peers, and suggested that the incentive to take the drug may be enhanced by its association with environmental rewards such as peer-group approval and acceptance (Johanson, Mattox, & Schuster, 1995). These researchers tested the initiation of drug use when drug taking was associated with an environmental situation that provided rewards of different value. Participants in this experiment received two different colored placebo capsules that were presented as different drugs (unspecified). Capsules were taken on different days and followed by a situation in which the performance of a task yielded a high monetary reinforcement after one capsule, and low reinforcement after the other capsule. When these sessions concluded, participants returned on additional days when no task was performed and simply chose which capsule they wished to take. Participants more often chose the capsule that had been associated with the situation that yielded higher monetary reinforcement. The capsules contained placebos, so no drug effects could account for these findings. Thus the authors attributed the development of these preferences to stronger secondary reinforcing effects acquired by the capsule associated with the more rewarding situation. The mechanism underlying these secondary reinforcement effects and motivating the choice of this capsule may be the expectation of a greater rewarding outcome.

Behavioral Economics. One approach to understanding drug consumption is based exclusively on principles of environmental reinforcement. Research with animals has shown that behavior maintained by the use of a drug as a reinforcer is similar to behavior maintained by other reinforcers. The ability of reinforcers to affect behavior declines as a function of the delay in reinforcement, and preference for a particular reinforcer depends on what other reinforcers are available (e.g., Johanson & Schuster, 1981). Behavioral economics applies these principles to drug-taking behavior, and proposes that sparse or weak alternative reinforcers, or restricted access to alternative reinforcers increase alcohol consumption by humans in their natural environments (Vuchinich, 1999; Vuchinich & Tucker, 1983, 1988). A related premise is that the maintenance of abstinence by drug abusers is a function of greater availability of rewarded nondrug activities (e.g., Bigelow & Silverman, 1999; Higgins, 1999; Vuchinich & Tucker, 1996).

"Community reinforcement" and "contingency management" treatments of drug abuse are based on the principle that any given reinforced behavior can be modified by introducing reinforcement for other activities and/or by penalizing the behavior by the loss of other reinforcement. These treatments place drug users in an environment where the availability of vocational, family, social, and recreational reinforcers is contingent on maintaining sobriety. Although no theory is offered to explain why this treatment should be effective, community reinforcement and contingency management essentially manipulate the associations between responses and their rewarding outcomes. An individual's experience of these relationships can engage associative learning processes that give rise to expectancies. It is possible that the effects of this treatment depend on the underlying mechanisms of expectancies. A consideration of how environmental events lead to the acquisition and change in expectancies could explain why this empirical treatment approach may alter drug-taking behavior, and could identify events in settings that lead to particular expectancies which may impede or improve the efficacy of treatment.

There is no doubt that the pharmacological classification and neurobiological actions of a drug provide a general indication of its effects. But there are marked individual differences in the response to a drug and its use. This chapter illustrated an approach to understanding these individual differences. A model of events in a drug-taking situation showed how associations between particular events allowed the acquisition of three types of expectancies that affect drug-related behavior. Because the drug-taking situations experienced by individuals are not identical, these expectancies could differ among individuals, and within an individual in different situations. Tests of the model have shown that social drinkers' expectancies about the types of effects alcohol exerts, and the consequences of these effects, predict individual differences in the behavioral effects of alcohol.

Little is yet known about the particular influence of each of these expectancies on drug use and abuse because interest has focused on the general finding that more favorable expectancies about a drug are linked to greater drug use. Research has identified an increased risk of alcohol abuse in groups with particular personal traits, or heritable characteristics, such as family history of alcoholism. But not all members of these high-risk groups develop alcohol abuse, and the disorder also occurs in the population at large. The gap in identifying those who are at risk remains to be explained. A learning analysis of specific drug-related expectancies could be helpful in determining which types or combinations of expectancies are more influential in determining an increase in consumption, and what types of events in an individual's drug-taking environment could foster the acquisition of these high risk expectancies. Unlike heritable or temperamental attributes of an individual, expectancies are learned, and can be changed. Understanding the influence of expectancies could contribute to developing interventions to diminish the risks of hazardous or undesirable behavior under alcohol, and prevent or reduce addictive behavior.

Notes

1. Stimulus events accompanied by an asterisk indicate that the stimuli have some important value for an individual. The use of an asterisk follows the convention of Bolles (1972), who used it to identify stimuli, such as food or shock, that function like a reinforcer.

2. The S_d*-R_d association has also been discussed by Kirsch (1985) who considered R_d as an involuntary or internal reaction to a drug. The R_d in this learning model is different, and refers to observable activity that is not reflexive.

References

Altman, J., Everitt, B. J., Glautier, S., Markou, A., Nutt, D., Oretti, R., et al. (1996). The biological, social and clinical bases of drug addiction: Commentary and debate. *Psychopharmacology, 125,* 285–345.

Baker, A. G., Steinwald, H., & Bouton, M. E. (1991). Contextual conditioning and reinstatement of extinguished instrumental responding. *Quarterly Journal of Experimental Psychology, 43B,* 199–218.

Beirness, D., & Vogel-Sprott, M. (1984). Alcohol tolerance in social drinkers: Operant and classical conditioning effects. *Psychopharmacology, 84,* 393–397.

Bigelow, G. E., Griffiths, R. R., Liebson, I. A. (1977). Pharmacological influences upon human ethanol self-administration. In E. M. Gross (Ed.), *Alcohol intoxication and withdrawal* (pp. 523–538). New York: Plenum.

Bigelow, G. E., & Silverman, K. (1999). Theoretical and empirical foundations of contingency management treatments for drug abuse. In D. T. Higgins, & K. Silverman (Eds.), *Motivating behavior change among illicit-drug abusers: Research on contingency management interventions* (pp. 15–31). Washington DC: American Psychological Association.

Bolles, R. C. (1972). Reinforcement, expectancy and learning. *Psychological Review, 79,* 394–409.

Bolles, R. C. (1979). *Learning theory* (2nd ed.). New York: Holt, Rinehart and Winston.

Brown, S. A. (1993). Drug effect expectancies and addictive behavior change. Special Section: Motivation and addictive behaviours. *Experimental and Clinical Psychopharmacology, 1,* 55–67.

Chutuape, M. D., Mitchell, S. H., & de Wit, H. (1994). Ethanol preloads increase preference under concurrent random-ratio schedules in social drinkers. *Experimental and Clinical Psychopharmacology, 2,* 310–318.

Colwill, R. M., & Rescorla, R. A. (1986). Associative structures in instrumental learning. In G. H. Bower (Ed.), *The psychology of learning and motivation: Vol. 20* (pp. 55–104). New York: Academic Press.

Curtin, J. J., Lang, A. R., Patrick, C. J., & Stritzke, W. G. (1998). Alcohol and fear potentiated startle: A test of stress response dampening and attention allocation theories. *Journal of Abnormal Psychology, 107,* 547–557.

de Wit, H. (1996). Priming effects with drugs and other reinforcers. *Experimental and Clinical Psychopharmacology, 4,* 5–10.

de Wit, H., & Chutuape, M. D. (1993). Increased ethanol choice in social drinkers following ethanol preload. *Behavioural Pharmacology, 4,* 29–36.

Easdon, C. M., & Vogel-Sprott, M. (1996). Drug-free behavioral history affects social drinkers' tolerance to a challenge dose of alcohol. *Journal of Studies on Alcohol, 57,* 591–597.

Engle, K. B., & Williams, T. K. (1972). Effect of an ounce of vodka on alcoholics' desire for alcohol. *Quarterly Journal of Studies on Alcohol, 33,* 1099–1105.

Fillmore, M. T., Carscadden, J., & Vogel-Sprott, M. (1998). Alcohol, cognitive impairment and expectancies. *Journal of Studies on Alcohol, 59,* 174–179.

Fillmore, M. T., Mulvihill, L. E., & Vogel-Sprott, M. (1994). The expected drug and its expected effect interact to determine placebo responses to alcohol and caffeine. *Psychopharmacology, 115,* 383–388.

Fillmore, M., & Rush, C. R. (2001). Alcohol effects on inhibitory and activation response strategies in the acquisition of alcohol and other reinforcers: Priming the motivation to drink. *Journal of Studies on Alcohol, 62,* 646–656.

Fillmore, M., & Vogel-Sprott, M. (1994). Psychomotor performance under alcohol and under caffeine: Pharmacological and expectancy effects. *Experimental and Clinical Psychopharmacology, 2,* 319–328.

Fillmore, M., & Vogel-Sprott, M. (1995a). Behavioral effects of alcohol in novice and experienced drinkers: Alcohol expectancies and impairment. *Psychopharmacology, 122,* 175–181.

Fillmore, M., & Vogel-Sprott, M. (1995b). Expectancies about alcohol-induced motor impairment predict individual differences in responses to alcohol and placebo. *Journal of Studies on Alcohol, 56,* 90–98.

Fillmore, M., & Vogel-Sprott, M. (1997). Resistance to cognitive impairment under alcohol: The role of environmental consequences. *Experimental and Clinical Psychopharmacology, 5,* 251–255.

Fillmore, M., & Vogel-Sprott, M. (2000). Response inhibition under alcohol: Effects of cognitive and motivational conflict. *Journal of Studies on Alcohol, 61,* 239–246.

Fillmore, M., Vogel-Sprott, M., & Gavrilescu, D. (1999). Alcohol effects on intentional behavior: Dissociating controlled and automatic influences. *Experimental and Clinical Psychopharmacology, 7,* 372–378.

Goldberg, L., & Havard, J. (1968). *Research on the effects of alcohol and drugs on driver behaviour and their importance as a cause of road accidents.* Paris: Organization for Economic Co-operation and Development.

Goldman, M. S., Brown, S. A., & Christiansen, B. A. (1987). Expectancy theory: Thinking about drinking. In H. T. Blane, & K. E. Leonard (Eds.), *Psychological theories of drinking and alcoholism* (pp. 181–226). New York: Guilford Press.

Goldman, M. S., Del Boca, F. K., & Darkes, J. (1999). Alcohol expectancy theory: The application of cognitive science. In K. E. Leonard, & H. T. Blane (Eds.), *Psychological theories of drinking and alcoholism* (2nd ed., pp. 203–246). New York: Guilford Press.

Grattan, K., & Vogel-Sprott, M. (2001). Maintaining intentional control of behavior under alcohol. *Alcoholism: Clinical and Experimental Research, 25,* 192–197.

Greeley, J., & Oei, T. (1999). Alcohol and tension reduction. In K. E. Leonard, & H. T. Blane (Eds.), *Psychological theories of drinking and alcoholism* (2nd ed., pp. 14–53). New York: Guilford Press.

Higgins, S. T. (1999). Potential contributions of the community reinforcement approach and contingency management to broadening the base of substance abuse treatment. In J. A. Tucker, D. M. Donovan, & G. A. Marlatt (Eds.), *Changing addictive behavior* (pp. 283–306). New York: Guilford Press.

Holloway, F. A. (1995). Low dose alcohol effects on human behavior and performance. *Alcohol, Drugs and Driving, 11,* 39–56.

Johanson, C. E., & Schuster, C. R. (1981). Animal models of drug self-administration. In N. K. Mello (Ed.), *Advances in substance abuse: Behavioral and biological research: Vol. 2* (pp. 219–298). Greenwich CT: JAI Press.

Johanson, C. E., Mattox, A., & Schuster, C. R. (1995). Conditioned reinforcing effects of capsules associated with high versus low monetary payoff. *Psychopharmacology, 129,* 42–48.

Jones, I. S., & Lund, A. K. (1986). Detection of alcohol-impaired drivers using a passive alcohol sensor. *Journal of Police and Science Administration, 14,* 153–160.

Kalant, H. (1975). Biological models of alcohol tolerance and physical dependence. In M. M. Gross (Ed.), *Alcohol intoxication and withdrawal* (pp. 3–13). New York: Plenum.

Kerr, J. S., & Hindmarch, I. (1998). The effects of alcohol alone or in combination with other drugs on information processing, task performance and subjective responses. *Human Psychopharmacology, 13,* 1–9.

Kirsch, I. (1985). Response expectancy as a determinant of experience and behavior. *American Psychologist, 40,* 1189–1202.

Kirsch, I. (1999). *How expectancies shape experience.* Washington DC: American Psychological Association.

Kirsch I., & Saperstein, G. (1999). Listening to Prozac but hearing placebo. In I. Kirsch (Ed.), *How expectancies shape experience* (pp. 303–320). Washington DC: American Psychological Association.

Lang, A. A., Patrick C. J., & Stritzke, W. G. (1999). Alcohol and emotional response: A multidimensional-multilevel analysis. In K. E. Leonard, & H. T. Blane (Eds.), *Psychological theories of drinking and alcoholism* (2nd ed., pp. 328–371). New York: Guilford Press.

Langenbucher, J. W., & Nathan, P. E. (1983). Psychology, public policy, and the evidence for alcohol intoxication. *American Psychologist, 38,* 1070–1077.

Leshner, A. I. (2001). Addiction is a brain disease. *Issues in Science and Technology Online,* Spring, 1–9. http://www.nap.edu/issues/17.3/leshner.htm.

Mann, R. E., & Vogel-Sprott, M. (1981). Control of alcohol tolerance by reinforcement in nonalcoholics. *Psychopharmacology, 75,* 315–320.

Marlatt, G. A., & Gordon, J. R. (Eds.). (1985). *Relapse prevention: Maintenance strategies in the treatment of addictive behaviors.* New York: Guilford Press.

Marlatt, G. A., Demming, A., & Reid, J. B. (1973). Loss of control drinking in alcoholics: An experimental analogue. *Journal of Abnormal Psychology, 81,* 233–241.

Mello, N. K., & Mendelson, J. H. (1970). Experimentally induced intoxication in alcoholics: A comparison between programmed and spontaneous drinking. *Journal of Pharmacology and Experimental Therapeutics, 173,* 101–116.

Mello, N. K., & Mendelson, J. H. (1972). Drinking patterns during work-contingent and noncontingent alcohol acquisition. *Psychosomatic Medicine, 34,* 139–164.

Mendelson, J. H., & Mello, N. K. (1966). Experimental analysis of drinking behavior of chronic alcoholics. *Annals of the New York Academy of Sciences, 133,* 828–845.

Miller, W. R., & Heather, N. (1986). *Treating addictive behaviors: Processes of change.* New York: Plenum.

Mulvihill, L., Skilling, T., & Vogel-Sprott, M. (1997). Alcohol and the ability to inhibit behavior of men and women. *Journal of Studies on Alcohol, 58,* 600–605.

Nathan, P. E., Lowenstein, L. M., Solomon, P., & Rossi, A. M. (1970). Behavioral analysis of chronic alcoholism: Interaction of alcohol and human contact. *Archives of General Psychiatry, 22,* 419–430.

Nathan, P. E., O'Brien, J. S., & Lowenstien, L. M. (1971). Operant studies of chronic alcoholism: Interaction of alcohol and alcoholics. In W. McIsaac, & P. Creaven (Eds.), *Biological aspects of alcohol* (pp. 341–370). Austin: University of Texas Press.

Panksepp, J. (1998). *Affective neuroscience.* New York: Oxford University Press.

Rawana, E., & Vogel-Sprott, M. (1985). The transfer of alcohol tolerance, and its relation to reinforcement. *Drug and Alcohol Dependence, 16,* 75–83.

Rescorla, R. A. (1987). A Pavlovian analysis of goal-directed behavior. *American Psychologist, 42,* 119–129.

Rescorla, R. A. (1990). The role of information about the response-outcome relation in instrumental discrimination learning. *Journal of Experimental Psychology: Animal Behavior Processes, 16,* 262–270.

Sampson, H. H., Slawecki, C. J., Sharpe, A. L., & Chappell, A. (1998). Appetitive and consummatory behaviors in the control of ethanol consumption: A measure of ethanol seeking behavior. *Alcoholism: Clinical and Experimental Research, 22,* 1783–1787.

Schafer, J., & Brown, S. A. (1991). Marijuana and cocaine affect expectancies and drug use patterns. *Journal of Consulting and Clinical Psychology, 59,* 558–565.

Schuckit, M. (1994). Low level of response to alcohol as a predictor of future alcoholism. *American Journal of Psychiatry, 151,* 184–189.

Sdao-Jarvie, K., & Vogel-Sprott, M. (1991). Response expectancies affect the acquisition and display of behavioral tolerance. *Alcohol, 8,* 491–498.

Sher, K. (1987). Stress-response dampening. In H. T. Blane, & K. E. Leonard (Eds.), *Psychological theories of drinking and alcoholism* (pp. 227–271). New York: Guilford Press.

Sharkansky, E. J., & Finn, P. R. (1998). Effects of outcome expectancies and disinhibition on ad lib alcohol consumption. *Journal of Studies on Alcohol, 59,* 198–206.

Siegel, S. (1989). Pharmacological conditioning and drug effects. In A. K.

Goudie, & M. W. Emmett-Oglesby (Eds.), *Psychoactive drugs: Tolerance and sensitization* (pp. 115–169). Clifton NJ: Humana Press.

Strizke, W. G., Patrick, C. J., & Lang, A. R. (1995). Alcohol and human emotion: A multidimensional analysis incorporating startle-probe methodology. *Journal of Abnormal Psychology, 104,* 114–122.

Tolman, E. C. (1932). *Purposive behavior in animals and men.* New York: Century.

Vogel-Sprott, M. (1992). *Alcohol tolerance and social drinking: Learning the consequences.* New York: Guilford Press.

Vogel-Sprott, M. (1997). Is behavioral tolerance learned? *Alcohol Health and Research World, 21,* 161–168. Washington DC: National Institute on Alcohol Abuse and Alcoholism.

Vogel-Sprott, M., & Fillmore, M. (1999a). Expectancy and behavioral effects of socially used drugs. In I. Kirsch (Ed.), *How expectancies shape experience* (pp. 215–231). Washington DC: American Psychological Association.

Vogel-Sprott, M., & Fillmore, M. (1999b). Learning theory and research. In K. E. Leonard, & H. T. Blane (Eds.), *Psychological theories of drinking and alcoholism* (2nd ed., pp. 292–328). New York: Guilford Press.

Vuchinich, R. E. (1999). Behavioral economics as a framework for organizing the expanded range of substance abuse interventions. In J. A. Tucker, D. M. Donovan, & G. A. Marlatt (Eds.), *Changing addictive behavior* (pp. 191–220). New York: Guilford Press.

Vuchinich, R. E., & Tucker, J. A. (1983). Behavioral theories of choice as a framework for studying drinking behavior. *Journal of Abnormal Psychology, 92,* 408–416.

Vuchinich, R. E., & Tucker, J. A. (1988). Contributions from behavioral theories of choice to an analysis of alcohol abuse. *Journal of Abnormal Psychology, 97,* 181–195.

Vuchinich, R. E., & Tucker, J. A. (1996). Alcoholic relapse, life events and behavioral theories of choice: A prospective analysis. *Experimental and Clinical Psychopharmacology, 4,* 19–28.

Wall, A-M., McKee, S. A., & Hinson, R. E. (2001). Assessing alcohol outcome expectancies in a naturalistic drinking environment: Faster, higher, stronger?*Alcoholism: Clinical and Experimental Research, 25(Suppl., 39A).*

Wall, A-M, McKee, S. A., Hinson, R. E., & Goldstein, A. (2001). Examining alcohol outcome expectancies in a laboratory and naturalistic bar setting: A within-subject experimental analysis. *Psychology of Addictive Behaviors, 15,* 219–226.

Wallgren, H., & Barry, H. III. (1971). *Actions of alcohol.* Amsterdam: Elsevier.

Wells, J., Greene, M., Foss, R., Ferguson, S., & Williams, A. (1997). Drivers with high BACs missed at sobriety checkpoints. *Journal of Studies on Alcohol, 58,* 513–517.

Young, R., Oei, T. P., & Knight, R. G. (1990). The tension-reduction hypothesis revisited: An alcohol expectancy perspective. *British Journal of Addiction, 85,* 31–40.

Zack, M., & Vogel-Sprott M. (1995). Behavioral tolerance and sensitization to alcohol in humans: The contribution of learning. *Experimental and Clinical Psychopharmacology, 3,* 396–401.

Zack M., & Vogel-Sprott, M. (1997). Drunk or sober? Learned conformity to behavioral standards. *Journal of Studies on Alcohol, 58,* 495–501.

Zinatelli, M., & Vogel-Sprott, M. (1993). Behavioral tolerance to alcohol in humans is enhanced by prior drug-free treatment. *Journal of Experimental and Clinical Psychopharmacology, 1,* 194–199.

Subject Index

Page numbers in italics refer to figures or tables.

Author Index